New Works in Accounting Theory

Richard P. Brief, Series Editor

Leonard N. Stern School of Business
New York University

The Auditors Talk

An Oral History of a Profession from the 1920s to the Present Day

Derek Matthews
Jim Pirie

LONDON AND NEW YORK

First published 2001 by Garland Publishing, Inc.

Published 2018 by Routledge
2 Park Square, Milton Park, Abingdon, Oxon OX14 4RN
52 Vanderbilt Avenue, New York, NY 10017

First issued in paperback 2018

Routledge is an imprint of the Taylor & Francis Group, an informa business

Library of Congress Cataloging-in-Publication Data is available from the Library of Congress.

ISBN 13: 978-1-138-86389-7 (pbk)
ISBN 13: 978-0-8153-3854-3 (hbk)

Printed in the United Kingdom
by Henry Ling Limited

Contents

Acknowledgements

This book could not have been written without a generous grant from the then Research Committee of the Institute of Chartered Accountants in England and Wales, which funded the programme of oral history on which it is based. A number of ICAEW staff also helped with finding interviewees and in drafting the questionnaire used in the project. Thanks are also due to Prof Dick Edwards who helped in securing the funding, gave support and encouragement throughout the project, also helped draft the questionnaire and read a number of the resulting chapters in their early form. We are likewise grateful to Roy Chandler, Prof Bob Parker and Prof Tony Arnold who also helped with the questionnaire and/or read chapters, and to Howard Mellett who offered advice with numerous accounting technicalities. Caroline Frame, Cheryl Morgan and Gill Powell handled the crucial job of transcribing the audio tapes with skill and perseverance and Roy Taylor also gave considerable help in the transcription process. Above all, however, we owe a huge debt to the retired and practicing accountants who not only gave up their valuable time to allow us to interview them but also read and revised the transcripts, in some cases lent us books, pamphlets, cuttings and other supporting material and were extremely patient in dealing with our often numerous follow up queries. Thanks again to everyone, and of course as usual any errors or weaknesses that might still remain in the book are entirely our responsibility.

Derek Matthews
Jim Pirie
Cardiff Business School
October 1999

Chapter 1

Introduction

In recent years, following financial scandals such as the collapse of the Maxwell empire, BCCI and Barings Bank, the issue of the effectiveness and value of the external audit of British company accounts has been prominent in public debate and was given due weight, for example, in the Cadbury Report (1992) on corporate governance generally. In this context, in 1996 the research committee of the Institute of Chartered Accountants in England and Wales (ICAEW) funded a project based at the Cardiff Business School investigating the changing nature of the company audit historically in Britain, a major part of which consisted of interviewing retired or experienced chartered accountants about their careers, with particular reference to their work as auditors. In other words an oral history of the issue.

Since its pioneering days, in Britain at least, in the 1950s and 1960s the use of oral history is by now well established, particularly among social historians, and its academic validity is accepted (Thompson, P., 1978). However, accounting historians have tended to use the technique sparsely and have been urged to use it more (see for example, Loft, 1990; Mumford, 1991; Collins and Bloom, 1991; Hammond and Sikka, 1996). This book is a step in that direction and in this chapter we discuss the setting up and carrying through of the project and the associated problems and issues surrounding the generation, uses and presentation of oral evidence and we set out the structure and aims of the book.

Setting up the project

The first job was to find respondents prepared to be interviewed. Surprisingly few people contacted refused, including those accountants still in post who could be expected to have a firm grasp of the opportunity cost of giving up hours of their time to talk to an historian. With regard to the choice of interviewees, a random sample of the profession was considered but rejected as this would have excluded some of the key figures who we felt it would be essential to interview. In the end we arrived at what Hammond and Sikka (1996: 88) have advocated, a 'purposeful' sample—adjusting as we went along the numbers in the various groupings within the profession which we felt should be represented. At the outset these categories were: the oldest accountants we could find (dubbed somewhat disrespectfully the 'golden oldies,' a number of whom trained in the 1920s); sole or small firm practitioners; accountants who had 'left the profession' but who could comment on their audit based training and on auditing from the other side of the fence as, for example, finance directors; medium sized or provincial practitioners; and the leaders of the profession (dubbed 'the great and the good').

Three categories were added at a later date in the programme: first, women, who perhaps inexcusably were only realised to have a separate story to tell late in the day; second, accountants personally involved in the major scandals past and present, dubbed the 'rogues,' among whom we found understandably more of a reluctance to be interviewed. Finally, we judged that, although this was a history project, the story would have been incomplete had we not asked the same questions to the present day incumbents at the head of the profession, which we hoped would enhance the practical relevance and usefulness of the project.

The next task was to draw up a list of questions. It appeared important at the outset that the interviews be rigorously structured to give consistency and to allow a comparison of responses to be made and analysed. Considerable research and discussion with accountant colleagues and ICAEW staff went into the drafting of the questionnaire, which by and large proved robust in that a core of substantially the same questions were asked of all interviewees. The questions could be broken down into: the social and educational background of the respondents; the nature of their training; and their experience in their mature careers, especially concerning changes they saw in the auditing process. Finally, all interviewees were questioned on their opinions on wider issues such as the purpose of the audit, trends in the quality of auditing and the causes of the recent problems, such as the apparent failure of prestigious firms of auditors to cope with the spectacular frauds, touched on above.[1]

Almost immediately, however, it was realised that rigour had to give way to flexibility in the structure of the questioning because of the heterogeneity of the respondents, obvious from the categories listed above. It probably should not have done so, but it came as something of a surprise that a sole practitioner was not talking the same language as the ex-senior partner with one of the big firms; they appeared to be almost in different professions. Self-evidently too, a somewhat different set of questions was required for a major actor in a financial scandal from those we would want to ask a woman who qualified against the odds in the 1930s.

Although all our interviews needed to be preceded by some research, an additional amount of background work was essential when interviewing the 'great and the good' and accountants, for example, with an inside knowledge of controversial audits or who had served as inspectors on Department of Trade enquires. People like Sir John Grenside, Sir Douglas Morpeth or Sir David Tweedie, for example, were, or are, major figures in the accountancy world, there has been a considerable amount written about them and their activities, and indeed they had often written a significant amount themselves, so clearly the interviewer needed to be conversant at least with the major aspects of their careers and works.

Prior research also helps guard against the throwing up of surprising remarks for which the interviewer is not prepared. It is a virtue of the interview technique that the unexpected fact or opinion can arise, but no matter how much preparation the interviewer has undertaken, this can be wasted or not made full use of due to his or her ignorance. To take the example of the Grenside interview (chapter 8), he states at one point that Peats would have nothing to do with Robert Maxwell after he had been branded as unfit to run a public company. At the time the interviewer was unaware that Peats had been doing consultancy work for Maxwell companies and Grenside should have been asked to clear up the discrepancy.

Obviously, the extent of this background research was limited by the time available. Fortunately, less preparatory work was involved for most of the respondents who fitted into the customary profile of the subjects of oral history in its function as the 'hidden history' of the unrecorded masses (Perks and Thomson, 1998: 1).

The interviews

The interviews had their technical problems. Tape recorders particularly of the modern miniature variety are treacherous machines, although when things went wrong human error was almost always the culprit. The interviews, which lasted from between one and three hours, were usually conducted in the interviewee's own home, although some respondents preferred to meet in the ICAEW head office in Moorgate Place. One interview was held in the front seat of the respondent's car in the middle of a thunderstorm. It was quickly realised that finding a quiet environment and the positioning and setting up of the tape recorder so as to give clear voice reproduction of both parties to the interview saves many hours later in the transcription and editing process.

With modern technology the taping of interviews held over the phone is an easy process and some were held in this manner but these were kept to a minimum after it was realised how much was lost in terms of rapport with the subject and in picking up visual clues from body language. However, the use of the taped telephone conversation proved useful for secondary interviewing, to clear up points raised in the initial interview.

The skills of the oral historian are common, of course, to all types of interviewing, summarised by Morrissey (1998: 48) as: the need for good preparation; establishing a rapport with the respondent; not interrupting but listening to what is being said and following up any points of interest; and asking brief but open-ended questions. Keeping respondents politely on the subject was sometimes difficult. Inevitably war-time adventures rank higher in interest and importance to most individuals than their auditing experience. Equally, knowing when to encourage respondents to pursue matters not in the script is an art form that the oral historian needs to cultivate. However, the accounting historian has the undoubted advantage in that almost without exception his/her respondents will be intelligent and articulate, with well thought out views on their profession—even if they are living through their tenth decade.

On a more philosophical level with regard to the interview process, Hammond and Sikka (1996: 79) have argued: 'that avoiding bias is impossible' and by implication should not be attempted. To them objectivity is merely a facade and in contrast to the traditional researcher who 'is expected to be dispassionate and detached, the oral history researcher is deeply involved' (Ibid., 88 and 91). We reject this post-modernist stance.[2] We take the positivist view that there is a real world outside the consciousness of the historian and his or her culture or language. The job of the historian is to find out what happened in this past reality and to explain it by a process of establishing hypothesis backed up by argument and evidence, which in turn can be substantiated or refuted by a similar process. Of course, complete objectivity is unobtainable and the historian is clearly subject to a whole range of social, cultural, political and not least economic influences about which he or she should strive as much as possible to be aware. Indeed, this alertness is seldom more important than in a project funded by the very professional body under investigation. Here the topic studied was not entirely in the hands of the historian from the outset and we discuss below a range of not very subtle pressures on us which continued to come into play until the book reached the publisher. However, it seems to us essential for the historian to strive, at least, for objectivity and to carry a professional commitment to reveal and explain the past in as 'dispassionate and detached' a way as possible. To do otherwise, to get 'deeply involved,' gives the historian it seems to us no professional guidance against getting 'deeply involved' in writing propaganda.

The practicalities of our viewpoint for the present project were that it was considered important, if not perfectly achievable, that, as Grele (1998: 101) has argued, the interviewer should try as far as possible not to insert his own views or ideology; or in legal terms not to 'lead the witness.' In our view any other approach to interviewing would have been intolerable, indeed almost unworkable.

Transcription and editing

The transcription of the completed interview tapes was fraught with difficulties. Understandably, audiotypists not having a grasp of the technicalities of accounting or the accounting business very often misrepresented what was being said (an amusing and recurring example of this was how many interviewees in the original transcript worked at 'Pete's' during their career). A good audio typist then can save the oral historian many hours of work, but, no matter how good the initial transcription, there will be errors and unclear passages requiring time-consuming editing by the original interviewer. More significantly, conversational English, even of well educated and articulate interviewees as ours invariably were, is grammatically and stylistically unacceptable, indeed almost unreadable, when transcribed *verbatim*. The degree of the editing then becomes an issue.

There is considerable discussion within oral history circles as to the extent to which, as Samuel (1998: 389) argues, the transcribed speech, warts (dialect) and all, should be retained, so that the 'original integrity' of what is being said can be preserved. We took the view in this project, however, that since, for example, body language and the intonation of the voice can never be captured in writing, which of course has a different set of conventions to the spoken word, a *verbatim* transcription is in itself a distortion of what took place in the interview. It was therefore considered only fair to the respondents (and to the reader) to make their words read fluently and with clarity, whilst trying to preserve the informality and vitality of the interview. Without this process most interviewees (and indeed the interviewer) would often have been made to appear foolish, which would have given the wrong impression. Equally, every effort needs to be made to preserve what the historian understands to have been the respondent's meaning or intention. There is no escaping the fact, however, that by the time editing has established readability in the text the prose has been substantially rewritten, and the extent of this process clearly at work in all forms of journalism and academic interviewing is often lost sight of. To give some idea of the process involved, and to judge whether the respondents' original intentions have been preserved generally in this book, we can take an extract more or less at random from the interview again with Sir John Grenside (not eventually used in the text) and compare the original and edited versions. Grenside was asked about rotating auditors as a solution to their getting too close to their clients. The original transcription read:

> One of the difficulties about rotation . . . we could all swap major clients of course, but the cost of that is very high to the company themselves and not only in terms of . . . perhaps not too high in terms of money but quite high in terms of initiation, learning the business, getting into the thing and so on. And it's not an easy option really. I think India had it over three years which seemed absurd that you could. . . . But I don't believe really speaking changing the auditors is terribly likely to disclose anything with any trouble that was there, because of course how often would you change them? I mean you couldn't possibly change them every year. Even if you did there was no great certainty that these sort of things would come to light anyway.

Edited this became:

> We could all swap major clients, of course, but the cost of that is very high to the company themselves in terms of initiation, learning the business, getting into the thing and so on. India have it [rotation of auditors] every three years, which seems absurd. How often would you change them? You couldn't possibly change them every year. Even if you did, there is no great certainty that these sorts of things [frauds] would come to light anyway.

In this way, every interview in this book has been heavily edited as to syntax, grammar and the avoidance of repetitive or redundant phrases. In addition, the editing process must also involve some rearrangement and regrouping of the order of the text to give a more fluent structure.

Of even more significance is what to do with the polished transcript. The uses of oral testimony range through a wide spectrum. At one extreme some practitioners argue that the oral record is history itself; the respondents create their own history which should be presented unsullied by the professional historian (Perks and Thomson, 1998: 1). Hammond and Sikka (1996: 91) want oral history 'to give voice to the people who have been excluded, oppressed and exploited in the onward march of the institutions of accountancy and accounting calculus.' In so doing oral history will 'question the very nature of dominant approaches to writing accounting history.' This leads them also to argue for minimum intervention by the historian since: 'Over-analysis can result in quoting informants only when their statements fit into the researchers preconceived theories, thus obscuring the contributions of the informants' (Hammond and Sikka, 1996: 89). At the other extreme is the presentation of oral evidence without using the words of the interviewees at all. The evidence is put entirely to the historian's own uses and into his or her own words, which need not of course mean any more bias is imparted to the source material. This is how Loft (1986 and 1988) has used interviews with cost accountants.

We attempt in this book to steer between these two extremes. The format of the discrete interview is preserved since the background and career of individual accountants are considered important in giving a context to the information and opinions they offer. Also the interviewees' own words are used wherever possible subject to the caveats discussed above. In these respects we took the books of Studs Terkel (1974, 1989) as something of a model. Yet in contrast to the 'minimum intervention' school of oral history we believe the historian must also do his or her job. Oral testimony is a primary resource similar to the documentary variety and it needs the historian to turn it into history. Oral history should not be another form of antiquarianism, which it can easily descend into if interviews reported *verbatim* include data simply for its own sake, rather than for the contribution it makes to an overall analysis or to testing an hypothesis.

Indeed, the main flaw with the 'minimum intervention' school of thought is that very heavy editing is unavoidable because there is simply too much material for the purposes of even the most dedicated student, not to mention the budgets of academic publishers. Transcribed, the 77 original interviews in this project came to well over a million words, the total for the edited interviews in this book comes to around 150,000 words, so the degree of necessary editing can be appreciated.

So if heavy editing is essential this raises the vital question as to the criteria on which it is to be based and these need to be made explicit. Much of the transcribed material (for example, wartime experiences) can easily be deemed irrelevant to the stated aim of the project. But much of the editing involves a fine judgment by the historian and a heavy onus is put on his or her skill and, indeed, the professional integrity discussed above. There is no doubt the editing process gives the historian scope to make his respondents look as foolish or wise, as craven or innocent or to tell more or less any story he or she (as propagandist) wishes, which is where the commitment to disinterested objectivity is essential. Oral historians must literally, in the great empiricist, E.P. Thompson's (1978:222) apt phrase, listen to the sources' 'own voices.'

What then were our editing criteria? Our overall remit was to focus on the changes that have taken place historically in the practice of auditing. Within that aim, our editing has attempted, first, to avoid repetition of information and viewpoints: stock answers are represented, but sparingly,—for example, the reader will only be interested in hearing that in the 'old days,' audit fees were strictly based on man-hours charged out a limited number of times. Much more interesting is the revelation in a number of interviews that in at least some firms, negotiation of fees with the client routinely took place at an early date. We also, second, gave priority to information or opinions not available elsewhere in the secondary literature. For example, John Whinney's original interview was highly detailed on the history of mergers in what has now become Ernst & Young, but since this material is already comprehensively described in Edgar Jones' history of the firm (1981), a great deal of this data was omitted in order to allow space for John to take us into previously unrecorded areas (chapter 7). Above all, third, we wished to give voice to experiences and views deemed to have wide interest and applicability and to facilitate the drawing of conclusions of general validity.

Transcription and editing therefore is an essential but inevitably problematic process. Because of this we considered it important that the original tapes and the *verbatim* transcriptions be made available, as is usual, to fellow researchers (with, of course, the express permission of the interviewee), so that ultimately they can judge the accuracy of the editing for themselves.[3]

ORAL HISTORY AND THE MIDDLE CLASS

There was a further complication before the final edited version of the interviews was arrived at. The interviews were conducted on the basis that the interviewees would be presented with an edited transcription on which they could comment and make additions. They were also given the right to withhold permission for any material that on reflection, for whatever reason, they did not want published. This process had advantages for the project and for the respondents. For the former it provided a check against the many inaccuracies noted above that creep into the transcription and editing process and also we could ask respondents to enlarge and elaborate on points of particular interest. The authors, neither of whom is a qualified accountant, were well aware of the number of technical howlers which could creep into the text and we have undoubtedly gained from allowing our material to be vetted by the interviewees.

We quickly became aware, however, of the disadvantages for the historian in allowing a middle class, articulate, professional group, protective of its reputation, the right to reflect on, edit and ultimately withhold publication of their own interviews; more stringent constraints than, for example, a journalist would usually accept. Whereas oral historians have traditionally given voice to the disadvantaged or the weak in society, who are usually given little say and have perhaps little interest in how they are represented, this was not the case with this project.

In seven cases, interviewees refused permission for their interview to be used at all, often after lengthy negotiation, and in one case a week before the book was due to go off to the publishers. Also, three of our subjects sadly died whilst the book was in preparation and, where in two of the cases their family so requested, these interviews too have been omitted from the book. Thus, in its final form, 68, rather than 77, interviews are represented here. The reasons given for withholding permission included: the fact that the interview had been given some time (over a year in one case) previously; the interviewee claimed not to realise despite the presence of the tape recorder that they were speaking on the record; they would breach client confidentiality; they feared some of what they said was libellous; they were concerned that what they said might influence disciplinary proceedings in which their firms were then involved; they did not know at the time of the interview the format or purpose for which the interview was to be put, clearly did not like what they saw in print, and editing the transcript would take too much of their time.

Evidently a major problem for oral historians with middle class interviewees is that they are for the most part people well able to write their own autobiographies (indeed one of them handed us an unpublished typescript of 250 pages), and the somewhat haphazard look of a transcribed interview (however well polished in the editing process) is not how they would choose to be represented. Interestingly, four of the interviews forced out were with retired senior (although not the senior) partners with firms in the (what was then) Big Six. One, an ex-Coopers and Lybrand partner, refused despite giving a charming and informative interview at the end of which he stated that he had no objection to almost all of what he said being ascribed to him. Rather unpleasantly he and another in demanding their interviews be withdrawn chose for the most part to correspond with the hierarchy of our institution rather than with ourselves. But in the end, despite repeated entreaties that the interviewees could take out anything that they were unhappy with, interesting interviews were lost. Indeed, initially, several more interviewees refused permission to be published and, since these hiccups occurred at an early stage in the process of distributing edited transcripts, it looked at one point as if we might not have a book left. Fortunately the vast majority of interviewees accepted the project for what it was and co-operated fully.

Unfortunately, the doubters and a number of others took the offer of self-editing their transcripts more seriously than was ideal. A number rewrote their whole interviews, often apparently merely upset by the awkwardness of the style or the grammar in the original transcript. Regrettably, this rewriting usually meant the liveliness of reported speech has been replaced by rather bland 'accountants' prose. Others, however, understood perfectly what was required. As Richard Wilkes (chapter 8) in a letter to us acknowledged: 'the informality of the interview situation should not be sanitised out of existence.'

More seriously, this self-editing has meant that interesting and valuable details and insights which we would have liked to share with the reader have been lost. In the cold light of print, many interviewees felt that their (unerringly) most interesting stories had to be suppressed. One of the present day leaders of the profession who refused at the last minute to allow his interview to be used, talked of his firm in the 1980s in the following colourful terms:

> there was a certain arrogance in the firm and in some of the things the firm did, all in a cocky, slightly unprofessional way. Our PR gave the press the wrong impression of a firm that was a bit 'Jack the Lad,' and a lot of the partners were enjoying the benefits of success in the 80s, partners with Ferraris, partners with Porsches and other expensive toys. Which again fitted the client profile quite well in the yuppie era . . . Driving a Ferrari you attracted other people who drove Ferraris, because no other accountants drove Ferraris. So you actually found that you got a whole influx of clients who were your type of people, so it worked very well.

Obvious and possibly libellous indiscretions were understandable candidates for the blue pencil; other deletions less so. For example, somewhat surprisingly one interviewee felt that his statement that he could always find the fraudster in any company by inspecting the cars in the works car park should be deleted. On another occasion, one of the contemporary leaders of the profession opined that Prem Sikka's mother must have been frightened by an accountant when she was carrying him; again, regrettably, this must remain unattributed.[4] Far more significantly, whole swathes of forthright critical comments on the performance of their fellow professionals in the great audit failures of the 1980s and 1990s, noted above, have had to go.

In the end it is a matter of judgment whether the advantages of giving interviewees an editor's or censor's role outweigh the disadvantages. Possibly with hindsight the authors should have established unequivocally the 'on the record' nature of the interviews—in writing. On the other hand it could be argued that interviewees should always be given the right to withhold what on reflection they do not wish to see ascribed to them. Oral history is not after all the art of luring respondents into indiscretions. What is clear is that the oral history of the middle class is a somewhat different animal to the traditional discipline.

Oral history: problems of use and interpretation

Oral evidence generates two types of source material for the historian-facts and opinions. The evidence gained by asking a senior partner to describe how his firm was run in the 1960s or if they circularised debtors is of a different nature to his thoughts about whether the quality of auditing had changed. The problems with oral sources lie more with the former than with the latter. An opinion is self-evidently subjective and can be taken as no more nor less than someone's stated view. In Portelli's (1998: 68) words: 'there are no "false" oral sources.' Even in these normative areas, however, the user of the material must be on guard since opinions change. For example, as a result of technical problems mentioned earlier it was necessary to reinterview one respondent. In the first interview the question: 'How good was your training as a preparation for your future career?' engendered the dusty response that auditing was a dead-end job and taught him nothing. Six months later the same question provoked the opinion that his training had been a valuable insight into how companies are run!

Equally, in terms of opinions, the response of one interviewee is obviously not statistically valid. The oral historian cannot claim to be conducting an opinion poll so the question will always arise— how typical is this respondent? It is hoped that here, however, the accumulated responses of 68 interviews add up to a useful set of data. As discussed above, the editing process has attempted to indicate where replies are typical or not. Also, of course, the value of a single response is enhanced by the importance in any given situation of the interviewee. For example, the opinion on their value of one of the prime movers in the setting of accounting standards, like Sir Douglas Morpeth, is clearly of interest in its own right.

With regard to factual accuracy, there are greater problems. Memories will be unreliable, especially of course among the many elderly respondents represented here, and particularly treacherous when interviewees are convinced of the veracity of their recall or believe their own experience to be typical when it may not be. The view of the individual respondent has to be subject to what Lummis (1998: 274) has called 'the normal process of maximum triangulation with other sources.' Also, even the keenest memories will lack the detailed accuracy that a considered and researched autobiography would contain. Regrettably, few British accountants since the war have published their memoirs (we know of only two: Henry Benson[5] (1989) and Sir Kenneth Cork (1988))—which is why oral history is important. Unfortunately, although there were some exceptions, understandably very few respondents did any preparation such as consulting their papers for the interviews and it was considered impertinent to have asked them to do this. Therefore, in the circumstances of impromptu recall there is inevitably a lack of close detail.

Another source of unreliability in the interviewee is the not unknown indulgence in outright dissembling, but more commonly the information may be slanted by omission either deliberately or by selective memory (Collins and Bloom, 1991: 26). This of course particularly applies to facts that show the respondent or his or her firm or profession in a bad light. Lapses of memory in key places in interviews will be found in this book, but clearly there is no way of knowing how strategic these were. In defence of oral evidence, however, the obvious point should be made that no sources the historian uses will be without deception or distortion of one sort or another, certainly not autobiography, minutes of meetings, newspaper reports or even, perhaps especially, company accounts.

Oral history, however, has a secondary source of possible bias not present in documentary evidence due to the fact that the interview is a two-way process and, as was discussed above, the interviewer comes with his or her own ideological baggage. 'Researchers often introduce specific distortions: informants tell them what they believe they want to be told' (Portelli, 1998: 70). In contrast, the 'content of the written source is independent of the researcher's need and hypotheses; it is a stable text, which we can only interpret. The content of oral sources, on the other hand, depends largely on what the interviewer puts into it' (Ibid.). As was asserted above, the best that can be done in this regard is for the interviewer to be aware of the two-way nature of the interview and to avoid its distorting effects as far as possible.

Oral history–the payoff

Turning to the advantages of oral history, these stem largely from the central point that, regarding both fact and opinion, the historian is often creating data that is not available in any other form. Oral history began on the basis of allowing the dispossessed to tell their story, groups who would have been hidden from history based on the documentary sources—in George Ewart Evans' phrase 'ask the fellows who cut the hay' (quoted in Perks and Thomson, 1998: 1). This role for oral history applies less in the relatively well-documented world of a middle class profession. Nonetheless, in the history of accounting there are still many interesting areas where there is no documentary evidence and Collins and Bloom (1991: 23–25) have suggested that, for example, the process by which accounting standards are set is one obvious area for the use of oral history. Issues previously less than fully exposed to the public gaze that these interviews throw light on, to name but a few, include: the attitude to women in the profession, the way the ICAEW examination pass rates were determined, the role of freemasonry, and the setting of audit fees. The range of opinions generated by oral history are even less likely to be available in documentary form, enhanced in value, as noted above, by the significance of the role in events played by the respondent.

Oral history puts the historian more in control of the data to be generated whereas the conventional historian has to take the documentary evidence he or she is given. In Hammond and Sikka's (1996: 86) words: 'Printed evidence is one-way, silent and unable to respond to comments, questions and observations.' In contrast, oral history gives historians the ability to go out and create the evidence themselves in the specific areas they are interested in and where other sources are lacking. Hammond and Sikka call for the use of oral histories 'to give voice and visibility to those marginalised or otherwise adversely affected by accountancy' which opens up an almost limitless field of potential interviewees. Our project had more limited aims. We judged that, give or take a few expletives, we would not have gained anything useful by asking a Mirror Group pensioner, a bank customer, or say a bricklayer their views on the audit process, however much they may actually have been affected by it.

We were guided by the expectation that specific information could be elicited where the documentary testimony is not available and it is not difficult to think of other specific uses of the technique in accountancy history. For example, colleagues have struggled hard with meagre documentary sources to identify what management accounting techniques, such as standard costing, were in use in Britain historically and when they were introduced (see e.g. Boyns, 1998). Finding and interviewing management accountants who were working in British companies from the 1930s onward and asking them what techniques they used and when and why they were brought in would probably solve the issue relatively easily.

A final advantage of oral history is that a response to a question might prompt a new line of enquiry. For example, Denza and Grenside's views in chapters 4 and 8 that the temptation in the decades after the war was to understate profit because tax rates were high and dividends were discouraged, is not an argument with which the authors were previously familiar and might well be worth pursuing. Equally, a change in auditing which would not be picked up by reading the audit textbooks at the time was Peats' view, voiced by Grenside, that: 'we should change significantly from just doing an audit to really trying to help the company to become a better company.' Again several interviewees named Graham Corbett as a major influence on the changing nature of accountancy in the 1960s and 1970s but Corbett would appear not to have been given full credit in the existing literature.

To sum up then, the interviews presented in this book illustrate the strengths and weaknesses of oral history techniques in general but particularly when applied to accounting history. On balance we hope the book shows that the technique could be more widely employed to advantage in the latter discipline. Our project on auditing has perhaps exhausted that area for the time being but this leaves wide areas of the discipline still to be covered. Moreover, the grim reaper carries off valuable historical evidence with every passing year.

Structure and use of the book

As can be seen, and was discussed above, this book is divided into chapters grouped loosely into broad categories of interviewee. The edited interviews are presented without editorial comment in the text but begin with a brief biography of the respondent taken from the interviews, other details provided by the interviewees or sometimes secondary sources such as *Who's Who*. In addition, endnotes have been provided to help with references in the interviews to people, processes or events which it was thought needed some elaboration or explanation, particularly for the non-accountant. The note is given where the issue, for example the Maxwell affair, is first mentioned in the book, so reference through the index is necessary where Maxwell crops up elsewhere. Secondary sources used are referenced in the normal way and refer to the bibliography in the back of the book.

The book ends with a somewhat extensive chapter which attempts to summarise and draw general conclusions from the evidence found in the body of the book. As discussed above, we believe the role of the oral historian includes not only choosing the interviewees, conducting the interviews and the crucial role of editing, but also drawing together and analysing the results. In line with our positivist and empirical stance, therefore, the concluding chapter attempts by induction from the disparate evidence in the interviews to make generalisations of wider applicability. In this way we hope we have demonstrated that the knowledge gained from the total adds up to more than the sum of the individual parts.

One of the advantages of the approach to oral history adopted here is that it can afford readers autonomies of direction in setting up their own lines of enquiry, which conventional historians quite rightly insist upon for themselves, but deny their readers because of the narrative structures they necessarily deal in. Indeed, perhaps the norm with academic books is for readers to pick at fragments like seagulls[6] and rush on, only to return for more later. So for those wishing to dip into our interviews as carrion we have tried to make the index particularly comprehensive to help the reader pluck out those aspects in which they have a specific interest.

Notes

1. Consideration was given to reproducing the original questionnaire here but lack of space was a deterrent, while probably no one respondent was asked exactly the same questions anyway. However, the original set of questions is available from the authors.

2. For good summaries of the post-modernist debate within history see: Jenkins (1995 and 1997) and Southgate (1996).

3. At the time of writing the final repository for the tapes has not been decided. Readers should contact the authors at the Cardiff Business School for further details.

4. Prof. Prem Sikka of Essex University is one of the leading academic critics of the accounting profession, and their role as auditors in particular. Some of his writing appears in the bibliography and has been a great help in focusing our thinking on a number of aspects of the subject.

5. Born in 1909, in South Africa, the son of the daughter of Francis Cooper, one of the four brothers who founded Cooper Bros. Benson qualified with the family firm in 1932, was made a partner two years later, and from 1946 ran the firm with John Pears, until his retirement in 1975. He was President of the ICAEW in 1966, knighted in 1964, made a life peer in 1981, and died in 1995 (*WWW*; Benson, 1989).

6. A metaphor made apt only by years of working in the environs of the Cardiff Business School.

Chapter 2

Small Firm Practitioners

The son of an "ordinary workman" on the railways, TOM SANDERS was born in Wellingborough, Northants in 1907. After receiving an elementary education, in the last year of which he started evening classes in Bookkeeping, Typing and Shorthand, he was engaged at the age of 13 as an office junior by Peter Octavius "Ocky" James, the only practising chartered accountant in Wellingborough. At the age of 16 he passed the Advanced Accountancy examination of the Royal Society of Arts and, unable to afford an articled clerk's premium, trained for nine years to gain an incorporated accountant's qualification as a so called, bye-law candidate (Garrett, 1961: 22). He qualified in 1932 and was engaged by Mr. James, combining this with teaching accountancy at Wellingborough (Public) School, and later some examining work for the ICAEW. His principal's deteriorating health led to Tom assuming increasingly greater responsibility for the work of the firm, and in 1939 he was admitted into a full partnership. Meantime, the rapid growth of the town as an industrial centre both enhanced the practice's client base and began to attract other firms of accountants. By 1956, this led to a merger with Baker of Leicester and Northampton, and an expansion of the practice into other towns. In 1958, a merger was arranged with Thornton and Thornton of Oxford, the new firm taking the name of Thornton Baker (now Grant Thornton.). Tom continued as a full national partner, running the Wellingborough office with two other partners until his retirement in 1968 at the age of 61.

When you started as an office junior in the 1920s, did your principal give you a lot of responsibility?

Absolutely.

Did he accompany you all the time?

Oh yes, yes. We went out together. Actually he had an old Ford Model T car, an old bone-shaker, and we used to go out to the various business places. He really took me under his wing. I've got him to thank for everything because he just took a liking to me. Then after I passed my R.S.A. exams, I was thought competent enough to cope, and under his instruction I used to take another unqualified bloke with me, and do the audit in a leather factory and many other businesses. Auditing was a matter of routine, really.

Did you physically attend stocktaking in those early days?

Yes we did that at St. Crispin's Mental Hospital. We checked the stock; we counted all the sheets, all the pillow cases and we went up ladders in all the stores all round the building checking the items on the stock sheet. The doors were locked to make sure the patients couldn't come in and create havoc.

Did you have any sort of systems of sampling? Or would you go through the lot?

Most of the firms in this area weren't terrifically large, so normally you checked the accountancy records but not the stocks.

What sort of clients did you have?

For example, Chamberlain's boot factory: they manufactured slippers, spats and that sort of thing. Next door was Page's that was a shoe factory. Then next to that was Metropole, another shoe place. We had a monopoly of audits, perhaps two to three hundred of them; though not many public companies in those days. Some of these small companies gradually developed into public companies. We also had up to 50 friendly societies and that was impossible for one Public Auditor, so I was appointed as a second Public Auditor by the Registrar of Friendly Societies.[1] The clients all became personal friends. The whole relationship was cordial. You were associated as Rotarians[2] or golfers or masons. In a town the size of Wellingborough, especially when you have been there all your life, everybody knows you. That's how you got your business. Of course, we were the only chartered accountants in the town for many, many years. Round about the thirties, Merrett & Son and Street, and one or two others began to filter in, because the town was growing and industry was increasing.

Overall then, your training was a useful experience?

Yes. And that's why starting from virtually nothing and only a basic education I was able to become a partner.

As a partner did you go out and lead an audit yourself?

Well normally the audits came to you. In the course of the growth of the partnership we had an audit department, a taxation department and an insolvency department but in the good old days you did everything in one or two rooms. But as things developed you had to extend the building and create departments for particular specialities in the profession. Nowadays, you get a specialist manager for a particular group. In my original days the partner had to know the lot.

Did you come up against much fraud?

So many of the frauds were Inland Revenue, taxation frauds. We had, I won't say dozens but a lot. You see after the First World War we had chaos because during the war you'd all cash transactions. People used to parcel crates of boots and shoes, and send them off to Petticoat Lane for £2–300 cash. The Revenue got wise if they built up bank accounts which could be traced. But that is something which an auditor finds almost impossible to get down to; there's nothing to show up. We did have cases where we detected fraud. There might have been one or two cases where directors were involved, but normally it was staff, cashiers and people in control of cash.

You have described an influx of other accountants after 1930? Did it get competitive, or was there enough work for everybody?

I'm sure that all the accountants made a living. That's why Baker & Co came to us for the merger. They knew we were the oldest established firm, with the clientele; we were the obvious people to approach. I made it a condition of the merger that my son be given a partnership when he was ready.

How did you link up with Thorntons?

As partners of the merged firm, we thought we'd go a bit wider. Oxford came up and somebody said,—I know old Jonathan, I'll have a word with him and see what he thinks. And it developed from there. Two partners went over there and had a chat, and agreed terms.

We used to have a regular meeting of partners in London. We'd go to an hotel and have a morning meeting, eat lunch, and then have an afternoon meeting. And it was a proper gossip with each other. We used to handle questions and answers, and queries that arose and all that sort of thing. It was a most friendly merger, and it set up the whole organisation. Lots of our former partners went into industry.

And then approached you to do the audit?

Yes, in some cases.

Do you have a perspective on some of the spectacular audit failures of recent years?

There must have been a lack of supervision by the principal partners. They depute too much work to their managers. The salaries of some leading accountants disgust me: how can anyone justify £750,000 a year?

And mind you between us I don't think they want to work as hard as we used to. All these blooming lunches they eat! I know they do business and talk business and so forth. But in the old days there was a time factor and we had three quarters of an hour for lunch. Otherwise we were slogging our insides out.

Born in Brighton in 1911, PARRY GOODWIN has spent most of his life and career there. The son of a journalist, he went to a grammar school and left aged 17 to take articles with a local three partner firm, Baldwins, whose origins pre-dated the formation of the ICAEW. He took second place in his final exams in 1934, was awarded the Peat Gold Medal, and moved to a 'high class practice' of incorporated accountants, Morgan Brothers, in the City of London. To this experience Parry added a spell in industry during the war, notably with the electronics company, Plessey. However, he returned to the profession in 1946 as a partner with his old firm Baldwins where he remained for the rest of his career. As a fellow of the Institute of Arbitrators he did many arbitrations, usually involving partnership disputes. Parry was prominent in the national Chambers of Trade[3] and in the ICAEW, including helping to organise the examination system. He retired in 1974, although even in his late eighties he, as he put it - 'still does a bit.'

Why did you go into accountancy?

We weighed up a lot of things. Chemistry was my best subject at school. I had an uncle who was director of the Federation of Master Printers, and he had designed their industry wide costing system. I don't think he had a formal accounting qualification, but he was a very able man and that was quite an important job in those days. I think he was a major influence in making me choose accountancy.

How did you find the firm that you joined?

My uncle came down and interviewed the senior partners of several of the local firms, and he felt that this one was the best of the bunch. It was a very old established firm, Baldwin and Son. The then senior partner, Baldwin, was one of the original members of the Institute.

What sort of companies did you audit during your training?

It's hard to think of anything that we didn't do. The county hospital, the forerunner of the Alliance Building Society, we did six or seven building societies and friendly societies. We also did the Brighton Corporation, down to little tiny concerns.

Were there any manufacturing companies?

Dubarry was a big public stock exchange company, manufacturing perfumery products. But I did a bit of everything. Even audited a football pool; an orchid grower, that was in one respect the most difficult one, because nobody knew how to verify the stock.

Can you describe a typical audit when you first started in the late 1920s?

We went out with a fairly detailed audit programme and started by sampling or checking or verifying. If you were doing a building society, you'd take the respective areas, the deposits, the share holdings, the mortgage advances, the investments, or a proportion of them. They'd call the passbooks in very often and you'd inspect a proportion and send out audit letters to members asking them to contact you if they didn't agree the balance. You'd look at the certificates for the investments that the society held. You'd get letters from solicitors who were holding deeds. You'd inspect a proportion of the deeds of the mortgaged properties, and you'd look to see that the mortgage deed itself and the title deeds were in order.

On what basis did you sample?

It would depend entirely on the particular circumstances. With the forerunner of the Alliance Building Society, the volume of accounts, transactions, and documents would be too great to look at all of them. So you might pick a week's sample or you might pick a certain alphabetical section. You would vary it from year to year and you'd make sure that the Society didn't know in advance which you were going to choose.

Who would be in charge of the audit and what would the hierarchy be?

One of the partners would be in ultimate charge. Then there was a qualified managing clerk, there were several qualified members of the staff; then there could well be an unqualified older clerk, and maybe a couple of articled clerks. Occasionally a chap in his final year of articles would be the senior in charge. And we always seemed to have one or two people just in the office to gain experience, who quite likely weren't being paid. We had one fellow with us who was the son of a lord and then he went into stockbroking.

Labour was relatively cheap. The salary of the managing clerk, who was a very well qualified, experienced, certified accountant was three pounds ten shillings[4] a week.

What kept up the quality of the auditing?

The quality was very high and the main motivation was protecting the reputation of the firm.

How did your career progress?

I qualified in 1934 as a chartered accountant and then I was given a qualification as a certified accountant. (I have sat on the T&R committee[5] of both ruling bodies). I then moved to a very well known firm in London, Morgan Brothers, the senior of which was a past president of the Society of Incorporated Accountants[6] and they had a very high class practice. It wasn't a huge one, but had very good clients. I did share transfer audits[7] for big companies, a very big prospectus for a share issue from a big estate development company called, New Ideal Homesteads, which I think is still in existence. Two men in their third year of operation made about a third of a million profit, which in today's money is a very large amount. I did wool merchants. What I very rarely did was a straightforward job! I helped in a case involving the shareholders of ICI, against ICI, in the High Court. It concerned the rights of the deferred shareholders.[8] When they merged the ordinary shares and the deferred shares, the deferred shareholders felt that they had had a raw deal. We came up against the senior partners of Price Waterhouse in that.

How did you come to leave Baldwins?

In 1937, I was offered the job of secretary and chief accountant of Raphael Tuck, the fine art and Christmas card publishers, which was a stock exchange quoted company with subsidiaries in the United States and Australia. Turquand, Youngs were our auditors. They had a brilliant chap who was in charge of our audit. Anyway, then war broke out. Tucks were having departments closed down. Then the London Blitz took three of our four premises out of action, and so I then switched through a friend of the family to become chief accountant of a thing called the Meat Transport Pool. This was a non-profit making organisation set up by the trade. It operated under the Ministry of Food and we hired all the fleets of meat transport vehicles. We undertook all the haulage of meat long distance throughout the country and the local deliveries in the southern half of England.

But I had no wish to remain a civil servant. I was way above their salary range. I then became the deputy chief accountant of the Plessey group. It was a very big, complex organisation with 15,000 employees. There were three qualified accountants at Plessey then and two of us ran the accounts department, and we also ran the cost office. We had two hundred people in the accounts department. I negotiated product prices with the accountants from the Ministry of Supply and I also used to sell all their scrap in my spare time.

Who audited Plessey?

The auditors were Deloittes and the manager in charge was Guy Densem, who became the President of the Institute.[9]

How long did you stay with Plessey?

About six years full time and then another five to six years as a consultant. I left them after the war had finished when I was offered a partnership in Baldwins back down here. This had repercussions because the next thing that happened, I went on the Oxford University summer courses,[10] met a lot of the top brass from the Institute and I got involved in giving lectures to returning service men.

Then I was invited to become an Institute examiner. I set the papers. I started with General Financial Knowledge and then it changed over eventually to Management Accounting, Accounts 3. I did it for 30 years, 62 examinations. It started with 700 candidates and the last one I did was just over 5,500. I had a team of people. I had two or three directors of American Express. Robert McNeil,[11] Ian McNeil's father helped me for a time, and Ian McNeil served his articles with us.

How did you go about the job of examiner?

You set the questions. You had another member as a moderator. Sir Harold Howitt[12] used to be one. His nephew, Tony Howitt, a cost accountant, also became one later, and Gordon Turner[13] was my first moderator. You'd agree the paper with him, then they would have a big round table meeting in Moorgate Place, with all the moderators, all the examiners and the chairman of the Examination Committee. Then you'd go through all the papers, one after another, no holds barred, no punches pulled, start at ten o'clock, and by about five o'clock in the afternoon, having worked through lunchtime with a sandwich and a drink, you'd end up with seven or eight agreed papers.

Then you would be responsible for the marking, with assistance. We did a very careful, 'audit' you could call it. A checking of the examiners' work to make sure that every page was marked, that the marks added up, and that they were correctly transferred to the summary sheets. I had a special system for doing that. With the university people, and there were one or two university teams, they always worked on the basis that the chap marked the whole paper for a small number of candidates. I found that it was terribly hard to get two or three people to mark to a sufficiently close standard. So I insisted that most people only marked one question. The same question for say 2,500 candidates. So to begin with you would have a team of two people per question and we would each mark a couple of hundred, something like that, until we felt we'd ironed out what to expect. We knew the likely responses, we weighed up in our mind what different approaches were worth, and we set out a marking scale. We'd sit down and agree that with each other. Then we'd forget the ones we had done which were in pencil, push them way back in the pile, start afresh and pick them up preferably in the second half. Then I'd have other teams doing the other questions and I would sit in on all the lot, and agree it with each team and then I would review a small number. As I said other people, like the university teams, had different methods, but the Institute had a review of it at one time and, without quoting names or quoting teams, our system was described as the best.

What was the pass mark?

We never knew it, thank goodness, because if you knew the pass mark you'd be going back on the marginal ones, agonising over whether to give them another mark or not. The staff settled that with the chairman of the exam committee, probably on a statistical basis.

They wanted to let so many through that year and so they'd make the pass mark higher or lower?

I'm sure numbers never entered into it. It was based on a system where they took the top couple of hundred or so, found the average mark there and then took 15 percentage points below that as the pass mark. It was pretty rigid and would only be varied in extreme circumstances.

Can you tell us about your partnership?

I had one other partner and in all the years we stayed together, we never remotely had a quarrel. The nearest we got to an argument was if somebody gave us one bottle of booze. I'd say,—you have it, he'd say,—no you have it. We brought junior partners in later on and they had a share but a much smaller one. We ended up with eight partners, and about 80 staff.

Can you describe the work you were doing as a partner?

We became very interested in the Chambers of Commerce and Chambers of Trade. My partner ran the Brighton Chamber of Commerce; I was a board member of the National Chamber of Trade and was on the committee of the British Chambers of Commerce. In fact, I did two years as national president of the national Chamber of Trade. So quite a bit of my time went on that, and the rest of it was nearly all the difficult assignments that other people didn't want, rescuing people who were in financial difficulties, very complicated deceased estates and that sort of thing. I was never good at saying no to people and I couldn't resist a challenge. If somebody told me I couldn't do something I liked to do it to prove them wrong.

What did you do in a rescue?

I'll give you two examples. One was the senior partner of a very big firm of estate agents. He had left well over a hundred thousand. Half of it went in estate duty and legacies, and costs took it down to forty thousand. We had a house for the widow that took thirty thousand. There was ten thousand left to invest. This was being administered by the solicitors but the thousand per year it earned wouldn't pay the boarding school fees for the young children. So I persuaded them to defer realising everything, and negotiated with the estate agent's firm and with everybody else in sight and persuaded them to keep the money in the firm. I still run it and it is now worth about three-quarters of a million.

Another one was a Midlander, a wheeler/dealer who had a lot of businesses in engineering and manufacturing; he was a member of Lloyd's, had interests here, in Switzerland, in Germany, and left a very complicated estate. He also left three women who each tried to bury him! He had a huge country house in Devonshire and a lady friend there who had a new Rolls Royce every year. He had another lady friend in Switzerland. She had to put up with a second hand one. And he had a wife in Surrey who had a Ford!

Well the solicitor was the executor and he ran a mile. The family was quarrelling. But I had been his accountant and I thought I was the only person who could possibly rescue it. It took me over ten years. I traced over 200 cars that he had owned, and farms, big ones, a big country house, accounts in the names of his lady friends, a son in Switzerland, and two families over here. I mustn't give away identifiable things. The hardest day of my life was negotiating in Switzerland, where he had a joint venture making office machines. The machines didn't work very well and the partners believed he was a millionaire and looked to him for payment. We'd looked to them for payment. I came out of it well in the end.

He also had a big business in the Midlands, a joint fifty/fifty venture with a German company. He had given a bank guarantee and the Germans wouldn't take it over. The chairman of the Bar Council advised me to call the guarantee in, the bank would have required its payment and that would have bankrupted the estate. So I went against the advice and in the end we pulled things round. There were also several lots of litigation which we resolved and in the end I shared out half a million between the family. I wouldn't want to do that again.

The other thing I did was to hold people's hands, and I found that I was taking work from our competitors because they wouldn't do it. What happened, for example, was a woman came to me. She had been left a business jointly with her brother when their father died and the brother wanted to buy her out, and she wanted somebody to see she got a fair price. So I negotiated a much higher price than she'd been offered. A year or so later, the brother's premises were being compulsorily acquired by the local authority and he didn't know what to do. He had been offered alternative, much more expensive premises. If he had enough business to pay the rent on the bigger premises, he hadn't got the capital to run the business and if he didn't up the turnover he couldn't pay the rent. He said he couldn't get any sensible advice out of his accountants, and could I help? So we sat down, we worked out a lot of budgets and the figures. I went along with him to the bank manager. We presented the case, the manager said,- help yourself, we are pleased to back you. It worked out almost spot on, and that bank manager recommended half a dozen other jobs to us. The firm that wouldn't or couldn't give the advice is now part of one of the Big 6. I won't tell you their name.

I got more satisfaction from that sort of thing than from auditing.

Did you do other non-audit work?

I also set up and ran quite a lot of self-administered pension schemes. I found that with this sort of service and holding people's hands the clients never argued about fees. Their question always was,—look Parry will you stay helping me? Now if they had one of the big firms of consultants in they couldn't get them out quickly enough because they were expensive, they disrupted the normal procedure, and from what I've seen of them their reports often weren't worth having. For a stranger to go into a business and think he can get the feel of it, get all the answers at once is nonsense. When I went into Plessey it was six months before I dared change anything, and I was working full-time. Although when I went into Tucks, they had got rid of the previous accountant secretary, so of course I had to take it on from the word go.

Was there any formalisation of the audit procedure in the 50s? Would you have an audit manual by the time you finished?

We didn't have an audit manual, Coopers did.[14] I remember talking to Henry Benson and their big worry was keeping control of the staff. There were huge numbers of people, they didn't know what they were getting up to, they were scared out of their wits and this was the origin of the audit manuals. Now where you had a small team of 20 or 30 people, they were so much in contact with each other that your techniques were passed down by example and instruction. The programme was written out and you would have a great thick file of working papers. Some you would produce yourself. There would be schedules of debtors and creditors, payments in advance and stock summaries and so on.

Did you ever detect fraud?

Oh yes, but it wasn't very common. One I detected because I was vouching[15] petty cash,[16] and there were a lot of bills for BP petrol and one I saw was for Esso, and it made me look at it again. I ferreted a bit and discovered that one of the staff was filling up his car and putting it through the petty cash as if it was the managing director's. We followed it through and we found a few other things that were fraudulent.

Another one was pre-war in one of the bigger building societies. We were unhappy about one branch, but we couldn't pick on anything definite. Anyway, we told the head office management we didn't feel completely happy. They sent a small team down to investigate, and they came back and said,—you needn't worry, everything is absolutely OK. Come the end of the year we made a point of sending out an extra large number of letters to depositors, asking them to report if they didn't agree with their balance. We didn't get a single reply from anyone for accounts at that branch, but we did from the other branches. Then a month or two later, it was spotted that a passbook disagreed with the ledger.[17] When we went down there we found about 40 accounts that had been fiddled. Instead of writing in as requested the people had all been in to see the manager who told them not to worry, it was head office's fault and he would get it sorted out.

So what was the fraud?

The manager was taking money and debiting it to members' accounts as if it was a withdrawal. He got prosecuted and went to prison. We were sitting pretty because we had warned them and they were a little bit red faced because they had been down there and said it was OK.

Do you think fraud has been on the increase?

I don't think so. Probably a two—way movement. In some ways people are less honest and some are a bit more honest. More people were strongly religious then. On the other hand there were a lot of people who almost lived by minor fiddling. Hotel staff, hospital staff, people like that.

Low paid people?

Yes. In one hotel they found sides of bacon and sacks of sugar were going out, disappearing, and they couldn't find out why. They weren't going past the front door. Then they discovered that from the store room there was a narrow window, about pavement level, which could be opened and things were being pushed out.

How did you assess audit fees? Was that on a rigid basis?

No, far from it. The majority of fees in relation to businesses that were relatively static were agreed in advance. It might be five hundred, a thousand, what have you. But if you had a business that was expanding rapidly or was a bit of a problem, then we'd expect it to be left until we finished and it could vary a lot.

When we did the New Ideal Homesteads, this was before the war, that expanded at an enormous rate and we found a lot of discrepancies which all took time. So we had to be that bit more tolerant when setting the fees. For example, laying out an estate, the builder draws up the plans. It is approved by the local authority and maybe he's got 50 houses on one side of the road, numbered from say, two to 100. Then they find they aren't selling as well as they wanted. They decide to take out some detached houses and put in semi-detached or a couple more bungalows, and now there are only 48. So instead of two—100, it's two—96. So the house you sold as 94, may now be 90, and we found one or two cases where they changed several times, and apparently the same house had a deposit as a bungalow and it had been sold as a semi-detached (laughs here). And it had to be sorted out. In one case we had to send someone down to the estate, knock on the door and say, excuse me, what's your name? It was simply very rapid expansion. They had to keep on taking on staff and it got a bit beyond them. They used to give 100% mortgages and a lot of people did moonlight flits. So there we erred on the cautious side. Then you had another sort of problem, particularly in Kent. A lot of the land there suffers from having holes in it and you can't tell whether you can build until you bored holes to make sure it was solid. So we used to value the plots only on the basis of those that had been proved buildable on. But they didn't want to do this in advance of having to because they were hard up. They were making big profits, but very little money in the bank, with a big overdraft. So with successive audits you'd have a new calculation and bring a bit more value into the picture. When we really sorted the thing out, we had more profit then we certified for in the prospectus.

How did you get clients?

A big mixture. Mainly recommendation. Strangely enough I found that some of my worst clients produced the best introductions. One or two people we were on the point of chucking out, came up with extremely good introductions.

Did other firms in Brighton engage in touting?

We used to get funny things. The worst were the insolvency people; they did a bit of what you might call touting. But before the war accountants had very little to do with each other. We didn't have any joint committees and it was on the cards that if you saw another accountant coming down the street, you'd cross over the road. They were much more secretive, although they knew each other.

Have accounts become more true and fair in the course of your career?

Again, a little bit of a two-way movement. There are more opportunities for distortion. There's a bit more opportunity to be untrue and there is another point I used to argue with them. You can't get rules to fit everybody. Look at the problem of measuring assets. If you have a company that builds a ship, say for the sake of argument it costs £1,000,000. It has enough money to start with and it doesn't borrow any. The next company starts building a similar ship, it has no money and it borrows the lot. Now do you capitalise interest on the construction cost? The first company has the money; you haven't paid any interest. The next one hadn't any money but it borrowed, so they capitalise the interest and it ends up costing say £1,200,000. Or you've written off £200,000 interest and you say the company lost £200,000 during the building period. But to say it lost money isn't true. The thing has gone according to plan; it may have gone better than planned. There is no absolute truth there. You've got more uniformity today but because of the absence of judgment, in many cases you get less real truth.

Do you have any views on the major auditing failures in the last ten years or so? Where do you think things went wrong with the Maxwell situation and Coopers and Lybrand,[18] *or BCCI and Price Waterhouse?*[19]

Maxwell was a very exceptional case. He was a very exceptional individual, who chucked his weight around and people didn't resist him. If they did they were out on their necks. The City didn't trust him. I had investments in his companies and I sold out in good time at a nice profit because we didn't trust him.

But Coopers and Lybrand trusted him?

Well the thing was very split up and he was the only person who had the overall picture. Without trust you get nowhere—it oils the works doesn't it?

When there was so much suspicion around, of all people, the auditors should have been suspicious, shouldn't they?

I would have thought so. Coopers were always looked upon as the tough guys who wouldn't bend to anybody. But senior partners change.

When Benson was in charge perhaps it was tougher?

Possibly.

How was it that Spicer & Pegler didn't see what was going on at Barlow Clowes?[20]

That didn't begin to add up. I saw all their adverts and took one good look and said,- this can't be right. So we never touched it.

You couldn't earn that rate of interest from government stock?

No.

So why didn't the auditors work that out?

Well in any sphere of life some are average and some are below average.

Uniquely in our study, ALAN FABES and his long standing partner and friend ARTHUR CHAPMAN were interviewed together (their contributions are indicated by their initials). Arthur was born in 1912 in south London, the son of a department store owner and was educated at Ardingly College, a minor public school in Sussex. He took articles with the four partner London firm of Thorne, Lancaster, qualified in 1936 and three years later joined a firm headed by Wilfred North, before going off to war. Alan was born in 1910, the son of a caterer in south London. He attended Abingdon, also a minor public school in Berkshire and was then articled in 1929 to the four partner London firm of White, Fairbrother & Steele. He qualified in 1935 and after war service, joined as a partner in Arthur's firm. In 1952, as North, Chapman they merged with Cork Gully and headed their audit section for many years. Alan retired in 1972 and Arthur did so in 1978 but continued some part-time accountancy work until he was 86.

What jobs were you asked to do in training in the 1930s?

AC For the first three years I was mostly in the office doing pretty menial jobs, but I was taken out onsite occasionally to audit, mostly to check additions. In the office it was usually brown paper parcel jobs,[21] which I had to check over. I was taught to sort things out and list certain items. When you'd taken your Intermediate you were given more responsibility. My first main client then was Boyd's who sold pianos on hire purchase: thousands of people buying at two shillings a week. I would go there two or three times a week to collect their cards, check them against the ledger, circularise the debtors[22] and send the cards back. You were a postage clerk really; it took weeks and weeks of your time.

AF My office duties mainly consisted in answering the phone. But because I was fairly bright I was taken out on audits; I was fortunate because after six months I was able to produce accounts up to trial balance stage.[23] These were always double-checked but usually accepted. By the time I took my Intermediate I was producing complete accounts: so much so that I was doing many a senior's work and I thought I knew it all. However, this caused my training to be neglected and I failed my Inter the first time. I told my boss that I'd failed and he allowed me a week off to swot for the resit. I said,—Is that all you can do? He replied,—O.K. You can have a fortnight and I'll give you a bit more money. Now go and see if you can cope.

How closely were you supervised?

AC You were under a senior's eyes all the time. Supervision was very close and it stemmed from the chap in charge of the job.

AF I was subject to the supervision of a senior until I qualified, although I was not accompanied on every job. Very rarely would I report to the partner. I was very lucky in having a good senior, who helped me a lot despite being very strict.

AC We had no audit managers but we did have a managing clerk and a lot of unqualified seniors who were very good at their job. You don't get them now but firms were full of them in those days. Good solid men in their 40s who taught you your job.

You rarely saw the partners unless you were on an interesting job. I was articled to the senior partner and I saw him exactly twice. When I passed my finals he sent his son to congratulate me. A very pompous old gentleman. The partners were not at all hands-on. I often wondered just what they did. They were shut in their rooms or out playing golf. They lived in a strange world.

Can you tell me about some of your clients?

AF One of our biggest clients was a chain of public houses with their offices in the Strand. Another firm produced their own accounts, and we used to audit them and we'd always do a half-yearly audit. We had a big flour mill on the Old Kent Road and a cork importer in Aldgate; an enormous business bringing in cork from Portugal, and all quite interesting. We had several firms in Mincing Lane that imported canned fruit, spices, coffee and tea. I enjoyed going to tea sales.

AC One of our clients used to perforate postage stamps and every sheet was initialled in order to prevent fraud. They had hundreds of huge cash sheets, and I was given the job because I could add up quickly.

It was nice to go away on a big job sometimes. If the client was big enough they wouldn't query the bill too much, and you could live quite well. There was a big firm up in Lancashire who manufactured cellophane when it first came out. They never queried your expenses, and I went there several times.

What happened after you qualified?

AC War broke out! I was one of the first in our firm to be called up in 1939, and I went to work in an ordnance factory.

AF I was newly qualified too and I went into the Ministry of Supply as an administrative assistant.

AC Round about 1943 I met my ex-boss and asked about becoming a partner after the war. He agreed.

AF I joined as a partner at the same time.

How did you work out the profit share as partners?

AC After costs and salaries it was divided equally.

AF But we never knew the senior partner's salary!

AC This share-out only happened once or twice because we were quickly bought out by Cork Gully and we became partners with them.

It all happened because a catering company had gone bust, when it had just won a tender for the Festival of Britain.[24] A key player in CG put my name forward to the investigators as a neutral accountant that knew something about the catering trade.

That's when I first met Kenneth Cork.[25] I went into his office and he said,—I'm very busy. Here's the paperwork. Get on with it. He must have been pleased with us because he gave us several jobs afterwards and then asked us to run the audit side of CG

So you both went into CG as full partners?

AC At the time, there only was Walter Tickler and Harry Cork. It is ironic that it all started because a tea bar went bust!

How did CG organise their profit share?

AC When we joined, we took a large salary hike as new partners, though the owners kept the lion's share. We were fairly treated by CG as the profit was shared equally, but your salary reflected your seniority in the firm, and they made it quite clear that there was no pension and you were expected to make your own provision for your retirement.

It was difficult for us running the audit section in an insolvency practice, since insolvency was where the money was. The insolvency partners thought they should have more money, and for a while this was reflected in salaries. This meant that if you got anyone good they could be lured away by the insolvency section. We solved this problem by introducing a scale based on seniority regardless of your discipline.

You must have seen great changes in the audit post-war?

AF When I was articled we never circularised debtors, but I had to in my first audit with CG. It was a big wholesale grocers in Maidstone who supplied depots, shops, hospitals and schools. We wrote around to all of them every year asking them to confirm their balances and about half responded, which is where the circularisation of debtors is useless.

Now Kent County Council was in the half that did respond, and accordingly their head accountant thought their accounts were gospel and insisted that we do the same for their audit. They had many depots that sent money to this chap King in the grocers who would store up the cash and every three months send off a cheque, so the banking always looked right. With circularisation of debtors, of course, the balances were shown to be wrong. King evidently hoped that debtors would not respond.

AC This was the chap who committed suicide.

Before or after he was caught?

AF It was in 1960 and we were instructed to do a special audit because there had been a take-over bid. I went along to see King at five o'clock on a Friday evening and said,- We've spotted a difference in the cash account. You're in on Monday, aren't you? I'm sure we can sort things out.

He knew we'd find him out, and when I went into the office on the Monday I was told that he'd shot himself on the Sunday. He was made to carry the can for a lot of things, and the firm trying to take then over was not best pleased.

Was attending stocktaking common?

AF We didn't physically attend stocktaking until well into the 1960s.

What brought about the change?

AF People became more interested in verifying the actual assets of a company rather than what was posted. It became the practice to attend the stocktake and see how they did things. We were very often faced with something we didn't understand and we would have to satisfy ourselves as to the accuracy of their methods, until we took more and more on board and became quite expert ourselves.

AC No one can know everything. Stock was obviously a place where fraud could be carried out. Although this was clearly the directors' responsibility, we had a watching brief and hoped that the powers that be were satisfied with their staff's methods.

Were there other changes?

AC Again, it was not the general practice in the early years to check the percentages or the rates of gross profits. Accountants were very lax in checking those figures, especially in the provinces. They were only interested in producing accounts for the tax inspector, as in,- here is your tax bill, Mr. So and So, and here is our bill.

Gradually we became more sophisticated; we would look at what a client was producing and conclude that they should be making a gross profit of such and such.

Before the war, many's the time I've argued with accountants in the provinces and said,- look your accounts are rubbish. The company ought to be making x% profit, why isn't it? How the hell should I know?—he'd reply. As the accountant you ought to know that certain types of business should make certain profits, and if not, why not. This philosophy became more prevalent after the war.

We're now in the computer age. Have auditors kept up with the fraudsters in the exploitation of IT?

AF It's neck and neck. We used to have a huge spreadsheet for accounts, but with computers this became a columnar sheet, which showed the same result but with less information of origin. Auditors could still ask for proof of this information though.

And the information on the audit certificate changed and things got much more complex. So much so over the last ten years that we now have a special Audit Certificate Committee within the Institute, who altered the whole thing and not necessarily for the better.

The auditor used to take responsibility for the figures he produced himself. Now he is more or less given the figures, and the responsibility for their accuracy sits squarely on the shoulders of the directors. But there is so much rubbish put into accounts nowadays to substantiate the figures that the directors don't get a chance to read them. As a result, the audit has become much more of a rubber-stamping exercise, and I'm not sure that's progress.

Born in Merseyside in 1914, GEOFFREY THORNTON *was the son of a timber importer. After secondary education at the minor public schools, Liverpool College and King William's College on the Isle of Man, he took up articles with the three-partner firm, Knox Hassal who, in 1934, became Liverpool agents for the Scottish firm, Mann, Judd, Gordon. The latter introduced more advanced auditing practices to Geoffrey and proved an enduring influence throughout his career. He qualified in 1938 and set up his own practice in Runcorn, Cheshire, just prior to being called up for war service. He resumed practice in 1946 and in 1951 moved to Bideford in Devon, where he set up again, with a partner in Barnstaple. This proved unsatisfactory and the partnership was dissolved. From 1955 onwards the expansion of his business enabled him to bring in a small number of partners, culminating in a merger with Turquands Barton Mayhew in 1974. He retired in 1980 following his firm's merger with Whinney Murray, (now Ernst & Young). Geoffrey's career has been painstakingly and entertainingly recorded in an autobiography he wrote for the benefit of his friends and family and some material from this source has been used here.*

Why did you decide on accountancy?

I listened to my father. I was very fond of my father and I knew that anything he suggested could only be for my ultimate good.

Did you have to pay a premium?

Yes. £250. I got some back as wages but they were so mean. Maybe that was the custom in those days but I never felt that there was any generosity. I also remember having a bitter argument over non-payment of expenses for working away from home which led to me walking out temporarily.

Can you give me a general idea of the kind of jobs you were asked to do when you were doing your articles?

I would not describe what Knox Hassal did as auditing. I do not know what you'd call it. But Mann, Judd did proper auditing and when we worked for them a colleague used to say,—We are now working for a very big, very important firm and we mustn't let them down in any way at all.

How would that involve you?

I worked with one other chap who was extremely nice and efficient who had learned a lot from his principal, whom I never met. When I first met him he was not qualified, but later on he did qualify and eventually became company secretary for one of our bigger audits in Liverpool, a wholesale grocer. I was lucky to work with him because otherwise I would have gone on messing around just sticking ticks on things.

What did 'proper' auditing entail in the 1930s?

Proper auditing requires knowledge of the system of internal checks and those internal checks should be thoroughly tested to see that they are in place and up to date. That was the essential thing. All the jobs we did were sizeable and there were many sizeable problems. Fortunately, most of the officers of the companies audited had been recruited or seconded from Mann, Judd and had very good training and they all knew each other. And the work I was doing was of practical use for my exam studies for the first time.

How did you go about testing controls?

When I went on an audit for the first time, I would be given a rough indication of what work was involved, what the supervision was, who were heads of the various departments and I would be taken to meet the directors, the secretary, the accountant, the assistant accountant and so on. The audit programme laid down sample checks on selected items, and if these were correct then it was assumed that the others were likely to be correct also.

How closely were you supervised?

There were various ways of doing things, and I was encouraged to use my initiative, but it was essential that any enquiries were dealt with properly. In the afternoon one tended to get a bit dozy. My companion would test me informally to find out if I was alert; he would deliberately give me a wrong figure, and if I accepted it then I paid a fine, and if the person being checked saw through it, the questioner had to pay a fine. And I would do the same to him. You'd have to pick and choose fairly carefully the challenge you threw out; you would not want to have to pay. Can I show you something? This is a dabber. (A pen-like object with a wooden stock and a metal tip.) As you see, at the end of the metal there is an initial. In my case it is G. We each had a dabber, which was personalised, usually with an initial. It might be a surname, might be a Christian name. And then you dabbed it on the inkpad and ticked any entry you had checked. It was very neat.

And that was standard for your checks?

Yes, that was part of our auditing equipment. You could see exactly who checked what. Each dab could do about three ticks. Very quick and unique to the user. And then there was a numbered rubber cancel stamp that went with it.

Did you come across any frauds when you were in training?

I remember one—Morris and Jones, a sizeable Liverpool company—because a director actually went to jail.

You qualified in 1938 and set up on your own in Runcorn. What happened then?

I was in the Territorial Army and was called up before the war started, so I had nearly a year to establish things. The only thing I could do when I joined up was to give power of attorney to a very good friend, who was a partner in another firm and much older than I was.

How did the practice differ when you moved to Bideford in 1951?

The work was mostly from incomplete records rather than auditing. The clients seldom had any financial controls and one could not do anything to persuade them to bring them in. They would say,- yes; but they had no intention of following the advice of the accountant. None at all. I was very keen on being properly organised. It was all-important to me. My attitude was to get the accounts completely right. No messing; no half measures. In the interests of the clients themselves, accounts should be as near to 100% as possible.

Did you ever in fact resign from an audit?

I had to resign occasionally. How could you do the job properly without the client being straight?

Did you ever have hostile relationships with clients?

Sometimes, particularly with back duty work.[26] If a client accused me of working for the Revenue I would suggest that if he had no confidence in me he should instruct another accountant.

Were there cases when you were denied information that you felt you were entitled to?

Oh yes, and I insisted on getting it. With back duty work you had to be positive. It was amazing the amount of information you'd get. Also, the first thing I did with a new client would be to interview him, have a rough idea of things. At that first meeting I'd get him to sign authorities for all his bank accounts; from that point on I could obtain all the information I needed.

How did you go about resolving disagreements over the presentation of accounts?

I cannot recall the situation ever arising.

You would expect the client to do exactly what you wanted?

Yes, that is right.

Did you ever have to formally qualify a client's accounts?

Occasionally. The difficulty arose because accounts must comply with company law. Clients had to obey the rules, and if they didn't I would report the fact.

Did you ever come under pressure from clients who threatened to go elsewhere?

I would tell any client that there had to be a sense of mutuality; that he must be satisfied that I was trying to do my best for him and that I must be prepared to act for him. If that mutuality did not exist, it would be better for him to go elsewhere. I do not think anybody would ever threaten me.

When you started in Bideford, how did you set about attracting new business?

Reputation and word of mouth.

Did you get involved in the Rotary Club or the golf club?

I was a member of the golf club.

But that was not significant?

No. I think the best way is being recommended by satisfied clients. Also, by solicitors and bank managers.

Did you have any problems from other accountants?

No.

Did you ever have to complain about another firm?

No.

How did you assess fees?

Purely by time and responsibility. You had to have proper time records. That was absolutely essential to any practice. There was a time when I used to account for every six minutes of my time.

Would you ever be gentle with an existing client who you saw was in difficulty by scaling down fees?

I did try to take into consideration the position of the client.

The son of a dealer in musical instruments, JOHN SIMPKINS was born in Barnstaple, Devon in 1920. After leaving Barnstaple Grammar School in 1938 he took up articles with the small Exeter firm of Orchard and Hamlyn, which merged one year later with the larger West Country firm, Ware, Ward. He took third place nationally in his Intermediate exam, first place in his Finals and was awarded many prizes. After qualification in 1943 John spent a further seven years with Ware, Ward before moving to Nevill, Hovey, Smith as a partner. This proved unsatisfactory, and he very shortly founded his own practice in Exeter, Simpkins, Edwards, where he remained as senior partner until his retirement in 1985.

What sort of firm were Ware, Ward?

Our head office was in Bristol, with branches in Exeter and Torquay and smaller offices in Sidmouth and one or two other places. They were, in the 1940s, by far the largest firm of chartered accountants in the South West, and a firm of very high standards; I was extremely fortunate to be articled with them.

What were you asked to do as an articled clerk?

Again, I was extremely fortunate because it so happened that just at the point I was articled there seemed to be a dearth of suitable applicants. Therefore the more interesting, more demanding work wasn't farmed out amongst all that many people and I got a much better experience than I might reasonably have expected. I was very much on the technical side, doing audit work and the preparation of accounts, but I also dealt with insolvencies and taxation; not all that many people were familiar with them.

How much supervision did you receive when conducting an audit?

After my Intermediate exam I took charge of the whole audit, reporting to the partner concerned, but very much left to my own devices. Even when I dealt with the local authority audits there was comparatively little supervision of the way I carried out the work. I frequently wrote audit programmes.

Would that be with new clients?

Yes or with existing clients who weren't up to date; their audit requirements obviously differ as time goes by. For example, I would sometimes be in a situation where there was something in an audit programme which struck me as thoroughly unnecessary, or that something we ought to do wasn't in the programme. To that extent I was responsible for drafting the programme and I also contributed to discussions about change.

Who were Ware, Ward's clients?

In addition to the local authority, we did a local savings bank audit, but I can't think of a single listed public company we audited. We did have a lot of private companies and we audited those very much to the same standard as we did the public companies. We did have a few public unquoted companies, perhaps half a dozen, the South West being predominantly non-manufacturing. Most businesses of any size were not based in the South West but in London or Birmingham or wherever it may be. As far back as 1939, if you looked at Exeter High Street there were hardly any shops that we audited, they were nearly all audited by firms in say, London. Eventually we reached a point by about 1970, when they wouldn't even keep the books in Exeter; they would just bank the money and send off the payment slips to show what they had banked, all the records were kept elsewhere.

Did things change when you set up on your own?

No. In many ways all the firms I was with were quite similar. With my own practice, I sought to follow the standards of the two practices in which I previously worked.

How many partners did you build up to?

By the time I retired, we were a fairly large firm in terms of work on purely private company audits; we ended up with about 10 partners and fees of rather more than a million.

What were the main changes in the audit over the course of your career?

Change lay primarily in the fact that the firms we audited tended to be smaller businesses because the larger ones were nearly all run from elsewhere. To some extent, the detailed checking gradually got less as things like the systems approach[27] came in, and supervision of the way the work was done tended to increase.

Did you find that you were more and more dealing with business that did their own accounts?

No that remained fairly constant throughout the 50 years.

A large part of the audit would still incorporate a basic bookkeeping role?

Yes indeed, there were firms who had their own in-house accountant and competent bookkeepers but they were sometimes faced with unusual situations that weren't dealt with in the way they should be, and as the auditor you knew where the problems were.

Did you find that computers changed the nature of the audit?

It must have done. We were one of the first firms in the South West to be dependent on computers and that made a difference to our staffing.[28] We also did some work on a bureau [consultancy] basis either for clients or for people who otherwise weren't clients. When we dealt with them as clients it simplified the audit because we knew where everything was.

Do you think the purpose of the audit has changed over the years at all?

A bit but not very much. I don't think the public's perception of the audit has changed much; they still look upon it as a device to catch out a bookkeeper on the fiddle. We always tried to make it clear that the prevention of fraud was as much the directors' own responsibility as it was the auditor's. But the larger the business the less practicable it became to do the checking in that way anyway. The primary purpose is still to get the accounts right.

What underpins the accountant's professional ethics?

First of all, when we prepared the accounts, or did the audit or whatever, almost without exception we then agreed the tax liability with the Inland Revenue; so to some extent there was a kind of cross check. In addition, the Institute had its own monitoring of standards, and then most clients were reasonably alert and they would decide if they were getting satisfactory service from their accountants or not, and if they weren't then they would go to somebody else. After all there was a free market.

Did relationships with client management ever get hostile?

No. If we fell out with the directors of a company they would appoint other auditors. That was the easy solution. Just occasionally, we told clients we wouldn't act for them any longer. It sometimes happened that at director level they falsified the books and hoped we wouldn't notice. I can think of two or three of those over the 50 years, which isn't a very high rate. There were a number of occasions where we came across fiddling by senior staff, but that was rather different.

Do you think fraud is more common nowadays?

I think, probably, it is more common. About 40 or 50 years ago most businesses were comparatively small and the directors were in control of what was happening. They were in a position to see that they weren't being defrauded by their staff. But times have changed and you have now got branches of national set ups, and I won't say the shop manager doesn't care if the staff are on the fiddle or not, but he's likely to be less alert because it's not his money they are fiddling.

Did you ever feel your independence as an auditor was compromised?

I don't think I ran into any difficulty. I don't think we were in a position that we had any client whose fee was such a large proportion of our total income that we had to trim ourselves so to speak. I'm sure we didn't.

How did you acquire clients?

I was a Round Table[29] member and one or two of our partners played golf or what have you, but I don't think that brought in much business directly. If someone else in Round Table was looking for an accountant then I would be one of the names he would think of. But in many ways it's a deterrent, because if I got friendly with a chap, he wouldn't want a professional relationship with a friend. I would know his wife and he would know my wife, and it would probably be better if we stayed completely at arm's length. But then, if you were reasonably forward looking, you were always looking for new clients, and if anybody turned up with half a whiff of a new instruction you took it.

How did you assess fees, was it man-hours booked out?

Yes, usually, but just occasionally it came to 'what the traffic would bear.' It's easy to say it's based on so much an hour and time spent, but what do you do when you have only spent an hour or so on something but that has saved the client £20,000? Do you charge him for an hour's time. Then occasionally it is the other way round: you devote a vast amount of time to someone and achieve nothing. It is basically your time you charge for, but it's modified by swings and roundabouts in extreme cases.

Broadly speaking we were expensive. We liked to think we were worth it; clients were buying a Rolls Royce, not a Ford.

What sort of dealings have you had with the Institute over the years?

My relationship with the Institute was always quite cordial. I held all the usual offices in our local branch of the Institute and I once presented a paper at a Cambridge Summer School and again at Church House in Westminster.[30] In the last year or two before I retired, I was the chairman of an organisation we set up to interview principals who took on articled clerks or students. Our remit was make quite sure their office was a fit and proper place for a student or articled clerk to get trained in.

Do you think Standards[31] have changed the profession for the better?

I don't think they have. I think the problem with the Standards and all the rest of it is that they're so convoluted. To some extent they have had to be trimmed to fit in with so many points of view that they are almost valueless. It should all be replaced by one standard, and that's,—you ought to get it right. Also, we should be careful that Standards don't become a substitute for original thought.

I've always had a sneaking fear that the temptation is to follow the audit programme mechanistically, and not bother to apply one's common sense. Rigidly set schedules are partly, if indirectly, the cause of the Maxwells and the Polly Pecks.[32]

Overall, do you think auditing has improved over time?

It's not necessarily any better, though the ground for it has altered. In the old days one was much more concerned with the prevention of fraud, and looking at things in greater detail, possibly checking everything; whereas now with a big client it's practically impossible, you can only do a test check. The approach is quite different.

STANLEY JONES is typical of the interviewees whose training was interrupted by the Second World War. The son of a civil servant he grew up and went to grammar school in Abergavenny and started his training in 1939, aged 19, with the well known south Wales incorporated accountants firm of Sir Frederick Alban. After war service in the Signals Corps he qualified in 1949 and in the early 1950s he became a partner in the firm which later linked up with a major national firm. Stanley finally set up as a sole practitioner in the early-1970s after refusing to move to a new branch in Cardiff. He played a part in the district and national affairs of the Institute, most notably as the examiner for the audit paper for 24 years. He retired in the early 1980s but still, in his late eighties, did the accounts and audits for some small concerns and charities.

How did your career start?

I scratched my head and thought about accountancy. My father said the only accountant he knew was Frederick Alban, who used to be in the civil service with him and was in practice in Newport. I came down to Newport in early 1939 and was articled there. I'd just about started finding my feet as a young clerk when the war came.

I came back in 1946 and because of my overseas service I had two months holidays due to me. Rather foolishly I poked my head in the office in Newport the first few days I was back, and they said,—Oh good, we're glad you're back, we're starting a new audit up in Crewe next week. So much to my disgust I was pitch-forked into it. That was the audit of Crewe Corporation. So I went up there and you can imagine how I felt. I had only been there a few months before the war, and then the partner told me to go and check on British Restaurants.[33] I didn't know much about anything, but I went out trying to look wise going round all these restaurants. I had to write a little report to the partner on each of them, pointing out weaknesses. Anyway I must have got by because I ended up carrying out the audit myself for many years.

What was work like in a post-war accountants office?

We were years behind in the practice. People's accounts had not been prepared because everyone had gone to war. As a result, we were working until eight or nine o'clock at night overtime in the office, just to clear the backlog. By the time I got back home to Abergavenny I was dead tired but I had to start studying at ten at night until one a.m. And catch the eight o'clock train in the morning.

You found the training tough?

Well, Frederick Alban's son was articled with me, and to break his heart, the first few weeks he was in he was given all these bound books, pages and pages of totalling, all done manually. For three weeks he did nothing but add up. They were harder on him than they were on all the rest; that was symptomatic of the training in those days. The most important thing was you had to cast[34] quicker than any client. If you were in a client's office and there was a problem it was considered a great disgrace if you couldn't add up quicker than the chief clerk; it was a matter of pride

What was the range of work?

It was a rather rarefied practice with over three-quarters of the work concentrated on local government or the Boundary Commission.[35] Albans published a lot of textbooks on local authority work. We were the editors of a journal, and also ran a correspondence course, which most borough treasurers in the country took. I started off mainly on the audit side. We did a lot of incomplete records brought in by small clients. We started off with quite a number of biggish companies, but after the war when mergers accelerated it seemed that I would be invited out to lunch somewhere and by the time I came back I'd lost another audit to one of the big boys.

What did an audit entail in those days?

There were very few public companies, everything was on a smaller scale. The essence of an audit was rather like driving a car in the old days. There were no rules but you were taught to behave in a certain way to other road users. You would wave people on if they were coming up hill and you were going down.

There were printed programmes of course—for every type of business. They were very elementary but there were procedures we had to go through. Then, if you suddenly got appointed to a tramway company or something, instead of having to start from scratch you had some idea. The person in charge more or less supervised things. He used all his team to do the essential work and kept himself free to flitter, and where he was at all troubled, he could delve. Then when he felt satisfied, the audit was over. It was very much a personal style. I still used it years afterwards when I used to go up to Crewe Corporation. They would say,—how long are you going to be there? And I would say,—I don't know. It varied between a fortnight and three weeks. When I went on my own, the philosophy was,—until you are satisfied, you haven't finished. It was a personal thing. You had to be satisfied that there was nothing adrift.

Did you ever have to qualify accounts?

We put some pretty horrendous qualifications on Julian Hodge[36] at one stage.

So you audited Hodge's companies as well?

I didn't personally. I used to do the group accounts of United Transport in Newport. I remember qualifying some and having to suck the end of my pencil to get the wording just right. I did it when things got a bit tricky, when there were doubts about the viability of a company. That [qualifications] came in a little more commonly in the end.

How would it go when you informed the management that you were going to qualify their accounts?

They didn't like it, but they couldn't argue. Being awkward would do them more harm than good. We knew that they would lose more by taking umbrage with us and by trying to get rid of us. We had standing in the profession in south Wales and if someone wanted us to go it wouldn't do them any good. They would lose more than they would by just accepting what we told them.

So you didn't feel under any pressure that by qualifying you might lose the audit and the business?

I didn't myself. Our business was fairly widely dispersed, and we had no particular audit where it was a case of sink or swim, we must hold onto it. In the 1950s and 1960s we lost most of our bigger companies to national firms because of mergers and take-overs.

What was the competitive relationship between accounting firms? How did you acquire new audits?

I am old fashioned, I wince when I see some of the advertising that goes on. In my day 99% of it was a client would recommend you. Sometimes there might be another accountant from another area, who would say,—if you want someone in Newport, go and see so and so. However, there was a person who I kept as a client for many, many years. I was sitting next to him at a dinner once and said to him,—by the way, one thing I have always been curious about is what made you choose us? He burst out laughing and said,—Easy, Alban's your name and A is the first letter in the book!

What was keeping up the quality of the audit work then?

Until you reached the point where you were satisfied, you didn't sign off the accounts. You could make mistakes. Once I was auditing a water board. We were a little bit suspicious of the engineer in charge because he had come in from a commercial firm outside and local government was always suspicious of that. I was going through his personal accounts and someone pointed out to me a sum of £5 for babies nappies. I knew that his daughter had just had a baby since I had seen the pram outside. So I said to him,—what's this figure here for babies nappies? He said,—I thought you would ask me that, and he pulled out a letter from his pocket from an irate housewife who had had her nappies spoilt by something in the water supply and part of his public relations role had been to reimburse her for the nappies.

Did management ever refuse to divulge information to you?

Occasionally; there was a storekeeper on an audit where we used to have all the certificates of stores apart from his. He had a chip on his shoulder because he felt it really wasn't his job to cooperate. So he would wait until we were walking out at the end of the audit, catch us in the corridor and say,—I think this is what you wanted. It became almost a joke.

Did you ever find any fraud?

Nothing in local government. The commercial one that comes to mind was when I was quite young. There was an outfitter with eight branches all around south Wales and we used to go around four every year. On one we had some reservations but nothing you could put your fingers on. I went down to Swansea to make tests and caught the manager when he wasn't expecting me; it was completely outside the normal audit time. I did an up to date check and all the receipts were dated for the following day. It took me some time to work it out, but at the end of that week he resigned and left. What he was doing was making sales, and using the cash personally. These things tend to mushroom and get out of hand; I think he had been doing it for a couple years, with the amount going up all the time. So you get some results from your audit in catching out people.

The audit was effective in detecting fraud?

The audit was effective where people had that rather old-fashioned approach to things, a personal feeling that you had to be satisfied things were right. It was possible with the smaller volume that there was before the war of reaching a point where I would have been very surprised to find that I was wrong in giving a clean bill of health to a company.

It was more a gut feeling?

Intuition. I had a partner once; a good accountant. He was Borough Treasurer of Neath when he was 23. You don't appoint someone treasurer unless he has got ability. He came into our firm as a partner and he came on a few of these Crewe audits with me. I remember being with him on one and he was looking at a ledger and he said,—I don't like this. So I came across and looked at it. I couldn't see anything and said,—it's alright. He said,—no, there's something wrong. I could see him shaking his head, and do you know he did find something. He himself couldn't say what it was that aroused his suspicions. He had a brilliant mind but he also had this sixth sense.

What changes have you seen in the audit process over your career?

It changed because clients changed. Things started moving after the war. So from 1946 to 1966, everything went up a scale and the number of transactions increased tremendously. As the volume went up and the systems and the nature of business itself became more complex, obviously the audit procedures had to change. You had, on the one side businesses merging, integrating, taking over, consolidating, and making technical changes, and on the other side you had the profession trying to keep up, and trying to build a new system to cope with the new situation. People were struggling to keep the lid on from the audit point of view. They were completely bogged down with the volume of things that they had to pick up to go in the accounts. You couldn't carry on casting all the books yourself. But technical improvements were keeping people at arm's length, whether it was through punch cards or computers. As an illustration, when I first went to the Crewe office I was faced with about 15 people in the cashiers' office, all with different types of receipt books; and any member of the public could go to anyone of these 15, and if they wanted to say pay their rates the cashier would reach for the rate receipt book. They had separate bank accounts and kept all the accounting figures separate. It was all done physically, like a woman keeping jars on the shelf and putting housekeeping in one jar and something else in another. Then they went on to punch cards and eventually onto computers.

Also when I went there in 1946 you walked into this room and it felt like walking into the Albert Hall. It was like a large church, and as far as you could see there were rows and rows of people, with their heads bowed down, and piles of paper all around them. They were all dealing with the accounting that this Borough Surveyor was doing off his own bat. There was no checking or balancing on these figures, whereas the Borough Treasurer's were all integrated into the financial accounts. So the Surveyor was advising his committee on figures that were often completely wrong.

Things improved when computers came in in the 1960s, and they were able to do away with all these hundreds of people working for them. When I left them they were as efficient as any local authority but the types of transactions were becoming more complex.

Did that cause problems?

Yes. I remember going to a very big audit. It was all on punch cards but they'd lost the records meantime; so you had a room full of files with every single expenditure neatly coded to be sorted out. But no way could I go back to check, because they'd mislaid the records. We did check where we could, but it was completely impossible to do a reconstitution of it overnight. Fortunately, we had been doing the audit for some years, and we knew things there. Also the comparisons with the years before were helpful as a guide as to whether what was coming through at the end was reasonable or not. So we were able to carry out enough checks to feel it was a genuine case of lost records, and not anything more serious. But the days when you could visibly see something in front of you were gone. You were a bit more apprehensive then about being able to get to the kernel of things.

So what did these changes mean for the auditor?

There were so many ideas coming forth which people were tending to swallow, hook, line and sinker; new ideas of being able to do this, and do that. So if anyone came along with a new idea, everyone would say,—Oh perhaps this is the answer. When I was on the London audit committee of the bigger firm they were very keen. They wanted everyone in different offices around the country to keep to a set pattern so it would be possible for someone to be posted from Swansea to Southampton and carry on as if he had been there all the time. I added a note of caution, saying,—keep your feet on the ground. Eventually they agreed to call in some of the working papers, and the people who were swearing how wonderful it was and that it provided all the answers saw there were a tremendous number of errors thrown up when we went into the nitty-gritty of it.

There was a period which alarmed me when people became slaves to paper. Instead of having that feeling of responsibility, if they ticked everything on the programme they thought they had done it all. Everything was so systematised that they were lulled into a false sense of security. People tend to fool themselves by moving responsibility onto the end product of an approach; for example, sampling on a statistical basis.[37] I always had great doubts about that. I was interested in it at one stage and went into it quite deeply. The illusion was that if you worked out the formula the chances of anything going wrong could be calculated. Although it could have been a great help, sampling was expected to achieve more than was ever possible.

Did you personally feel you were losing a bit of control?

I still feel the danger that we get carried away by the ticks on every page as being the be all and end all when it isn't. You have got to have someone there, a responsible person who makes it a point of honour, if you like, to reach that sense of satisfaction with the audit, over and above the ticks on every page.

DAVID HADDLETON is still active in his two-partner firm of Elverstone, Tomlin in Coalville, Leicestershire. Born in 1933, like his brother (who features in chapter 4) he took his articles with Thornton and Thornton, (now Grant Thornton), of Oxford, initially working out of their small office in Thame. After qualifying in 1957, he spent two years in Canada auditing for an international firm of accountants, before returning to his home town of Birmingham where he worked for four years in industry. He then moved to Coalville. He served for many years as a Conservative councillor in his adopted home district of Shepshed, Leicestershire and remains a formidable critic of the profession from the inside, keeping up a voluminous scrapbook of the 'goofs' he has observed.

Do you think your articles were a good preparation for your career?

We had to go and work in the real world. The one thing that became apparent to us when we met people who had done a university degree was they were much better educated than we were, but they knew damn all about the work. And it became obvious that some people were very good at recognising their ignorance and other people weren't.

What happened after you qualified?

A bit of wanderlust I suppose. When you qualify you think the world's your oyster. You read about it and it's not true is it? I went off to Canada for two years to work for an international firm.

Was it mostly audit work?

It was mostly audit work and in my opinion it was not up to the standard of the firm I had been working with. It was demonstrably lower. I was surprised and disappointed about work in Canada I must say. But I did have much bigger clients to deal with—manufacturing, servicing, shipping, insurance.

So when you came back from Canada after those two years, where did you go then?

I worked in Birmingham for about four years and then came over to this very room. I've been here ever since—an awfully long time.

In your experience in Coalville, how common was it to make up a client's accounts prior to auditing?

I can think of perhaps one or two cases where there were accounts and we just audited them. But in my whole career, I can only think of a very, very small number where all I did was audit. Almost invariably we either put the whole thing together or we up-dated it for year-end. Or we put errors right and so forth. Small companies cannot afford to have an accountant on site to put the accounts together. It's got to be a fair old size to pay somebody whatever they pay nowadays: twenty, twenty-five thousand pounds to put their accounts together. I was such an accountant [working in industry] in Birmingham, so I did see it a bit from the other side. But small companies invariably use their auditors to put their accounts together, which is not a bad thing.

How would you go about planning your sort of audit?

The sort of work I've always done has involved me in going through their accounting records in great depth. If it was a small family company you'd talk to them and you'd notice whether they got on with each other in the family, or whether father or granddad was boss and that formed a view in your mind.

If it was a family company with one outsider in it, you thought the family will know each other, how well do they know him and can they trust him, and does he trust them? Then of course if you moved onto a great big company where nobody knew each other to start with and nobody has any reason to trust or distrust, you are completely back to square one, aren't you? I think a lot of the background in our kind of auditing is knowing the people.

As opposed to the paperwork?

Well, I have seen management letters[38] which said exactly the same thing year after year. They would say,—there appears to be a weakness in your incoming goods department: the same chap does the same job every week and he only gets relieved for four weeks of the year when he goes on holiday. And the client would reply,—it's all very well for you, you're just the auditor. He is the best man there is, I trust him and I've known him since he was a kid and all the rest of it. There is far more to the control of a company than any apparent theoretical perfection, which questions whether we should place so much reliance on what somebody might say in a management letter.

I have had people say to me,—I want your management letter. I then say,—why? Oh well because the tax department wants to see it. I'd say,—all right, I'll write you a management letter: 'Dear client, we've completed your audit and there were one or two minor things that we found which you've corrected. We find nothing material to draw to your attention.' And I repeat the same letter next year and presumably the tax department thinks,—Ah, the management letter, they've done their job.

So what is the purpose of what you do?

I think the general public may wonder about it. Unfortunately, they think that accountants are boring and auditing is probably even more boring, and they only get excited when they stuff their hard earned savings into some crappy overseas company and get mad when somebody runs off with the money. Where's the auditor?

I can remember one executive of a financial institution. I said to him,—aren't you bothered Frank, I come in here and get under your feet every year? No, he said, because when you go away, you give me a clean sheet and that's why I want you in and want you to check everything. I want the directors to know I am honest. So he understood the purpose of an audit. I don't know about anybody else.

And what keeps the auditor on the straight and narrow?

I think the effective pressure is fear. I don't want to be sued, I don't want to lose my qualification, otherwise I won't be able to audit anymore. I don't want to lose face in front of my friends. I think there's another one and you come across it occasionally,—I'm not going to let this rogue push me around. I've lost audits for that reason. I think we've all got to be prepared to lose work for that reason. Maybe I will lose an audit but at least the next guy will get my honest opinion, if he asks for it. If he doesn't ask for it, he won't get it. Mind you, I've got one client who said,—it's like coming to the dentist, coming in here.

How have you got on with clients?

I think all the time we subconsciously weigh people up. It's far easier doing business with somebody straight. People who are difficult make it awkward for themselves because it lengthens the job and it doesn't go through so smoothly. Life is easier when you can trust people. But because you trust people, it doesn't mean to say you don't do your audit work. And some people say,—why do you want to look at that, you've seen the bank statements? And I say,—because that's what we have to do. We had to write to your bank and ask them. I'm sorry it cost twenty-five quid, but that's what we had to do. We had to write to your bank because a long time ago somebody typed some duff figures on a bank statement and the auditor was fooled. So to make sure it doesn't happen, we had to write to the bank.

Have you uncovered any significant frauds in this way?

I can't say I've found anything that related to the senior management of a company. Although I can remember one time when I was asked to audit some stock and they said it was fabulous stock. I think it was worth more than gold, this substance. I laughed and said,—getaway. I knew what he was going to say,—if I got the chief chemist in, would that convince you? So we went to get the chief chemist, and I deliberately prolonged this discussion and eventually I think I got the managing director. I had three senior people discussing this item, and I thought,—either there are three crooks or they are all honest. So I said,—can I take a sample and have it analysed? They said,—if you insist. I said,—how much would I need? I'm an accountant, I know damn all about analysis. But the point was, by getting three people talking in front of me, in effect I had done the audit work. We didn't analyse it.

But it's much more difficult with a big client. On our sort of audit we can go in, look around and say,—those shelves look a bit bare. With just one room it is evident to you. But if there are 50 or 100 shops you've got to work harder. Which is why the big firms do have a harder job than we do.

In what circumstances have you qualified accounts?

Bad debts are probably the favourite or if for whatever reason we haven't seen all the records. Or there is something like the books have been burned. You can't give a clean audit report if the books have been burned. There may be absolutely nothing wrong with everything else, but you can't give a clean audit report. This is where differences of opinion can come in.

Have you been pressurised by a client who wanted to avoid qualification?

Nothing I couldn't handle. But I once bought some shares in a company which was audited by an internationally known firm of auditors. Their audit fees were about £1m and their consultancy fees £13m. I wanted to go to the AGM and stand up and ask a question. I thought they were inextricably interested and could not possibly be seen to be independent auditors. But they said they were. We would never allow that. If the accounting or consulting fees that we got from a client got anything like that big, we'd say,—look we can't carry on auditing your accounts because we might want to say something that you don't like, and we'd lose all this other money. So do you want us as auditors or do you want us as financial consultants or for payroll preparation or whatever? I cannot imagine how any qualified accountant can get thirteen times as much in consultancy fees as his audit fee and maintain his independence. I think it's laughable.

You don't think highly of the big firms?

Big firms? What do they do? I suppose there will always be people who find it necessary to drink in bars and play sport, and take people along to watch cricket matches. And if it works for them, why shouldn't they? One year I was asked by the secretary of the cricket club,—would we like to sponsor a match? I said,—what do you mean? Well the sponsor usually buys the match ball and we put his name in the programme. I said,—oh that sounds interesting but I'm not allowed to advertise, I'll ask. So I wrote to headquarters and told them this tale and they wrote back and said,—yes you can certainly buy the cricket ball but your name mustn't appear on the match card or on the ground. I felt,—well what's the point of doing it, if we have to keep it a secret? And yet not so long before I'd been to a county match and there was a tent on the far side with the name of a certain international firm of accountants on it and their clients were in there. They definitely advertised before they were permitted to advertise. There was no doubt in my mind. We never did. We hardly do any advertising now except in the Yellow Pages.

Have you lost clients through unfair competition?

It doesn't happen very often. When it does happen, you've usually seen it coming and you can explain why it's happened. We always say to a new client,—we are happy to see you, we are not going to charge any less than your previous auditor, and we want you to know up-front that we don't poach, we don't tout and we don't do cheap jobs. We think we do a reasonable job.

How do you assess fees?

In the old days everybody assessed their fees in the same way. They used a thing called the Treasury Scale. This was abolished some years ago when the Office of Fair Trading said it was an illegal monopoly or cartel or something.[39] And we were disappointed because we thought it made sense for the heads of the accountancy bodies and the civil service, and the minister to get together and determine what were reasonable rates for London and less in the provinces. I think we invariably charged less but we had some sort of measure. And our clients could see what the Treasury Scale was. When it was abolished nobody quite knew where they were, did they?

I can remember saying to a plumber,—you ought to charge more than six pence for changing a tap washer. He said,—Oh the washer only cost tuppence. I said,—that's not the point, it's your twenty years' experience they are paying for. You should charge more and I think we all try to follow that. We try to charge what the work warrants, which is hard when somebody hasn't got much money. We are gentle with all our clients especially if they are in difficulty but we expect to be paid promptly. Some that go on for a year we put them through the courts. You must remember that we are in competition with unqualified people.

The government has not seen fit to give us the protection that they have given to doctors, dentists, architects and others, whereby you can't be one of these things unless you are qualified. Anybody can set up as an accountant and some of them probably do a very good job, and some of them screw it up don't they?

What sort of dealings have you had with the Institute over the years?

Oh we fill their forms in regularly and sign them and send them back on time. We always pay our subscription and they don't hear much from us, and we don't hear much from them.

The Institute has come out with a number of guidelines, standards and codes of practice over the years. In your opinion has that been beneficial?

Yes and no. Have you seen the latest book [of Standards]? It used to be a loose-leaf book. Then one year they bound it and I wrote in to the President and said,—it's very nice but I much prefer the old one. I got a very nice letter back saying I was unusual in my criticism since most of the people he spoke to thought it was a splendid idea. He didn't actually say get knotted. But what I used to like about the old book was every three months we got a parcel and we opened it up, and we had to read nearly every word to update ourselves. Then we filed it away and that was it. But when we get this, it's much harder to find out what's changed. This only comes out once a year. It's months out of date when it comes out.

I think this illustrates the difficulty of having any influence even if you want to have influence. The Institute regularly goofs by not knowing what the members think.

We read the stuff that's new and of course it's in *Accountancy*. But sometimes it doesn't seem to tie in with what we find is happening. It's not practical; it's not relevant. A family company is a different animal from an international company. What I am saying is, I feel a lot of the work we do is pointless. That cupboard behind you is full of files which weren't there before. Each limited company file starts 100 pages thick and then we have 50 pages on the permanent file, and then there's the latest edition of the checklist, the tick list to make sure we have got everything right. The old one used to run to ten pages. The new one runs to about 24 pages. Now most of them are perhaps 20 questions down the page and on most of them you would tick the not applicable column. Does that really contribute to a true and fair view? Are you as an investor happier because of it? I don't think so, because you could never invest in my family companies anyway. You are not allowed to, they won't have you.

Born in south west Wales in 1932, ELWYN TUDOR JONES, whose father was a company secretary, was educated at Llandovery College. He trained with the six-partner City firm, Black, Geoghegan and Till and qualified in 1958, his training having been interrupted by National Service. After two years post-qualification experience with the same firm he spent a short time with a smaller firm in the City before setting up on his own in Epsom in 1963. His firm prospered and by 1983 had expanded to three partners. He retired aged 61 and now lives in a Somerset village and still enjoys watching rugby football, having given 15 years service as treasurer of the London Welsh club.

What was your original motive for wanting to be an accountant?

My father was secretary and financial accountant to Chanel, Barbara Gould and Bourgeois, the scent people, and I went with him for two or three weeks during the holidays and met John Lawson, the auditor of those firms; and as a result decided I was interested, and in fact joined John's firm, Black, Geoghegan and Till. And an excellent all round firm it was too. Very good experience there.

How did they set about training you?

Initially we had a father figure, Armitage, if I remember rightly. He wasn't qualified. He was just there through experience and he took us round on four main audits. One was the Royal Bank of Canada, and another one was the artists' supplier, Reeves, up in Dalston; Lillywhite's, the sports shop, is another that comes to mind.

Then I did quite a few other things as I progressed. I was very fortunate in that I was sent down here [to the West Country], on the audit of Lord Beaverbrook, the newspaper owner's, farms. He had six down Illminster way. This was the era when rich people owned derelict farms solely for tax purposes, but he built them up and they in fact were very successful. I got involved just as the farms became profitable and were formed into a company. So that was a bit more interesting than just routine farm accounts, since it involved quite a lot of tax work.

Do you mind me asking how much was your premium?

None, nil. I was the very first in the firm not to pay a premium, basically because my father refused to do so, and of course it was just at the very beginning of premiums going out of the window in any case.

Did they pay you a salary?

I joined on the 15th August at a pound a week, seventeen and eleven pence net,[40] two and a penny national insurance. But I had a hundred per cent increase on the 1st January, to two pounds, and I can't remember how it went after that.

What did you do when you qualified?

I was with Black, Geoghegan and Till for a couple of years, and then decided to move on and joined a three-partner firm in Chancery Lane. Typically for those days, one partner was the boss and the other two were yes men, but again I had excellent experience there. I had to stand up for myself, because I was the first qualified accountant they had taken on. They'd all trained right the way through and been there for years some of them and they really were yes men. I had a few stand-up rows with the boss and that again stood me in good stead. I was asked to join them as a partner, but I wasn't going to be a yes man.

I lived in a place called Tadworth, close to Epsom racecourse on the loop line, and it was an hour and a half's travel each way. So I decided I could give myself two years to start off on my own and if it didn't work out I was young enough to go back up into the City. Fortunately I didn't have to do so. From that point on I was in my own firm in Epsom.

Were there any major changes in audit procedures in those years?

The major one arose from America over stock. The Americans went into far greater depth than we did, and even now I don't think we have gone as deep as they do. In 1959–60, I was involved with a take-over of a company in marine corking; a product was developed called polycyanate, a wonderful word. It involved a system where a liquid was sprayed onto rudders and other parts of boats, forming a hard sponge-like substance which protected them. It was very typical of what used to happen. The inventor built up a very good business in Woolwich, and then of course it was wine, women and song, and the company went down and down. It was duly taken over by one of the big companies in the Midlands, and I had to go and prepare the final accounts. The deal hung on the loss not exceeding £10,000. After the take-over, I had to meet the auditors of the new company who were shocked that I hadn't done very much on the stock. So I said,—Wait a moment, I can look at a five gallon drum of what I'm told is polycyanate, but I'm not qualified to tell whether that is polycyanate or liquid cement. As far I'm concerned they both look the same. Then it came out that in America they would have had chemists in. In general stock became more important during my time. We came to do far more stock checking, sending chaps down on the final day to check the count, a lot more than we used to in the old days.

Did relationships with client management ever get hostile?

Oh it has been. Take this company down in Woolwich. I couldn't trust any of them, except for one person, and they were trying to hoodwink me the whole time. That was a battle royal. But in general, no problems at all. I got on reasonably well with everybody. We had our differences and sometimes we had to put our foot down, if you like, and say,- well I'm sorry but we are not going to sign the audit certificate unless . . . But that was reasonably rare.

What steps did you take to ensure that an audit was being conducted to your satisfaction and to your specifications?

In the early days, I would be the one who would prepare the audit programme and then I would go down either on the last day or perhaps the day before. I used the gambit of asking the clerk if he understood the procedure. The clerks would initial that they had done this, that they'd done that. I would look to see that what had been signed off had been checked, and generally also have a chat with the client to find out how the clerk had performed and were they happy with him. Most importantly though, the working papers ensured that if work had not been done, this would show in the records.

Did you come across interesting frauds?

I was involved in a charity, which was very fortunate in that I wouldn't accept what the treasurer told me. I wrote to the chairman and found that he was claiming non-existent expenses amounting to a lot of money, and how glad I was because he went down for five years. I thank my lucky stars that I had done a check and I always insisted on having the return cheques. When I found these had been made out to the local pub, obviously my suspicions were aroused.

But I have had far more experience of non-company fraud. I have had four solicitors go down for misuse of clients' funds. I have had two or three other cases where money was being pinched. One was a doctor's practice, but they were all partnerships not companies.

You sound as if you relished all of this?

I was always amazed that even my colleagues didn't like unpleasantness and I found even before I was on my own that I was the one acting as the trouble-shooter with my partner or boss sat beside me. All right, partly because I had uncovered things personally and had the facts at my finger tips but my partners' reluctance to get tough always amazed me, but again good experience for me.

Perhaps half a dozen times over the 30 years, having examined the books, I realised I had a dishonest chappy sitting in front of me. I would say,—I'm sorry Mr A but I think you'd better go and find another accountant or auditor. But again, they were usually the small one-man companies or husband and wife companies, never big time concerns.

How did you go about resolving minor differences with clients over accounts? What was the procedure there?

It was always resolved; a lot of it was ignorance. It was just diplomacy that was needed most of the time. Quite a few used to be about stock; perhaps getting the client to agree that some of the stock was obsolete and therefore, should be either ignored altogether or slashed in value.

How frequently did you have to qualify clients' accounts?

Not very frequently. Work-in-progress was the one area where we qualified two or three times. That was in the building trade where we just couldn't delay the finalisation of the accounts until a project had been completed.

We had to qualify because in our view the project could end up making a loss, which couldn't be reflected in the accounts at that time. It was very rare. Obviously we had to qualify when a company was heading for insolvency; a 'going concern' qualification.

How did you build up the number of your clients?

When I started, I got myself into the Rotary Club. There was a businessman's luncheon club called the Friday Club, and I also fairly soon became secretary of the Chamber of Commerce to get myself known in Epsom and around. There were a number of friends who said,—come on you can take over our accounts or audit. It then grew from contacts made in Epsom like solicitors and banks. You saw the bank managers in those days of course and knew them all, and if there was a change they would come and see you. That's changed today of course.

Then I was very unfortunate. I won't go into details. After about 18 months I joined up with another accountant and found out that this was a very big mistake and went through a very unpleasant six months unravelling it. He was an active mason who spent 90% of his time on lodge work. A lot of his work was substandard and I had to put right one or two of his clients' problems. As a result I took over quite a few of his clients, so that helped. People don't tell you before hand, but of course when I parted with him everyone said,—Oh thank God. It was as a result of this that one of our biggest clients, said,—You've got rid of him . . . right you can take over our audit. That was quite a big job, and I quickly had to find another qualified man to join me. He is now the senior partner. That's how it grew.

Were you ever aware of competitor firms touting for business?

Oh yes, oh yes. We have reported two or three firms to the Institute because of what they were up to. Posting letters to our clients and so on. I mean, the clients would be up in arms too.

Were fees strictly based on man-hours booked out?

The only exception was on a take-over when I was involved with the City Take-over Panel.[41] It was a hell of a lot of work including weekends and I had no idea what fee was appropriate. I got onto the chap who had been my third articled clerk, and who had become a partner in Peat Marwick, and got advice from him because I was taking on far greater responsibility than anything I had met before. I must admit I was a little bit horrified by the size of fee he suggested but I gave that figure and it was accepted. That was the only occasion when I switched from the standard hourly rate.

Did you ever tender for an audit?

I had two occasions where I was asked to give a quote for subsidiaries of American companies. The local fellow was trying to cut his costs and he'd one of the Big Six as auditors. He was furious because the answer came back from the holding company in the States,—Oh no we want the signature of the Big Six firm and we've got to stick with them—which made me laugh.

How do you find the proliferation of Standards in contemporary auditing?

Very irritating, and all we are doing it for is the Institute, quite frankly. I can quite see from the experience I've had with other firms that they haven't been of the same standard, and I have no compunction about saying that, as we did set very good standards. So of course we found it all extremely irritating, and in fact my partners still anxiously await their first JMU[42] visit on the audit side. It's all a lot of work. If I'm honest I don't think I've taken too much notice of the Institute.

In recent years we have been appalled at the standard of work that the Big Six have carried out, when we took over some of their smaller clients. On one occasion we found logbooks for non-existent motor vehicles. In fact, I can think of two occasions where I said to the client,—sue them. And they were compensated, purely and simply for money lost.

I can well imagine the new regulations have increased the standards overall, but for our firm the only genuine improvement in our practice came from the introduction of peer review,[43] which does allow you a good objective overview.

ROY KEMP *was born in Devon in 1943, the son of a production manager. He attended St. Marylebone Grammar School, and then took up a training contract with the long dissolved four-partner firm, Thomas How. Qualifying in 1968, he went abroad for two years, acting as a "travelling" auditor in Europe, before returning to Thomas How for a further three years. A proposed partnership there fell through and after the firm merged in circumstances which Roy found uncongenial, he moved to another firm, from where he was head hunted as financial director by their largest client, ICC Information Group Ltd., remaining there from 1977 until 1988. Subsequently he worked with another small firm of accountants and then for a short time he was the Director of Financial Administration with a firm of solicitors. In 1990–91, he served as a senior inspector with the Joint Monitoring Unit, carrying out approximately 60 visits to firms of accountants. Since then he has run his own consultancy business from his home in Pinner, Middlesex, providing support to accountancy practices of all sizes in compliance monitoring, quality control and practice management. He is a regular contributor to* Accountancy Age.

When you were an articled clerk, how was the audit organised in the 1960s?

There were no commercially available audit programmes that I was aware of. We developed our own systems from job to job. Sample checking was very different to what it is today; we mainly did block vouching, where we concentrated on one month of the year, usually the last one. Nowadays you're expected to cover the whole year.

What was the range of clients?

Mostly one-man bands and small limited companies. But we had a group who were a subsidiary of Taylor Woodrow [the builders]. They were involved in plant hire and sand and gravel exploration, tool hire, and the various needs of the building industry. As our largest client, they required interim audits[44] and depot visits.

Can you tell me about your experiences with the JMU?

The decision to set up my own consultancy in 1991 was very much based on experience gleaned in those 12 months with the JMU. The style has changed since I was there, but the visit remains a three-stage process. Firstly, the inspector carries out an overview meeting with the firm to gather as much information about the practice as he possibly can. Stage Two is the thrust of the visit, the review itself, which can take from a day upwards, depending on the size of the practice. Then there is the closing meeting between the inspector or inspectors and the partners, in which the firm is taken through the findings of the visit.

What weaknesses were most prevalent?

That's an impossible question to answer. I'm not being evasive, but they were so varied. Most firms made a genuine attempt to comply with the standards laid down. No firm was perfect, and human nature being what it is, you wouldn't expect that. At the other end of the spectrum, there were firms who made no real effort to comply. Probably the vast majority was somewhere in the middle, operating to their own standards.

What feel did you get of the morale in the profession?

As you know, audit registration came in 1991, and was largely unwelcome to practitioners. Investment registration had come in 1988, so accountants had had three years to get used to it. The combined impact affected everybody in a markedly negative way. They had never been overseen before and quite understandably they didn't like it. Even to this day a good proportion of my generation will say they don't get the same enjoyment out of the profession as they did in the early years. But there's no point in kicking against it; you just have to live with it.

There was an awful lot of form filling that involved time and cost, which got increasingly difficult to recover from the client. Accountants do feel that things have become too bureaucratic, but they have to realise that auditing standards, particularly at the small firm end of the market, left an awful lot to be desired, and that regulation has met the objective of raising standards and I'm exposed to professional accountants every day of my life.

But you are there at their request now?

Yes, I'm not forcing myself on them.

Is your role largely educative?

There is a large educational element. Frankly, if our clients didn't learn from what we gave them I wouldn't regard it as giving a proper service.

How would you assess the changes brought about by computerisation and other technical changes?

Used intelligently the computer can serve to make the audit less tedious. It is very rare to come across someone in practice who actually enjoys doing an audit. So with the increase in computerisation, the advent of the switched-on FD, the move towards risk-based audits[45] which is very much in vogue at the moment, all serve to make the audit more meaningful and less tedious, and add value for the client. The vast majority of clients feel that the audit is imposed on them by statute and regard it as a financial burden that they have to suffer, and really they don't want it. This is the profession's fault in that they have failed to convince them of the value of the audit.

And what is it that underpins an auditor's professional ethics? Older accountants tend to place a great deal of emphasis on their training as a source of professional ethics.

That's entirely understandable, the older the accountant the more resistant he is to regulation. I've been in the profession 30-odd years, and I'd resent some of the impositions. So there is an attitude out there,—Who the hell are they to tell me how to run my practice? The problem is that what your client wants from you and what your professional body requires don't sit very well together. In fact, they usually pull in opposite directions. Take stocktakes: for years auditors didn't attend them, and then suddenly came to realise that they couldn't get away with that anymore. The client then says, not unreasonably,—Why have you never done this before? You can come in, but don't charge me any more. So the auditor has to bear the cost of those extra couple of days, and that's an example of how he's pulled in opposite directions. On all kinds of issues the client is much more switched-on to what he wants and what he doesn't want, and is far more likely to kick hard if he doesn't think he is getting value for what he is paying.

And much more likely to sue?

Litigation has never been a huge problem for the practices I advise, but clients are nowhere near as naïve as they were when I started. They know their rights and if push comes to shove, they are much more likely to serve writs than they were 20 years ago.

Have the firms you advise come under more pressure from clients who want to avoid qualification?

Not really, but they are always very reluctant to qualify, since they want to retain the audit. Independence is always a matter of perception.

And what has been the impact of increased competition in recent years?

There is no doubt that the audit is the most price-sensitive service we provide. The reality is that auditors get a lot of other work from clients and the audit is sometimes regarded as a loss leader to secure other work.

As far as tendering for audits goes, we have almost reached the stage where clients realise that judging the value of an audit purely on cost is not always a good thing.

What has happened to the quality of the audit?

Accounts are now of a far higher quality produced in compliance with much more tightly worded standards by far more technically competent people. So the opportunity to produce false accounts that don't give a fair representation has undoubtedly been reduced.

Notes

1. Under the conditions of the Friendly Societies Acts, unless the auditor was a public auditor appointed by the Treasury the accounts had to be certified by two auditors, although they could be partners in the same firm of accountants (Magee, 1951: 137).

2. The first Rotary club was set up in America in 1905 by Stuart Morrow to promote charitable works and high ethical standards in business. Membership is by invitation and drawn specifically from the business and professional classes. Today there are 1,800 clubs in Britain with 61,000 members (Rotary International in Great Britain and Ireland, 1997).

3. Chambers of Commerce were local organisations formed by industrial and commercial companies to discuss, give mutual support or campaign on issues of common interest. The first permanent chamber was set up in Jersey in 1768 and others followed in Manchester in 1794, Birmingham in 1813. Subsequently they spread throughout the country and today number 60. In 1860, a national association was formed which is today the British Chambers of Commerce. Chambers of Trade are similar though smaller organisations for the retail trade, and nationally their organisation has recently amalgamated with the Chambers of Commerce (Ilersic and Liddle, 1960: chap. 1; information from British Chambers of Commerce, Head Office, London).

4. £3.50 in today's currency.

5. The Taxation and Research Committee of the Institute was set up in 1942 (originally as the Taxation and Financial Relations Committee, now the Technical Advisory Committee) and began publishing its Recommendations on Accounting Principles, the start of the accounting standards setting process (Garrett, 1961: 236–237; Jones, 1995: 201).

6. Set up in 1885 as a rival to the ICAEW, with somewhat less stringent entry requirements, but with which they merged in 1957 (Garrett, 1961).

7. A special audit which may be called for by a company's directors to see that the transfer of ownership of a company's share certificates has been correctly carried out (Bigg, 1969: 243–246).

8. Shares where the holders have a lower priority claim over a company's profits than the ordinary shareholders (Parker, 1992: 88).

9. In 1964–5 (ICAEW, *List of Members*, 1966).

10. The accountants' summer schools were started at Cambridge University in 1934 by the Society of Incorporated Accountants and Auditors (SIAA) as short residential courses for their junior members during the university's summer vacation. About 150 participants were given lectures by visiting luminaries on current accounting issues, and then split into discussion groups. The courses also came to be held at Oxford and after the Second World War the practice spread to the ICAEW (Garrett, 1961: 194–196).

11. Qualified as an incorporated accountant in 1925, became a partner with Nevill, Hovey, Gardner of Hove and was President of the Institute, 1965–66 (ICAEW, *List of Members*, 1966).

12. Born in 1886, partner with Peat, Marwick, Mitchell, 1911–61, helped lead the firm from the 1930s to the 1950s; ICAEW Council member, 1932–61; President, 1945–6. He wrote the history of the Institute in his retirement in 1965

and died in 1969 (*WWW*, 1961–79; Wise, 1982: 15, 17 and 19; Howitt, 1965: 255–6).

13. Qualified 1927, partner with Armitage & Norton in Huddersfield (ICAEW, *List of Members*, 1966).

14. Coopers' *Manual of Auditing* was apparently written by Henry Benson and issued to staff in 1946. Designed to grow with the firm it was held together with extendible brass screws so that sections could be added. The original areas covered included: liquidations, investigations, taxation, company accounts, auditing, and executors and trustees (*C&L Journal*, No. 31, June 1979: 15). It was not published until 1966 (Cooper, 1966: vii).

15. Checking that original documentary evidence, e.g. an invoice, correctly verifies the entry in a company's books of account (Parker, 1992: 300).

16. Cash balances held in the form of notes and coin rather than bank balances and used for minor expenditures (Parker, 1992: 218).

17. A book or other record containing accounts (Parker, 1992: 175).

18. Maxwell's publishing empire collapsed in 1991, when he died falling from his yacht. His companies, where Coopers & Lybrand were the auditors, had reported debts of £1bn, and he had plundered their pension funds (*Financial Times,* 7 Dec 1991, 17 June 1992; Greenslade, 1992: 278). Previously, in 1971, following an investigation by Price Waterhouse, a report by Board of Trade inspectors, including Ronald Leach, senior partner with Peat, Marwick, Mitchell, concluded that Robert Maxwell, as head of Pergamon Press, was 'not in our opinion a person who can be relied on to exercise proper stewardship of a publicly quoted company' (Greenslade, 1992: 42; Russell, 1991: 87). Leach in retirement stated: 'I said he wasn't a suitable person to be in charge of a public company. It was his capacity to regard the world as his own which we thought was extremely dangerous' (Greenslade, 1992: 381). Coopers & Lybrand were fined £1.2m by the Joint Disciplinary Scheme (JDS) in 1999 for serious failings in their audit (*Guardian*, 3 February 1999).

19. The Bank of Credit and Commerce International (BCCI) was founded in 1972 by a Pakistani, Agha Hasan Abedi, with Arab funds (Truell and Gurwin, 1992: chaps, 1 and 2). Management was lax and the bank lent huge sums to the Gokal family of Pakistani shipowners. When the Gokal fortunes waned in the late 1970s, BCCI was almost certainly insolvent and fell to robbing customers' accounts to plug the losses (Kochan and Whittington, 1991: 15, 47 and 212; Truell and Gurwin, 1992: 198). Up to 1987, Price Waterhouse shared the audit with Ernst & Young, but then took over as sole auditors (Adams and Frantz, 1992: 319). Not till 1991 were PW apparently finally alerted to the full situation and the Bank of England closed the bank with estimated debts of $13 billion. In 1999, Deloittes, the liquidators, settled their suit with PW, E&Y and others for £117m and the JDS began an investigation (*Guardian*, 8 January 1999).

20. Barlow Clowes was a private company set up in 1973 to invest client's funds in gilt edged securities, but in fact diverted them to the use of the founder, Peter Clowes (Department of Trade and Industry, 1995, vol. 1: 35). By the time the fraud was uncovered by the Stock Exchange in 1988 the misapplication of funds, some of which were never found, led the government to pay compensation to 18,000 investors equal to £155m, and Clowes was jailed for ten years in 1991 for theft and fraud (*Financial Times*, 3 November 1992; Department of Trade and Industry, 1995, vol.1: 35). The liquidators sued Spicer & Pegler, the auditors, and

other parties, and settled in 1995 for sums reported to run into tens of millions of pounds (*The Times*, 27 November 1992; *Accountancy*, February 1993: 13; *Guardian*, 25 May 1995). The crucial failure in Spicers' performance as auditors seemed to be that they never audited the off-shore client accounts, the main source of the losses. (Department of Trade and Industry, 1995, vol 1: 322–31, and vol.3: 1470). Touche Ross were also apparently at fault in their audit of James Ferguson Holdings, a related company. The case represented the biggest issue to date for the JDS and in 1995 after an inquiry lasting six years and costing £4m they expelled a Spicer partner, Julian Pilkington, (also ordered to pay £100,000 costs) who was, in 1988, chairman of the investment businesses sub-committee of the ICAEW Auditing Practices Committee (APC) (Joint Disciplinary Scheme, 1995; *Guardian*, 12 April 1995).

21. Small jobs with often incomplete accounting records, so called because of how the client often presented them to the auditor.

22. Correspondence with debtors asking them to confirm the amount of their debt (Parker, 1992: 65).

23. Debit and credit balances are extracted from the ledgers. Two lists are then made—one debit and one credit, which should be equal in value (Magee, 1951: chap. II).

24. 1951, organised on the South Bank in London on the occasion of the centenary of the Great Exhibition.

25. See, Cork, 1988: 82.

26. Back duty is tax which should have been paid in the past but where a person has failed to give correct or adequate information for an accurate assessment of liability to be made (Lewis, 1977: 471).

27. Checking a company's own internal accounting control system rather than directly checking the primary accounting records (Woolf, 1997: 20).

28. Sales of electronic computers in the UK only exceeded 50 per year in 1957 but reached 1000 per year in 1965 and grew rapidly thereafter (Kelly, 1987: 9).

29. Formed in 1927 in Norwich by Louis Marchesi as local, non-political and non-sectarian organisations for men aged from 18–40 (recently raised to 45) to get together socially and raise funds for charity. There are now 968 active Tables with some 13,000 members in the UK; 3,500 clubs and 55,000 members worldwide (information from Round Table head office, Birmingham).

30. Church House was a conference centre.

31. After the GEC (General Electric Company) take-over of AEI (Associated Electrical Industries) in 1967, AEI's forecast profit for 1967 of £10m emerged in new accounts as a loss of £4m, caused by the new management team taking a less optimistic view of stock valuation. (Jones, 1981: 248; Edwards, 1989: 245–6). Public criticism resulted from this and the Pergamon scandal from among others Eddie Stamp, professor of accounting at Edinburgh University, which he published in *The Times* in 1969. These attacks focused on the lack of consistency in the way accounts were presented, and the ICAEW under the leadership of Ronald Leach established the Accounting Standards Steering Committee (ASSC) in 1970. Its job was to reduce the variety in accounting presentation by publishing authoritative Statements of Standard Accounting Practice (SSAPs), which have multiplied down to the present day (Edwards, 1989: 247–8; Aranya, 1970: 284).

32. Polly Peck, built up by Asil Nadir, was one of the fastest growing conglomerates of the 1980s until it collapsed in 1990. The company (audited by Stoy

Hayward in part relying on the audit of the Cypriot operations by the Erdal brothers, a small local firm) had been built on bogus profits and creative accounting. In 1984, the *Financial Times* drew attention to the fact that Polly Peck appeared to be earning profits from Turkish Cyprus greater in value than the country's entire exports (Hindle, 1991; Barchard, 1992; Gwilliam and Russell, 1991). Nadir escaped criminal charges by skipping back to his home base in northern Cyprus in 1993. In 1994, Stoy Hayward were sued for an estimated £400m by the liquidators but settled in 1998 for £30m; a JDS investigation followed (*Guardian*, 21 July 1994; *The Times*, 3 July 1998).

33. British Restaurants, formed in 1940, was a government war operation to provide cheap nutritious meals for working families.

34. Add up (Parker, 1992: 54).

35. A body independent of government which determines constituency boundaries for local and general elections.

36. Sir Julian Hodge, himself a certified accountant, built up a large financial empire in the 1950s and 1960s based in Cardiff. Apparently he made many enemies in the City of London, and his methods were said to be surrounded in controversy and based on 'probing and imaginative accountancy methods' (Baber and Boyns, 1985: 286–290).

37. Statistical sampling involves checking only part of the accounting records under the auditors scrutiny on the basis that the sample chosen is statistically representative, and therefore the error in the whole can be accurately calculated (Parker, 1992: 29).

38. Letter sent to a company's management by the auditor, usually after the conclusion of an audit, suggesting improvements to the running of the business (Parker, 1992: 183).

39. Up to the Local Government Act, 1972, the Treasury issued scales of payments for audits of public bodies and friendly societies. Firms could use these scales for fee setting with private clients since they indicated that they were not being over-charged (Edwards, *et al*, 1999: 189; Helmore, 1961: 115; Wood, 1976: 140).

40. 90p.

41. Panel on Take-overs and Mergers, a City self-regulatory body set up in 1968 to administer the City Code on Takeovers and Mergers (Jeremy, 1998: 217).

42. Joint Monitoring Unit (JMU), an arm of the Audit Registration Committee (ARC) both set up by the ICAEW in 1992, under the Companies Act 1989, to register and monitor auditor firms. The JMU visits a certain number of the 12,000 or so firms registered as auditors each year to check the quality of their work (Woolf, 1997: 358; *Accountancy Age*, 12 May 1994: 11).

43. The appraisal of the quality of the work performed by one firm of auditors by another firm (Parker, 1992: 215).

44. Phases of the audit conducted during rather than after the end of the accounting period (Parker, 1992: 159).

45. Designed to concentrate the audit effort into those areas which are perceived to have the greatest likelihood of material misstatements occurring (Woolf, 1997: 165).

Chapter 3

Pioneer Women Accountants

MARGARET PEARCE was born in Portsmouth in 1907, the daughter of a local chartered accountant. She was educated at a private school in Portsmouth until the age of 15 and then at Bournemouth Collegiate School. After matriculating at the age of 18 she took articles in her father's office in Portsmouth, and qualified in 1930. She was not made a partner until 1935 having to wait for her brother to qualify so they could become partners together. She continued in the practice until retirement at the age of 65, in 1972. She never married, but has lived since the early 1950's 20 miles outside Portsmouth, in Liss.

Was it considered unusual in the 1920's for a woman to want to be an accountant?[1]

Yes, it was. But I had never considered anything other than accountancy. My father didn't push me, but when he asked me if I wanted to go in for accountancy, I was interested. When I qualified, I was asked if I would like to join an organisation of women chartered accountants. There were about 100 women chartered accountants in 1930, but I wasn't interested.[2] People didn't seem to find anything really strange about dealing with a female accountant. I never encountered any prejudice; and in fact during the 1930's I had another girl as an articled clerk. She came to me because I was a woman, and we're still in touch.

What did you do during your articles? How did you learn the job?

I learnt through my BCA[3] correspondence course, and, of course, my father helped me to begin with. When I was articled, I helped audit a large general drapers on the Isle of Wight, a firm of blind makers, and a wholesaler in London. I remember going across to Cowes, and picking up all the draper's records, and bringing them back to the office. We also had some small local concerns. We always made up the clients' accounts before we audited, and we generally did people's tax returns as well.

What sort of firm was your father's?

My father had started the firm in 1904, just before he got married, and he was good at attracting clients. He died in 1955, at the age of 75, so then there was my brother and I, and eventually three other partners. My brother had to get rid of one of the chartered accountants we employed, who had been pinching money. I didn't get directly involved because by that time I was up here in Liss working from home. We were never approached by any of the big firms wanting to take us over, and we never considered merging with anyone else. But the girl friend, with whom I eventually set up house in Liss, had a father who had trained as an accountant in Portsmouth. He was a partner in Deloittes, and was responsible for setting them up in Brazil.

Of what did your daily work consist?

It was more or less a rule that I would work on a client's books in my office. A complete job would take a fortnight or more, and you might have to make a couple of visits to the client in order to get all the information you needed. Bank reconciliation[4] was an important part of the job, but we didn't get involved with circularising debtors in those days, and we never attended stocktaking; all the details I needed were there in the books in front of me. And, as I say, the accountancy work led directly on to the client's personal taxes, and there was also some business consultancy involved. When I was working from the office in Portsmouth the hours were long because I would bring work home. I would work on the train, and then I would often work till 10 o'clock at night, and take the work back down in the morning. Sometimes, I would work here in Liss at the weekends. Spring and also the January 31st. year-end were particularly busy periods. Fortunately, my friend was here to keep house for me.

What changes in the practice did you see in your career?

Things didn't really change much—there was probably an increase in the amount of tax work. As far as auditing was concerned more of our clients grew and started to form themselves into proper companies, and we helped them with that. By and large, things went smoothly. We kept busy right up to the time I retired—in fact, towards the end we were still attracting new small clients, mainly offices. Some of our clients came from personal contacts made through our Baptist church in Portsmouth. We never had to turn business away because we were always sufficiently well-staffed to take on new work. After I retired I kept on a dozen or so personal clients, doing their taxes mostly, apart from this small sweet shop in Portsmouth that I did the complete accounts for. That was until the friend I shared the house with fell ill in 1990. So I really carried on working, even in my 80's.

What was your relationship with clients and the Inland Revenue?

Because I kept a strict diary, and I would always charge fees strictly in accordance with time spent, I never had any squabbles with clients over fees. We kept clients and we attracted new ones because we were prepared to work hard. The blind makers stayed with us almost up to the time I retired. They left me because he tried to put some repairs to his private house through the company's account and I was expected to be blind to this. Well, I didn't do so. I charged that to his personal withdrawals and he wasn't very happy with that. I didn't come across much fraud, though, in my professional life. We also developed quite good relationships with the tax inspectors—we would go up and visit them for the day in London, or wherever. We got to be friends with some of them and we always seemed to come to an amicable agreement.

Have you had much to do with the ICAEW over the years?

I went around to begin with. Before I qualified my father used to take me. My brother was a representative for Portsmouth but I never took that on. As far as the standards and recommendations that came from the Institute were concerned, I relied upon my father and then my brother to keep me up to date, but I never got too tied up with them.

What did you do in your spare time?

I was a founder member of the local Soroptimist Association[5] branch in Portsmouth. I was invited in about 1953 to start it by two people who came to Portsmouth to live. It was a female equivalent of the Rotarians; in fact, the Rotarians came to me for help when they set up their own local association. I was secretary for 27 years. We only had one member of any particular line of work—one accountant, one solicitor, one . . . About thirty in all in the branch, something like that. And then we thought we must do something and formed a housing association for the retired. We had five houses which kept me very busy, even after I retired. They are still going and I am a member still but I don't do any work or attend meetings or anything like that. One way or another I seem to have been kept busy all of my life.

KATHLEEN PATERSON was born in Cardiff in 1909, the daughter of an incorporated accountant. She left Cardiff High School at the age of 18 with her higher school certificate and she took articles at her father's firm, Wentworth Price, and qualified in 1932. She worked for three years in the accounts department of Mars, the chocolate bar makers, in Slough, before returning to Wentworth Price, and staying there throughout the second war. Soon after the war, the firm was taken over, and after a short spell working for the new regime in Cardiff's docklands, she went to work for Gilbert Shepherd,[6] a small accounting practice. In 1958, she transferred to Marment's, a department store, as accountant and company secretary and worked there until her retirement in the late 1960's. She never married.

What made you want to be an accountant?

All the girls in my class at that time were doing odd things like dentistry or landscape gardening, so I thought,—what can I do that's unusual? I suddenly said to my father,—supposing I come down to the office and take the accountancy exam. He said he would be very pleased; so that's how my career was settled. I didn't know what I was getting into, and I wouldn't recommend it. People say, you must have been good at maths and I say,—no I wasn't. I just did one or two figures because everything else we did on the machine if we possibly could.

So you went to work with your father. Where did he work?

Wentworth Price, it was just a small firm, with four partners, but it was the best firm in Cardiff, I think, so it was a good place to train. Wentworth Price was the Victorian founder, and when he qualified his father Peter Price, who was an architect, set him up and arranged for Lawrence Dicksee[7], the writer of the textbooks, to have contact with him. Every day Wenty used to write up all the things he had done in the office and send off a letter to Dicksee. Then Dicksee would write back and tell him what was right and what was wrong. So it was very good training for Wentworth Price. He had a very high standard of work and passed that on to everyone in the office. Of course, Wentworth had retired by the time I got there.

Did you have to pay a premium?

No because I was articled to my father's partner but nothing was paid to me either. Five years without a penny and my parents had to keep me the whole time. But think what you'd get when you qualify. What did I get? Well, two pounds a week! But I got very good training. My father and the other partner were very determined that everybody had to go through every job in the office. He used to say,—how can people run their own office if they don't know how to do the jobs themselves. In loads of offices articled clerks had a sort of special position and didn't do the ordinary jobs. I even had to keep the postage book when I started, and do everything properly.

Did being a woman make a difference to your training?

Within the firm I was accepted as a woman, but for my first year I wasn't allowed to go out on an audit. It was felt that the clients would never have seen a woman on an audit before and they thought I wouldn't have been received very well. On some of the jobs you had to go away and stay, say down to west Wales, but again I never went away because I was a woman. Of course, the war changed all that, with so many men being called up, clients had to accept women accountants.

I never felt that to succeed I would have to be better than a man. We did have another woman in the office, training to be an incorporated accountant, who was senior to me and took me under her wing. She was very good and we used to go to each other's student society lectures. I found that trainee incorporated accountants were much friendlier than trainee chartered accountants, who thought they were 'it,' and were not that easy to get on with. I think there had been women incorporated accountants from the start, but it was an odd thing for chartered accountants to have women.[8] In fact I think I was the first one in south Wales.

After I passed the Intermediate exam, I started going out more on audits, and taking charge. We had a good variety of jobs; hospitals, gas companies, department stores like David Morgan's and Marment's, everything really, and that was a good training. I remember meeting an articled clerk with another firm who complained to me that he'd been doing nothing for nine months but working on one railway company's accounts. We didn't have any jobs as big as that so there was more variety and better training.

What did the audit consist of in the 1920s and 30s?

It was very much basic bookkeeping and the preparation of accounts. Actually, I had a lot of trouble at first understanding how journals[9] were kept and what they meant. We had strict [audit] programmes to work to, and round about August, which was a quiet period when people were on holiday, articled clerks made up what were called skeleton accounts, which could then be taken down to the job so the figures could then be blocked in. Later, when I worked for Gilbert Shepherd [in the 1950s], he did things backwards, by working from the balance sheet, but the old-fashioned way was to go along with the skeleton accounts and audit everything. Unless it was a very small job, which could be done entirely in the office, there were always senior clerks or managers around to supervise and check that working papers were being kept straight. Some people found the bank reconciliations a real trouble, but that was something I found easy to manage. On most of our audits, the partners' would specify what specimens they needed checked. You couldn't do everything, unless they saw something suspicious, and then you did a complete check. We didn't do much circularising of debtors, but we did have this bill book in the office; a big machine copied the bills onto fine paper, and you checked off all the bills to see if they were paid. It was routine to attend stocktaking, because we needed the figures for the balance sheet; I got quite good at that.

We were encouraged to use the audit as a means of suggesting useful changes to our clients' business, but some clients were resistant to change. Others were very good. I remember a small grocer who told me that the changes I made enabled him to understand his own accounts for the first time ever—so that was gratifying.

How long would an audit take in the 1920s and 30s?

On some of the larger jobs, we did interim audits, to suit the client, but generally, the length of time an audit took depended on the state of the client's books. If they had good records, everything in apple pie order, we could work fast; if they didn't, it meant an awful lot of work for us. I remember in the early days it was very important you got the balance sheet correct. On one job I remember one of the clerks moaning because he had been out with the partner and he said he had spent all day looking for tuppence. You see, it might be a big figure one side and a big figure the other side but there was a difference of tuppence!

My father's high standards stayed with me though, throughout everything. I remember him saying of someone associated with the firm that if headquarters knew how he operated he would be struck off. I also remember that when Wentworth Price were awarded the audit of a local gas company their accountant committed suicide the night before the audit started, because of the reputation of my father's firm. Standards were high in the old days. Client confidentiality was so strict that you weren't even supposed to say who your clients were, that was all secret. And auditors were very proud of their independence.

How did you get on with clients?

In general we had a good relationship with the clients, even if they thought we got under their feet and made a nuisance of ourselves. That was just an incentive for them to cooperate, so as to get rid of us as soon as possible! Usually, though, we avoided clients who were likely to give us trouble and I can remember my father resigning from one job because they were doing something on the accounts that they shouldn't do.

Was there much fraud in those days?

I never came across fraud in the course of an audit myself. I think fraud is much more common these days because standards have fallen. Some clients you could take at their word, in the old days; although you developed a horse sense about who you had to be careful with. My father was very good at that, putting his finger on something wrong. Again, we weren't so scared of being sued as accountants are nowadays, and we tended to get our own way with clients: the auditor was the great god.

How did Wentworth Price build up its clientele?

It started with Wentworth himself, who knew a lot of people and was very influential. Personal contact with people in the business community was sustained even after he died. I never got involved in the social side of meeting potential clients. Some of the partners kept up their golf clubs, but I don't think that a lot of clients came out of that. My father was always very clear that he would never join the masons, for example. He used to say that if his work couldn't stand on its merit then he didn't want the job. Competition was never a problem then. I remember when we lost the Medical School audit to another firm my father was annoyed but he did not make a fuss, and he certainly did not consider complaining to the Institute.

How were fees assessed?

As far as fees went, some of the younger accountants in the office thought that we weren't charging enough for what was being done, and they moved on. The firm always believed in giving real value to the client. I suppose that was how we were competitive—providing an exceptional standard of service, at reasonable rates.

You qualified in 1932, and you stayed with your father's firm?

Yes, I stayed with them. Of course my father wanted me to stay all the time but I wanted to get away and have a job. So I started applying for jobs and I used to go to interviews. Then I got this job with Mars Bars. a big American company in Slough. All the desks were laid out in rows in the office, and you did your own work. You were not supposed to do anybody else's work. I thought it was very unfriendly, not being able to help other people and other people not helping you. When we finished our own work we could go home if we wanted to. If somebody else was bothered with their work you couldn't stay and lend them a hand. I was only there about two and a half years. As the war was coming on my father said,—I want you back in the office. So I was a good girl and I came back.

He wanted me to become a partner, but I said, I'm not interested. All I see you doing is bringing work home from the office. I've got other things to do with my spare time. So I wouldn't be a partner. I ran the office, handling all the details as they came in and going out on the occasional audit myself.

How did your career progress after the war?

After the war, my father died, and the firm was taken over by March's who moved us down to Cardiff docks, which I didn't like, after working in the city centre. So I went to work for Gilbert Shepherd's in town. Then in 1958, I moved to Marment's, the department store, as accountant and company secretary for the last eleven years of my career. Of course, I continued to see the audit from another perspective, if you like. March's audited Marment's, and they were always very complimentary about the accounts we produced for them, although we might have been a bit old-fashioned. I enjoyed it at Marment's because it was a big enough firm for me to have something really interesting to do and it was small enough for me to be able to poke my nose into everything that was going on.

What changes have you seen in the accounting world?

Well, I was aware of increasing regulation. One day I said to Mr. Marment, himself,—am I working for you, or the government?—because of the number of forms we were having to fill in. So things have definitely gone overcomplicated. At the same time, I remember from the grocer who I helped to understand his own accounts for the first time, accounts have never been simple for ordinary people. As far as the Institute is concerned, my father had this trick of reading the *Accountant*, and marking down the initials of whoever in the office needed to read a particular item; that was how he kept everyone up to date and up to scratch with changes. In general, I think things in the profession have changed for the better because now accountants are encouraged to look at the whole picture, rather than go into the ridiculous detail we used to have to do. Mind you, if you get the broader picture wrong, then you get the Maxwells and so on.

What have you done in your retirement?

Retirement, over thirty years ago now, was a blessing and has been enjoyable. I did keep up some work for charities, but not a lot. If I ever had the chance again I wouldn't have done accountancy. I didn't like it very much. I would have liked to have done domestic science. That would have been interesting. In fact, we audited the cookery college. The University College accounts was one thing we did. We used to have the boardroom for auditing and I remember going up there when my sister was at the university and one day at 5pm the door opened and there was my sister and my best friend. Are you coming country dancing with us? So I dropped the job and went country dancing with them. It was all so easy then.

IZETT HELEN PARTRIDGE was born in Dover in 1909, the daughter of a regular soldier in the Royal Army Pay Corps. A peripatetic childhood (her First World War years were spent in Malta), and restricted educational opportunities for girls, saw her leaving elementary school at 14, initially being apprenticed to a poultry farmer. After a long struggle, and various night school qualifications, she obtained accountancy work at a chartered surveyor's office in Newbury in 1935, qualifying as a certified accountant in the following year. During the war she entered her brother's practice, while continuing to work part-time in Newbury, and in 1952 upgraded her qualification to chartered accountant. In 1964, she established her own practice in Newbury where she worked, unmarried, until her retirement in 1984. She then sold out to another local firm, but carried on working in retirement for a number of personal friends into her 80s.

What did your education consist of?

I left at 14. In those days parents were funny. Girls weren't expected to do anything except to eventually get married. My father decided he wanted to be a poultry farmer so I was apprenticed to a poultry farmer. I carried on there until I got fed up with the work and around 1930 I went to study bookkeeping in evening classes. I went to the Wokingham evening classes and I was the first person there ever to get a Royal Society of Arts Advanced Certificate in any subject. I had it for bookkeeping and arithmetic. I then went to the Gregg School, a secretarial college in Ealing, to do shorthand typing for three months. Then I came back from there, got a job in Reading and went on with my studies. The headmaster at Ealing suggested that I was more suited for accounting than as a secretary, so I did accounting as an advanced subject for the R.S.A. Then my teacher suggested that I studied for the London Association of Accountants[10] by correspondence, which I did and qualified in 1936.

So how long did it take you to qualify for the LAA?

About three years. Well, you can't do it in three years unless you are prepared to put in a lot of time. Too many people think it is going to be handed to them on a plate. Well it isn't and then they fail. At that time the average percentage passing was about 30%. I then got myself a job as an accountant in Newbury. I fell rather fortunate there. My boss Mr Fowlie was not averse to women. At that time it was an awful job for a woman to get a foot in anywhere. They didn't want women. But he was not of that sort. He thought, —if a woman could get the same qualification as a man they have a right to the same job. In fact, when I got the job there I was competing against a man but he chose me for rather peculiar reasons. I had taken and passed all my exams at the first attempt, the letter of application that I had typed had no mistakes in it, and the third reason was the way I kept my shoes. As I sat there he could see my shoes were highly polished and the heels weren't run down.

Tell us about the firm in Newbury. Were they chartered accountants?

No, actually they were estate agents, chartered surveyors. But I used to do their accounts and shorthand and typing as well but soon the business started expanding and they got somebody else in to do the shorthand and typing and I concentrated on accounts. At that time estate agents tended to do the accounts for farmers because it was a large farming area and there was a shortage of accountants, only about three in Newbury, while there were about six estate agents. But from 1944 onwards I was also working in Reading at my brother's chartered accountants firm, Taylor's. His boss died suddenly and there was no one to carry on. I was only a certified accountant but in the circumstances during the war the Institute accepted for me to take over. After the war, I decided to take the matriculation exams and then because I was in my brother's office I could take my articles and I passed the exams and became a chartered accountant myself in 1952.

You would have been 43 wouldn't you? One of the very few women to qualify in that period.

I was. When I went up for my exams in the Horticultural Hall there were ten women for the Intermediate and six for the Finals.

Did you find the chartered exams more difficult than the certified?

In some respects yes but not in others. The certified exams were quite tough and they covered more subjects—statistics, economics. But we didn't take the other individual subjects in quite so much depth. Otherwise they were much the same. I took the Intermediate without taking any course, just revising a few things in the books. For my finals I took a course with the School of Accountancy, Glasgow.

What work did you do for Taylor's?

Anything and everything there was to do. It was an out and out chartered accountant's job.

So what sort of firms would you be auditing then? Could you name some?

I could give names but I do not see why I should. They were medium size companies, private firms, shops, builders, farmers, all sorts. Relatively small manufacturers. You didn't just do one thing in those days. You had to do everything.

So tell us what you did in a typical audit. What would you do first?

Make sure you had got everything. All the books. Very often you hadn't. There were incomplete records very often. Some would have their records more or less complete. But we always prepared the accounts because they had not got the qualified staff to do that.

How long would an audit take?

Well you did them all in together. We did not go down there and sit down and spend several days. We had only got three staff and anyway they didn't want you there all day, everyday. The only one where that would happen would be the solicitors. You would be there for say a week. They could not have the books taken away. All the others used to bring the books in themselves. When they were ready they would ring us up and say—Can you have our books now? And we might say,—Not for a couple of days. If you want them done at once bring them in next Monday or next Tuesday. In that case we got down to it straight away and dealt with those. They would come in and say,—Here you are. If you want anything else come down and see it. Then we would send the books back when we had finished so they could carry on with them.

Would you do things like circularise debtors?

That didn't really arise on most of them. We used to get the actual bank statements, the whole lot. It was all there in black and white if the bank statements didn't tally with the accounts. We didn't usually attend stocktaking. Not all of them required stocktakes. But we had all the stock sheets in and checked them.

What was your relationship with your clients?

Friendly. It did not matter if it was a private, personal matter or whether it was a business matter. You would be surprised what they would ask me . . . even about their marriages! We did all we could for them if they wanted any help. Gave them advice if we thought they were doing the wrong thing. Some of them didn't take any notice though. I had one case, he was a builder who had his eye on a property owned by a company which had planning permission to convert it into several flats. I told him to go and buy the property but they wanted him to buy the company. I said, don't do that you are going to take over their tax liability. Still he went ahead and bought the shares instead of the property. So they walked off with their profit on the shares and he got the property at what they paid for it. It was only a matter of a couple of thousand pounds but still why should he pay somebody else's tax?

We were always the intermediary with the Inland Revenue. We had a very good relationship with the Revenue. There was one inspector where we would sit at opposite sides of the desk and go at it hammer and tongs and afterwards we would laugh and we were the best of friends again. They would say,—It is all very well saying he only lives on so and so but it really ought to be a bit more. So we would have to go a short way towards conceding that. Too many clients were a bit careless sometimes about the way they recorded their personal expenditure. There were some borderline cases where the Revenue made an awful fuss and bother about things and had a client up but hardly ever was there anything in it. Sometimes they queried private use of vehicles, these sorts of things, and we just agreed an amount and that was that.

There was a major case with a coal merchant, where it did seem as if his percentage[11] was not right. But I don't think he should have been caught for the amount the Inland Revenue claimed because I think that he had been having money and coal stolen. Roundsmen not handing in all the money they should. But the Revenue of course picked up the fact that the percentage was lower than it ought to be.

We were always having that sort of argument about the percentages. Take pubs, the Revenue would take for comparison one of these brewery-owned pubs with a manager in. Well their percentages are quite different from what they are compared to the small private public house with probably only one bar. But they expected them to provide the same percentage of gross profit as the others. There was an occasion I actually met an inspector of taxes in one of these Oxfordshire village pubs and he had to agree that things were not quite as the Revenue thought.

Did people in your business dealings look askance at the fact that you were a woman?

No, strangely enough they didn't. With clients, if they came to me there was no question about it, they were quite happy. Sometimes they even came to me because I was a woman. One of them told me to my face. He said he went to the Inland Revenue and asked them who they recommended as an accountant. They said they could not recommend any particular person but there was so-and-so and so-and so, and when he saw that I was the only woman amongst them he thought that if a woman was able to compete with all those men she must be good. A few people looked askance when they saw they had a woman to deal with. Once on a liquidation case one of the things I had to do was to go to a garage and see their managing director, and when I went in he said,—I expected to see your boss. I laughed and said,—Well, I am the boss. Oh, he said, I am pleased to meet you. I have never met a lady chartered accountant.

Did you ever come across any prejudice against woman in the profession?

Oh yes. In the early days, there was terrible prejudice. There didn't appear to be any prejudice once you got established. I was all right because I had done my articles with my brother. So I got in, but I wouldn't have got in otherwise I am quite sure of that. While I was in business, about 1960, I had a letter from a young lady in Basingstoke. She was at her wits' end. She had been trying to get articles for months and had written hundreds of letters and been to scores of interviews and never managed to get in. She had some foreign connection, so she said,—Do you think it was because of that that they wouldn't take me on? And I said,—No. It's because you're a woman. That poor girl, I could not take her on as I had already got one trainee. I did sympathise because at that time there was terrible prejudice and there were only two women chartered accountants in practice in this area, me and another woman and both of us in Newbury.

How did the business progress?

After I qualified as a chartered accountant I bought out the accounting side from old Mr Fowlie. I stayed together with my brother until 1964, when he moved to Brighton and I set up my own business. I took a few clients from Reading and all the ones from Newbury and the practice grew very considerably based there.

How did you acquire clients?

Recommendations from other clients and from the Inland Revenue.

A lot of accountants acquired their clients by the golf club, the Rotary and so on.

Oh, no. I never had anything to do with that. Never had time for it.

Did you ever audit a quoted company? On the Stock Exchange?

Oh, no, no. We didn't aspire to that sort of thing. We hadn't got the staff for that sort of thing. Beside we didn't have quoted companies in Newbury any way. I did not have all that number of companies at all. They were mostly private firms and partnerships. But the company business was coming on—here in Reading in particular. Half of them should never have been turned into companies but if they wanted to I arranged it for them. I never recommended it because in nine cases out of ten it just does not help at all, not for the husband and wife sort of business. If they want more money they've still got to mortgage their house. And so they have got all this extra expense to no purpose.

Did clients change at all in terms of becoming less honest, less scrupulous?

I think it has always been very much the same. You had to be on the ball with them. For instance, although shops have a cash register they often never put a till roll in. At the end of the day they counted up the money in the till and put that down, and they carefully noted in the out-goings books all the things they had paid out, but I found they omitted to add what they paid out during the day in cash from the till. Of course, when you came to it you are hundreds of pounds out. That's nothing new. One of the funniest things was we used to find it difficult to get answers to queries from people. We used to send a list of queries with space for the answer against each. And on one occasion I put: The £50 you paid off such and such an account, did you pay cash or did you use somebody else's cheque? And the answer came back—Yes. Not very helpful.

Did you train up staff?

I used to be able to manage one articled clerk but that was not always very successful. The big firms got all the best material. If you went to the local education place the people they sent along were just hopeless—the ones who couldn't find a job elsewhere. Half of them could not write, they could not add up. When we asked them if they had got the necessary GCEs—they hadn't. It got worse as it went on because Newbury was a growing area, companies coming down snapped up all the best school leavers. The grammar school girls and boys seemed to disappear into thin air.

What was your relationship with the other firms? Did you ever meet socially?

They were all right together. But as I said I never had any time for a social life. Travelling to Newbury every day doesn't leave you very much time for social life. Saturday, some of the small companies had their AGMs on a Saturday afternoon so that all the directors could be present. Some would have it in the evening for the same reason. It would probably be 10 o'clock before I got home.

Did you ever have any relations with the Institute?

Not really. I belonged to the local branch, of course, and I went to their meetings when I could. I found it difficult to attend meetings; only one or two would be in Reading itself and the others would be out of the way. When you have already worked a 12-hour day you are not going to add to it.

When did you retire?

I planned to step aside at 75 and in 1984 I sold out to Lewis's, which was a very old local firm. We merged but eventually as part of the agreement at a certain date I retired altogether. But for about another five years after that I just kept one or two people who did not want to go to the other firm, they would rather stay with me. Just a few of them, made a few hundred a year that's all.

MARJORIE BURGESS was born in Coventry in 1918, the daughter of an automobile engineer and motor racing driver who died when Marjorie was 11 years old. She was educated at a small private school in North London, and became articled in the late 1930's to a small City practice of two women partners. Qualifying in 1941, she saw war service as an accountancy officer in the WRENS,[12] and upon demobilisation, became an accountant in the Ministry of Supply. A long civil service career followed, in which she was employed in the investigative accounting work necessary to the supply of government contracts, mostly in the aircraft industry. She rose in seniority, eventually becoming the Director of Accounts (Aircraft) for her Ministry. She never married, retiring in 1977, and continued to employ her accountancy skills by assisting with the finances of her local church.

What made you want to be an accountant?

The school wanted me to go on and get a degree and teach mathematics, that was my strong point. I was my mother's problem child, because she was widowed of course by then, and I didn't want to teach; I didn't want to become a secretary; I didn't want to go into a bank; and I didn't want to go into nursing. I didn't want to do any of the things that a girl usually did. My mother talked to the parent of a school friend, who knew a woman who was articled to an incorporated accountant. I thought,—that's a good idea. I hadn't heard of any girls doing that. Enquiries were duly made, and in those days you paid a premium and received no salary at all. With no social security or anything it was fortunate that there were enough funds left by my father when he died to keep us going. When my mother went to see her solicitor he said,—Waste of money Mrs. Burgess, she'll get married by the time she gets qualified. My mother said,—Well I was widowed young, and if there hadn't been sufficient funds we would have been in trouble, I'd nothing that I could turn my hands to. At least if she gets married, she'll have something behind her.

I was then articled to this incorporated accountant, who was probably one of the first women incorporated accountants to qualify. Unfortunately, she died within the year. She had been collaborating with Lynette Harris,[13] who was a chartered accountant, and it was suggested that I might transfer to her. Noises were made at the Institute as to whether the year that I had worked already would count towards my articles, and they said,—No, start all over again. So that caused a bit of a problem with funds, but in the meantime I was articled to Dora Hamlyn and later transferred to her partner Lynette Harris. In those days, women were a small band, and they all knew each other and mucked in together. A premium was paid for my articles and I worked for nothing until I passed the Intermediate, then I got the handsome sum of five shillings[14] a week. I was due to go out to Switzerland as a reward for passing the Intermediate because there was an English school there we audited, but the war broke out and I didn't go, much to my disgust.

Did you find it a problem being a woman at any time?

You got warned against the clients who were awkward. Possibly they raised eyebrows when they knew it was a woman who was coming to do the audit. They were used to having a fellow. Some of them had to be pre-prepared that a woman was coming along. The other articled clerk Lynette Harris had was male, but the very nature of the practice probably had its influence because if they were prejudiced against a woman they wouldn't go to a practice of women partners.

What sort of jobs were you initially asked to do?

I remember very well the first one. I went out with the other clerks, and I was handed a nominal ledger[15] and told to take out a trial balance, simple as that. It was a great mixture of clients. We had restaurants, doctors' practices, approved schools, small firms who paid last year's audit fees when the next year's audit was due! Some were obviously attracted by the female nature of the firm. I used to do the audits of the Business and Professional Women's Association.[16] I also remember one Italian woman who did dress designs and clothing. Because she had no idea of keeping records everything was dumped on us once a year and we had to fill in the cash book,[17] and write up the accounts, and agree with the Revenue how much she'd got to pay.

You did an awful lot of vouching in those days—one was looking for malpractice amongst employees, checking the balance sheet, and verifying assets. Bank reconciliation was one of the first things you did. We had audit programmes, and the job was to keep them up to date. You were going back to the previous year's working papers. You had to check off that you had done everything necessary and added anything else that became necessary.

Did you circularise debtors?

Yes, with verification of assets, depending how major the debtors were. This was how I came upon someone who was helping himself to some of the company's funds by paying some of the monies coming in into his own bank account. He was collecting money when it came in but not banking it. It was about the beginning of the war, the poor devil reckoned he could probably try to tuck away a bit of money for himself against what might happen. It was a considerable sum he was managing to tuck away nicely, and this came out through verification of debtors. What brought it to a head was when he suddenly found I was going off to XYZ limited, saying,—Confirm you owe X pounds, and you haven't paid any money; or, you've only paid a small amount of money over six months, that sort of thing. He'd only been at it for about a year, but it was quite a substantial sum in relation to the business.

What were the rules about sampling?

Do a dip—and not necessarily the largest items, a selection across the board as it were. Our programme would indicate what the proportions were. We might change them each year. You might sample in a certain area one year, and then say,—OK, that's been sampled; we'll sample somewhere different this year, again according to the size of the organisation, and what was going on. It was much more rule of thumb to be quite honest, than statistical.

Was there an equivalent of the management letter?

No, unless there was anything we discovered which we thought was radical, which was putting a question mark over it. We had one or two interim audits, I don't think we had any big enough to warrant a monthly investigation. The idea of interim audits was more that we wouldn't sit on our backsides.

Did you get to travel?

Mainly in the south. Sometimes you found yourself having to stay away. I was very lucky really, you could take your books with you. There was a war provision, allowed by the Institute, that if you were within, I think, six months of the end of your articles, you could take your finals, even though you hadn't completed the full five years. It meant I could take my finals in 1941, earlier than I expected to and I remember writing to Foulks Lynch,[18] saying I'm going to take my finals. They wrote back,—You are very ill advised because you are behind in your studies. In other words they wanted to hang on to me a bit longer. So I wrote back and said it would be a good trial run, and when I was successful they wrote back and said,—This brings to an end a satisfactory partnership to our mutual benefit.

What controlled the quality of the audit?

I think we were pretty independent of the client. One of the first warnings that you got as an articled clerk was that you were outside the organisation, and don't let yourself get entangled into it in any way, because if anything goes wrong you've got to be able to stand your ground as it were. One was conscious of the fact that if you hadn't done your job properly it could be trouble. You've got at the back of your mind that the last thing you wanted to do was to say that you considered the accounts were showing a true and fair view of the company's affairs and find a few days later something would come along to prove that they were disastrously wrong. That would do your firm absolutely no good whatsoever, or your own professional reputation. So one was guarded. Obviously there were times it would depend how strongly you felt. If you felt that the thing was absolutely basic and quite wrong then you'd dig your toes in. But if you felt, well, OK it's not going make an awful lot of difference. If he wants to say that let him have his way. Sometimes I had to put my foot down. You'd make yourself unpopular then and say,—Look, I'm asking for it and I will not be happy till I have it. You had the professional threat of,—Well if I don't get it you're going to have a qualified certificate on your accounts and you're not going to like that, are you?

What did you do after you qualified in 1941?

They didn't know what to do with fresh young women accountants. You were called to the Labour Exchange. In those days there was one for men and one for women, so I went to the women's one and they were absolutely astounded; they didn't know what to do. So they said,—you had better go round to the men's, and see what they say. I got round there, and they looked at me as if I was a most peculiar creature. So they said,—we suppose we could put you in a factory as a cost accountant. I thought,—hang that for a lark. I don't fancy going to a factory, having seen it from the other side. At that time the navy were looking for women to come into the WRENS to do accounting officers' jobs to let the men go to sea and they welcomed me with open arms.

What happened after demob?

They were in the process of bringing in a new Companies Act and I knew that I was out of touch with the professional side of things and I had got to get myself back in. There was an advertisement in the *Accountant*, they were looking for accountants in all government departments, one of which was the Ministry of Supply. I thought,— if I can get a job for six months then I can have a look around and find out what is going on in the profession, and see where I go from there. Much to my surprise I was offered the job. I can always remember the first day that I arrived there, the Director who was in charge said,—you realise that you're the only woman professional accountant in the Civil Service, and there's 300 men. Well, I said, —no I hadn't realised it, but anyway here I am, so get on with it.

I was fortunate, because I was working for a Scottish accountant in the first months. He was a very good chap and I settled into the aircraft industry, and perhaps the influence of my father came in in the sense that I enjoyed walking round a factory and saying,—well this is where you've got expensive machines, and you've got a high cost area here with a high labour force. And then you'd walk into the assembly shop and you've got large spaces, but not the expensive machines, therefore this would be reflected in your overhead rates. Well, some women wouldn't enjoy it. I remember the chap who was in charge of the whole section the first week I was there saying,—I like my chaps to come back and tell me about the factory and how many football pitches they reckon would go into a shop floor, would you be able to do that? I said,—I won't be able to tell you how many football pitches, but I can tell you how many hockey pitches!

Did you ever meet hostility as a woman accountant in the Civil Service?

I wouldn't say hostile. Apprehension to start with, until I got known. They used to have to break it to contractors that there was a woman coming. Very early on I walked out of a firm. I was sent up to this place and was given nothing but trouble. So I said,—OK, I'm going back, and much to their astonishment I came back to London. The next thing they knew they'd got an army up there including senior accountants and technical people who really did crawl all over them. The chap concerned soon conceded. I continued going up for some years after that. Once we were going for lunch at an hotel when he saw somebody he knew. He said—sorry, I must go over to that chap and tell him that I have the Ministry accountant with me and she is a woman. Otherwise he might get the wrong idea!

We did have a man who refused to work with me, about three years before I retired but usually the attitude was,—there's a woman there but it's all right she does the same thing you'd expect the chaps to do. I was able to work along with the fellows and not be resented by them and the fact that they were all fellows didn't worry me at all. When I went out to the firms concerned I was always in trouble with the secretaries because one could never remember their names. I was dealing with their bosses and because I was a woman they all used to think I ought to remember them. So it was always the secretaries I was in trouble with.

GLADYS WINCH was born in Beckenham in South London in 1909, the daughter of a bookbinder turned secretary of the local co-operative society. After a central school education, Gladys left school at 16 and got a job with the Co-operative Wholesale Society. She became a comptometer[19] *operator but disliked the work and studied in the evenings to improve herself. She qualified as an incorporated accountant in 1943 and continued working for the co-op until the mid-60s when she became a partner in a private partnership created by ex-co-op accountants. Gladys retired from the partnership in 1975 but continued active voluntary work until recently. She never married.*

How did you become an accountant?

My father used to do odd audits for certain benefit societies like the Hearts of Oak[20] and he used to get me doing the adding up, all the awkward adding up like the four-pences and five-pences whilst he did the easy ones. I left school at 16. Girls couldn't get their matriculation because they had to sew instead of doing the science. Some stupid school teacher had said,—you can offer geography instead of a science. But of course you can't. So I had to go and start off again. I went to the Sir John Cass Institute,[21] a branch of London University, just off of Aldgate Pump. It was mainly for sailors I think, but a lot of people who hadn't been able to get their matric at school went there. So I was working and on the way to being 21 by the time I matriculated.

What was your first job?

There were no jobs in 1925. It was dreadful. My father said I could go teaching, but I didn't want that at all and so he said,—Well, I think you had better go up and see if there's a job in the CWS. This was then in Leman Street, London, and I went up for the interview and sat the little exam and passed. After a time I got a transfer to the Co-op Audit Department which did the audits of the Co-op Societies. I was a comp operator.

What is that?

Well, comptometers, are they not used now? There were copy invoices with a slip at the back and I had to check the arithmetic. I never really knew the whole system. Do you know what a plus adder is? It's a much smaller version of a comptometer. I can show you one. You just punched in the numbers with the buttons. It used to have a farthing, ha' penny and three farthings and shillings and pence, and pounds buttons.[22] They were concave or flat so you know exactly which one you are on when you are really working. You feel it like a typewriter. You can do all the arithmetic. But you had to know all the decimals of every farthing of a pound. Working on the comptometer for long hours you would get the most awful pain up the arms, but you just had to get on with it.

I made a ghastly error once. It was one of the small Co-ops. I hadn't been in the audit department terribly long but I've never forgotten it. I was scrutinising the stock sheets and I hadn't picked up a colossal error. I was absolutely stupid because it was a terrific amount. It meant a tu'penny dividend[23] to this small place. The auditors accepted our scrutiny with the comptometer and it wasn't picked up until after the audit. I should have had my mind on it and realised that such a large stock of tea is not reasonable in such a small concern, it's obvious. That's the trouble when you use a machine, if you haven't got your mind on it and the decimal point is in the wrong place you get it 10 or 100 or 1000 times too big or too small. That was where the old system of checking everything was so bad.

How long were you a comptometer operator?

I hated the work I was doing. It was very hard and monotonous. Just adding up for other people. Well after I got my matric I thought I would do an external Bachelor of Science at the evening class at the Regent Street

Poly. That was quite cheap then. Then after two or three years I was getting so fed up with my work I thought I would qualify as an accountant. I stopped the degree but I had to get permission from the Secretary of the CWS in Manchester, permission from umpteen other people and wait and wait. I got so browned off with each year younger boys coming along ahead of me and I thought—Oh crikey if they can do audits I knew I could. I know it sounds big-headed. Finally I got permission and was signed up for the incorporated society. I didn't pass my final accountancy exam until 1943. It took me a hell of a time because I didn't really have any experience other than adding up. But I used to do odd things for the man in charge of the auditing department and when I did start to study (I'd learned bookkeeping at school) we used to talk in notes. He taught me how to tell him what was wrong in a note, which was extremely helpful. But I was never allowed near any top work at all.

What was the first exam you did in the Incorporated?

Well the matriculation took you straight into the Intermediate. I took my first Intermediate up in London, just off of Liverpool Street, but I failed that one. I wasn't very good really. My second time, because the war was on, we had to go down to Taunton, in a public school there, to take it, with tin hats on, gas masks on and everything else. There were three women and we were put in the sick bay and the cold water cistern ran all night and we couldn't sleep properly. And when I took my finals I was the only woman and I stayed in one of the empty houses in Taunton.

How difficult did you find it studying for your exams?

It was hard for me. I don't think I should have been signed up because I never had any real practical experience of getting anywhere near a balance sheet except small ones. But I finally realised I needed someone who had done wider work. During the war, up at Westminster College, there was a man from the Treasury who taught me. He was trained as a chartered accountant in the mining and cotton industry and he was the first one who said,—If you don't do your job properly or do the audit thoroughly, beware. I think you should be put away. We did adjusted accounts in the audit department, and that course really did help because he spoke of it in the wider area. I also did the correspondence course run by a bright set of men who set up in competition with Foulks Lynch. You had to sign the forms. I just used to put G. M. W. and one came back saying "Cute." That's how you got treated. These days, long before I retired, the blokes with me thought nothing of getting my tea and coffee, whereas that was all I was expected to do in the earlier years.

You mentioned that there was a certain prejudice against a woman doing higher grade work in the Co-op?

The unqualified men wouldn't work if I did the audit. The departmental head just couldn't use me, so I had ten years after qualifying either working for others or on the comptometer, which was delightful! The men did all the auditing side, although they had introduced girls just after the war on the Burroughs machines to save them adding up. I got onto the audit but as a comptometer operator only, except that we used to do stock. They used to send the stock sheets in and I did a spot of stocktaking, very useful. I could do audits on my own though. I did depots in the Port of London for a number of years. I didn't need anyone. I was a comptometer operator so I did both jobs. If it was a very big job I would have another girl with me. I used to do Club and Institute Unions. They came mainly under the Industrial and Provident Societies Acts.[24] I also had one or two of the craft trades unions. Unfortunately I had to wind them up as they went into bigger unions.

How did you finally work your way into auditing?

Well they hadn't enough men to go round in the 1950's. When a senior man retired, the younger man coming up didn't care who I was and straight away he gave me a whopping great round of audits to do. All over the place. I went up to the south Midlands, Peterborough, Yarmouth and west to Oxford and Reading. We did Ruskin College.[25] We used to stay away on a regular basis. For Peterborough we got the 8:30 from King's Cross, get there about ten o'clock and then we would work until nine o'clock at night on Monday, Tuesday and Wednesday. Thursday was their half day, so we left at five and had a night off. Then the staff went home mid-day Friday but if there was a meeting it was my job to stay over and come back Saturday.

How would you go about auditing?

Well I called it "tick it and touch." You checked everything, every total and every item. I think it was ridiculous because we used to work very long hours and at the end of the day it was a job to keep your mind on it—in fact, it wasn't half the time. We didn't check every single item of stock though. With the comptometer, just by the look of it you would know if it was much out. Then came statistical sampling with random numbers and flowcharts. Those were the intelligent audits, a big improvement to the old "tick and touch" business. The old one where you did everything wasn't intelligent and you didn't pick up everything—you don't, you're human. I used to go to the Incorporated and Institute evenings and one evening course, run by the London Business School which used an American book, introduced us to sampling. But this was almost at the end, when I retired in the 1970's.

What would you say was the purpose of the audit?

Mainly to give the members an idea of how their organisation was at the balance sheet date, I suppose.

Would you say it was specifically to detect fraud?

No. You don't go in thinking of fraud. You just work through and if it hits you then you would have to investigate. I had that dinned into me. You don't look around for fraudulent people because most of the time they are not. Mind you the last thing I did before retirement was to put somebody in Holloway for two years. I think they damned well deserved it too. It was in Ruskin House in south Croydon, which was like a club set up by a collection of local trade union branches. About 1972, they had taken this person on who I should have suspected from the beginning because immediately she wanted a PAYE[26] refund. It was a lovely job for her, all she had to do was keep the books and pay the wages. Then one day I had to get an interim audit in before Christmas. She said it wasn't suitable, but I said,—I'm coming. I realised straight away what had happened. I went straight to the bank. The Co-op Bank in George Street had an elderly manager then and he always kept cash cheques for wages if they were altered. She was writing out the wage cheques and altering them and the CID bloke from Bow Street said he'd never seen a quicker one. She got through nearly £10,000 in three months. I was determined they were going to take it through the courts but all the committee were Councillors, and it was kept fairly quiet. I don't know how they did it; because the lady pleaded guilty I suppose.

I've had one or two other frauds on the way. What always puzzled me was—why did they use a cheque? Take this huge laundry in Dartford, which used to do the Chatham Docks. I think it came out of Dicksee, because that was my first Bible, but I always used to do a test, and take just a simple little cheque. In this case it was for about £4 and I got one of the boys to trace it through to the ledger, and it wasn't posted, so I made enquiries. But when you think of a laundry, it's mainly cash isn't it? We might never have known if they had taken £4 cash would we? It has always beaten me why they use a cheque, it doesn't make sense. I think I'd make a good fiddler!

How frequently did you have to qualify accounts?

Well, that was when I was a partner. We would have a meeting on a Saturday morning and discuss it with the other partners. I did one or two Club and Institute Unions. We did one [qualification] over depreciation, that was our usual one. Co-ops nearly all had depreciation rates in their rules and then if they didn't keep to it you automatically qualified it.

Were you doing anything else besides auditing in the 50's and 60's?

Not often, except the Club and Institute Unions, you always had to do their balance sheet and sort out their stuff. Most of the time it was just plain auditing. Mind you I hadn't got my coat off one day in Peterborough when they said,—Come and look at this, we can't balance. Auditing Industrial and Provident Societies, we were never under the Companies Act so we never got the 'true and fair view.'[27] Once the Companies Act was extended to I. & Ps., it was ghastly because the Co-op societies were riddled with secret reserves. When they made more money they felt that they had to put it by for a rainy day. So it was a big struggle because we realised that it was only a matter of time before we got the true and fair view. When this came in there were dreadful struggles. I had a hell of a row with the editor of the *Morning Star*. I tried to push them to declare the hidden reserves and we finally got them to agree.

With regard to clients, was there any trouble with you being a woman?

When I first appeared there might be some horror really, but when we got working together and they found I was a human being same as they were it was fine. I had a spot of bother with some London cabmen in Brixton. They wanted to know how they could go to the toilet if I was there. But I said,—I wouldn't be stopping them would I? They got over that and I got on very well with them. I did have the misfortune to wind them up though, and they'd been in existence since the First World War.

What other changes did you see?

Well again the big change around was with the 1965 Act. We in the audit department were considered to be too near to the trading interests of CWS Ltd. That meant that we couldn't work for the Co-op. So we were flung out and asked to form our own partnership. So in middle age we went out into the big wide world. It was called English and Partners because the chairman's name was Mr English. All the qualified people had to be the partners so they had to take me as a partner. That caused problems I can tell you because I was the only woman in the partnership. I had 19 brothers! Some of them never got over it, but most of them were all right. The chairman spoilt me; he went to the other extreme.

Did you have much to do with the Institute?

They were very helpful if you wanted anything. When I retired they did a very good course at the Institute on voluntary work which was just what I wanted. It was a bit high brow, but they did the tax very thoroughly. I don't have anything against the Institute except I did go to that one meeting when we turned down the Council over the introduction of an inflation balance sheet.[28] Oh, that I did enjoy. I couldn't help it. The Council had a shock but I think it did them good. That was another thing, when I went to that meeting at Moorgate they weren't expecting a woman. In the cloakroom, they said: May I have your coat and hat, sir! Then when I went in they said,—Have you come for somebody?—which didn't please me. I did belong to the Chartered Accountants Women's Association[29] and went a few times. At the beginning women accountants were nieces or daughters or friends of chartered accountants weren't they? I think Miss Fox[30] is one of the few that wasn't. We had an occasional meeting and an annual dinner. But I didn't belong really. They were nearly all from public schools and I came up from the bottom.

Have you any thoughts on any of the scandals that have gone on in the accountancy world in the last 10 years or so - the big Maxwell case?

I just don't understand it. It was absolutely disgusting wasn't it and so are the two sons. They knew what was going on. They must have done. They are not stupid. But on the other hand when you see the thing afterwards it's easy isn't it? When the thing comes out and it's put in front of you, you think,—Oh, how could I have missed it? I only did small pensions, although I did qualify one Co-op pension.

Did you have any hobbies?

Well the only thing I did with the help of a certified accountant and a solicitor was set up a centre for free legal advice run purely by the Labour Party. 46 years we ran it at the Congregational church.

What year did you retire?

I think it was 1975. We didn't have a pension in the Co-op. I was never one to bother much about money. The Institute offered me a first class broker to arrange any capital I had to invest. I put it into annuities, which gave me a small supplement to the old age pension. I did voluntary work after I retired and actually I only gave up auditing the Grove's Community Centre this January.

So you were still working when you were 87?

Yes, I'm afraid so. But my sight isn't all that good and I have slight tinnitus and that made it a bit difficult.

Born in Gedling, near Nottingham, in 1928, CHRISTINE BURDETT, *was the daughter of an unqualified accountancy clerk. She attended a girls' public day school until she was almost 16, and was then articled to Sands and Sands, in Nottingham, in 1945. Qualifying in 1950, she worked for the Nottingham accountancy firm, Mellors, Basden & Mellors, and a Nottingham hosiery manufacturer. In 1961, she married a consulting engineer and moved to Lincolnshire and then in the late 1970s, with a grown up family, to Sheffield, where she worked for a small practice until she retired in 1996.*

Why accountancy?

I wasn't a great mathematician but I was interested in business and accountancy. An uncle was the senior partner of Sands and Sands and I was interviewed by them, and joined them in 1949, when I was still only 15. I was articled at 16.

What was an audit like when you were training?

In those days accounting and auditing went hand in hand. Our firm prepared the accounts from the business records and we verified the information provided by the business. In the very early days there was no written audit programme; largely it was a matter of co-ordinating the records. But we always felt that though the audit didn't follow a particular form, the work done was very comprehensive and didn't require the completion of a whole lot of forms. Of course, clients were much smaller and we gained a good knowledge of the business, its staff and management.

Would you have attended a stocktake?

No, another thing that wasn't extensively checked in those days was stock and work in progress. We looked through the stock sheets and you got an idea, but that was all. Quite honestly, as I got older, even when I attended the stocktakes I thought,—how reliable is this? They can tell us anything. Stock is an extraordinarily difficult thing. The result of the year depends on the stock. When I was being cynical I felt that the accounts are only as true and fair as the stock figure is reliable. Nor did we circularise debtors in those early days. The bank was always considered to be the most important item but I don't even recall that we confirmed the balance with the bank. We would have the bank statements and prepare bank reconciliations and verify subsequent months.

Did you ever feel that you were denied information that you were entitled to?

On one job we speculated that they had two sets of books! One set was put away as soon as they saw us coming. There have been a number of things in the course of my working life that I have picked up through intuition. I have never been an extremely systematic person. I have always found an easy relationship with staff —no problem.

Did you ever get involved in interim audits or monthly checks?

We would always do interim audits. If we were preparing the business accounts the client wanted to know what the position was as soon as possible after the year-end.

How did things develop?

About 1951 three of our clients went public, so we had inspecting accountants in. We prepared the accounts and all the documentation and it was at that stage that more detailed records started to matter. The inspecting accountants questioned the dates of the invoices and we were picked up on this point. It was quite harassing. We had wrongly assumed that all work was completed when it was invoiced but on this particular job it was the customary practice of the firm concerned to issue an invoice for one particular process before the work was done. I have to say that this was the only error that required adjustment and it involved a minimal figure.

What were your biggest jobs?

When I moved to Lincolnshire I worked for a practice which audited a variety of agricultural distributors. These were gradually bought out by large national companies and we then worked with joint auditors representing the parent companies. It was at that stage, about 1965, that I was introduced to questionnaires.[31] The first such joint professional colleague, a Sikh, was a splendid person and we worked very well together. But there was another man who was very difficult, and we had numerous arguments about details and procedures. He seemed to be more concerned with ticking all the boxes on the audit programme than with carrying out an effective audit. There were a number of problems. There was a stock and debtors' defalcation,[32] which we found after the stock had already been audited. We found it as a result of talking to the client's accountant and cashier at lunchtime. The client wanted to make things look better than they were. Their accountant was under tremendous pressure.

You seem to have had varied experience after you qualified?

Within limits. All within the profession with the exception of the period with the Nottingham hosiery manufacturer in the 1950s.

When did you notice things changing, like clients having their own accountants, internal controls, and computers?

When I came to Sheffield in the late 1970s, only one or two of the big accounts had their own internal controls, so they still relied on us tremendously. I wasn't computer literate at first but became knowledgeable about the advantages and limitations of computers through experience. We still prepared the accounts for all of those firms. One firm in particular which had computerised their records were in great difficulty as a consequence and I had to devise a manual back-up system which was successful in restoring order to chaos.

Did you get involved personally in scientific sampling techniques?

This only happened latterly. When I had to do it I just followed a ritual and thought it was stupid. I wasn't at all happy.

What sort of relationships did you used to have with clients? Did it ever get hostile?

Not really, I don't think it did, because we made sure it didn't. We would ring and say,—we are coming up tomorrow, and I do not recall any objections by the client. The firms I worked with were fairly adept in ensuring that a true and fair view was the result of their work.

Did you ever personally uncover a fraud?

No.

How did fees change over the years?

In the early years there were no time sheets, no records at all, and we had some very good accounts. Not much inflation and there were no staff salaries of much consequence. When the ex-servicemen came back the practices didn't have to pay them as the state paid for their training for a number of years. But in Lincolnshire, later on, the practice always felt that they were bedevilled by these early years, as they then had to pay realistic salaries and hence had to charge realistic fees. In Sheffield, one or two clients insisted on discounts.

How did you ensure an audit had sufficient depth and quality?

In the early days, without forms, that the whole of the assets were verified and the liabilities were recorded. I think that really summarises the procedure we practised. I have to say that this was fully supported by detailed working papers and equally detailed comments.

How much initiative would you allow juniors on a job?

I always found it difficult because it depends very much on the person concerned. In Lincolnshire in the 1960s I never checked what the staff did because the people who worked there, including the comp girls, were as competent and reliable as I was. The firm I worked for later didn't use juniors.

Have you thought about some of the scandals that have hit the profession lately?

Yes. I think an audit is only as good as the people on the spot who carry it out. You can have a terrific capability as a partner, but you are still reliant on the staff on the site. But I found it very difficult to understand, for example, how the Maxwell pension funds were allowed to go 18 months without an audit, particularly as it was already known that the auditors were dealing with a man who had previously been adjudged unfit to hold office as a company director. Subsequent events have certainly confirmed these views.

Finally, did you ever feel you were discriminated against as a woman accountant?

No, I was spoiled really, just because I was a woman. I never looked for a partnership, because my family came first and I was quite ill after the birth of my first child. I always enjoyed the company of and working with both men and women. I have greatly enjoyed the variety and stimulus of my professional working life.

PATRICIA BURLINGHAM was born in Hertfordshire in 1926, the daughter of a chartered accountant. She was educated at Hitchin Girls' Grammar School, and Lady Margaret Hall, Oxford, where she read History. She then took articles in her father's firm, qualifying in 1951. From 1952 until 1958, she worked for Peat, Marwick, Mitchell in their London headquarters, spending two years on secondment to their Nairobi office. She left Peats to marry, and has brought up three children continuing with a small amount of part-time work. She also served for some years as a Justice of the Peace.

Why accountancy?

I came down from Oxford knowing that I must have some other qualification. I thought I had much the same sort of brain as my father, who was a very successful provincial accountant, and we both thought it would be a good thing if I was articled to him. Of course being a graduate I went in at an advanced level, which was one factor.

What was the name of your father's firm?

S. McCombie and Co, in Hitchin and other offices as well. At that time there was only my father, but I think there was another partner taken in later, after my time.

Can you give me a description of the sort of jobs you were asked to do when you were training in the 1940s?

I went in at the bottom. I did things in the days before calculators; it did wonders with one's mental arithmetic. A lot of the work came into the office. You were in fact under quite close supervision. You were working in a large office with all the senior clerks around you, so there was never any difficulty about getting advice on anything. Ultimately, the accounts were seen by my father who went through them with you, and he was an extremely thorough professional. Going out to jobs, you would have been always alongside, or in touch with, a senior. As you gained experience you worked up to trial balance. With small or medium sized firms you did all the work for the accounts, and the tax work. Under those circumstances you were also doing the audit, you didn't divide the two. We didn't circularise debtors and we didn't attend stocktaking. Not with our farming clients, remember we were in a rural area, and I didn't go round and count the cattle! But one always had to make judgments as to whether their idea of what was there was reasonable. I imagine that there was some sampling of stock, and that kind of thing, with the larger clients. I didn't have very much to do with those, possibly because I couldn't drive.

What clients did you have?

We had quite a good range, there were a lot of small clients, all sorts of retailers, and one got a very good grounding in incomplete accounts. We had bookies. There was a tribe of related people who ran the local bookmakers and the chip shops, and they offered me a job. They said,—We've found it very difficult to get honest accountants—would you like to come and join us? I just did their accounts. But my father also had good connections with some bigger firms like Herts Pharmaceuticals in Welwyn Garden City. He had directorships and he was the secretary of the Hitchin and District Chamber of Commerce.

Did you find any resistance among clients to you because you were a woman?

No, I was my father's daughter, and they had too much respect for him to have any nonsense like that.

So what did you do when you qualified?

I knew I wanted to get wider experience and, being only 30 miles from London, it was obviously a good place to start. So I made enquiries about jobs there with my father's co-operation. I think I only enquired about three jobs. I never saw anybody in the first one, but there was a partner known to my father, and he said,—Oh we don't employ qualified ladies. Then I had two more interviews, one was a firm who would have taken me, then I went to Peats for an interview and I settled for them.

It must have been interesting to be in Peats in the 1950s?

It was an interesting place to be, because you were in the City of London in its respectable heyday. Peats dealt with Slaughter and May; that was the level—top accountants working with top solicitors. And the articled pupils in the office: one was connected with the Stock Exchange; one with the Baltic Exchange. There was a network, and it was a small world. And there was a wonderful buzz about that. One of the amusing things in my time in the office was that there was a long series of brewery amalgamations and we had to do reports before the amalgamations, and the men did most of that because they liked the beer—it was that sort of atmosphere. You were working under pressure, and often in some quite interesting clients' offices. You tended to get pushed into the small back room without much in the way of comfort. But a lot of people never had anywhere else to put you. And there was great variety of work from doing hop merchants' accounts in Southwark, which were very hierarchical, and traditional family businesses, up to doing Moss Bros. and Radio Rentals.

What was auditing with Peats like?

With Peats one was doing everything, mostly big stuff, and obviously they had audit programmes. The only really close involvement with things was cash counts, counting the Moss Bros. cash, and weren't they surprised! That was when I was a senior. I can't remember physically doing any stock-taking. Some businesses are not amenable to it. If you do Radio Rentals, what are you counting? I can remember doing something with stock lists in some engineering business and being rather intrigued by 'galvanised female elbows.' You also did all the client's tax work.

How close was the supervision at Peats?

Your work was scrutinised. But with a good audit programme they weren't going to stand over you. But it was tight on a personal level. You went through it very carefully with your manager, and he asked the questions and you had to be able to answer them. Then you left it to your manager to sort out if he wanted to take things any further. We didn't see a lot of the partners. They had a life of their own. Peats was very departmentalised. You knew what was going on in your own department to a large extent but what was going on in other people's departments you didn't hear very much about. But once the manager had been through the accounts with you, you did actually see your number one partner. So I got to know him quite well but he was the only one I actually had anything to do with. Except, we were allowed to see Sir Harry Peat's coronation robes in his office in 1953.[33] He was reputed to go round at the side door of Buckingham Palace to count the petty cash.

What sort of relationships did you have as a woman with client management?

Oh fine, I got on very well with clients. I think that's why Peats liked to have women because they got on well. There were three girls in the firm. One of them hardly got into the office at all because she was always being borrowed as a company secretary. She became a permanent sort of temporary. Once they'd got used to the idea of a woman most of the clients were far too well mannered to say anything. There was one exception, a chap I never actually saw. The audit was for a government-funded research establishment and I rang him up with some questions and the voice at the other end said,—I've never had a lady deal with my accounts. So I finished our conversation rapidly. That was the only time I ever had any reaction. With most of them I reckon I got on better than the men because I'm hardly ever abrasive and I knew I had Peats behind me if they were being awkward.

What underpinned the quality of work at Peats?

Having to retain their credibility. They've got to deal with the Revenue. They've got to deal with everybody else. They've got to be ethical. I think that's one of the attractions of the profession, wanting to do what's right. Most of the clerks did leave because they'd have families to support and they could make more money going into different areas of commerce, but they weren't going to have that in-built requirement to be ethical.

You said there was a special quality about the City of London at the time. Was there a culture around that you could take people at their word?

In the City, yes. After all it was a fairly small world then [the 1950s]. So I think there was a considerable degree of mutual trust. There were quite a lot of family businesses where they had a personal relationship with the partner. But, of course, auditors never take people at their word. Peats did do a lot of investigations where companies were being taken over. They were going to look at those companies very hard indeed and they may well have found funny things going on there, especially if they were in the provinces. Londoners never thought the provinces were trustworthy.

How did your career develop?

I went out to Nairobi for some time doing audit work there. I was obviously marking time, although I had a very nice time out there, and saw interesting things. Nairobi was at 6,000 feet, and physically it didn't suit me, so after a period I came back again. It was as simple as that.

What sort of clients did you have out there?

Tea estates, sisal estates, retail businesses, farmers. I was in a sense going back to my earlier experience. You were working with a very mixed lot; the standard was not as good as in the UK. They [Peats] had difficulty getting professional staff. You very often went out and stayed on a farm out in the outback, or tea estates. It was just after the Mau Mau troubles.[34] It was still risky, but it didn't affect me very much.

Did you become a partner yourself?

Good grief, no. I was a clerk, then I went out to Nairobi, and when I came back I was a senior clerk. A very small number went on to be managers and they normally ended up as partners. Well, I could see that the actual physical strength and the mental abilities you needed to be a partner were way beyond me. You did need to be awfully good at it, and very tough. So I was already looking round for something else.

I stuck to my last and made sure I did the job properly, but I was never one who sat down and thought about things in a very constructive way. It was one of the things that made me realise that I wasn't going to go all that much further. Someone who joined at the same time as I did, James Butler,[35] was in my department and subsequently became the senior partner in Peats. I knew he was going to the top. I think if I had been good enough and tough enough, I would have stood a chance of becoming a partner but you don't know until you get to that point. The ethos of the place was very favourable for a female. I could have stayed there. Peats were very good employers, and they specifically liked having women, and they made it quite clear I could have stayed there more or less forever, but I decided I ought to move, and then I got married.

Notes

1. Women were only allowed into the ICAEW after the Sex Discrimination (Removal) Act of 1919, and the first woman to be admitted by examination was in 1924. Women until the 1970s were mainly employed as secretaries, comptometer operators and more rarely as audit clerks, and even then up to the Second World War were expected to leave on marriage. In 1945, the ICAEW membership still had only 105 women members (0.8% of the total); by 1960 this had grown to just 342, or 1%. Even by 1986 the proportion was only 7%, although it is over 30% today (Matthews, *et al,* 1998: 74–78).
2. Margaret is clearly in error as to numbers here, although there were about 100 women qualified in all accountancy societies (Matthews, *et al,* 1998: 76). The organisation to which she refers could not be traced and perhaps never got underway.
3. British College of Accountancy, the main rival to Foulks Lynch as the correspondence course for articled clerks (*Seventy Five Years of Progress,* 1955).
4. Agreeing the record of transactions in the client's accounts with the statements from their bank (Parker, 1992: 170).
5. The first Soroptimist Club was started in 1921 in California by the American, Stuart Morrow, who had also founded the Rotary clubs. The first club in Britain was set up in London in 1923 with the aim 'to bring together outstanding women of different professions and trades to enjoy fellowship, provide mutual

support and benefit and work together in service to the community, both national and international' (Soroptimist International of Greater London, 1995: 15–18).

6. Gilbert David Shepherd, MBE, was President of the ICAEW in 1947–8, and in 1950 his firm had three partners practicing as Shepherd (Gilbert), Owen (ICAEW, *List of members*, 1950).

7. Born in 1864, a leading accountant at the turn of the century and writer of one of the first and most heavily used textbooks on auditing, first published in 1892. Kitchen and Parker (1980: 54–56) tell a somewhat different story to Kathleen, and say that Dicksee was in partnership in Cardiff with Peter Price (from 1889 to 1892 when Price died) and acting as principal to Price's eldest son, presumably Wentworth, until Dicksee returned to practice in London in 1894; that is, after Wentworth qualified.

8. In fact the SIAA only allowed women members in 1918, a year before the Institute did so (Matthews, *et al,* 1998: 75).

9. Books of prime entry in a business which record individual transactions on a day to day basis. Journals usually cover transactions not picked up by other books of prime entry (Parker, 1992: 170).

10. The London Association of Accountants was formed in 1904 by accountants in general practice but who could not meet the entry requirements for the ICAEW or the SIAA. They introduced their own examinations in 1919, and formed the core of what is now the Association of Chartered Certified Accountants, largely formed by merger with other societies in 1939 (Matthews, *et al,* 1998: 64 and 67).

11. Percentage rate of gross profit on which tax was paid.

12. Women's Royal Navy Service.

13. Lynette Harris qualified in 1927, and her partner Dora Hamlyn, related to the well known accounting family, qualified a year later. They had an office in the City and must have been two of the first women chartered accountants to set up in practice on their own account (ICAEW, *List of Members,* 1950).

14. 25p.

15. Book into which postings from the journals and other books of prime entry are entered under various categories of revenues and expenses, and from which a trial balance can be extracted (Parker, 1992: 198).

16. Business and Professional Women's Association could not be traced.

17. Book of prime entry containing a record of day to day cash receipts and payments (Parker, 1992: 51).

18. Founded by H. Foulks Lynch, a solicitor, in 1884, as a spin off from his teaching lawyers. The firm provided the leading correspondence course for accountants throughout the period when most of our interviewees trained (Jones, 1981: 240; *Seventy Five Years of Progress,* 1955).

19. A mechanical adding machine operated by pressing keys and pulling a lever, the leading make was the American, Burroughs machine, first used widely in Britain in the interwar period (Campbell-Kelly, 1989: 7–8; Jones, 1995: 166 and plate 58).

20. Hearts of Oak was a mutual insurance club made obsolete by the 1946 National Insurance Act.

21. Named after the 18th century City father who had endowed an educational foundation, it was a college which opened in 1902, modelled on the London-wide network of polytechnics. It aimed to meet the educational and recreational needs of working class men and women mainly on the basis of evening instruction. It is now part of the London Guildhall University (Glynn, 1998).

22. A quarter, half and three-quarters of an old penny, where 2.4 old pennies = 1p. One shilling = 5p.

23. The dividend was a bonus paid to Co-op customers based on their total purchases for the year, and calculated as so much in the pound; e.g. as here, two old pennies in the £ would be a bonus equal to a 120th of the value of their total purchases.

24. Industrial and Provident Societies Acts, the first of which was in 1893, (unlike the Companies Acts, which applied to joint stock companies) imposed on savings clubs standard forms of accounts, which gave a measure of comparability and a reasonable level of disclosure, and therefore greater protection for investors (Edwards, 1989: 214 and 264).

25. College in Oxford specialising in adult education for the working class.

26. Pay As You Earn, a method of paying income tax out of weekly or monthly salary and therefore the responsibility of the employer; first introduced in 1942 (Glynn and Booth, 1996: 152).

27. Their special status meant the Industrial and Provident Societies did not come under the Companies Acts, which from 1948 laid down that auditors had to give their opinion on whether the accounts were 'true and fair,' and meant previously secret reserves had to be disclosed (Jones 1981: 203). The Industrial and Provident Societies Act, 1965, however brought these societies within the 'true and fair' audit requirement.

28. The system for coping with rapid inflation called current cost accounting, which the Sandilands committee imposed on the Accounting Standards Committee, was rejected by the Institute's members in 1977 (*Accountancy Age,* Dec. 1984: 25; Edwards, 1989: 253).

29. No record of the Chartered Accountants Women's Association could be traced.

30. Miss Barbara Fox, FCA, of Deloitte, Plender, Griffiths, qualified with the SIAA in 1936 (ICAEW, *List of members,* 1966).

31. A list of questions sent to a company's management as part of an audit to test their internal controls (Woolf, 1997: 100).

32. The misappropriation or embezzlement of property belonging to another person (Parker, 1992: 87).

33. Peats had been the auditors to the monarch since before the First World War (Wise, 1982: 16).

34. Mau Mau were the secretive and violent organisation fighting for Kenyan independence from Britain, eventually won in 1963.

35. Born in 1929; educated at Marlborough College and Clare College, Cambridge; qualified with Peat, Marwick, Mitchell in 1955, partner, 1967; senior partner in the late 1980s; CBE, 1982; member of the ICAEW council, 1992–94 (*Who's Who in Accountancy*, 1987: 41).

Chapter 4

Accountants Who 'Left the Profession'

HAROLD EDEY was born in 1913, in London, the son of an Inspector of Taxes. He was educated at the Burton-on-Trent Grammar School and the High School for Boys, Croydon, and, aged 16, he was articled to a small firm of accountants in London. Qualifying in 1935, he moved on to work for Deloittes for a short period. Contacts made there led to employment with Whitehall Securities, (now part of the Pearson Group), where he began part-time studies for the Bachelor of Commerce degree at the London School of Economics. His studies interrupted by war service, he graduated in 1947. Increasing involvement with the LSE led to him becoming a full-time academic in 1949, culminating in a full professorship. He retired in 1980 and lives near Brighton.

What happened when you qualified as an accountant?

I was offered a clerkship in the firm at £150 per year but I thought that this was not enough, and since grandfather knew Lord Plender,[1] the aged senior partner at Deloittes, I was invited to go around for an interview. Lord Plender for some reason did not turn up and I was interviewed by one of the other partners. I was offered a clerkship, and I joined at 200 guineas a year in 1935.

Was it mostly audit work that you were doing?

I was only at Deloittes for a short period, and during that time I was employed entirely on audit work, mainly on the Pearson group of companies[2] like the Whitehall Securities Corporation Limited. I was under the supervision of a senior audit clerk, who himself was under the supervision of a more senior audit clerk, who was under Russell Kettle.[3] I did not see Kettle at all, as far as I can remember, until the time when I was actually leaving the firm.

What made you leave Deloittes?

As I said, I worked on the Whitehall Securities audit; it couldn't be much more than a year. They employed a lot of chartered accountants, and I was told by my senior that they would like to take me on, and I was to take this to Kettle and ask him if he had any objection. He said I might proceed although he did not seem very excited about it. I became an employee of Whitehall Securities in 1936.

And it was during this period that you did your external degree.

I decided after I had been at Whitehall Securities for a short time, and I was not working at full stretch, that I really wanted to do something more with my spare time. So I decided to consider a part-time degree. I knew about the London School of Economics, and obviously a Bachelor of Commerce degree was relevant to my accounting work, so I registered as an evening student in 1936. I was in the Navy from 1940 until 1946, so I did not actually graduate until 1947. Then in 1949, Professor Baxter[4] got in touch with me, saying there had been some alterations in the degree and would I be interested in a lectureship? So I said,—well, yes, I would on the understanding that the salary was adequate.

As an academic, did you maintain a close relationship with the profession?

The relationship has changed enormously over the years and I believe is now very close. I would have said that in the very early years the contact would have been very limited, because there were virtually no benefits for graduates in terms of the professional exams at that stage. The Council of the ICAEW, itself, was not interested in the universities. There was a small number who were particularly interested. After the amalgamation with the incorporated accountants, that was carried forward by Mr Nelson[5] in particular who had always been very closely interested in the university side.

What perspective has being an academic given you on the technical changes in the audit?

I could see that computers were going to be crucial, so I took steps to have a short course with Ferranti's, who as you know made one of the first computers. As we approached 1980, I spoke to one of the lecturers, who is now one of the Professors, and said,—I think we ought to consider putting on exercises in computerised accounts.

I took an interest in statistical sampling a little bit earlier because I had the elementary knowledge through my B. Com., and I kept in touch with the statisticians at the LSE. Of course, it was unknown in chartered accountancy, and at one stage I was asked by one of the firms in the early 1960s if I could provide them with some advice. Again, this was something that we could see coming and we opened courses at the LSE.

Do you think the purpose of the audit has changed?

It is difficult to be very precise about the purpose of the audit unless one knows the size of the client. Probably due to public pressure there has been a reversal recently to an earlier way of looking at things. In my day, quite a young man in my 30s, one would have thought of the audit very much in relation to fraud, the prevention of fraud, internal or external fraud, and much less to anything else. One would not have been thinking of it in terms of ensuring that the accounts when read would enable people to decide whether to buy and sell shares.

One is almost inclined to wonder if the ICAEW should just be concerned with the big audits, for big clients, and leave the certified accountants to do very much the same things that were done by chartered accountants before the war. My own suspicion is that this is happening already and may continue to happen, perhaps because of the way graduate students are being recruited and deployed by the big firms. I must admit if the present level of auditing and accounting requirements is continued by our Institute I would be tending to advise someone who wanted only to do small businesses to become a certified accountant. This is linked up with the fact that the very big firms are more than just accountants now. Therefore what they want, what they need, tends to be more than the small firms or clients need; this of course is bound to cause tension and cost money.

Has the standard of auditing got better or worse?

Auditing is like everything else. There come periods in all businesses, in all activities, where people slacken off a bit, and bad things happen, so we tighten up again. That is the way life runs. That is what is happening with auditing. I do not think auditing is worse or better, I think it is different. It is directed more towards understanding clients, understanding what is going on, and perhaps in recent years not enough attention has been paid to fraud.

The son of an import/export merchant in the City of London, who was bankrupted in the 1929 crash, REGINALD KEEL was born in north London in 1920. He was educated at the Froebel Institute (now Ibstock Place) and then to matriculation at the West Kensington Central School. Joining Thompson, Levett in Holborn, London in 1937, his training as a chartered accountant, after passing his Intermediate exam in 1939, was interrupted by active service in the Second World War, delaying his final qualification until 1948. He then moved on and after five years left the practising side of the profession and moved into industry, working in increasingly senior positions until his retirement in 1980. From then until 1997 he practised as a sole practitioner from his home. In 1952 he first became involved in Institute affairs serving on many committees and the Council of the ICAEW from 1963 to 1977.

What did Thompson Levett put you to do when you first started in the 1930s?

Douglas Levett (my principal) was a director of a lead works, The Du Bois Co. Ltd., based in Kings Cross, London, with overseas associate companies. I spent quite a lot of my time working at that company under the direction of Mr. Levett. I was also involved in various audits of small to medium size companies, often including the preparation of books of account, taxation and final accounts. These included a large laundry group in north London with many branch offices, a big printing works in Sydenham and a number of businesses in the City of London. We worked from pre-prepared audit programmes and the audit process was one of completing those programmes. Most of the audit work (where we did not do the bookkeeping) was on a sampling basis. If the company's own controls were strong then the sampling would be limited. If they were weak then the sampling was much more extended. We'd probably select a month or two and having worked through if too many difficulties, errors or weaknesses did not occur we would accept that evidence. On the contrary if the outcome was unsatisfactory checking would then be extended.

When you were demobbed did you return to your old firm?

Yes I did, I stayed with Thompson, Levett until I passed my finals in 1948 and at that time hoped they might offer me a partnership. They thought it a better idea if I went somewhere else and got some wider experience. Although I was disappointed at the time I subsequently came to the conclusion they were right. They didn't need any more partners anyway. So I left and joined a medium sized firm in the City—Holden Howard.

How did your work change then?

One of the first jobs I did there was the audit of the Odeon Theatres Group which was part of the J. Arthur Rank, film and cinema empire. The senior audit clerk was in charge of the first consolidation of the group of over 400 or so companies, required for the first time following the 1948 Companies Act. I was very much involved in the audit of a major section of the group's companies and also in the innovation of consolidation.

How long did you stay with that firm?

I stayed with Holden Howard for a year. I then felt I needed to move on and find something which would stretch me to a greater extent. I joined another City and long established firm, Champness Corderoy (today part of Saffery Champness), as their senior managing clerk. I stayed with them for four years. My general feeling at that time was that I should stay in the practising side of the profession for about five years after qualification and then review my course from there. I thought if there was an opportunity of a partnership I would take it and if there wasn't I might move out into industry. I was the managing audit clerk on the Carreras, the major tobacco group, (now part of Rothmans) audit. I still prepared their accounts first, although they were a quoted public company in the early 1950s.

At Carreras, were you attending stocktaking, because stocktaking must have been quite a big thing in the tobacco trade?

Yes we did attend. The point about stocktaking tobacco is that most of it is held in bond anyway—there was a bonded area within the factory. Tobacco carries a considerable amount of duty which is subject to moisture content. Duty having been paid at a particular level, the moisture content can then be increased with greater revenue being obtained from the customer!

How was Champness organised? It was a medium sized firm then, wasn't it?

Yes, it wasn't a large firm, although it had some other quite significant clients such as the Reed paper group and the estates of the Duke of Westminster. There were a number of partners responsible for groups of audits and a number engaged on tax work. One audit I had was that of the estate of the Earl of Berkeley. It involved a six monthly visit to Berkeley Castle on the banks of the Severn in Gloucestershire. The Countess had been widowed in 1942 and had been left a so-called 'tax-free' annuity, which actually involved tax being payable on the tax-free element—ad infinitum! This monstrosity was alleviated somewhat by her being resident in Italy and by investing most of the capital funds in 3% UK Transport Bonds (laughter).

Tell us something about your work in the Institute?

Having served on the Committee of the London Society of Chartered Accountants, in 1963 I was elected to the Institute's Council and I served there for 14 years (my life seems to go in 14 year sequences). One of the major things that I did was to spend a great amount of time, effort and enthusiasm on the ethics side of the Institute. I took up the torch at Council and later by chairing a committee of inquiry on support for members working in industry. The idea was to give advice and protection to members working say for domineering tycoons who might come under pressure to act unethically or even fraudulently. I met severe opposition from the Institute secretariat but nonetheless in due course the Industrial Members Advisory Committee on Ethics was set up and has thrived and even spawned parallel services for members employed in practice. IMACE now has a network of some 80 advisers all over the country and a full time director on the Institute staff. More recently legal advice and insurance protection have been added. Over the years many members have gained from such help and many lessons have been learnt from the experience of the advisers to the benefit of the profession.

After my semi retirement in 1980—with the background of my IMACE experience and that of service on the Ethics, Investigation and Disciplinary Committees—I served on two JDS disciplinary inquiries. The second being that concerning the role of the auditors and accountants in the notorious Barlow Clowes Affair. The latter sat for over eight years including the Old Bailey trial and appeals against the committee's decisions. Three members were excluded from membership and costs imposed totalled many hundreds of thousands of pounds.

What went wrong in the Barlow Clowes affair?

Spicer & Pegler the auditors left the responsibility to a single partner. He failed critically in the exercise of his judgment of the actions and word of Peter Clowes, the chief fraudster. He gave unduly unquestioning support to Mr Clowes being more than prepared to accept his assertions without adequate and reliable evidence. Touche Ross the auditors of Ferguson and the reporting accountants on the acquisition of Barlow Clowes failed to recognise the fraudulent use made of overseas unaudited funds. They should have insisted upon the audit of all funds as did an earlier intended audit firm who then, because that was not available, refused to act.

Who was it that turned down the audit?

Josolyne Layton-Bennett.

So why weren't the offshore accounts audited?

The Gibraltar operation, which was a late development, and had a limited role and controlled only a small part of the overseas funds, was audited. The main funds though were controlled by Mr. Clowes through a partnership registered in Jersey, which was not required to be audited.

It would seem that the slightest bit of delving would have uncovered the fact that it was all just a house of cards?

The auditors and the other external accountants were prepared to believe Peter Clowes. There was no question of them being involved in the fraud but they did give credit and credibility where it was not due. It was indeed unbelievable that persons with such points of view could be effective auditors and reporting accountants and the JDS Committee of Inquiry said so and held them severely to account as a result.

The Department of Trade and Industry (DTI) Inspectors' report said that both Spicers and Touche did a tremendous amount of work. How could they overlook the completely bogus sale of software to the non-existent Hermes?

The Inquiry pursued this avenue very thoroughly. The auditors went so far but not far enough. Touche traced Hermes in the records to an accommodation address in Jersey and got their local firm to actually visit the address, a firm of solicitors who happened to be close associates of Peter Clowes. But from there no action at all proceeded. Barlow Clowes was purporting that Hermes was a live operating business but it had never ever existed.

There were two parts to the saga. Initially Touche were not involved since they, as I already have said, were the auditors to Ferguson. The latter had come under the control of Peter Clowes who then used it (being a small converted shell quoted plc) to acquire Barlow Clowes. The Touche audit partner was also the reporting accountant on the Barlow Clowes acquisition. While he did well on Ferguson he left the Barlow Clowes audit aspects entirely to Spicers, who had performed disastrously. Peter Clowes kept most matters to himself particularly the receipt, allocation, transmission and expenditure of cash.

There were many employees in Barlow Clowes who suspected wrongdoing but being in receipt of generous salaries and many promises, and under the tyranny of Peter Clowes, were averse to take any 'whistleblowing' action. Two such were Institute members and were asked at the JDS inquiry whether they had contemplated seeking help and advice from the Institute's IMACE service. They hadn't even been aware of the service but even if they had used it they said they were more than certain that their jobs would have been lost. Such help by IMACE would have been confidential and could have curtailed the scale of the disaster incurred through the fraud.

To what extent do you think that the auditors turned a blind eye in order to keep hold of a lucrative client?

There was no question of any of the auditors turning a blind eye. Both firms were big enough and of sufficient integrity not to have succumbed in such a way. They were more concerned that they had a very difficult client and didn't want to give up on the handling and presentation of the many problems that were thrown up. The Spicer partner never called in a second partner despite all the serious and major difficulties he encountered. The firm's system was that there should be recourse to a second partner if the operating partner considered there a was a need for one. The Inquiry considered this inadequate control on the part of the firm.

Did you interview Hooper who was in charge of the audit of the Gibraltar Company, and who did investigate to some extent the situation in the Barlow Clowes Geneva office?

Yes we did see Mr. Hooper but under the then JDS rules we only had jurisdiction over UK based conduct and we weren't able to pronounce upon overseas practice. Under the amended JDS rules that position has been corrected.

Mr. Hooper was more than aware that the affairs of Barlow Clowes were in disarray. He had intimated such to Spicers in London but no action had transpired as a result. He confirmed that the Geneva operation was merely a post office, monies received there from 'overseas' clients being sent on to deposit accounts of the Jersey partnership. In fact Jersey never invested, they spent these funds otherwise. In the plans for the overseas development of Barlow Clowes, Geneva would have been closed and the operations would have then been carried on by Jersey and Gibraltar.

During your career in industry you would have dealt with auditors of your enterprises. In particular taking your time with Price & Pierce who were the auditors there?

Touche Ross.

And what was your opinion of the job they did for you?

They did excellently. The partner in question for most of the time was Peter Stilling who sadly died recently.

As the finance director what did you look for in a good auditor?

Primarily I expected a good and thorough understanding of the business under audit, the organisation of the firm and the management running it, and naturally also a good and experienced command of the audit process. As the finance director I would always go one step further towards the auditor than they would expect. I would without being asked provide management accounts, budgets, future plans as well as the accounts and other statements under audit. I would also discuss all of these matters with them in order to build a sense of goodwill and confidence. As a result they would have a better and more constructive view of what was happening in the business and any difficulties with which they might be faced. In turn I would be able to judge from their reactions to the information I was providing as to the outcome of the audit. Such pro-active interaction provided considerable benefit.

WILLIAM BRITTAIN was born in Birmingham, in 1925, the son of a crane driver. He attended King Edward's Grammar School in Aston, and after war service with the RAF he did three-year articles with the firm of Warrender in Birmingham, qualifying in 1950. Within the year he left to join ICI's Metals Division in Birmingham (latterly Imperial Metal Industries), starting in the internal audit department and rising to finance director before the age of 35. He retired in 1987.

What made you want to become an accountant?

Money. Well, I came out of the Air Force when I was 22, more or less, and I hadn't got a job. As ex-servicemen we could have three-year articles instead of the usual five and that seemed the quickest way to getting money. So it was the sheer logic of money.

Would you describe to me the jobs you were asked to do while you were doing your articles?

It was a small firm of chartered accountants and, basically, you did everything. As your level of competence or knowledge increased you did more. I suppose the thing that I remember most of all was coping with boredom, which has stood me in good stead ever since. I think everybody should have a two-year course on coping with boredom (laughs).

It was 99.9% audits, you know—ticking. Most of the clients didn't really keep books to the final stage, so a large element of the audit was bookkeeping, and bringing the books up to date. You were bookkeeper/auditors. You started off just ticking, ticking, ticking, ticking, and then after a while you were allowed to use your intelligence in simple things like say, balancing the bought ledgers, the purchase ledgers[6] and trial balances, and getting a set of accounts out. It was basically drudgery.

Was there always a strict system of audit programmes and working papers?

No strict systems at all. You just went out and did the job and nobody told you what you'd got to do. Whilst you were under articles, for the first two years you were always with somebody who was qualified, or a senior. So, you were supervised in that sense, but there were no tight audit manuals, as in—you've got to do this, you've got to do that. The man in charge of the audit you were on told you what to do and you did it. In those days there were very few qualified men. So, predominantly, it was senior clerks, unqualified men, supervising you. And, of course, we used to work Saturday mornings in those days. That was the time when you filled in your expenses and came up to date. You did very little work on a Saturday, apart from exchange ideas.

Can you remember some of the clients that you were involved in auditing?

They were largely small traders and then there were lots of small manufacturers in the jewellery trade, making badges and things like thimbles. I suppose a lot of them have gone out of business now. Small manufacturers were ten a penny fifty years ago because there wasn't a concentration of power in industry as there is now.

Did you have to pay a premium?

I didn't pay a premium, but that emphasises how things changed, because I spent a few months with this particular firm, in between leaving school and going into the Air Force, and they did want a premium. Four years later, they did not want a premium. So in 1942 they wanted a premium and in 1947 they didn't.

How much did they pay you?

That's a little difficult to say because they paid me for the three years of my articles, £2.50 a week. But over and above that, as an ex-serviceman, the government gave me another £1.50 a week. So, effectively, I got £4 a week, for three years.

Do you feel that doing articles was a good preparation for your future?

I think the strengths, largely, were discipline and indoctrination. This is why I'm not keen on people training in industry. I would prefer all auditors of public companies to be trained in a professional firm. There was very little input from the client in those days. Auditors were treated with more respect in that the auditor was the sole arbitrator of what was true and fair. There was no negotiation because you had to get it right without fear or favour. In my day, the auditor was a semi-god. I know it sounds daft but even as a humble clerk you could go and ask for information, and you got it.

What sort of changes did you notice in the way audits were conducted when you went into industry?

I didn't get too involved with them because I used to say to the auditors—do whatever you want to, and ask for whatever information you want to. I used to give them the freedom of the house because an audit to me was an audit, and I didn't want to put any constraints on them. As a customer of auditors I was fairly relaxed because I always kept a good set of books anyway. I suppose it was really pride. My figures were right, and it wasn't my job to dress the figures up for shareholders or directors.

I suppose the only thing I noticed from a distance is that over the years the auditors became more disciplined and more professional. Then a lot of the routine work was taken out of play by sampling.

Did you ever come across fraud?

We had fraud in the firm when I was finance director. We usually found them by accident, not by design. I remember once a fraud of petty cash where somebody was forging his boss's signature and going to collect the cash for expenses. The way we picked that up was good luck, with a system whereby one in a hundred examples of expenses for cash were returned to the manager of the department for verification.

Actually, the first thing I did when I became finance director was to close the internal audit department down. The fraud it might be saving was less than the cost of the department. So I'd rather have the profit on the department, and stand the fraud.

We've also had a managing director of a smaller subsidiary cooking the profits to make his main directors happy with his profit, but you pick it up.

How did you pick that one up?

Well, the auditors picked that one up, and we prosecuted. We didn't think it was part of our responsibility to hide people, and we thought it was a good warning to anybody who read the newspapers as well.

Did you have an audit committee?

My firm was one of the first in the country to set up an audit committee of non-executive directors before it became fashionable, probably over 20 years ago. We said,—look we've got non-executive directors, we really ought to have them meet and meet the auditors, without any of the executives there.

And did you find that fruitful?

Well, it was only fruitful in the sense that the auditors could always go off the record and say something about something they didn't like to the non-executive directors in the annual audit committee meeting.

KENNETH MOORE *was born in Sevenoaks in 1926, the son of a Post Office clerk. After attending a grammar school in Wembley, north west London, he was articled to the small three partner firm of Stammers, Martin, Williamson, in Victoria, London. His training was interrupted by war service, but on demob, he managed to pass his finals in two years, in 1950. He very shortly moved on to work for British Oxygen, occupying a number of senior positions at home and abroad, ending his career, at 55, as chairman and managing director of BOC's Indian subsidiary.*

Can you describe your early experiences?

My training fell into two parts because I started my articles and did nearly a year, and then I was called up into the army for three-and-a-half years, and then I went back again. For the first year, I was mainly involved with keeping the accounts of two or three hotels in the West End of London. I did quite a lot of basic things like learning to add up columns of figures; very mundane work. And then when I came out of the army I virtually had to start again because I didn't remember much of what had gone before.

The business of that particular partnership was practically all sole traders and small companies. We had no large company business whatsoever. And I was doing audits, taxation, and incomplete records. There was not a great deal of pure audit. Immediately after I qualified I joined another company in the City for more money, and there I was involved in rather more audit work and rather larger but still not really large companies. I was there for about nine months.

Did you have any larger clients?

Perhaps the biggest audit we had, which was a pure audit, was an air services and charter company operating at that time out of Croydon airport. And, we had a chemical/pharmaceuticals company too.

Would audits like that take longer?

They would take longer, about six weeks, partly because the companies were bigger, and the sheer volume of records was bigger, and we used to do quite extensive sampling and checking. You must remember there were no computers in those days.

Was there always a fixed audit procedure of working papers, or was it more informal?

We had a fixed audit programme written up by the partners for each particular client. We didn't have an audit programme blue print which applied to everyone. But we worked according to a fixed programme, and we would be involved in doing things like being physically present at year-end stocktaking. The programme would establish for instance roughly what percentage of sampling and other checks was to be done. It would be part of the programme to list discrepancies, missing documentation and missing vouchers, which was perhaps the most frequent discrepancy. Then either myself or the partner in due course would go back and investigate.

Was there a culture in those days of taking the client at his word?

So far as the limited companies are concerned, no, I don't think so. Your relationship with a sole trader or a partnership was rather different. The smaller the organisation and the more rudimentary its system and its records the more you were required to rely on the explanations that you were able to obtain and to try and satisfy yourself that they appeared to be reasonable. I can think of one or two of our clients, where that wasn't so. One of our customers was a Turkish restaurant in Soho (laughs). If we had relied solely on what we had been told there we might have produced a different answer.

How did both the firm that you were articled to, and the firm that you went on to, go about acquiring clients?

Well, clients came to them in two ways that I can recall. One, by recommendation from other clients, and, secondly, in one or two cases, by buying out other practices.

How often did that happen?

During my articles, I think we bought out two other practices.

How were the clients' fees assessed?

Basically, on time spent, and on who had worked on the job. Obviously, the partner's rate would be higher. Certainly not on any perception of what the business might stand, although we might make some reduction of fees if we perceived the client was in considerable financial difficulties. We might be sympathetic in that sense.

Would you say it was always the case that when accounts were certified you were happy in your own mind that they were a true and fair record?

We would not have certified them if we were not satisfied that they gave a materially correct picture. Having said that, I can remember the accounts of some of our sole traders, which were prepared for them from incomplete records as much for the purpose of the Inland Revenue as for any other purpose, where I wouldn't have felt quite so confident.

Overall, did you think that doing your articles was a good preparation for your future career?

Yes. Although I didn't have the experience of large companies, I was given a great deal of freedom to work on my own and to do as much as I thought I was able to tackle. And that gave me independence. I think there is nothing better than working on incomplete records. It gave you a basic foundation of accounting. It prompted you to think about what is missing, what was not as I would expect it to be, and what needs to be probed into.

After you left to work for British Oxygen in the early 1950s, what was your relationship with the external auditors?

I find it difficult to answer that directly. We had our own internal audit department, with the operations of that department directed by our chief internal auditor and by our finance director. I was never directly involved.

There certainly was a close working relationship and a high degree of consultation over internal audit programmes between our own staff and the external auditors. No doubt the external auditors to some extent planned their programmes on the basis of ours, but they had agreed with what we were doing and had verified that we were actually carrying it out. I suppose that the fact that our chief internal auditors were independent of anyone else on the accounting side, except the finance director, was also helpful in that respect.

Was there ever a possibility, because the company was so big and powerful and its systems were so sophisticated, that there might be a temptation for the external auditors to rubber stamp the internal audit?

Not when you are audited by Cooper Brothers.

Have you had much to do with the Institute over the years?

Not really. But then, if I hadn't been a member I would never have been employed by BOC in the first place.

One of the relatively few subjects with a working class background in our study, EVAN DAVIES was the son of a coal miner at the Great Mountain Colliery, Tumble, Carmarthenshire. Born in 1924, he was educated at the local grammar school and after leaving the RAF in 1947 took up articles with a three-partner firm, Frank C. Bevan, in Swansea. He qualified in 1951 and worked for two years with Deloittes in Swansea, before moving into industry, working for Guest Keen and Nettlefold (subsequently Allied Steel and Wire) in Cardiff, until retirement in 1984.

Can you tell me what sort of work you were asked to do when you were training?

One did a fair amount of quite varied work. The hours were good and suited me because the articled clerks didn't start until ten in the morning, and I had about an hour's journey to get to Swansea. We finished about five and this enabled me to devote a whole evening to studying. One did the work initially of a junior, worked up to semi-senior, and eventually senior status. I remember at one stage during the course of my articles I was seconded to the National Coal Board, who had recently come into being, and there was a tremendous amount of accountancy work arising from the merger of various units. This provided me with new experience, and my principals received payment for my services.

A lot of the work the firm did, obviously, was auditing. However, in those days auditing and accountancy went together. The firm had few pure audits. Generally, the smaller the client the more likely it was we would be doing the total job. If the client was bigger then quite often it would have a trial balance, or possibly even full accounts for us to work on.

Were there audit programmes for every client?

Audit programmes started becoming more fashionable towards the end of the 40s and early 50s. Many accountancy practitioners introduced printed audit programmes, and these included questions aimed at ensuring that internal checks were properly in place, with a view to avoiding fraud and making sure the accounts showed a true and fair view.

Perhaps you can take me through some of the stages in the course of an audit in those days?

Once you qualified you were given a number of companies or individuals to look after and you virtually then did the lot, with the help of some supporting staff. You worked out your own programme unless there was one already available which was accepted or modified. We tended to start with the purchase journal, sales journal, cash book, debtors and creditors ledgers. These were generally written up by the clients. Sometimes a client would have completed the nominal ledger also but occasionally we would either have to complete it or write it up totally. Having worked our way through all the books of prime entry we would have a trial balance to check or we would have to prepare one. Having finalised the trial balance we were in a position to check or prepare the final accounts. Occasionally, we came across very small businesses where we were handed a box full of vouchers, bank statements, cheque stubs, plus perhaps a cash book, petty cash book, together with one or more rough notebooks. In those circumstances one had to pool all the information together and prepare final accounts. One endeavoured to prove the accuracy of the accounts as best one could. It was then a case of computing the tax, discussing things with the partner, and finally presenting and discussing the accounts with the client. The tax computation would be submitted to the appropriate Inspector of Taxes, and any subsequent correspondence dealt with.

Did you attend stocktakes?

This was regarded as a standard requirement. Certainly in the firms that I was involved with there was a great emphasis placed on the accuracy of stocks held and their valuation. All too often more emphasis was placed on the accuracy of petty cash than on the stocks, which invariably represented far more significant value. It was important to ensure that stock control was effective. Stock valuation was another important issue, and one sometimes came across conflicting views. One occasion I shall always remember. We were doing the audit of a furniture store and whilst checking the stock one of my colleagues knocked over a bottle of ink, which ruined a baize-top table. Instead of apologising he had the insolence to say to the owner that the value of the table should be written off. This was an articled clerk, a bit younger than me, and he had a right earful from the owner.

Did the audit programmes specify sampling methods for the individual audit?

Yes, we carried out sample checks on all the books of prime entry and the personal ledgers.[7] Invariably we would take randomly selected months and check them in some considerable detail. Initially, the office manager or the partner would state which particular months you had to check, or you would be told to select one month in each half year. Sometimes we'd do an interim as well as a final audit.

Were there a lot of interim audits?

The bigger the client the more likely we would do an interim audit. Many of the clients were uncertain as to how well or badly they were doing until the interim or final accounts were completed and presented. Some judged their progress on the basis of cash flow but this could be misleading. So the interim accounts were useful in that the clients learnt how they were doing without having to wait for the year-end results.

Would you send out anything like a management letter?

Yes. I wouldn't say it was standard, but they were quite often sent. They would be sent if we had come across some aspect that was considered unsatisfactory and was a means of alerting the client that the deficiency had been spotted and had to be rectified. I did not come across these letters much when I served my articles since matters of concern were communicated by word of mouth. This was because we dealt mainly with small companies, particularly small manufacturers, shops, solicitors, and ship-brokers. We also did a lot of estate work for titled people. They invariably owned lots of farms and they had rentals coming in from fishing rights and so on.

That must have been interesting?

It added to the variety of the work. I remember on one occasion, a very wealthy man wanted to get his hands on some of the capital in exchange for a proportion of the income the estate generated. He came to an agreement with his successor and we, in association with solicitors, set up the mechanism to cater for this change, having regard to the estate duty implications.

And after you qualified?

As soon as I sat my finals I left Frank C. Bevan & Co., since they depended to a large extent on articled clerks. I went to Deloittes in Swansea. It was a one-partner office at the time, with three other qualified accountants. On certain jobs it was necessary to have support staff to help with the detailed checking. The clients I dealt with were generally bigger than those I had come across during my articles. One company I dealt with employed over 600 and there were a few with more than 200 employees. On the bigger audits the work could extend over a couple of months. One was given a portfolio of jobs to be responsible for and this meant making the best of one's time since it had to be logged on a daily basis. I was there for two years and was given a fair degree of freedom although in regard to some of the letters sent to clients, one would seek guidance and/or clearance from the partner. And if one wanted to do something radical one had to consult the partner and get his approval. This might be something to do with an argument with a client in distinguishing between capital and revenue. One also always discussed a client's final accounts with the partner before they were released. In spite of the latitude one was given, it was good to have someone to turn to for guidance and advice. I worked on the Swansea University audit and that was quite demanding. After completion, you had to go to the Senate to present the accounts and submit yourself to their questions.

When you were with Deloittes did you ever have problems with client management?

We occasionally did with matters such as stock valuation, when a manager in a client company would value goods on a basis that we could not accept. Or there could be inconsistencies in the year under review compared with the previous year. In other cases you might have felt that there were contingent liabilities that should be reported. On certain occasions it would be necessary to threaten a qualified report in the event of failure to convince by argument.

Was there never any prospect of you becoming a partner there?

I don't think so, and in any case I was not interested. I wanted to go into industry. I left for GKN in Cardiff, and was with them until I retired. I had worked my way up to being Chief Accountant (South Wales) in 1966 and then moved on to commercial and marketing activities. I ended up as a Divisional Managing Director.

When you were chief accountant you must have seen the audit from the other side. Which firm was it?

It was Carter & Company, in Birmingham. They were subsequently taken over by Coopers & Lybrand,[8] who continued as auditors. Coopers brought in lots of documentation which in the main ensured that the internal controls were sound. This aspect of an audit became increasingly important in the late 50s. There had long been a great deal of emphasis on internal controls within GKN.

What sort of changes did Coopers introduce?

The biggest change was probably their emphasis on a balance sheet audit. Otherwise they seemed to follow the style and practice established by Carter's; more a change in emphasis than anything else. They placed a lot of emphasis on stocks. We used to do stock checks in great detail ourselves and would always have independent managers present during stocktaking in every department. The audit staff attended some of the stocktaking, even though this was usually done at weekends. They also examined stock valuations in considerable detail.

What sort of dealings have you had with the Institute over the years?

Not a lot. When I was articled and also with Deloittes, we used to go en bloc to the local Society meetings. When I came to Cardiff, my boss was a member of various committees, and I occasionally attended as an alternate. I attended two Summer Schools, and tried to attend local meetings including the AGM. However, as time went on I did less and less due to other commitments. My job was demanding in terms of time, and I was increasingly involved in several trade associations as a committee member or chairman. So in consequence my involvement in the affairs of the Institute, has, regretfully, been poor.

JOSEPH KENWRIGHT was born in 1925, in Liverpool, the son of a tram conductor. After a secondary school education in Liverpool, he started articles as an incorporated accountant, moving to the chartered firm of Whitehill, Marsh and Jackson, in Birmingham. He qualified in 1951, his training having been interrupted by a spell in the army. Immediately he went to work for Bake-a-Lite, who were pioneers in the techniques of data processing (he became member number 24 of the British Computing Society in 1953), and subsequently worked for the accountants, Arthur Young, as a consultant, English Electric, the Valour Oil Heater Company, the Neville Merchant Banking Group, and finally, a small group engaged in computer marketing. In semi-retirement since 1984, he has never married, and has kept up the same flat in Sutton Coldfield for the last 35 years. It is next to 12 square miles of parkland, where he can indulge his favourite pursuit, walking.

Why accountancy?

It just seemed to be a better way of earning a living than if you just got an ordinary job like a clerk or an engineer. It was a professional skill and the only one that was open to me at the time. That's why there are a lot of accountants my age, because the law and medicine required all sorts of different things.

I was lucky, in the sense that the war was on. I would have had little chance of getting into the accountancy profession had I been born five years earlier, because after school, even if you'd got a good school certificate, you'd frequently be unemployed. It wasn't a reserved occupation and a lot of clerks were whistled off into the services. So they were looking for people, and premiums weren't applicable.

Can you describe what jobs you were asked to do when you were training in the 1940s?

Basically, you trained yourself. You didn't get very much training in a formal sense at the office. You just did what you were told. When you first started off you spent six months to a year doing very little more than adding things up, cross-checking, doing stock calculations, and things like that. Which is why people of our generation can do sums without a calculator. That was taken as a thoroughly basic thing; everybody had to have skill with numbers. Then, thereafter, you picked it up as you went along. You went out on a audit, there would be seniors, semi-seniors and juniors, and the juniors would just do all the dogs-body work. We had a comptometer operator on the larger jobs. But he wouldn't come on the smaller audits, so we had to do our own casting. You just picked it up as you went along. You'd learn all the elements of bought ledger auditing. You'd learn how an audit was initiated, the documentation or the recognition of the order, the invoicing. There were a lot of changes in auditing, with sampling techniques coming in and possibly spending more time looking into systems, but fundamentally we did the same job.

By seniors do you mean that there were always qualified accountants with you?

Not necessarily. There were a lot of audit clerks who were not qualified. A lot of the seniors would be unqualified people, with a lot of experience. They might have been doing auditing for many, many years. They'd probably been with the same firm for 20 or 30 years and the same job for the same clients for a similar time, and they just knew what was going on. You learned from their experience.

But they were always there, you were never sent out to do jobs on your own?

Not as a junior. The first couple of years you were a junior, and then you'd have a couple of years as a semi-senior, as they were called. Semi-seniors would do small jobs on their own. For example, I would do solicitors' accounts on my own, because I would be the only one who'd read all the books and knew all about the law on solicitor accounting. In the main you would be pushed up as fast as they thought you could go.

Was there always a strict system of working papers?

When I first started, they would have an audit programme and you would just work through the list. Later on, in Whitehall, Marsh, Jackson, they started introducing a more formal system of documenting the audits. You'd have a section on debt, a section on credit, a section on stock, fixed assets, and so forth. Then, you'd have specific tasks that would need a printed layout sheet, stating what were the fundamental points of that particular section, and that would then be developed into a more detailed specification on what would be applied in the company's accounts.

Can you give me some examples of the clients that you went to when you were training?

J. & J. Cash of Coventry—they were the name-tape people. They were a good old fashioned, almost feudal company, with the works on the top floor and the employees living down below. Cannon Iron Foundries in Bilston—it used to be a well known brand name—gas fires and things like that. I think they were the largest company we did. There was a firm out on the Coventry road called Harcourt's, they were part of Smith's, the electrical company. The London office did the Smith's group audits, so we picked up the local audits for them. Benson and Stone were quite large, making brass irons. Then there were a whole host of small manufacturing companies in all the metal trades in Birmingham. There could be anything from ten employees up to about 30 employees, and that of course was the heartland of manufacturing. In Birmingham there were many small companies who processed bits which fed up into the larger manufacturing companies.

How did your career progress?

I became a semi-senior, then I became the senior, and then I became the audit manager, eventually. Then I qualified and got out, because I never was particularly interested in the profession. I'd no ambition to stay in the profession and become a partner. I was always interested in getting out into business.

Do you think articles gave you a good business training?

The accountancy profession, apart from the modern business school, is still the only formal way of getting a business education in this country. It's the only way people learn to actively run a business. The extent to which accountants have infiltrated into industry is formidable. You learned things, particularly as an audit clerk. It was really boring stuff, but you didn't half get round. You'd get into production control—how processes were priced. I'd specialise in 'stobble' bits.[9] We all learned about standard costing techniques.[10]

What were the main changes you've observed in the audit?

I don't think the principle of auditing has changed much. But in those days labour was cheap. I got paid seven and six a week[11] when I first started, and when I came out of the army at 22 years old and I was a senior I got three pounds a week. An audit could be much more labour intensive than it is today and I think we would take on a lot more detailed work than would be affordable today. I think the main changes have been determined by the fact that labour has got too expensive to be able to give a blanket coverage on transactions, so there has been a tremendous reliance on sample checking and nowadays a more detailed survey of the way systems work, the integrity of systems. I think there's quite a lot of disadvantages in the fact that they just do not do the work and I imagine an awful lot of avoidable frauds take place.

Do you think the purpose of the audit has changed now?

I suspect that there is a lot of cynicism about auditing at the moment, both by the auditor and the people they audit. I don't think the arrival of the auditors is taken as seriously as it used to be in the old days. When we used to go in people knew we were looking for trouble. We were in there and if anybody had been naughty they were going to get caught. I think there was quite a strong terror that has gone nowadays. I think fraud has gone up market, you are talking big stuff now. I think there is more fraud at high levels now than there was in the old days. In the old days, I think, it was a lot of petty stuff.

The profession has gone through a pretty tricky time, with businesses going through a tricky time too, and I think that the audit has changed its emphasis a lot. Go back to the old days and it was pretty straightforward. There's a set of accounts, they have got to be reasonably right and if anybody in there is fiddling, or people are not doing their job properly, or not accounting properly, find out and get something done about it. Today, businesses are too big, the volume of transactions is so high. There's a lack of transparency now—computers have made it very, very difficult to be able to trace an awful lot.

Has the quality of the auditing declined then?

Well put it this way, with the businesses I've been with throughout the years, I'm going back 20 years, the audit has not been taken as a terribly serious matter, really. We were very keen to get the accounts out, the auditors rubber stamped them, and you've got that out of the way. I don't think people nowadays expect auditors to find that there's as much wrong as there would be in the old days. I think we were there to make sure that people who handled the company's assets were doing it in an honest and proficient way. The way we used to audit, using cheap labour, meant you covered a pretty high percentage of transactions. In a solicitor's office, you'd do every transaction. You'd check everything through. You checked every transaction through client accounts, and you'd make sure you reconciled all the accounts, and everything was properly disposed of. They were very detailed audits. I haven't noticed anybody seriously checking enough transactions in the businesses I was with to really get down to whether anybody was on the take or not. I'm not talking about BCCI type fraud. We're talking about people that pilfer. But then, it's not stopping them which leads on to the big stuff.

Has the beneficiary of the audit changed?

It has always been company management. We know all about the rights of shareholders, but that has always been notional. You are employed by the managers of the company, and they are aware that they are in the same spot as everybody else—they can't modify the routine of the audit. But in the main they were, at least in the companies I was auditing, very keen to make sure we did our job properly. They supported us in our audit reviews. Where we thought there were weaknesses, or where we found areas open for exploitation, they wanted to know.

When you worked in auditing were you ever involved in a situation where your company's accounts were formally qualified?

No, but going back 30 odd years, my company had an overdraft with the bank of about £2m under circumstances where the bank was not happy with the way it was done. The company was going down, down and down, and the bank was getting more and more restive. We did have a situation with the results for one year where we had to use all our influence, and all our arguments and persuasion, to allow the auditors to pass a set of accounts that presented a slightly more favourable view than a more strict one would have called for. We argued that it would be in the interests of the shareholders and the employees, and everybody involved, to take a slightly more favourable view of the company. Which they did I'm glad to say, and the company went on to be highly successful. That's why sometimes it is very difficult. If the auditing rules had been applied. If today's rules had been applied with their full rigour on that occasion, that company would not have survived, and a lot of people would have been out of work. It's very difficult.

JOHN HADDLETON was born in Birmingham in 1931, the son of an advertising manager in the motor industry. He was educated at Solihull (Grammar) School, and in 1948, was articled to H.J. Anderson, a father and son firm of chartered accountants in Birmingham. He completed his articles in 1953 with Thornton and Thornton, (now Grant Thornton) in Oxford, and after National Service, unlike his brother David (who featured in chapter 2), moved into industry where he occupied a number of senior positions and directorships.

Did your parents have to pay a premium?

At that time in the late 40s most parents still had to pay two or three hundred guineas for their sons', (never daughters) articles of clerkship. This was refunded as pay to the clerk as a salary of £2 to £5 a week for the final two years of their five-year apprenticeship.

What were your first impressions of the job?

Well, the first real job I was given was a chemist's accounts, where the manager had altered the figures on the receipts. I looked at those in surprise and discovered that he had changed the dates, and it turned out he'd been on the take. He'd been stealing the money, then putting the next month's money into the cash book for this month. He'd done it very crudely, and I picked it up. That was the first exciting find I made. It was also the first big shock I had about public morality, in that, when we got the owner of the shop in and the lady was told what I had found, I got as big a ticking off as I have ever had. How dare I impugn the honour and integrity of her manager, in whom she had absolute faith. She completely ignored the handwritten alterations to typed receipts! I then discovered she was living with him, and that was the first part of my understanding of how auditing works.

Can you say how audits were conducted when you were doing your articles?

We went from jobs where you would make up the books. You would get vouchers, receipts, cash books, bits of paper, and, first of all, you would turn them into a set of accounts for the year. And we went right up to the jobs where the accounts were presented to you by the firm. We went from little shops in Birmingham up to quite large companies. But we did much the same thing to both of them, as we put the figures together for the little ones we audited them as we thought best, and with the big ones, much the same, and when we finished we'd say,—audited and correct. Which would frighten the life out of anybody today.

Were working papers always kept in the late 40s, early 50s?

They were not big files. There were no intricate detailed reports to make and for published accounts, six/ten pages were quite sufficient. Everybody understood what was in it because it was simple and straight forward, and could be understood by the client. That was because the early audits that I was doing were still based upon the 1929 Companies Act, which was simple, four sheets of paper, a balance sheet and profit and loss account,[12] and that's what people could understand. Then, later on, it was the 1948 Companies Act which was a lot more complicated. At that point, people ceased to understand, on the whole, what was going on.

Did Anderson's specialise?

The firm, being small, took everything that came to it. Being in Birmingham, we had quite a lot of public companies in the metal bashing or general engineering industries. We had Stanley Brothers' Brick and Tile Co. in Nuneaton. Now long gone but which was quite a substantial public company audit. We discovered the same sort of things going on there as I had discovered in the little chemist's shop.

Why the move to Oxford?

Half way through my articles father's job was moved from Coventry to Oxford. So, I moved to Thornton and Thornton, as it was then, and which was much the most substantial accountancy business in Oxford. There were about 60 or 70 people in the Oxford office, and also offices in London, Banbury and elsewhere. There was a very much wider range of companies, like BUPA, and many of the Oxford colleges, Morris Motors and the Nuffield Organisation, which consisted of 32 different companies and we audited them all in detail. Each company had an accountant, but only two of them were qualified accountants. I think Morris Motors' head office accountant was qualified; and the British Motor Corporation Spares Division had a qualified accountant. I later joined Nuffield's after my later Air Force days, and it was standard that most of their companies were run by unqualified people, who could produce accounts but they didn't really go much further than that.

What were Thorntons like to work for?

You had very tight schedules indeed. In Oxford, the work depended so much on how awful the papers were that you were given, and you were under great pressure if you took much longer than other people. One of my colleagues, however, calculated that his average rate of pay, for the five years of articles, was a farthing an hour, and he decided that that set the rate at which he was going to work, if he was put under pressure. Then as now, the audit bill was based on time taken, so it was inevitable that there should be pressure. There wasn't any competition from other people to take the audits away from you. That came much later. So the pressure was really applied by the principals on the staff to the get work done as quickly and as cheaply as possible, for the sake of the cost.

If you audited Morland's Brewery, the new boys would always be taken down by the kind ladies who bottled the sherry downstairs, and the unsuspecting auditors would walk through and be offered a drink; but before they got to the end, they were flat on their backs, unconscious. It wasn't the drink, it was the fumes, and everyone went through that.

What was the background to Thorntons' business?

The original partner set up with a solicitor to help Billy Morris make motor cars. So, of course, he became the auditor of Morris Motors. Thorntons were very shrewd actually, they did their marketing. They had Morris, which was the biggest, fastest thing in Oxford, and each time Morris took a company over the audit came to Thorntons. All the local breweries, nearly all the pubs, cinemas, and various motor industry offshoots, like Hartwells, came after this big initial start up.

Oxford University didn't permit its colleges to have local auditors, so Thorntons opened a London office, and all the colleges, because they found it so cheap, appointed the London office to do the audit, which London then sub-contracted to Oxford. Every college was within five minutes' walking distance of the Oxford office, so travelling and hotel expenses didn't exist.

Did you discover any frauds with Thorntons?

Yes, when I went to a local borough council and found that the housing manager had stolen the rents. The manager was not prosecuted, he was allowed to resign. I wasn't allowed to complete the audit and I was not at all happy that the audit was completed. The council produced a clean set of accounts, and should not have done so.

You did your articles, and then you did national service? Can you give me a brief resume of what happened after that?

Well, I went back to Thorntons. I was not happy. I had been earning £14 a week in the Air Force, which was a fortune, and I came back in 1955 to be offered £9 a week, but I desperately wanted £10. This was refused, and I was told that I needn't look elsewhere in Oxford, which is where I lived, because all the firms in Oxford paid that sort of money and had an agreement not to accept each other's staff. It was still not feasible to leave home unless you went to London, and you couldn't realistically go to London until you had post-qualification experience. To my surprise, I was offered a job, within the month, by the financial administrator of the Nuffield Organisation, as his assistant, on £700 a year, £14 a week, which was a colossal rise—it shook the firm. When I asked the man why he chose me, and not other people, he said,—well, you are bright enough, but not experienced enough to want more money than we are prepared to pay. He was a very realistic man, and a very good man to work for.

What did you do at BMC?

The British Motor Corporation centralised all the spares from Austin's in Birmingham and Morris in Oxford into one place, in Cowley. They had lost a third of their spares in consolidating and they took me on to deal with the discrepancies. BMC Services was the only part of the corporation at that time to be making a profit, so it was important. I looked at this vast amount of paperwork, and I looked at the place and I thought,—this is ridiculous, they are never going to find anything. So, I took a different tack. I took the biggest area of losses which was lorry and car engines. I got one list of a particular set of lorry engines which had come down from Birmingham but there were only two-thirds that many lorry engines in Cowley. Everything was checked in, I had seen that. Then, the penny dropped,—the drivers were paid by the load and the lorries were driving in with their loads, being checked in, driving out, driving around the Oxford by-pass and driving in again with the same loads. We hadn't lost four million pounds' worth of parts, we'd never had them. I was thanked embarrassingly by the accountant and by my boss but not another word was ever said, and I moved back across the road to the Nuffield head office. I wonder if that sort of thing is as easily picked up today, by people going through endless computer lists, because, unless you have your stock sheets, and you know what it is that you ought to be comparing, you can never find it.

You moved up to board level didn't you?

Yes. My first directorship with a public company was with a pharmaceutical wholesaler called Barclay and Sons Ltd. It was set up originally in the 1700s by a branch of the family who set up Barclays Bank. Their accounts were qualified because it was not possible to verify the value of properties in Northern Ireland. That was my first audit from the other side as a director. I was responsible for increasing the profits of that group by 50%—from very tiny to quite big. Sometime previously at Cope Allman, I had had my first experience of inadequately trained, university-qualified, auditors when one came to audit my group accounts and told me that I'd got the figures on the wrong side of the sheet. This was a qualified auditor, full of his own importance, who was entirely wrong. It was the first experience I had of overconfidence and a total lack of understanding of the basic elements of bookkeeping and accounting, which I have noticed ever since. That was in 1959/60, when I first saw this problem arising. It should have been dealt with by the Institute requiring auditors, requiring all accountants, to conduct work at a very low stage in the game, and to actively prepare accounts properly—before they qualify.

You sound disenchanted?

Company accounts are less true and fair than they have ever been. More has meant less. The more detail brought in meant the less being understood. You can't believe a word of a set of accounts. You can't understand a set of accounts unless you took part in putting them together. The only way of understanding them is to smell them really, the ratios and proportions. It is so easy to hide absolutely everything, and to give a different picture. So much is opinion on matters of great scale that you often just cannot tell. When Guy Motors, a big company making nice lorries, was about to go bankrupt in the 1950s, I looked at the accounts of 1958 and said,—God, they are going bust. I looked at the accounts of 1959, and thought,—this company is bust, it's going to have the receivers put in, and I bought a put option[13] on the shares. It was obvious it was going bust and sure enough it went bust. I made £500—a fortune! I laughed, because the accounts were so transparent. You couldn't be that precise about accounts today.

And what about auditing?

Computerisation is in everything now, so it has to be matched by computed auditing to a degree. Auditing ought to be all about checking systems, and particularly people, accurately. I don't believe that now takes place in too many places. But, I think it has got a lot worse, in that they have totally missed the wood for the trees. Barings[14] is a case in point.

The son of a personnel manager with ICI, KENNETH JACKSON was born in Huddersfield in 1929. After secondary education at Huddersfield College, he took up articles with the small local firm of incorporated accountants, H.N. Bostock, in 1946. His training was interrupted by National Service, and on qualification with the Society in 1954, he moved south to Gloucester and worked for another firm of incorporated accountants, King, Scott, Dicks, for ten years before moving into industry, becoming chief accountant with the Phoenix Assurance Co. He served for some years as secretary to the ground committee of Gloucester Rugby Club.

What did your job entail when you did your articles?

In the beginning I did menial work. I did National Service for two and a quarter years, from 47–49, and after that more senior work. But these were small firms and pure auditing was uncommon. We did basic accounts because the taxman or the banks wanted them. We checked invoices, postings from day books[15] to ledgers, cash books to ledgers; we checked bank statements, and sometimes carried out physical checks. When you did bigger jobs, which were few and far between, we still produced the accounts. Your auditing really came in checking the books before you produced accounts. I don't mean we were never given accounts. I can recollect one client that had an accountant, but I was too junior to get to see whether he had produced the actual balance sheet.

What kind of clients did you have?

Builders' merchants, hardware wholesalers, garages, a majority were shopkeepers, farmers, estate agents, solicitors. I can't recall any manufacturers.

After you qualified, what happened then?

After I qualified I thought I would like to try my luck somewhere else, particularly down south, because the start of my life in National Service was in the air force near Swindon. Eventually I moved to Gloucester, that was in November 1954, to King, Scott, Dicks & Co.

What was your relationships with the management of client firms?

People were sometimes reluctant to show younger people information they considered to be personal, but they would produce it, perhaps, for a partner who was older than them. I remember once, even though I was senior clerk at King, Scott, Dicks, I sat in my office looking at something and not liking it and when a partner came in, who was 20 years older than me, I suggested that we go up to the top man in the company. And yes, there was fraud going on. If I had gone to the lower down man, I think I would have cottoned on anyway but I might have got a lot of waffle and it might have been stalled for a while.

Was the discovery of fraud a frequent occurrence?

No, that was a serious one, and the man got sent down. He was a cashier and he was putting money into his own pocket. He was foolish, he wasn't the only one, but sometimes they weren't quite so foolish and the firms didn't really want to make anything of it. They might get restitution and they would leave it at that. I think that was the only one I can recollect going to prison.

Did you ever come across management fraud or fraud on a large scale?

I think I did, but I couldn't do anything about it. I couldn't prove anything. It was a case of,—we'll keep the stock down so we don't pay so much tax. This comes out in the long run obviously, but it might well be that by the time it came out, the tax rates had gone down, and the boost to profits was secured.

JULIAN EVANS was born in Cardiff in 1933, the son of a bank manager. After attending Hereford Cathedral School, in 1951 he became Peat, Marwick, Mitchell's first ever articled clerk in south Wales. After qualifying in 1956, he did National Service, and then for two years he worked on audits for Peats at their head office before leaving to work in industry. He worked first with the steel makers, Richard Thomas and Baldwins, in London and Swansea and then with AB Electronics, where he remained for 26 years, the last 19 as financial director, until his retirement in 1991.

What sort of work did you do in training with Peats?

Well, it was mainly audits. At that time there were very many steel companies in south Wales, some of which were still nationalised. I was involved in many of these audits. We audited Richard Thomas and Baldwins in Ebbw Vale and four other locations in south Wales. We audited Briton Ferry Steel, which owned about 13 old-fashioned tin plate works, which were subsequently closed down when the large modern strip mills were built for the Steel Company of Wales nearby. We audited the Electricity Authority and also many manufacturing companies. So the work was mainly auditing but in addition there was considerable tax work and a few investigations. At this time many foods were still rationed and their prices controlled, so we did many investigations for the Ministry of Food on suppliers of eggs, meat and milk. This necessitated visits to large suppliers as well as to very small butchers' shops and dairies who were at the end of the supply chain. It was very interesting comparing the costs of various units throughout south Wales and also compared with the rest of the U.K.. Also the senior partner was a very well regarded accountant in south Wales, and in the aftermath of nationalisation of the coal industry in 1947 he represented the interests of the various coal owners in their claim for compensation.

Were you closely supervised during your training?

As a new articled clerk for the first couple of months I was located in the office, being taught the office routine, the names and businesses of the clients, etc. Then when I started visiting the clients' offices on audits I was always the junior audit clerk performing the most mundane tasks under the supervision of a senior auditor. Each job had an audit programme listing the work to be carried out on each area of the client's organisation: for example, purchases, sales, wages, etc. This programme would be initialled by the members of the audit team after they had completed the work, indicating the extent of the work done: for example, 20% of purchase invoices, 10% of sales invoices, etc.

When the final accounts had been prepared, each item on the balance sheet was checked in detail and supported by a comprehensive schedule which explained the make-up of all the individual items. Peats had a very good system of producing these schedules, based on the 'grandfather, father, son' principle: prepared by junior staff, scrutinised by a senior, and in due course reviewed by the partner in charge.

If there were any questions the manager asked which you weren't able to answer that was a little bit of a black mark. It was inevitable that he'd think of something you hadn't because of his experience, but if it was something very obvious that was a black mark. Then they'd sit down side by side, the partner and the senior auditor, and go through all the papers, and, if after two or three hours he still hadn't found anything important that was obviously wrong and he couldn't be provided with an answer straightaway, you knew things were going well. But it was a nervous time when the partner came along and checked all the work that you and all your colleagues had been auditing for the last two or three weeks or so.

How did Peats go about auditing a new client?

The standard for Peats in those days, in the 1950s, when they won a new audit or they were auditors of a new company, was the first year a senior would go in and review all the systems and all the books, and possibly make a note of all the personnel involved in the accounting areas, as well as the directors, and keep all this as a permanent record. He then concocted an audit programme, which would comprise all the work that had to be done every year. That would list what proportion of items you checked, the cash book, the purchase ledger and sales invoicing; all the various aspects of accounting. So that in subsequent years, if you personally hadn't been to company X before, you could look up last year's papers, look up the audit programme and the permanent files, and have a feeling for the people, what type of organisation it was, before you arrived there. You could talk with a little bit of authority about the organisation, which is good. You didn't have to go in there and ask the same questions every year. You made sure that the things are the same, of course, but from there on in you can immediately give the juniors on the audit some work to do, counting the petty cash, that sort of thing.

Was it tailored to the individual types of clients?

Oh indeed, and the work involved was very much based on the strengths and weaknesses of the accounting departments of these organisations. The big operations would tend to have much stronger controls, some of them would have their own internal audit department, and they would do certain work. Our work would very much bear in mind the work the internal auditors had done. We would read their internal audit reports, which would cut down work that we had to do and reduce our audit fee. That's why, of course, they have their own internal audit.

From your perspective as finance director, have you seen major changes in the conduct of the audit?

Yes. In my early years as an auditor a great deal of detailed checking was carried out. Far too much sometimes but, of course, few clients had sophisticated computer systems with built in checks and counterchecks in those days. Nowadays, auditors of major companies concentrate on balance sheet audits and place much more reliance on statistical analysis, comparisons with budgets and forecasts, etc.. In addition, probably more reliance is placed on materiality.[16]

How did you end up at AB Electronics?

I was working for RTB in Swansea, when I saw an advert in the *Sunday Times*, and I applied for it. Having had the interview, I rang up Bob Martin, who was by then the senior Peats Cardiff partner, to whom I used to be articled. Since Peats were AB's auditors, I asked him what the firm was like, and he gave me a bit of background. At the same time, before they offered me the position, AB had seen I had actually been articled to Bob Martin. So they rang him up, and asked about me. Well he said I was OK. So they actually used their auditor to act as a referee for me. It was only later that I realised that this procedure was more common than I thought.

And the association with Peats continued?

Yes. I just happened to always be associated with Peats all my life. My eldest daughter qualified with Peats in London. So I was happy to go along with Peats as auditors because I knew their approach, I knew they were a top firm, and they were an ethical firm. I think the relationship with auditors is very important and my approach when I had been at AB a few years was, if I had problems with anything in the presentation I'd just sit and discuss it with the senior person involved in the audit. I'd say,—look, I have three matters this year which I think are contentious. You might take an opposing view to me, so let's discuss them.

Would this be at the start of the audit?

Yes, at a very early stage. Things have changed, but they always used to plan the audit. Assuming they hadn't done an interim, when the year-end was imminent the manager or partner would come and see me and say,—look the year-end is due and we need to check the stock. Let's confirm which factories we are going to. They would say,—what is your programme for completion of the accounts? We would say we could get things out in two and a half weeks. Then we might be talking through the finalisation of inventory valuation, and they'd say,—OK, that seems all right, and then we'd go through other matters, and then I would raise any points which I thought might be contentious, which they might or might not have raised. So we'd just kill those off at an early stage, in principle.

How were discrepancies dealt with?

As far as I was concerned, from the other side, timing and materiality were the two factors. I used to prepare the accounts and if, for example, the result was a profit of a million and they found an error up or down £10,000, you wouldn't bother to alter it. It's one percent or whatever it is. It's peanuts. It is not material to the profit. If we found £40,000 or £50,000 within a week of the auditors coming then we would alter the figures. But as you got near the end and you'd done all the schedules, and maybe you'd presented the interim figures to the board, the materiality of the figures would change. If they found £50,000, then you might not alter it because it's in relation to the profit last year of say £900,000. OK, this year it should have been £970,00. It is still showing a profit increase, and the right trend; so we might say it is no longer material in terms of the profit or the balance sheet, and so don't alter it. That was the way I presented it to the auditors for the last 25 years and they would accept that without any problem, because that's the sensible approach, looking at the overview of the results.

IAN ENGEL was born in St. Albans, in 1931, the son of a London furrier, and was educated at St.Paul's public school in the City of London. He took up articles with the small incorporated London firm of Edward, Blinkhorn, Lyon, qualifying with the Society in 1956. After a year as audit manager for another smaller firm, he set up his own practice which eventually expanded to three partners. After 14 years, he left the profession and studied at the Institute of Education and Brunel University in London. He then lectured in Accounting at the Polytechnic of North London for many years, with one year in New Zealand. He has served as an examiner for the ICAEW, and on four occasions was sent by them to East Africa as part of a team charged with setting up a new system of professional qualification. Since 1979, most of his time has been occupied as finance director for ORT, a world-wide Jewish charity operating from offices in Camden Town.

What work were you given when you were doing your articles?

It did vary. We had small public company audits at one end of the scale, and the incomplete records at the other end. With one of the partners, the clientele was almost entirely in the field of light engineering, manufacturing of precision tools, handbag frames and other forms of metal accessories. Another client was one of the largest glaziers in the country. This was where I would say the good auditing practice was carried out. Where there was a responsibility publicly to the shareholders and we acted as a form of both external and internal control, because none of these firms had any staff that dealt with the internal control of their organisations.

But this was only part of the firm. On the other side there was anything from the small clothing manufacture and the sweet shop, the little garage around the corner where there was no auditing carried out at all. You were basically preparing accounts that would be suitable for the Inland Revenue. I'd say my time was equally divided between routine audit work and the incomplete record side.

Were you very closely supervised?

With clients of any size there was an audit manager or a senior member of staff present, and I being the most junior would start at the bottom, and then as the years went by and I completed my articles I became what was known as a semi-senior. When I qualified and went into practice on my own, then I was paddling my own canoe.

Were the programmes strictly worked out and tailored to the individual client?

Very much so. They were fairly well defined and there was a substantial list of different jobs to be done. There were a number on the list that we would only do periodically as random checks. Unless of course during the audit you felt there was anything that needed to be attended to in much greater depth.

The firm kept extremely good documentation of the work they had performed. So there was always continuity for the next generation of audit clerks to follow. The audit manager would go through the audit programme, and then would come down maybe a week or so later and find out what you had been up to and what the problems had been.

Did you find it hard going during your articles combining work with your correspondence course?

It was a very poor way of studying. You really were cramming and it was very tough. In my case I had to do a lot of travelling, living in St. Albans and having to travel into London every day and possibly out somewhere again. Coming back from a long day's auditing say 40–50 miles away wasn't conducive to study.

But you were motivated by the fact that you had only a certain period to do the work in. You had to get through it; otherwise you couldn't sit the examinations. But there was no personal relationship and it was all centred on trying to find out what sort of questions were going to be asked in the exam.

In general though, were your articles a good preparation for your future career?

I think so. I was very fortunate to work in a smallish firm, because of the variety. I would have hated to have worked for a sizeable firm where probably you only got two or three clients, or the tiny firm just doing the sweet shops. But there was no real education and training by the senior members of staff other than on the job.

What did you go on to do immediately after you qualified?

I was an audit manager for a year in a small practice and that's when I really got to know small businesses and it was extremely useful experience, particularly as the following year I went into practice on my own. And there the majority of clients were on the smaller side but we did have one or two medium-sized audits.

Can you go through what was involved in a typical audit at that time?

Bank reconciliation was number one on the list. It was very important to make sure the bank was in order. Then we would laboriously check a certain amount of the bank statements for probably two months out of the year, and if we weren't satisfied then of course we would do a full check. I thought we spent a lot of unnecessary time on checking copy sales invoices, and I can remember on one occasion there being half a dozen missing and the chief accountant saying,—one minute, I'll get them typed out and give you copies. Also there was the checking of outstanding amounts due to the client and following through the trail on payments in. We were paid badly, and time wasn't of the essence. If you spent another week or so on an audit, it wasn't a question of being cost effective. The important thing was that you looked reasonably smart, and wore a suit, white shirt and tie. Your periodic presence there was very important as a form of control. We weren't particularly liked around the place as we slowed up the client's work.

That was the basic work done by a junior audit clerk. As you progressed up the scale you were then very much more concerned about balance sheet audits; starting from the end and working backwards, and that's really the sort of check and control that I developed when I was in practice myself. I had to be satisfied that the accounts looked right and there didn't appear to be any manipulation or any funds going astray. So, for example, we would check the gross profit ratios, comparing them with other clients or even using information from the Inland Revenue. Looking back, extensive checking was done but a lot of short cuts could have been followed at the time. The process was too laborious—maybe to justify the fee.

It was more of a cash control check than anything else, to see that funds went into the right slots and that there were no frauds among the staff themselves. That appeared to be the main objective—to be satisfied that to the best of our knowledge the books and records were in good order.

Did you get involved in interim audits?

Even monthly audits. We had a very big second hand car retailer and we would send one or two clerks down to the firm to check the books on a monthly basis. This was to satisfy the owners that monies and goods hadn't gone astray, because it was the sort of business where all kinds of things can disappear, and big money was involved.

How did you ensure the quality and depth of an audit in your own firm?

Being a very small practice we were top heavy; there were three partners to eight or nine staff. We were very much hands on, so we were in control. And where we did have larger clients, like the second hand car dealer, we would regularly go down and work with our staff on the job to ensure the quality of the work being carried out.

Did you ever have to formally qualify a client's accounts?

There may have been the odd case. Certainly it was always in our armoury if the client insisted on non-disclosure. My attitude was always,—if you're not satisfied with our reporting, go elsewhere.

Do you think qualifications have become more frequent over recent years?

I think so because of the whole question of indemnity insurance and the tremendous liability put upon the larger firms of auditors, and there they go through a tremendous amount of stress. It also reflects on the fees charged to cover such enormous policy costs. In my day, there were a number of large firms but not anything like the size they are today. And today audits are global. So it makes a very big difference.

How did you build up your business when you went on your own?

Because of my experience during my articles I tended to attract people in light engineering. I attracted a lot of second hand motor car dealers because of my knowledge of the trade and Edward, Blinkhorn, Lyon had dozens and dozens of dentists, so I also attracted dentists! But it was purely by recommendation, word of mouth and clubs, pubs, sociability. And doing charitable work. We had quite a number of clients where there was no charge, voluntary organisations, and I am sure that helped. It's the wideness of your own circle that matters.

Were you ever aware of other firms actively touting for business?

We always worried as our clients grew that we would lose them to the Big Four or Five at the time, firms like Price Waterhouse and Deloittes, and in fact we did lose our biggest client because we just couldn't cope with the work. That was always our major worry. On the other hand we did get clients from the larger firms. We used to get their cabbage, their small clients, because it wasn't economic for them to undertake the work. That came from knowing a lot of practitioners in the larger firms.

What is your view of the proliferation of standards governing the profession?

Standards are extremely important and I think that the Institute has been slow in developing them. I'll give you an example that I'm close to: charity accounts. In the United States there have been standards of accounting practice for probably 30 or 40 years, and it's only now when you are dealing with one of the largest industries, if one could call it an industry, that this has been developed in this country.[17]

But I think the codes of practice and the standards and the regulations are of paramount importance. The big minus against the accounting profession is in the stupidity of its membership remaining isolated in six or seven compartments, where you've got the Institute of Chartered Accountants in England and Wales, separate from Scotland and Ireland, separate from management accountants, not to mention certified accountants. There are all these bodies, we don't speak with one voice and it really is to our detriment that we are not universal. Although the Institute has tried very hard, maybe they should try a bit harder. They should bring the bodies together under one umbrella and could then speak with one voice for 250,000 members.

Some small practitioners complain that standards have over-complicated the audit?

They are just making excuses.

Born in Rugby in 1934, CHARLES RAWLINSON is the son of an electrical engineer. He was educated at Canford School and then read the Law Tripos at Jesus College, Cambridge, after which he took articles with the three-partner Rugby firm of A. E. Limehouse, qualifying in 1958. He then worked for Peat, Marwick, Mitchell in London, Toronto and Milan before leaving the profession in 1962 to pursue a career in corporate finance with Morgan Grenfell, where he rose to become chairman. A Council member of the ICAEW from 1995 to 1997, he is chairman of the Industrial Members' Advisory Committee on Ethics,[18] *is a member of the JDS Executive Committee and the Chartered Accountants' Joint Ethics Committee (CAJEC).*[19] *Since he retired in 1993, he has acted as senior adviser to West Merchant Bank, the London subsidiary of Westdeutsche Landesbank and is deputy chairman of the Britten Sinfonia.*

Can you describe the jobs you were asked to do when you were articled in Rugby?

In the early days I was very much a dogsbody. There was a chief clerk who was very old-fashioned, so the bookkeeping and accounting was very nicely done but mostly by writing in ledgers, day books and cash books and so on. A great deal of our work was incomplete records: cardboard boxes of dirty pieces of paper delivered by farmers on their way to market and we had to turn them into accounts. I remember visiting farms and counting cattle as part of the inventory check. We handled all the tax affairs of these people, sometimes having to argue with the Revenue at General Commissioner or Special Commissioner level. But I think there has always been a difficulty with the smaller businessman trying to persuade him that an audit is actually something that he needs, rather than something he has to have because the law says so; and because they had to get their tax affairs agreed, and the best way to get that done was if a firm of chartered accountants or similar signed the accounts and said they were correct. So the audit was something imposed upon the client, something of an expensive nuisance and I suspect today that there is still an element of that at the smaller end of the business.

So it was that sort of work, which was a very good basic grounding in the profession which I found very helpful when I went to Peats in London. Immediately one was working on public companies and much bigger things, but still the principles were the same.

Can you tell me about your experiences with Peats?

I was based in the London office in one of the general departments of the firm that did whatever came. We did investigations of companies for merchant banks who were proposing to float companies or to make a takeover bid. And we did audits for companies of a variety of sizes. At the end of 1960, I managed to persuade the firm to send me to the Toronto office of PMM because I wanted to get across the Atlantic and learn something of what went on in North America. In those days, there was no way I could work in the United States because of work permits, but they would allow me to go to Canada where my qualification was accepted by the Canadian Institute. I worked in the Canadian office of PMM for about six months doing very much the same sort of work I was doing in London.

Were there any interesting contrasts in the way things operated over there?

The Canadian firm was run more on American lines than on British lines. A lot of the Toronto clients were subsidiaries of American companies, so naturally we were having to do our work the way Americans wanted it done. We were a bit more advanced in the use of accounting machinery, and many of the developments of accounting machinery at that time were essentially American, the early electro-mechanical equipment, which preceded the electronic methods of doing things.

Where else were you sent?

Well, in 1959, a leading Italian industrial company wished to have a listing on the New York Stock Exchange and they had to produce the documents required by the SEC.[20] PMM were asked to go to Italy and oversee this process, but it was not easy because the attitudes of the Italians were hard to reconcile with the requirements of American regulations. It was an early and interesting example of the way in which a change in accounting attitudes and theories is driven by the capital markets.

I believe that the way to drive forward accounting standards is to start from the profession, rather than by government action. There is a drastic change coming in the way in which financial statements are being produced throughout the world, whether it be in Japan or in Europe or elsewhere, driven much more by the requirements of the international capital market than by legislation. Because, if in fact German firms, for example, wish to raise capital on the international capital market they have to produce financial information which is acceptable to the international investment banks and stock exchanges. That is driving things together, and therefore I believe the best way forward in developing standards, both of auditing and accounting practice, is to encourage the private sector to deal with it. I've been very impressed with the efforts being made by IFAC[21] and FEE[22] in these areas. In bodies like CAJEC, we find ourselves spending quite a lot of time thinking about what is happening abroad, and I'm glad to say that the papers produced by IFAC seem to have a very substantial relationship with ours.

What do you see as some of the most problematical issues in auditing?

We had one client company at Peats which was researching and developing very advanced electronic equipment for scientific measurements and other things. They were very much at the edge of technology and one of the great difficulties of auditing the accounts was that nobody really knew whether the work-in-progress at the end of the year had any value at all. So the only way we could complete the audit was to have the directors take a very strong position on the valuation of work-in-progress, which was the company's largest asset. We had to take a very careful approach as auditors. I believe it raises a very fundamental question, which I don't believe has ever been totally addressed in subsequent years, as to what is the role of a balance sheet. Is it a statement of value or it is a statement of—what I was taught as a student by the finance director of GKN in Birmingham—the balance remaining in the books of the company after you have drawn up the profit and loss account, no more no less?

Subsequently, there's been a whole debate about inflation accounting, people constantly trying to move towards putting a value on the balance sheet, and I believe that that is a mistaken approach. And having been a corporate financier of a merchant bank for 30 years, and having recently been involved in selling a company which had net tangible assets of about £1m, when it was worth more than ten times that. The most valuable asset which the company had was intangible and not valued in the accounts at all, and it makes you realise just how the figures in the balance sheet do not, and I argue are not, intended to show what is the value of the business.

What perspective has your career in merchant banking given you on the audit process?

I had a very wide view of it because of our clients. I dealt with an enormous range of clients, some of whom were modest in size, but some of whom were extremely large even on a world scale, and in all these cases we were issuing and in many cases we were producing documents for issues, and there were merger or take-over documents. One was doing a lot of very complex accounting work, involving accounting theory and sometimes developing new concepts, for example, merger accounting. Our clients' businesses were becoming more and more international, and the capital markets were becoming international, so one was dealing with preparing accounts in a variety of currencies. One was having to cope with the problems, for the first time, of how to reconcile accounts prepared in accordance with American principles with accounts in accordance with British principles, let alone Italian or Japanese. It was only in the 1960s that the Eurobond market developed and suddenly you had people from all over the world wanting to issue bonds providing financial information. Well what financial information? In those days Japanese companies did not prepare consolidated accounts, there was no such thing in Japan. And yet you could make a pretty good argument that unless accounts were consolidated they weren't very meaningful.

We had to wrestle with a lot of very difficult and complex issues even in the accounting of the bank. Morgan Grenfell had more than half of its business denominated in foreign currencies. However, the capital and reserves of the bank were in sterling, and legally the accounts had to be prepared in sterling. It was very difficult because we had endless devaluations, the currency fluctuations were enormous, and this was beyond our control. So we then had to start thinking very imaginatively about how to manage this situation.

What is it that underpins an accountant's professional ethics? It is not anything as clear cut as a doctor's, is it?

I think it's just the same. Let's suppose you are the chief accountant of a business and the books are in a muddle, the accounts are in a mess. The managing director wants to know what it costs to produce a left-handed widget and you tell him, but actually this proves to be absolute rubbish because you didn't do it properly. Or when the accounts are produced at the end of the year, you tell him that he's made a profit and then you get audited and the auditors say you haven't made a profit at all, you've made a loss. Some people get it wrong by mistake or by incompetence, other people are dishonest. It's always been the same, in every walk of life people will bend the rules. But in the end, coming back to market forces, whether you are a 14th century wool merchant in Ghent or Bruges or you are trading on the London Stock Exchange in 1998, if you get a reputation that you are rather sharp and tricky to deal with, it won't be good for your business. And so maintaining integrity, objectivity and independence of mind is something which is a chartered accountant's stock in trade. He must be somebody that people instinctively rely upon and trust. That is what the individual accountant trades on, and that is what firms of chartered accountants trade on.

Given your experience on the JDS, do you think there is any problem with the profession policing itself?

There is a problem of the members' perception of what their professional body is doing. There are members who complain that the Institute is too much a regulator and not enough a trade union. They'd like it to be more of a body representing them and helping them to get business and they resent the fact that the Institute has a disciplinary role. I'm afraid a profession must have a self-regulatory function. No matter how many external regulators there are, if you are a civil engineer or a chartered accountant or a doctor, your own professional peers are the best people to decide whether you're doing it right or wrong and behaving yourself appropriately.

The other problem that we have in the disciplinary area is the difficulty of regulating on an international basis. The ICAEW does not yet have an entirely satisfactory regime for regulating people who are members of the Institute but are operating outside the UK. There are, for example, people practising outside the United Kingdom who are members of the Institute, and I believe they should be regulated by their own professional body, quite apart from whatever other rules or regulations there may be in the territory where they function. If in fact you practice in Jakarta and you say that you are a chartered accountant then I think you should be subject to its discipline. The disciplinary processes are competent and sound, but I do believe that they are hobbled at the present time by the difficulties of operating outside national boundaries. That is not the fault of the profession. In some cases, it is the fact that foreign governments will not permit information to be made available to examine what went on. That's been the case in many countries for a very long time.

ROGER BERRY was born in Manchester in 1936, the son of an engineer. After Manchester Grammar School and Oriel College, Oxford, where he read Agricultural Economics, he took articles with Peat, Marwick, Mitchell in Manchester, qualifying in 1961. He then audited for Deloitte, Plender, Haskins and Sells, in Paris, and Deutsche Treuhand Gessellschaft, in Germany, before returning to Britain to take up a career in industry with

Fisons, and other companies. He then taught accountancy at university level in London and in Glasgow but now lives in Swansea and works as a property developer.

What was your job when you did your articles?

Audit clerk, basically. We had a file, and two or three of us would go out and do an audit, and then the file would be checked through by a partner. First of all, you got the bank statements, worked out a bank reconciliation, because very often they couldn't even do that, and then checked out all the banking side, and thereafter, it was purely a balance sheet audit. Looking at, and checking out, debtors' lists, getting debtors' confirmations, checking liabilities, stocktake, making sure all the goods in stock had been properly either paid for, or else accruals[23] had been made for the liability to suppliers of goods taken into stock. And then, you checked the fixed asset register.[24] When I was first doing that, there weren't too many difficulties in setting up the accounts. We didn't have a prescriptive set of accounts like you have nowadays, and the legal paraphernalia of checking that all the provisions of the Companies Act were met.

Who were some of your clients?

Granada Television, Chloride Batteries, and there were some smaller businesses in Manchester.

Did you ever detect a fraud?

Oh, yes. It was in connection with a payroll where a cashier was fiddling around collecting monies. There always has to be a problem in the internal control. That is something the auditors have to be concerned with—to see that no one person really is in a position to carry certain defalcations over a long period to any great extent without the possibility of collusion. And in this case, the internal control was definitely defective, not our audit. Once we discovered what the mechanism was, and when he admitted things, he was wheeled into their managing director and suspended on the spot. They didn't even bother taking him to court. Apparently he was a freemason. The freemasons found him another job somewhere else.

How would you characterise a true and fair view?

The expression 'true and fair,' is one which I've considered as an academic. In Germany, for example, it just means that accounts conform with the legal requirements, and that's the way I think it should be. You really shouldn't have a term which defies analysis, but which makes philosophical assertions about quality and truth which simply are not there. The whole idea of accounting is to make the recording of transactions within businesses a whole lot easier and to give a bird's-eye view of the business, albeit an incomplete one. But what accounts mean at the end of the day really can't be expressed in terms of: this is the right value of the company.

That was another thing—the way accountants were called in. I was involved in a conference once, working out a price to pay for a business acquisition. I don't think accountants really have much to contribute there at all. The idea that the price for a business is a multiple of so many years' profit averaged out does not seem to be a particularly sensible way of valuing a business. In that context, you have to think about accounting principles and the amounts you're prepared to report by way of profit—whether you should write off goodwill in the profit and loss account, or against reserves.[25] The price/earnings ratio[26] resulting from this exercise is judged to be important, but it should be far less important than a price derived from a detailed analysis of current and future trading prospects.

Has accountancy theory got to grips with this?

I feel that the accountancy theory that I grappled with was misguided; and too many claims were made for accountancy theory when it was mostly just specious talk. I'm not happy with the whole idea, for example, of consolidated accounts[27] because you are putting together accounts of companies which are separate legal entities. The Companies Act specifies that the holding company and the subsidiary accounts are to be consolidated as if they are the accounts of one company. One company, if it has got a wholly owned subsidiary, can let that company go to the wall and have unsatisfied creditors. In the case of that subsidiary, there is nothing anyone can do about it. And this consolidation is all done with the idea of giving a better, more true and fair view, and I don't think it does. In fact, whole numbers of transactions really ought not to be allowed, on the grounds that you cannot account for them in a realistic manner. A whole number of transactions have been devised in order to play around with profit and loss in accounts.

The grammar of accountancy ought to be law, and I don't think there has been too much real heart-searching, outside the accountancy profession itself, about what companies should be allowed to do. Take the simple example, does your average customer of a bank know what sort of risks bank directors can take? They don't. They haven't a clue, and yet their banks are in the market, and taking enormous risks, and you wouldn't think a bank would do that. But no, they have got the power to do that. I think company directors are a self-perpetuating oligarchy with far too much power, far too much pay, and the whole matter ought to be taken in hand.

What is your opinion of the guidelines and standards that the Institute has come up with?

I think they have been disastrous. I think they haven't stood the test of time. They have chopped and changed enormously, and I think they have been put together by people, Tom Lee[28] and Tweedie (qv) are prime examples, who get on to topics and try to make an awful lot of them, and the topics really don't justify what they try and make of them. Over time the Institute have been politically inept, and most of the accounting guidelines have had to be revised quite drastically. Current cost accounting hasn't stood the test of time, and that was a fairly dodgy exercise anyway.

The adoption of standards has improved nothing?

No, I don't think so. Accountants have adopted certain techniques, like double entry or self-contained matrixes[29] nowadays, which have provided an enormously valuable practical framework for dealing with business transactions. But what you make of it in terms of reporting and giving people an inside sense of the business is very limited. In order to protect your average shareholder and creditor from abuses, you ought to make sure that: a) the currency doesn't devalue too much, because inflation accounting is certainly a very inferior substitute for having a stable currency. And, b) because accountancy has its limitations various practices which are developing in companies ought to be stamped on.

Do want to give some examples?

Well, all the lease-back operations.[30] I think that property companies are into all sorts of dodges on reporting. Goodwill should never have been allowed to be an accountancy issue. It ought to have been just an inexplicable residual value; it ought to have been written out of the accounts, written off against reserves. Otherwise, if a limited company couldn't afford to take over another company because of this writing off of this residual value, (if it didn't have the reserves to do it) they shouldn't have been allowed to make the take-over bid. Creditor protection is severely dented in a lot of these take-overs, and for no good reason. I don't think companies should be allowed to have whole tiers of subsidiaries and sub-subsidiaries. I didn't see any reason why a quoted company should have more than one legally recognised identity in one country. They can use brand names instead of separate corporate identities to differentiate their types of business.

You've seen no improvements at all then?

I can't say I've seen any particular sign of progress. I think most of the developments in accountancy theory, I'm not saying they've been regressive, but they haven't really tackled the issues properly. Really, you can only tackle the issues properly by saying accountancy is enormously important. It is a technique which has proved its worth over hundreds and hundreds of years. It has a good future, if you like, but it has limitations, and those limitations ought to be recognised. Company law ought to be very, very cautious in allowing anything innovative because there are so many people out there who will use it in a manner to further their own ends. And a lot of conglomerates seem to have been built on the basis that they can make their progress look good by continual take-overs. But once they hit a flat period, the whole thing falls apart.

What would change things for the better?

We need a complete overhaul of company law and everything has to be made a lot simpler. The number of transactions, the number of the things that directors can do has to be reduced significantly, and their powers and limitations more clearly set out. I'd even go so far as to say that levels of remuneration should be no more than, say, ten, or even a maximum of 15 times the average salaries that they are paying. That should be put down in the articles of association. People are paying themselves (that's effectively what they are doing) millions of pounds per year, and all sorts of options in shares, irrespective of achievement. That is a social scandal; I don't see how a capitalist society can progress with that sort of carry-on. I think it ought to be rooted out lock, stock and barrel, and that can only be done through changes in company law. Auditors' best practice is a small matter by comparison.

Auditing is impotent in the face of these abuses?

I do know in a place like Swansea, half the small accountants write out accounts to order. Just anything that will minimise tax liabilities. It is the only way they can get the business. There's an awful lot of that going on, I would say. Swansea is a bit like the wild west—there are all sorts of dodgy types in business. I'm quite cynical about it.

LORD PATRICK SPENS comes from a famous accounting family, although his paternal grandfather had been Lord Chief Justice of India, and his father, previously a barrister, served as an army officer in India where Patrick was born in 1942. He was educated at Rugby and Cambridge, where he read economics and law and 'scraped' a third. He qualified in 1967 and after two years moved into merchant banking, spending ten years with Morgan Grenfell, before taking over as managing director of Henry Ansbacher. He was forced to resign over his part in the Guinness scandal in 1987, although he was acquitted at his trial in 1993.[31] *He has returned to practising accountancy, despite suffering from ill-health and attempted to sue the Bank of England in 1999 for their alleged part in his dismissal but failed to get legal aid.*

The Spens family is well known in the history of accounting. What was your relationship to Ivan Spens?[32]

Ivan Spens and the others were cousins of my father, who became an accountant late in life because of Ivan. I simply went into his firm. I became an accountant because it was a job I could go into immediately. I'd started as an articled clerk before I went to university, in my gap year. So I continued my qualifications with Fuller, Wise, Fisher, a small City firm with some big audits, people like De La Rue, Express Dairies—it was very enjoyable. They eventually merged with Touche Ross.

What did they put you to do?

We were sent off as junior members of the team on some of the big audits. The training itself was very practical—there was very little theoretical training, and absolutely no computer training at all. I think it showed me how a business worked. They were also very good at teaching their students on small operations where you had incomplete records. So you had to physically write up all the books using double entry. You learnt accountancy the hard way, as opposed to the theoretical way. I specialised in investigation work after I qualified and I very much enjoyed that aspect because one was seeing what made a business tick. So it was good fun. I have no complaints about my training. It was much better than some of my colleagues who went straight into BP or whoever, and never saw the light of day.

Could you describe a typical audit in the 1960s?

Well, the Hays Wharf audit was one of the most fascinating, because in the beginning of the year, which was 1st October, we used to go onto the wharves, the coal wharves, the butter wharves, the tea wharves, to count the cash. And from there onwards it was basic auditing. Literally every entry in the books was checked, for this huge conglomerate! The journals and everything else were hand written still; there was very little mechanical work other than on the big machines for debtors, creditors, and stock control. It was such good grounding that years later, when I was financial advisor for Hays Wharf, I knew the business better than some of the directors, and, of course, I got to know the chairman and the chief executive whilst doing the audit.

You give the impression that there was no sampling or anything like that involved in the audit.

Sampling was very rudimentary, in the sense that we took a month and checked everything.

Did you do things like attend stocktaking?

Yes. But we also developed new methods of stocktaking. We helped Fords of Dagenham who were exploring new methods of stocktaking, trying to save costs by using statistical analysis, as opposed to physical counting. And it did seem to work. You could find a discrepancy fairly quickly if the statistics did not agree. We could get a three week stocktake done in under a week.

Did you circularise debtors?

Yes, but I always considered those awful routines of circularising debtors to be a total waste of time. The debtors never replied. You didn't need it because in most cases we could follow the process through so if the debtors were fictitious you could very quickly find out. If no cash came in, you were then automatically suspicious because it was not hidden in the way it is in computers now.

Did you find any frauds?

One or two, yes, mostly very small. The bigger frauds that we found were often when I was acting as an investigating accountant. Prior to acquisitions, people would pump up their figures, and we would always go in with a slightly jaundiced viewpoint. We would find some woeful miswriting of the records—I think that is the best way of describing it. So we had to get rid of the dross and uncover the business down to its reality. And that was a technique which stood me in good stead for the rest of my career.

What would you say was the purpose of the audit at that time in the 60s?

I do not think the purpose has changed today. It is to put your name to a set of accounts to present to the public which in theory have been independently verified. It's a difficult one that. Since the company pays the bill, it largely controls the operations and the extent to which the audit work is done. I can remember most of my life as a senior manager was spent in arguing about the bills. The audit fees were always too large from the client's point of view.

Overall, there are two types of audit: the 'waste of time audit' from the ground up, checking the invoices and so on, and then there is the 'top down audit,' where you start with the directors and check them out first. That's the only one that's worthwhile. The factual accuracy of the figures down to the last pound, shillings, and pence is not the problem of the audit. We spent weeks adding up with comptometers. All right, so they were a few pennies out but it did not prove anything. It did not solve any problems. It just proved that human beings are fallible. Very often, management and systems and other aspects can be overlooked relatively simply in an audit. If you are not careful, they can come up and bite you. Systems weren't really closely vetted in my time.

How did you justify your fees?

Try a figure—if it works, it works; if not you had to negotiate a compromise. I think it has always been done on that basis, even today.

What was your relationship like with clients?

Generally, very good. Because I was a public school, Cambridge graduate, I was able to go and talk to the chairman quite easily. We had some difficult situations during take-over bids. I remember when Ranks were trying to take over De La Rue, the directors wanted to have their profits much higher than they should have been. I remember vicious arguments about that.

Who won?

In the end, the directors won, they always do. They are probably right because it's ultimately their responsibility. Although you can threaten to qualify, you never do. You always reach a compromise. I have never seen qualified accounts, except in very obvious situations.

Would you say that auditor independence is a problem?

Yes, I think closeness to management is a difficult problem. You can never get away from it as long as auditors are paid by the company—and that means by management. Unless auditors are paid by an independent committee and the management has absolutely no say, it is impossible to break the chain. But the simple fact is that the audit is always behind the times;

it is always historical. By the time the event happens, the auditor can do nothing about it. And that is why we have major collapses.

Is there a solution?

Yes. I did a lot of take-overs with Arnold Weinstock[33] in the early 1970s. He ran his companies on the basis of a statement from the bank to him from every subsidiary on a Friday morning. By lunchtime, he had all their bank statements for that week. They came straight to him, independently of management or the accountants. Their figures had to agree with what he saw on the table in front of him. His basic tool was to run things on a cash control basis. He taught me that if you have profits going up, stock going up, and overdrafts going up, the business was bust. If you are making profits, you should be making cash in the bank. If each subsidiary does not increase its cash balances on a weekly basis, there has to be a reason—capital expenditure, whatever. If the cash isn't growing, profitability isn't growing, and it doesn't really matter how you devise your accounts. I think that's a much simpler and more effective way of auditing; getting independent input from the banks, controlling the cash, and then you know whether the business is working or not.

Can we summarise your views on what is needed to improve the audit?

So long as directors appoint auditors and pay them the auditing system can never work effectively. I think that all companies should be required to put a certain percentage of their assets into a fund to be paid to auditors and controlled by a committee of shareholders, and that means the institutions. There are plenty of good institutional bodies, like the National Association of Pension Funds, that could do it. The auditors would report directly to the shareholders, and bypass the directors. These audit committees and remuneration committees are nonsense. They are all self-appointing.

Why did you leave Fullers?

I was tired of being on the historical end of the decision making process. In other words, I had been dealing with situations where decisions had been taken. I wanted to get in at the end before the decision making process started. So I went to become a merchant banker, and I joined Morgan Grenfell in 1969, and stayed there ten years. I may say that Spicer & Pegler were Morgan's auditors in the 1970s and I never came across them. Never saw them. Ever.

Eventually, I became managing director of Ansbachers in 1982. Peats were Ansbachers' auditors—it was actually Sheila Masters, now Dame Sheila Masters, the head honcho at the Court of the Bank of England.[34] We got on fine. No problems. We used to have good intellectual arguments. They [Peats] were enormously helpful. Running a merchant bank is never easy because there are always a lot of transactions and valuing these transactions was never an easy job. They used to suggest ways of managing that. It was really risk management—where they were way ahead of the game. So I have great respect for them.

What was your involvement in Milbury[35]

I was criticised in the DTI report for not putting one of our people on the board. Well, I said it wasn't my job to put a director on the board. It was the Stock Exchange's job. They were the ones who'd said Raper was OK.

But you were up before the Institute's Joint Disciplinary Scheme over it.

Yes. It lasted a day, but they couldn't understand why I was there. I was completely exonerated.

You have suffered at the hands of DTI reports on more than one occasion. What is your view of DTI inspections?

Most DTI inspectors, with one or two exceptions, have very limited knowledge of the markets or companies or anything else. It depresses me that the quality of the DTI's Q.C.s is so low. The inspecting accountant has a very secondary role. They rarely ever ask the questions. I also have a problem with the emotive content. I don't think the DTI inspectors should ever be asked for an opinion. They should stick to the facts—that is what people want to know. As a factual analysis of what happened the Guinness report is pretty accurate, but where they put conclusions in, and say, in our opinion, then I think it is very wrong. The world should decide its opinion, not be told. You didn't see the interim report did you? I have got a copy of it and it is so emotional—it was mind blowing.

Let's discuss the role of the auditors in some of the other fraud scandals that followed Guinness.

You have to distinguish between criminal acts and those which are a normal part of the market mechanism. The first type of so called frauds, which are regulation frauds if you like, breaches of regulations, should not be criminalised. Regulatory frauds like Guinness or Blue Arrow[36] should be handled by the regulators, whoever they are.

The second type of fraud, like BCCI and Barlow Clowes, where the money goes walkabout, should always be left to juries. Now there the auditors clearly are involved. They aren't involved in any of the other ones. There are no crimes being committed.

In BCCI money had gone walk about on a major scale. On a scale that everyone in the City knew about in the early 1980s. They weren't known as the Bank of Commerce and Crooks for nothing.

It's the same old fallacy of all audits—if you accept an audit, by definition you trust the directors. And if they ask you to trust them, you feel you have to do so. Obviously, auditors trust the boards less these days, although I expect the wheel is going back full circle, and the next recession will bring out a whole lot more horror stories, where the auditors have failed, simply because they have gotten out of the habit of distrusting the directors.

As a banker, do you agree with Ian Brindle's assertion that you cannot qualify a bank?[37]

I think that is true because the qualification of accounts is always bound to have an impact on the quality of the deposits, and no bank can survive if its deposits go. I remember in the early 1970s when Nat West's accounts should have been qualified.[38] The auditors were under great pressure from the Bank of England, who ordered the accountants not to qualify. I do not know what indemnity the Bank of England gave them but I guess it was big.

What are your views on the Maxwell scandal?

Bob Maxwell was a client.[39] We did a lot of business with him. I had a lot of fun with Bob Maxwell. I don't subscribe to the anti-Maxwell view. In the days when I knew him he certainly wasn't a crook. He became a very sick man—I don't know if he had a brain tumour, or something. But then, after 1987, I never saw him again. Remember, he challenged the DTI's statement that he was unfit for the stewardship of a public company and won in court.[40] I think he did not believe he was doing anything wrong. I don't think he had any intention of taking any of the money away. He believed that people's pension funds were invested by him, and providing he was investing them he was looking after their funds.

Even when he was losing money hand over fist?

Well that may be why he jumped off the boat. It may have gone too far.

Guinness also used their pension fund in the share support schemes didn't they?

Yes they did and what a good investment that was.

Isn't that a reprehensible thing to do?

I want pension funds to be managed by the individuals themselves and then they only have themselves to blame. What has happened in the past is that the employers' contribution was many times the contribution from the employees' side. As a result, directors felt that they had an entitlement to these funds, and sometimes felt that the funds should be invested in their own business.

But Maxwell had previously been using dubious methods, moving money around subsidiaries and pension funds.

All audited by Coopers, yes. I have no comment to make. It's the same as saying,—who should have picked up the money that went from Barings, London to Barings, Singapore? The auditors picked it up and got nowhere on it. Again—trust the directors.

Would you still support self-regulation?

I think self-regulation is a nonsense, a real nonsense. It's a bed of patronage. If you are one of the boys you are in if you are not you are out. Unless you are big you have got no hope of getting anywhere. The paper work which is thrust on you, the conditions you have to comply with to get a registration are making it very difficult for individuals to make any progress. We need a situation where decisions in the self-regulatory system are justifiable in court. The Securities and Exchange Commission in America has demonstrated how to work a statutory system effectively. Any decision taken by an SEC equivalent could be challenged in court under judicial review, so they have to act properly. The danger of the self-regulatory system is that if the authorities act improperly it is very difficult to do anything about it. With the statutory system you can always go to court, and if you are right you can get justice.

Do you have any views on the accountants' regulatory bodies.

I think accountants are doing a remarkable job in an impossible climate. There is great hatred in government for the accounting profession. No one can understand how fees being charged for the liquidations cost that much, government in particular. I think the accounting profession is probably finished as an independent profession. I guess it will come under statutory control very quickly. Like the Police Complaints Authority no one really believes that the professionals can discipline their own profession.

ROBIN ATKINS is another son of an accountant who came to Britain with his family from South Africa in 1954, aged ten. He went to Clifton College public school, and after A-levels briefly pursued a banking career. He then took articles with Thornton, Baker in Oxford, where his father was a partner and he moved on to Peat, Marwick, Mitchell in the City of London on qualifying in 1967. In 1972, he became an audit manager with Harmood Banner, but his career there came to an abrupt end when he resigned after a disagreement with the partners over the audit of the notorious London and County secondary bank, which subsequently collapsed in 1974.[41] *Rejected by the profession, he moved into industry, working in relatively senior positions, for amongst others the British National Oil Corporation and Courtaulds, until going into the import and export business with a partner in 1983. Since 1992, he has been in an accountancy practice with his brother, specialising in expert witness work and consultancy. Robin was elected as a town councillor in Alresford, Hampshire in the 1999 local elections.*

Why did you do your articles with Thornton Baker in Oxford?

My father was a partner there. There were eight or nine partners. My brother is also a chartered accountant, slightly younger than me, and we both started there. We were all interested in cricket and accountancy!

I was very lucky in Thorntons because we had large audits, like Morris Motors in Cowley which was the main audit Thornton Baker did in Oxford, through to medium sized jobs and small incomplete records. So I had a whole spectrum of jobs, and in a small office of about 80 people one learns a hell of a lot. I also think their standard of auditing was pretty good. To me, in the early 1960s, Coopers dominated auditing and since they were joint auditors of the British Motor Corporation (which included Morris Motors) we followed their audit manual and so they were very influential on my auditing. My father had been with Coopers for four or five years in the 1950s before he joined Thorntons, so he was well ahead of his time in the way auditing was done.

Were you actually on the Morris audit?

Yes, the first job I did was with Morris. Within a month of joining I was verifying stock of £110m, which was a big number back in 1963. Physical stocktaking took about 14 days during the shut down period. We then expanded the auditing procedures and I got involved in things like sample testing and detailed verification work. Stock was one of the key areas, as well as creditors. In a big job like that each individual audit clerk was given a different section to audit. A lot of different people in Thorntons were involved, because Morris Radiators, Morris Cowley, later Pressed Steel

Fisher, were part of the BMC Group. We probably had 20 to 25 people involved, which was roughly 40% of the Thorntons office.

What was the breakdown of personnel on the audit?

There were two partners, one of whom was my father, and the senior partner was Harold Tonge. They covered the Oxford audit. We would probably have a couple of managers, Brian Plumridge and Michael Roxburgh, and then on each of the audits there would be seniors reporting to these managers.

What sampling techniques were you using at Morris?

We had simple sampling. We predetermined, for example, what we wanted to count. So, say there were 100,000 stock items, we covered the high value items as well as random sampling. We then compared the actual stocktake with the book figures we had obtained and you could calculate the deviations. We were pretty sophisticated considering it was 35 years ago. We didn't sample check invoices. That was mainly a question of test checking. You couldn't check everything or else you would still be doing it! No, you would just select a series over a period of a month or a day, or whatever. There was no actual sampling technique as such.

Obviously, costing was important. In those days you could be seconded to industrial firms as part of your training and I spent six months at Pressed Steel Fisher mainly looking at the costing side and management accounting. That gave me an insight into what the 'other side' did rather than just checking numbers. So I had a very good all round training.

How long did the Morris audit last?

It was fairly continuous at Morris Motors. You basically had staff down for most of the year non-stop. Internal auditing was also fairly important because you could establish some sort of rapport with the internal auditors and see what they did and it would form the basis of your work. We did not have a continuous audit in the sense of 52 weeks of the year but during the actual year you may be down there three or four times. The actual year-end audit would last I would guess two months.

What was the relationship with management in those days?

Fairly good. The audit brought practical value for management, for example, where you find where systems were wrong. But also we had some very tough discussions at certain stages. I remember whole fields of Vanden Plas cars they were not able to sell and having to review what sort of write-down there was going to be. On the auditing side the profession was reasonably well regarded and most of the adjustments one wanted were reflected in the accounts without resorting to the threat to qualify.

Were there any problems with other clients?

Yes there were. When companies aren't doing well you have a problem of trying to persuade them to make the relevant figures fit the facts, rather than what they want them to be, and it becomes very, very, personal.

Did you ever have to rely on the uncorroborated word of management?

I never believed in that. You have to get third party verification and if you don't get it you have to take a view as to where you've got to. What management says has some relevance but you need to back it up with detailed facts. You take, for example, the sales of Vanden Plas. If they say they are going to sell brilliantly and you see at the half year-end they don't sell at all, then you have to make a provision, unless they can convince you otherwise by producing other evidence.

Was fraud an issue in those days?

Only minor frauds, mainly on things like social and athletic clubs. I remember finding one in Llanelli, the Morris Radiators branch, where the person who was running the club wasn't banking some cigarette and bar takings, and the gross margins were unrealistic.

How long did you stay with Thorntons?

I stayed until I qualified in 1967. My view was that I had got as much as I wanted to out of Thorntons, and given that my father was there I thought it was a sensible move to go to London and join Peat, Marwick, Mitchell. Peats was a great firm. Towards the late part of the 60s, they were way ahead of all the other firms, because they encouraged people to work, make decisions, and where you did have problems they took it seriously. Ronnie Leach was the senior partner but although I was stationed at Peats' head office in Ironmonger Lane I never really came across him. I worked for Frank Hancock,[42] who was one of the old brigade of managers who had been there all of his life, had a massive amount of very practical experience. He ran a department of 30–35 people in a very autocratic way. It was quite simple and it worked really well. In the department you used to work for a whole lot of different partners who were responsible for the jobs they did. Each particular job had a partner or two depending on how big it was and Hancock's department worked for about 15 different partners. Mr.

Hancock got the job to a stage where he was happy, the senior then took it to the partner.

I worked for John Grenside (qv) on the EIS Group, an engineering concern, and with Graham Corbett on the Rolls Royce receivership in 1971 and they were extremely good people to work for. They had a massive amount of knowledge, and they were very quick at picking things up—at that level it's like being a barrister. Corbett was pushing through major changes—internal reviews, sampling, checking, the way auditors looked at the job. The audit was evolving in terms of trying to get more independent.

When I left it was as an assistant manager, which probably wasn't meteoric but it was reasonably good.

Why did you leave Peats?

I wasn't sure if I was going to be promoted to manager at Peats. There was a lot of competition and with the limitation on partners to 20[43] there was quite a big block at the top. One could go out into industry and although I did eventually I would have liked to have stayed in the profession all my life. So in 1972, I went to Harmood Banner.

How long were you there before you got involved with the London and County episode?

I think something like seven or eight months. Nick Pitman became Group Chief Accountant, he was previously a manager of the London and County Securities audit team at Harmood Banner and in about April 1973 it fell on me to take over his role as audit manager.

What was your impression of the company?

I wasn't too impressed. The actual people who ran the company didn't seem to be fully in control of it and didn't really know what was happening. There was the question of whether the books of accounts were properly kept and the whole job was riddled by a series of manoeuvres to bolster the profits of the company. There was money being lent to a company called Capebourne, of which the chairman Gerald Caplan was a major shareholder, apparently to buy London and County shares, and that was only one of the problems that had arisen previously.

Would you describe that as fraud? Another accountant has said to me that it's just a manoeuvre and no one outside the financial world really suffers. Also one of the partners involved has said to me that he had doubts that there was a fraud at London and County.

I think that's absolute rubbish. How a chartered accountant cannot know what fraud is I find difficult to understand. Fraud is more than actually taking money. If you are actively manipulating share prices to create the aura that the company is doing well, people are buying shares which are worth nothing when the company goes bankrupt. If that's not fraud then I'm a Dutchman. People went to jail, so presumably the courts weren't very happy either.

One of your colleagues at Harmoods takes the view that on audits you were a fanatic looking for fraud where there wasn't fraud?

Well I think that it is superficial opinion. He can only have known me for a few months. Yes, I had strong views but I am not a fanatic. I believe in the truth coming out and that things are done properly. I don't think everyone is fraudulent. Fraud is only one small element of auditing. If one looks at the numbers and they indicate that there is something wrong, one checks a bit deeper until one is satisfied.

So how did the London and County audit go?

What happened is that one has audit packs for each part of the audit and these packs are signed off and are then used for consolidating group figures. When it came to my having to sign the audit pack I refused because I was not happy that the accounts were true and fair or indeed complied with the Companies Act. Plummer, the partner on the job, was out of his depth. I don't think he was strong technically. One had to spend a lot of time with him on things like Section 54 on directors' loans,[44] and I don't think he had the strength of character to stand up to people. But Hugh Nicholson, the senior partner, Matthew Patient and another partner, Mr. Percival, as well would have discussed it, and were obviously happy enough to sign the accounts without qualifications. But no one could have possibly signed that set of accounts on a true and fair basis. It was just impossible.

After that there was only one way forward and that was to resign which I eventually did at the end of June 1973.

Why do you think the Harmood partners signed it?

Well, it is conjecture really. Certainly, there must have been discussions at that stage with Deloittes on the merger which was announced very shortly thereafter. London and County was one of Harmood Banner's biggest audits, perhaps 10% of the London office fees, and if they had qualified the accounts there must have been some chance that they would have lost the audit and lost the fees. And if you were going to merge you don't want your major client to be doubtful.

It is highly unusual for a junior auditor to resign from their firm on a matter of principle, was it an easy decision for you?

I don't think any of these decisions are easy. I am lucky in that I have an accounting background and one could talk in sensible terms with my father and my brother. It is very difficult to stay in a firm where trust and confidence are important if you disagree fundamentally.

When did you decide that you were going to make a show at the London and County AGM?

Before the AGM there had been quite a lot of publicity. I just went to the AGM. I didn't speak but I got involved when the press outside asked me questions and that led to the headlines the next morning about my resignation. I was summarily dismissed by Harmood Banner the next day.

What did you do then?

Well I needed to find a job and it became very clear that I certainly could not find one in the profession. I would hazard a guess that Harmood Banner had made it very clear with the Institute and everyone around that I was *persona non grata*. The Institute eventually did an investigation based on a complaint by Harmood Banner for breach of confidentiality but I was vindicated.

What did you think of the DTI report and of DTI inspectors in general?

I think you have to look at each inspector on his merits. Their firms certainly get a lot of money from the Department of Trade. Hobson (qv) of Coopers, and Leggatt, the QC, regarded my involvement as somewhat off centre and they concentrated on other things. If I had been writing the report I would have taken a much stronger view on the deficiencies I found and I don't know why they didn't. However, they got the message across.

Banking and other laws were changed in the areas where the London and County accounts and controls were deficient.

How do you explain the recent scandals in the profession?

People can be very good technically, there are many more graduates joining the profession now, but they suffer from a lack of judgment. It's a skill. If you can't judge the whole picture, it does not matter if you know every single section in the Companies Act, the accounts will still be wrong.

How do you train judgment?

By actually having the right sort of people at the top giving an honest lead, so students follow the right trend on what to look for. It is very sad because what you have lost are the big people, the Leaches, the Peats, etc. You seem to have got a whole load of top people now who are very keen on mergers and making a mass of money for the partnership and themselves. Honesty has gone down dramatically in the profession, in the widest sense. You look at the big firms now, they charge ridiculous fees—£300 an hour. It is just not acceptable and it drives them to bend over backwards to manipulate their own opinions to justify things, do the thing as quickly as possible and make the biggest profits, rather than actually sit down and ask whom are you trying to protect. Because money drives them, the big firms haven't got the independence. I don't think they see themselves as having a public duty.

I got involved as a consultant in the last five years with an oil-related British controlled quoted company winning contracts with massive bribes running into $3 million. I had an hour long meeting with the audit partner of one of the Big Five firms of accountants and told him all about them, but he was quite happy to let that go through and sign an unqualified report. You could say, so what, no one is hurt by it. In fact, the shareholders probably did quite well out of it not being disclosed in the accounts. But is this the way to behave?

The right wing element, without being too political, in the Institute is also very bad for the profession. You haven't got a mix of people. They need to stop the inbreeding, and get some external people in with different views.

Since you were involved in a bank scandal, what do you think of Ian Brindle's argument that you cannot qualify a bank?

What does Brindle think you are doing the audit for in the first place? Why do an audit if you are not going to qualify if matters are wrong? Of course banking relies on confidence, but so do a lot of firms. Sometimes you do qualify and the thing resolves itself by someone taking them over. Take Barings, if their accounts had been qualified in earlier years, what would have happened then? Perhaps its total demise because of fraud could have been avoided.

With BCCI, Price Waterhouse were told there were certain accounts they were not allowed to look at.[45] *Why should they have accepted it?*

I think they accepted that because as long as they don't get caught, and they can get the fees, to them that was more important than doing an honest job. If I didn't get total access to what I required as an auditor I would qualify on that point alone.

Clearly, you do not seem to believe that self-regulation is working. What in your opinion would work?

If you are going to get to the stage where you have a limited number of accounting firms, I would go for state control, which I advocated some 20 years ago. You have to have independent bodies looking at the particular problems and taking fairly direct action, like suspending accountants from ever auditing again. If you take a strong enough line initially, as has happened to an extent in America, it cleans up malpractice. You have to clean up auditing; you have to give the people who rely on these accounts some confidence. What you can never do is paper over the cracks, and go from there.

Accountancy is not just something for accountants, it's for everyone. If audit opinions aren't worth anything, like Brindle said on banking, then what the hell are we doing?

Notes

1. Born in 1861, William Plender was, from 1904, senior partner at Deloitte, Plender, Griffiths; president of the ICAEW in 1910–11 and 1911–12 and again in 1929–30; he was knighted in 1911, made a baron in 1931 and died in 1946 (Edwards, 1985: 736–44).
2. An early conglomerate built up by Clive Pearson in the interwar period (*Stock Exchange Official Yearbook*, 1935 and 1999).
3. Sir Russell Kettle, qualified 1910, senior partner with Deloitte, Plender, Griffiths and President of the Institute in 1949–50; wrote the history of his firm in 1958 (Howitt, 1965: 234 and 262).
4. Born in 1906, educated at George Watson's College and articled to Scott Moncrieff in Edinburgh. He taught at Edinburgh University in the 1930s and became the first professor of accountancy at the LSE in 1947, where for 26 years he taught a number of the future leaders of the profession (*Accountancy*, September 1996: 62–3).

5. Bertram Nelson, CBE, president of the SIAA, 1954–56, and one of the driving forces behind the amalgamation with the ICAEW in 1957, had initiated the summer schools at Cambridge in 1934 (Garrett, 1961: 194).

6. Both bought and purchased ledgers were otherwise known as the creditors ledger, containing creditors' accounts, subsidiary to the general or nominal ledger (Parker, 1992: 77).

7. Ledgers containing accounts with persons, usually separate ledgers for creditors and debtors (Parker, 1992: 217).

8. In 1960 (Matthews, *et al*, 1998: 292).

9. Capstan lathe drill bits used for producing pipes and gun barrels in the west Midlands engineering industry.

10. The management accounting technique where the cost of what a product or process should be is determined and the variance between that and the actual cost is used as a control over operations (Parker, 1992: 267).

11. 37.5p

12. The final accounts together with the balance sheet in the double entry system of bookkeeping. The profit and loss account is the statement of a concern's revenues, expenses and profit over the accounting period. (Parker, 1992: 226). Prior to the 1948 Companies Act the accounts of even the largest companies could be set out on no more than four sides of paper.

13. A contract to sell securities in the future at an agreed price (Parker, 1992: 233).

14. Barings Bank, one of the oldest merchant banks in Britain, crashed in 1995 as a result of the losses of over £830m incurred by Nick Leeson, a so called 'rogue trader' operating on behalf of the bank on the Singapore futures market. The bank's auditors, Coopers & Lybrand, were sued by the liquidators, Ernst & Young, regarding the weakness of the bank's internal controls (Leeson, 1997; *Daily Telegraph*, 30 Nov. 1996).

15. Specialised journals of prime entry filled in on a day to day basis (Parker, 1992: 84).

16. An item in the accounts is material if knowledge of it is likely to influence a user—usually determined by its size and the context (Parker, 1992: 186).

17. Charities, under the Charities Act 1960, were under no obligation to produce a profit and loss account or balance sheet or to be audited (Waldron, 1969: 133). The Accounting Standards Committee issued a SORP (Statement of Recommended Practice), 'Accounting by Charities,' in 1984 (Parker, 1992: 56).

18. See interview with Keel (chap. 4).

19. Set up in 1991, issues ethical guidelines (for example, on conflict of interest) on behalf of the English and Welsh and Scottish and Irish Institutes (Chartered Accountants Joint Ethics Committee, 1994: 2).

20. Set up under the Securities Exchange Act 1934. SEC has some 11,000 corporations under its jurisdiction. It registers securities and has the duty of ensuring disclosure of all material facts concerning them, has the legal power to determine accounting principles and initiates legal action against fraud (Parker, 1992: 253–4).

21. International Federation of Accountants, formed in 1977 to develop a coordinated international accountancy profession (covering about 80 countries) with harmonised standards (Parker, 1992: 162; Benson, 1989: 112).

22. Fédération des experts comptables européens (or the Federation of European Accountants), formed in 1987 by a merger of two bodies dating from the 1960s, to represent accountants' collective views to the EU. In this it has been successful in influencing European directives on company law and accounting practise (Parker, 1992: 119, 142).

23. The accounting principle that income or charges are accounted for in the accounting period of the transaction regardless of the date of receipt of the related cash (Parker, 1992: 13).

24. A record of an organisation's fixed assets, including a description, original cost, scrap values etc. (Parker, 1992: 125).

25. Goodwill is an intangible asset representing the difference between the market value of a concern and the current fair value of its net assets recorded in the balance sheet, and arises from the concern's reputation etc. On merger or take-over by another company the value of goodwill is capitalised and amortised, that is, written off over a period of years to the profit and loss account (Parker, 1992: 140).

26. The price of a share divided by the earnings (or profits) attributable to the ordinary shareholders per share. The higher the P/E ratio the more the stock market thinks of the share as an investment (Parker, 1992: 223).

27. The incorporation of the financial position of a parent company and its subsidiaries into one set of accounts, made compulsory first in the 1948 Companies Act (Parker, 1992: 66–68).

28. A leading Scottish academic and writer on accountancy issues.

29. An alternative to double-entry accounts (with its credits on the right hand side and debits on the left) in which the elements of the accounts are arranged in a matrix of rows and columns (Parker, 1992: 186).

30. An arrangement whereby a company sells an asset but immediately leases it back (Parker, 1992: 250).

31. During Guinness, the brewers,' £2.7bn take-over of Distillers, the whisky group, in 1986, in order to ward off a competing bid by Argyll, the supermarket group, a 'concert party' of Guinness supporters, including Lord Spens, was organised to buy up Guinness shares, so forcing up the price and assisting the bid. This was against the Companies Act 1985, the DTI inspectors were called in, and in 1990 Ernest Saunders, the Guinness chief executive, and others were imprisoned, although the former was released early on health grounds. Subsequently, based on a ruling by an unofficial City court in 1988 that share support schemes were legitimate, the European court of human rights ruled that the defendants' human rights had been violated (Pugh, 1987; Kochan and Pym, 1987; Department of Trade and Industry, 1997; *Guardian*, 4 August 1999).

32. Born in 1890, a Scottish CA, and from 1919 a senior partner in Brown, Fleming & Murray; he died in 1964 (Jones, 1981: 161 and 169).

33. Later Lord Weinstock, managing director of GEC from 1963 until 1997 (Cowe, 1993: 283–287).

34. Sheila Masters qualified with Peat, Marwick, Mitchell in 1973 and was made a partner in 1983. She has been a member of the ICAEW Council since 1987, a director of the Bank of England since 1994, and became the first woman President of the Institute in 1999 (*Who's Who (WW)*).

35. Milbury, a house building group controlled by Jim Raper, was suspended, then reinstated by the Stock Exchange, and finally collapsed in 1985. The annual accounts for 1984 showed a profit of £2.1m, and interim results indicated increased

profits, just before the company collapsed with debts of £15m. In 1992, the JDS found that the auditors, Arthur Young, should have qualified the accounts, and fined them £100,000 with £40,000 costs (*Financial Times*, 18 February 1992; *Accountancy*, March 1992).

36. In 1987, Blue Arrow, an employment agency, made a heavily under-subscribed rights issue and to conceal this, David Reed, a chartered accountant at the merchant bank, County Natwest, and others, agreed to buy up some of the remaining shares and sell them subsequently. The plan came unstuck with the stock market crash, and Reed and three others were charged with rigging the market, but the initial finding of guilty was quashed on appeal (Department of Trade and Industry, 1989; Department of Trade and Industry, 1992; *Guardian*, 11 Oct 1994; *Accountancy*, Nov 1992: 26).

37. In 1991; at the time Brindle was senior partner with Price Waterhouse (*Financial Times*, 15 Aug 1991).

38. This is presumably a reference to unsubstantiated rumours in the City that the Bank of England had secretly rescued the National Westminster Bank in 1974 (*Accountancy*, January, 1975; Reid, 1982: 123–5).

39. The same company, associated with Ansbachers, involved in the Guinness share support operation, had previously bought shares for a similar purpose in the British Printing Corporation, a Maxwell company, in 1986 (Department of Trade and Industry, 1997: 96–7).

40. Maxwell issued writs against the DTI inspectors at the time they published their three reports on Pergamon Press from 1971–3. In one of these hearings a judge was critical of the inspectors, although this judgment was later reversed. On this basis Maxwell maintained subsequently that the DTI reports had been overturned by the courts (Greenslade, 1992: 42).

41. London and County Securities Group had been built up by Gerald Caplan, a barrister and typical overbearing tycoon, in the 1960s, but it collapsed along with the property market in 1973. In fact the bank had been run dishonestly (Department of Trade, 1976: 253 and 258). The Harmood Banner, audit partner, Matthew Patient, (who went on to become chairman of the APC) questioned the accounts, but was replaced as auditor (*Accountancy*, March, 1976: 3). Robin Atkins resigned as audit manager on the issue of the 1973 , and made press headlines when he attended the bank's AGM. The DTI inspectors, including David Hobson (qv) of Cooper Bros, found that the accounts for 1973 materially overstated profits by the inclusion of unearned income, while the bank had also made loans to its directors to buy its own shares (Department of Trade, 1976: 131 and 240; *Accountancy*, April 1976: 17). In 1977, the bank's liquidator, Spicer & Pegler, sued Harmood Banner for negligence, which was settled out of court for £900,000 in 1980 (*Accountancy*, March 1980: 16).

42. Qualified in 1948 (ICAEW, *List Of Members*, 1966).

43. The previous Companies Acts limited the numbers in a partnership to 20 but the Companies Act of 1967 ended the restriction (Boys, 1994: 22).

44. Section 54 of the 1948 Companies Act prohibited the granting of loans by a company, not in the 'ordinary course of its business,' for the purchase of its own shares (Magee, 1951: 371).

45. Price Waterhouse knew that Naqvi, the chief perpetrator of the fraud at BCCI, kept a set of separate files, but accepted that they were not allowed to see them (*Financial Times*, 16 November 1991; Truell and Gurwin, 1992: 289).

35. [illegible] found that [illegible] had [illegible] and then [illegible] were £40,000 [illegible] (Accountancy, [illegible]).

36. In 1972, [illegible] Arrow [illegible] scribed rights issue and to conceal this Peter Kerr [illegible] merchant bank, Keyser Ullmann, and [illegible] agreed to [illegible] up [illegible] ing shares and sell them subsequently. [illegible] Kerrick and Reed and three others were charged with rigging the market, but the initial finding of guilty was quashed on appeal (Department of Trade and Industry, 1989; Department of Trade and Industry, 1992; Guardian, 11 Oct 1990; Accountancy, [illegible] 1992: 26).

37. In 1991, [illegible] Brindle was senior partner and Price Waterhouse (Financial Times, 15 Aug 1991).

38. This is presumably a reference to [illegible] in the City that the Bank of England [illegible] rescued [illegible] Westminster Bank [illegible] (Government [illegible], 1978; Reid, 1982: 83–95).

39. The [illegible] company, associated with Arnold [illegible], involved in the [illegible] share support operations, had previously [illegible] shareholders [illegible] a similar purpose to the Pergamon [illegible] Maxwell's company, in 1969 (Department of Trade and Industry, 1973: 66–7).

40. [illegible] Maxwell [illegible] the DTI inspectors [illegible] reports on Pergamon Press (1969–1971) [illegible] judge [illegible] was unfair to the inspectors, although this judgement was later reversed. [illegible] Betty Maxwell claimed subsequently that the DTI reports had been [illegible] by the courts (Greenslade, 1992: 42).

41. London and County Securities group had been built up by Gerald Caplan, a barrister and typical [illegible] tycoon of the 1960s, but it collapsed along with the property market in 1973. In fact the bank had been run dishonestly (Department of Trade, 1976: 237 and 258). The Harmood Banner audit partner Matthew Patient (who went on to become chairman of the APC) questioned the accounts, but was replaced as auditor (Accountancy, March 1976: 8). Robin Aitkins resigned as audit manager on the issue of the 1973 and made press headlines when he attended the bank's AGM. The DTI inspectors, including David Hobson of Cooper Bros, found that the accounts for 1972 materially overstated profits by the inclusion of unearned income, while the bank had also made loans to its directors to buy its own shares (Department of Trade, 1976: 131 and 280; Accountancy, April 1976: 12). In 1977 the bank's liquidator, Spicer & Pegler, sued Harmood Banner for negligence, which was settled out of court for £300,000 in 1980 (Accountancy, March 1980: 16).

42. Qualified in 1948 (ICAEW, List Of Members, 1966).

43. The previous Companies Acts limited the numbers in a partnership to 20 but the Companies Act of 1967 ended the restriction (Boys, 1994: 22).

44. Section 54 of the 1948 Companies Act prohibited the granting of loans by a company, not in the ordinary course of its business, for the purchase of its own shares (Magee, 1951: 371).

45. Price Waterhouse knew that Naqvi, the chief perpetrator of the fraud at BCCI, kept a set of separate files but accepted that they were not allowed to see them (Financial Times, 16 November 1991; Truell and Gurwin, 1992: 288).

Chapter 5
Practitioners in Medium-Sized Firms

The son of a clockmaker, RICHARD PASSMORE was born in Sidmouth, Devon in 1918. He attended a 'small, very good' grammar school eight and a half miles distant from the family home and then trained with the two-partner Exeter firm of John Orchard, qualifying as a chartered accountant in 1939. After war service he became the third partner in a previously incorporated firm, Bishop Fleming, in Torquay in 1946. Largely thanks to Richard's efforts the firm expanded remarkably, rising to 12 partners and over 100 staff, with offices in Torquay, Paignton, Exeter and Plymouth. A leading light in the Institute in the West of England, at one time he served as a member of a national sub-committee dealing with the small audit and lectured on the subject throughout the country. He retired in 1982.

What was it like to train in Exeter before the war?

It was the big local centre. At that time the biggest manufacturer of gas meters was in Exeter, and they came to us for professional advice. We used to get people from Dorchester down to Land's End coming to Exeter. It was a big medical centre; it had local chambers for barristers because of the High Court and the Assizes, and with all the new hotels being built a tremendous number of people got business doing the decorations and furnishings.

I did the accounts for wine and spirit importers. They had ships coming in from Germany and the Bordeaux area and sherry would come in small casks, which in other words was not duty-paid. Every time a ship came in, the directors in the board room would say,—this is good, three-tenths of this and five-tenths of that and one-tenth of something else, and so on, that'll make our so and so sherry. They would be blending it in front of you. I also had a soft drinks manufacturing business, a cider factory and two or three sweet factories. To prepare monthly management accounts, or quarterly and annual accounts was therefore very interesting.

How much initiative were you given as a clerk in all of this?

You made up your own audit programme for each job. You recorded the system and what gaps you thought there were in the system, but I can't remember any textbook that laid out audit programmes in the way they do today. Rigby who came in as the junior partner was a good accountant. He devised systems that we put into retail stores. At the beginning of the year you very carefully worked out the anticipated gross profit for each department. Then at sales times you made sure they recorded the reduction. At the end of the year or the end of six months, whichever accounts you did, you looked at the management accounts and the final accounts to see how they compared. Though there shouldn't be major discrepancies there would obviously be differences. If there was a major discrepancy you would start to look at what was wrong and the first thing would be to make sure that the system was right, and if the system was right, then somebody was on the fiddle in one way or another.

Did you employ sampling techniques?

We'd sampled something to make sure things were all right and if any part of the sample turned up looking fishy, then you increased the size of your sample. We were doing that before the war. I was horrified when one of our ex-articled clerks joined Price Waterhouse and, talking to him a year after he qualified, he reported he was doing massive checks of quite large businesses and the rationale was,—we can spare the time because the fee is large. But I don't think the massive checks that they did were any more effective than the samples we did. Among other things the auditor would get so bored doing them that he might miss something.

Was there anything similar to a management letter in those days?

We did that in 1934. It was one of the things that the partners insisted upon, and we were very much judged on the quality of what we wrote.

Did you actually call them management letters?

No. It was a letter that went out with the final accounts and the audit report. It might say,—we think that your recording of petty cash is rather loose and it may well be that if you ever change your existing petty cashier, then a new person coming in could take money which would not have been recorded and never been seen.

Was fraud common in the 1930s?

Dishonesty was rare in businesses. There was very little change of staff—for instance, a sales ledger clerk would have been there all her life; a bought ledger clerk might have been there for a long time; and the office manager would probably have moved in from another commercial undertaking. They weren't particularly well paid, but at least most of the jobs were secure and people didn't do silly things because they didn't want to lose their job. Once they had lost a job they certainly couldn't walk straight into another one, so perhaps people were much more honest than they are today because fear kept them honest.

When did you join Bishop Fleming?

At the end of 1946. I came in on condition of becoming a partner.

Did you have to bring any capital in?

Oh yes, I was conned. I was so anxious to get in that I paid far too much to old man Bishop. Coming back from the war was a traumatic experience, certainly as far as I was concerned. I did not realise how things had changed. I paid Bishop three times the profit that I was going to get: that was standard practice before the war. Bishop was then 69 and had said he could not retire because of the war. Tucker [the other partner] hadn't gone away to war. Bishop said he would hand over all his clients to me, but 12 months later profits started to rise and he hung on as long as he could; in total for five years. Then he sold his share to Tucker who then became the senior partner. He got it at half the price I'd been charged. I arranged with Tucker that he would then sell me a further share in five years time at the same price that I paid Bishop initially. In other words if the profits continued to go up I wouldn't pay any more. In fact with taxation at 50% it meant that it was far too many years before I was paid back, which was quite unreasonable.

How was the profit share allocated?

One third each.

Was there competition among the firms in those days?

Immediately after the war, other than Ware, Ward & Co., who later were absorbed into what is now Ernst & Young, and another firm, a forerunner of KPMG, who audited China Clays in St. Austell, there were no firms of any size in Exeter. There were no national firms of accountants west of Bristol. We were asked to do two things for the large London firms: we were asked to audit subsidiary companies and we also at times supplied staff. They would send a manager down to do an audit and we would second staff. All the time, we were looking at their audit programmes and improving ours and picking their brains to make sure we were up to date.

But you had amicable relations with the other firms?

Relationships were very professional. When I first came to Torquay there was a firm which grew very rapidly after the war, but it only had one partner, and he had a very forceful managing clerk who effectively did the partner's work. A number of people came to us saying they would like us to take over their accountancy work because they never saw the partner. On each of those occasions, I went to this partner and I said,—look if you are not careful you are going to lose such and such; if you call on him now within the next two days you might be able to retain him, and invariably that happened. If you got a client coming just because he didn't get on with Mr. X you took him, because if he didn't come to you he was going to go to somebody else.

Were there ever hostile relationships with client management?

It depends on the business. If you audited a national company, there was no doubt about it that initially there would be a feeling that we were there to cause trouble. It was up to you to show them that this wasn't necessarily so, and the way to do that was to go around and say,—if you do so and so and so and so then it will be more efficient and will take you less time. It was O.K. as long as you were telling the staff,—we are helping you to reduce your workload; for instance, persuading people to have a small computer and a programme that will do most of the donkey-work.

Again, one of the things that we gained on was that if you took over an audit from a national firm, after a couple of years you would have the manager saying,—Oh thank God they've sent the same people. Price Waterhouse would send in a different team every year and they would have to be shown how the business worked and how the checks worked and the system and so on. So we sent in a proportion of the same audit team for three years' running and this helped the relationship between the client's staff and ourselves.

Obviously when you found things out that were wrong then you started to check the innocent as well as the guilty. For instance, we did the audit for the House of Fraser for ten years in the West Country and there were always people in every store who were suspect. Eventually we lost the audit when Fraser died and his son took over. Touche Ross were the major auditors and they pressed to take over the subsidiaries. We then got departmental store managers coming to us saying,—look something is wrong. We had to turn around to them and say,—sorry we are no longer your auditors.

Did you ever have any problems getting hold of information?

There were times when I've said,—I'm sorry, I've gone half way through this audit and I'm not happy. I think you had better find another firm of accountants to act for you and we will not charge you for what we've done so far.

What kinds of problems might you find?

There are businesses where off-cuts of one sort or another have a saleable value and they've been taken away and sold off. A plastic moulding business, for example, means waste. When the machine starts in the morning the first half-dozen pressings will be faulty and they're thrown out. But there was a market for that waste because it can be ground down and resold; there are things like that. Even computer printout paper has got a high scrap value. You would usually find that a member of staff had been selling these things. An even more difficult problem was the director who charged private costs to the company.

So if you accept an audit the first thing to do is walk around and understand exactly what goes on. The second thing is to sit down with the senior staff, without the management present, and find out if there's anything that management haven't told you. And you do that before you finalise your audit programme.

How would you design an audit programme?

Eventually Peter Frost came to us from Coopers, we had a very good relationship with them, so I then got Coopers' system from him. They did things more formally than we did so we incorporated all that in the sheets that we sent out.

Did you ever have to qualify a client's accounts?

Yes. In the very early days we qualified them on the basis that the records were such and the internal controls were such that we had to accept the directors' assurances, and the Institute was horrified at this. There were other times when we qualified accounts, but to be blunt about it nobody seemed to take any notice of the qualification.

Stock valuations are based on cost; now if you then decide for one reason or another the stock should be valued at a lower figure, it really is a matter of opinion. If your client says,—no, no I'm sure I can sell this at full retail price, you could only turn around to them and say,—look you haven't. If the client refused to amend his figures, in those circumstances we might even have a full partners' meeting, but you would then qualify. It may be as a result of the doubts in your own mind as to whether the client knows his own business, that you put something in that alerted others to the problem. You see, if you thought the stock should be at a lower figure the taxman wasn't going to bother because as long as the figure was higher he was getting more tax. If it was a small family business, then if that business continued satisfactorily then it didn't really matter to the client.

I picked up a case after I retired. I was asked to run a large motor facility by a bank acting as trustee. I found around 150 cars on the forecourt. They were in the accounts at cost although obviously worth a lot less because some of them had been on the forecourt over a year, but nobody had qualified the accounts.

How did you set out to build up your business?

80% was client recommendation. At one stage we had a bank manager who sent us a lot of clients. He was building up his branch quite aggressively, taking on dubious clients and sending them to us. The attitude was,—you make sure that these people toe the line. If there was any danger that they were not going to be able to repay the bank he really wanted to know. We explained to him that we were employed by the clients and not by the bank. And mostly in the end it was a success, there were problems but we made sure that they were dealt with by the client very promptly. If you had any doubts about clients, you went to the bank and said,—if I were you I would insist that you have three-monthly accounts.

How important was your social life to building up the firm?

In the early days, incredible. I made sure I went to Chamber of Trade meetings and I made sure I went to the Hoteliers' Association; we became their auditors, things like that. Although in the end I don't think that sort of thing did very much good.

Would you ever drop a fee to attract clients?

Very rarely. There were unqualified people who cut fees, and the answer to that was that with their bad workmanship eventually you got Inland Revenue investigations. As far as you could you pushed the line with clients,—if you had gone with a qualified man and paid a bit more money, you wouldn't be in this state. Eventually, the clients came back to us. Mind, you would get a nice client but when you want to put the fee up all hell would break loose.

To what do you ascribe the recent troubles in the profession?

I think the honest answer is that the big firms have become too big, their turnover of staff has become too quick, they are too anxious to make money. If I saw somebody was putting money into his pocket I would say,—I'm terribly sorry you're not the sort of person I want to act for. I can't see that happening in the larger firms. They want their pound of flesh all the way up through. The terrible thing is that it's the people from the large firms who staff the Institute, because they can afford the partner time.

The son of a tax inspector from Shropshire, GEOFFREY WILDE was born in Devon in 1926. Ill-health in childhood led to what he describes as a 'mixed' education, latterly at Newton Abbot Grammar School. He was trained at the single-partner firm of incorporated accountants, Peplow's in Newton Abbot, qualifying as an incorporated accountant himself, in 1949. He then went to work for Bishop Fleming in Torquay, at that time a mixed three-partner firm, one of whom was Richard Passmore (qv). After ten years' service as office manager, he became a full partner himself when the Society merged with the ICAEW in 1957. Eventually he took over as senior partner and retired in 1987.

Why did you decide to become an accountant?

My education really. My English spelling was bad but I liked figures. Training as an accountant was one of the few ways of getting a qualification in the 1940s, and this was an opportunity to use my arithmetical ability. I entered the profession in a haphazard manner since Charles Peplow and my family were both from Shropshire, there was that connection. I remember my articles themselves were hand-written.

Did you have to pay a premium?

It was hard to find staff due to the war and my premium was reduced from several hundred pounds to £25, but that represented two years' salary.

What sort of jobs were you given to do?

There was an awful lot of copying documents by hand, even bank statements were handwritten in those days, and this was a very laborious process. It was mostly simple bookkeeping and routine audit checks. There was nothing resembling a pure audit. By the end of my training I had covered practically all aspects, including tax.

The war made a tremendous difference to a rural area like Devon because farmers, who previously had been taxed on the value of their land, now came under Schedule D.[1] Hordes of farmers used to descend on the office on market day armed with brown paper parcels, saying,—sort out my accounts. The practice really mushroomed.

How closely were you supervised during your articles?

You were left to get on with things within the hierarchy, but Charles Peplow himself was very good at getting the articled clerks around him and explaining things. He would go through all the schedules and he was well capable of producing a set of accounts himself when the pressure was on. The clerks would work in groups of two or three with either a senior clerk or a manager. We really worked as a team. 99% of the work was done in the office; we didn't get out and about much to start with, although as time went on this did change.

What was the procedure of an audit in those days?

There were only very rudimentary audit programmes, not like today. You always started with the bank account and you satisfied yourself about that, and routinely did a reconciliation. You took control of the petty cash and went through the invoices. Then you looked at the stock sheets; with clients like garages that could be very painstaking. Life used to be very simple and very basic; the clients really had the minimum of controls.

Did you actually attend the stocktake yourselves?

Not at this time, no.

Did you circularise debtors?

No. That was not a practise that was seriously taken up until the 1960s.

How long would a typical audit take in those days?

In the early days, you are talking two to three days, although the actual work could be spread over two to three weeks.

Were there any interim audits?

We did some monthly checks if the client was anxious to know whether he was making a profit. We produced interim accounts for some of our larger clients to maximise the efficient use of manpower. Gradually, the spreading of year-ends became more common. Clients sometimes wanted their figures no more than three weeks after the year-end and that put a lot of pressure on the team.

How did things change after you qualified?

Change was slow because of the small size of a lot of our clients. However, we did start to do work auditing subsidiaries of national companies, who were audited by the big London firms. In the late 60s, when we were starting to lose those subsidiaries to the big City firms, we set up a technical committee in our firm for the purpose of improving standards.

From the early 50s on, we audited British Transport in Devon and Cornwall, whose records were properly controlled by a qualified accountant on the premises, and then our audit programmes became much more directed towards examining their systems. Our working papers would be structured to meet the needs of the organisation we were checking. Mechanisation gradually started to come in. I remember a wholesale chemist introducing punch cards, which greatly speeded up the production of invoices.

A percentage of the small garages we serviced were reasonably well organised, actually trying to budget their profits, and we would do things like spot checks on their tills. This is where physically attending stocktakes really started: they introduced bin cards for incoming parts and we would do spot checks on their stock control systems.

Is this when the management letter started to come in?

No. It only became an integral part of the audit in the late 70s, although it was originally called a report not a management letter. It came from the Institute laying down standards, mainly on checklists, which were cross-referenced to make sure nothing was missed. Everybody now had hard and fast rules to counter fraud, which was becoming much more sophisticated. Before, fraud was much more a matter of people stumbling over loopholes in a firm's systems.

Did you personally uncover a lot of fraud?

Only the petty kind really, although I do remember a transport company where we thought the fuel costs were very high compared to the turnover. The excuse was that local runs over Dartmoor involved a lower MPG than the average maker's estimate. By researching the consumption of individual vehicles, we found that some drivers had an arrangement with garages at a distance to invoice more fuel than was put into the vehicle, and then the difference was split between the garage and the driver. The company management had been too scared of the men's union to look too closely at it, and if it hadn't been for local knowledge we would never have discovered it. A close knowledge of the client's business was what auditing was all about. On the whole though, fraud is more sophisticated now, mainly because of computers.

Were you ever aware of hostility from a client?

The relationship was usually pretty good. Any hostility tended to arise from a client feeling the audit was an expensive burden, rather than through any desire to deceive, although I did occasionally break off relationships when they lied to me about tax matters. This never actually happened on a strictly auditing issue.

Was the formal qualification of accounts a frequent occurrence?

I quite often had to qualify on the grounds of incomplete records and that sort of thing, or because of weak internal controls. It became more and more common as time went on, because standards were becoming so much more rigorous, and because of the increased threat of litigation, which was never a concern when I started. On the whole though, clients didn't take qualification seriously because they did not bother to consider what it meant.

You never felt your independence was threatened?

In my experience at Bishop Fleming we never had a client that was big enough in relation to the total fee income. I do worry though about the size of some of the clients the big firms have now.

How did you set about building up the business?

Mostly through personal recommendation, and we always got on well with the local competition. There was no point in being over-competitive because you ended up with difficult clients you didn't want. And there was the social side: the Rotary Club, the Round Table and the local Conservative Party for example.

What about fees?

We stuck strictly by the book. We wouldn't shave fees and that made the firm comparatively expensive. Equally, we wouldn't pad out fees for a particularly prosperous client. When I retired, tendering for audits was just coming in and that was purely a form of clients resisting the greed of the big firms.

What do you think maintains the accountant's professional ethics?

First of all you've got the Institute with its disciplinary powers which accountants take more seriously than you might imagine. Then there's the fear of litigation now; no one wants to be sued. And finally, there's peer group pressure; pride in the profession, if you like.

In general, do you think the profession is heading in the right direction?

All these new Standards are a burden on the small practice and mostly irrelevant in any case. But they had to come in because people are so eager to sue these days. I do worry though about the independence of the big firms, and a tendency towards sloppy, mechanistic checks. You really need a nose for things to audit properly.

The son of a Lancashire cotton yarn merchant, JOHN GILLIAT was born in Whalley Range, Manchester in 1923. He attended Hulme Grammar School, and after war service briefly took up articles with the three-partner Manchester firm of Parkinson Mather (later taken over by Turquand, Young). In 1948, he interrupted his articles to study for a BA (Com) degree in Accountancy, before returning to complete his articles. In 1953, he qualified and went to work for his uncle's practice, Dearden Gilliat in Manchester where he remained for the rest of his career, becoming a partner after four years' service. He saw the firm grow from a four-partner concern to one of over 100 partners, with offices throughout the U.K. and overseas through a process of mergers; in 1976 taking on the identity of Dearden Farrow and eventually in 1987 being subsumed by Binder Hamlyn. Always an enthusiastic ICAEW member, John has been

President of the Manchester District Society and was on the national Council for 14 years, where he served on the Examinations and the Disciplinary committees. Now retired from practice, he works as the Bursar of a private school in Cheshire.

What attracted you to accountancy in the first place?

My uncle was the most important consideration. He had a practice in Manchester called Dearden Gilliat, and he said,—before you go in the army come and work for me. I thought,—I like this. Now it's not everybody who gets that sort of opportunity.

And so when the King said,—well I've had enough of you working for me; I thought,—I'll go back to accountancy. But my uncle arranged that I would not be articled with him, which was a very wise decision, and then when I qualified I would join his firm and then later, perhaps, become a partner.

What was the work like when you started?

Menial tasks. Adding up. Computers hadn't been invented. My uncle could add up pounds, shillings and pence in one line. Now I don't think that's a meritorious competence and I never could do it and I wouldn't even try to do it. But you mostly did the routine stuff as an articled clerk, working with what we called a senior, who may or may not have been qualified. Checking sales ledger balances, adding up the sales table, nothing of any responsibility at that stage. I remember having a fair amount of experience doing monthly accounts for a client, in other words accounting rather than auditing, which was very helpful I think. I enjoyed it all; I've got to tell you that. It was never a chore to me.

Who were your major clients?

We did have a number of public companies. We were the auditor for Chloride Electrical Storage Company, which gained a certain amount of notoriety later on when Michael Edwardes became chairman. We were the auditors of Mather and Platt, which was a big engineering company, that was eventually taken over by Wormolds of Australia, and all its subsidiaries around the country. We had staff there 52 weeks of the year. We also had a big client called Lloyd's Packing Warehouses. That was another job where if you were in the office, apparently doing nothing, you would be told,—get off down to Lloyd's and check the sales ledger balances. It was a sort of running bolthole.

How did you find studying for your exams?

I was never very good at getting up in the morning and doing it before I went to the office. But a lot of people said they did. In fact I failed my finals twice. The second time the results were published on my wedding day, which is a lovely way to learn. But then I was married and passed the next time

Did you have to pay a premium?

I was the first person in Parkinson Mather who didn't pay a premium, but I didn't get paid. My parents lived in north Wales at the time. I lived in the YMCA building in Manchester and my father financed me. All the people who lived there were students. It was quiet at night; we were all in our little rooms beavering away, or in the pub. It was highly convenient. It was within about 300 yards of the office and about half a mile from the university, but I was always the last to arrive in the office and I was always the last to arrive in class!

You took a degree and then did articles. How did they complement each other?

It couldn't possibly have been better because the university was highly theoretical and you learnt the principles and the economics and so on, which you would never learn in an office. Then you'd go to the office and you'd learn the practicalities. That is an ideal way round and I would recommend it to anybody, if it is still possible.

What changes have you seen over the years? In fraud detection for example.

I don't think that one really thought of fraud in the early days. One didn't think of it so much as one has to nowadays. It's an investigative job as well as being an approving job, as the audit certificate is a statement of approbation. I remember saying to someone not very long ago that the whole essence of auditing was to determine for yourself in advance what it was that the guys are up to, because they are up to something and I have got to find it. I'm not so sure that was all that predominant in my training and in my practice for many years, but it became apparent to me later on in life that that's what you've got to do, because you could wake up one day and find one of your clients had gone bust and you didn't know why.

So scrutiny became the key word in terms of methods, did it?

It certainly became so in the 70s and 80s. I think in the 50s it probably wasn't so apparent, to me anyway. For example, attendance at stocktaking was rare in my early days. It became much more common. But I was never very happy about it because I hadn't got sufficient knowledge to know what the hell was going on. Another Manchester firm had a big client who once actually wrote the stock down by 90% and the auditors didn't spot it. Now that sort of thing was an eye opener at the time it occurred in Manchester, probably about 1955. So it began to sharpen up the wits a bit.

The notion that we are not bloodhounds but watchdogs[2] is really outdated now. I think you really are a bloodhound and you have actually got to discover what went wrong with the likes of Barlow Clowes, and you have got to find out what it was before it went wrong. That's expensive and the directors don't want to pay for it. But you've got to force yourself. It's a different job.

And what is it that keeps an auditor on the straight and narrow in these circumstances?

There is a degree of excitement that you might find something, which is a spur that keeps you on your toes. When you actually do come across something it then becomes extremely interesting as to what you are going to do about it. I had a big public company in London many years ago. The chairman was an Irish accountant who always used to talk about 'our trade union.' He was very strong willed and he was up to something in the consolidated accounts. I could not get him to shift and I eventually went to my senior partner and said,—come and help me. We went at quarter past eight in the morning to Broad Street and faced him down and he said,—yes I give up. Now that was an extremely rewarding experience. I had recognised that there was a fault, I was supported by my partner, and we were right. Now I can't say that happens more than once in a hundred years but it does happen and it is satisfying. I don't think I ever look at anything that I do as being dull and boring, in a sense the unexpected is what you are looking for.

Did you often have to qualify clients' accounts?

It wasn't frequent but it happened. It was such a serious blow that they usually caved in. What tended to happen was the other way round, when we would decide we were dissatisfied with a client and resign. That in itself was a very stringent course of action to take because the next auditor was bound to write to you and say,—is everything all right? When the reason you resigned was because it was not all right.

In all though, the one disappointment I have about my life is no one ever tried to bribe me, but it's not too late if you want to start! If somebody had it would have been lovely to see what I would have done.

Did you ever uncover outright fraud in the course of an audit?

No, but I had a major catastrophe with a client who was being deliberately fraudulent. He didn't go to prison. He was lucky, but he certainly went to court. He was giving certificates to a bank in respect of non-existent stocks that he was purporting to hold on behalf of a third party. Then the bank called in the security and of course the balloon went up and that blew it. But I don't think in that particular case any auditor could have found out.

But there are frauds where the auditor ought to have smelled a rat?

Well, for instance, Peter Clowes had an extraordinary life style. He never went on holiday without chartering a jet, just for the family. So you naturally said to yourself, and the auditors should have said to themselves,—how can this be on? The auditors ought to have said,—this doesn't tally with what the business is doing; there is something wrong.

Did the increased competition in the profession seriously affect your own firm's relationship with clients?

No I don't think it did. I think that clients were loyal because they were getting a service. The whole essence of the client/accountant relationship is service: being able to see a partner when the client wants to. They may not be able to these days but they certainly did in my day. They were happy and they would stay with you. I remember somebody once said,—I don't want Dearden's as my accountants, I want John Gilliat. Which is not quite the right thing but that's what they thought. They only knew me.

JOHN BEARD comes from a line of Sheffield chartered accountants, his grandfather setting up in practice there in 1905. His own father, however, after going into the merchant navy started a drapery business in Gillingham, where John was born in 1932. The business failed and the family moved to Southport where John went to King George V Grammar School and was articled in 1948 to a firm called Davies and Crane. He qualified in 1954, did two years National Service, and then joined the family firm of Knox, Burbidge, Henderson, one of the largest firms in Sheffield, where his uncle was senior partner. Within a year John was made one of five partners and as a result of his work as secretary of the Sheffield District Society, he met a partner in Franklin, Greening, with whom they merged to form a 12 partner firm in 1965. Finally, in 1972 they went in with what is now Pannell, Kerr, Forster, where John played a leading role, and was also on the Institute's national Council in the 1980s before his eventual retirement.

Tell me about Davies and Crane in the 1940s?

The firm was one of the leading practices in Southport (there were probably only five or six firms there), a two partner firm with an incorporated accountant as manager, who subsequently became a partner when integration happened. They had a fairly wide variety of clients, all the main hotels in Southport; I spent many hours ticking off hotel books. There were one or two public companies: one was called Ainscoat's who were large, and that was one where you were pure auditors. There was a brewery in Ormskirk; and the City of Liverpool Hide, Skin, Bone and Fat Co. who had offices in Liverpool and Belfast. In my early days I spent two weeks of the year auditing in Belfast, before the troubles, but they still regarded it as a bit odd coming from England. We also had a number of solicitors. So I was familiar with solicitors' accounts.

What did a typical audit consist of when you were doing your articles?

Well, I suppose it was the old vouching audit really. Not with printed programmes but we used to have long notebooks where the programmes were written out by hand and were fairly standard but tailored to the particular job. My memories of my first days were adding up a day book in a wholesale provision merchants where they actually still had farthings in those days (laughs). Checking additions for days and days. Balancing the bank was the first thing you did, working with old written bank passbooks and no machine accounting. There was some batch testing, but very often with a small job you did the lot. I can't think of many clients where we were given a balanced set of accounts. If you got the personal ledgers balanced that was a tremendous thing, because very often part of the difficulty was reconciling the sales and purchase ledgers to get them to balance and constructing control accounts.[3] Looking for differences in those days, you worried if you were tuppence ha'penny out, even though there could be compensating errors you might not spot. We had a very good grounding in double entry bookkeeping, which helped us no end, and this is my fear of today's students. I can understand how things have got like they have, but some of them don't understand what basic double entry or the end product is all about.

When you started who was in charge? What was the hierarchy?

I was articled to an old boy called Joseph Aloysius Bond. He was an interesting man because what happened when you presented him with a final set of accounts was he would say,—no I think we'll have it like this, and so you would change everything. Then the next year you'd go in with it set out like that and he would say,—no I think we will have it like that, and change it back to what you had in the first place.

He seemed terribly old to me. I suppose he would be in his 60s, maybe even 70, and his son, James Bond, who was then probably in his 40s, and they were the partners. We had an incorporated accountant called Bertrand Bramwell, who was very able. And we had seniors, unqualified men generally speaking, because once you qualified you probably didn't stop because of the salary levels.

Did you have working papers in those days?

Yes, what you would have was a very thin file, what you would probably find now in an incomplete record job. You would have a bound reconciliation statement, control accounts, lists of balances that you had ticked off, bad debts provision,[4] a list of personal ledger sales and debtors, stock tests, a trial balance, analysis of nominal accounts, where very often you would do the nominal postings for yourself, a closing trial balance, because bear in mind you always wrote up the accounts in the back of the private ledger[5] and laboriously closed off to the nominal and private ledger accounts. This was very good because that was a job you used to give to fairly junior people, and they then understood what double entry bookkeeping was about.

The actual audit programme itself was in a long book, which you kept from year to year, using the same book. You'd tick off each item and if you did a month you'd put down which month you did and so on. You ticked off using different coloured inks or rubber stamps with your own tick mark. Mine was a pig's tail. Of course, as you ticked everything you tried very hard to get things beautifully lined up down the sides of the paper, because sometimes clients would say,—what are all these awful ticks on my beautiful copperplate book?

Did you want to stay with Davies and Crane after you qualified?

Just before my National Service in the RAF, I went in and said,—I want a proper salary. Now the going rate in provincial cities like Liverpool and Manchester was around £8–9 a week for a newly qualified accountant in 1954. I went in and I thought,—well if I went to Manchester or Liverpool there would be the train fare and lunch. I managed to go home for lunch in those days; it was the sort of thing you did in a small provincial town. I can remember the senior partner saying,—how much do you want to stay with us? I said,—£6 a week. There was a sharp intake of breath but he said,—well all right then, you're quite a good lad, mind it will make some of our other salaries look a bit sick (laugh).

When did you leave Davies and Crane?

I left in October 1954 to join the RAF, came out in October 1956 and as had always been the idea I joined Knox, Burbidge, Henderson in Sheffield, where my uncle was senior partner.

So how long were you with the family firm?

Until I retired, basically. It went through various changes. I came in as a senior. There were two other qualified people who had come back from National Service, two years and one year before I joined them, and they had been promised a partnership. So in fact having joined the firm in October 1956, I became a partner at a very early age on the 1st April 1957. I suppose it was the family connections that did it. But I held my own all right. I think probably had these two boys not been waiting to come into the partnership I wouldn't have gone in, but they took all three of us in together and two of the partners then retired. The retiring partners were a chap called Freddie Young who was the original partner that my grandfather had gone in with, and Arthur Dawson. That left my uncle, R. G. Beard, Julian Young, Freddie's son, and Raymond Ward. Derek Hughes and I came in as junior partners. So we were a five-partner firm.

How did things change when you came to Sheffield?

Sheffield has never been a commercial centre; it's always been an industrial centre. It was a different practice altogether, mainly manufacturing, steel, cutlery, rather different from hotels. There were larger jobs all over the country, because we had clients in London, Scotland, Wolverhampton, Ireland. A number of public companies, which I wasn't used to. Big clients like Neepsend Steel and Tool Corporation; Star Aluminium in Wolverhampton, which was not a public company; also Wallace Heaton, the photographic company in Bond Street, now owned by Dixons.

I was amazed when I got to Sheffield that the audit programmes that we were using were nowhere as good as we'd been using in Southport. I think what had happened was, when the war started and a lot of senior qualified staff had gone, evidence of work done had rather gone by the board. It had never actually been taken by the scruff of the neck. I was quite horrified in certain cases, and so I started instituting programmes. OK, they had done the work, the working papers were there, but there was no evidence. So I started, certainly on the jobs that I was doing, to bring programmes in.

Can you tell me something about how the partnership was organised?

We paid goodwill to one of the retiring partners in six years' instalments of £300, so we paid £1800 for goodwill, and at that time we were on a share of profit of £1000 a year. Which was a lot more than I had been getting before—£1,000 a year wasn't bad in those days. Remember that two years before when I qualified I would have been on about £400–500 a year. But out of the taxed income I had to pay this £300. I always remember I felt a little bit put out and so did the two other boys who were in it because in fact this chap who retired as a partner continued to act as a consultant, and more-or-less drew the same amount that he had been taking out as a partner. But it was good in the long term. I think that was about the last amount of goodwill that was ever paid in the firm. We certainly didn't bring any capital in, so the existing partners really bankrolled the firm. We had money in the bank in those days, which was quite amazing! We were quite prudent in our drawings policy and that allowed us to build up our capital within the firm.

So you paid yourself a salary?

No, monthly drawings.

That was equally divided was it?

No. There was some differential, I think. They were very fair and looked after the younger partners quite well. We probably had a turnover of about £40,000, which was a lot in those days.

How did the firm progress?

We were a young firm. I was only 23 when I was a partner; my three other junior partners were 25 or 27, and my uncle was in his early 50s. So we were a young thrusting partnership. But round about 1961 or 1963, I suddenly found myself on the committee of the Sheffield District Society of Chartered Accountants. I think my uncle had put my name forward as a bright young lad who would be interested in doing something. I had been on the committee about a year when the President said,—we are looking for a new secretary and fixed his gaze on me. So I thought,—in for a pound in for a penny, so I became secretary. The previous secretary was Mark Shepherd, who had a firm called Franklin Greening. Mark was a very go ahead sort of chap, and although I was just a junior partner we talked together. Mark would say,—we really ought to get a bit bigger, and I've looked round and I think you are about the only firm that we'd be happy to go in with. So we started merger discussions and merged in 1965 to form Knox Franklin a 12 partner firm, with 110 staff. We were one of the leading firms in Sheffield around about that time. They had a lot of good clients.

What was the motive behind the merger?

We were seeing mergers in the industrial world and clients were getting bigger. There was also more emphasis on technical training. You really needed to have the resources to devote to training.

So we decided we would get together and that was very successful. I was responsible for looking at a lot of our systems and comparing them to Franklin Greening's and pulling them together. We were fairly large and we could start our own standard accounts. Although they were a partnership, the partners were running their own little practices within the firm itself. They had their own little foibles. We could see that we had to move with the times and standardise. We brought a standard printed audit programme out, which everyone didn't agree with because of the old argument that you shouldn't have printed programmes, you should dovetail them. OK, you should, but it was better to have something there in black and white than nothing at all. We got together what we called 'A client,' which was a standard form of simulated audit programme showing what should be done. So we lifted our standards considerably in the 1960s, when it was happening throughout the profession. Generally we looked at things in much more detail.

What was the competition in Sheffield?

Sheffield had always been on its own, very proud and independent and one of the founding societies in the Institute; we had our centenary before the Institute had its centenary.[6] The big boys were not in Sheffield. Peats came in the 20s on the back of the trade associations that were being formed, but they were a bit sleepy at the time; they weren't dynamic in Sheffield in those days. Coopers didn't come in until about the late 1950s. Price Waterhouse have never been here and still aren't today; Leeds is their centre in Yorkshire. Whinney Murray weren't in, although they did come in later. So there wasn't an awful lot of big competition. In addition to what was then the Big Eight, there were one or two medium-sized firms getting together.

So we were one of the leading firms in Sheffield when we merged.

How did you come to join with Pannells?

Well as time moved on and we had clients who were growing all around the country, we could see that whilst we were big for Sheffield, we were at risk from the big boys, particularly with our public companies, although we weren't actually losing clients at that stage. But we were eager for work in America and other places so we looked around for people who might be interested. We didn't fancy the idea of being swallowed up by the Big Eight. We did talk to Thomson McLintock in Manchester, but they only offered us a sort of alliance. We also got on very well with personal connections in Coopers. We had a joint consultancy, Coopers and Associates, North Midlands, where we put consultancy work Coopers' way and shared the profits. I was a partner in that with Henry Benson and Pears[7] but it was really just so we could get our consultancy work done. Had we had fewer partners I think we could probably have merged with Coopers, but 12 partners was far too many for them to consider taking.

Then there was Thornton Baker who are now Grant Thornton, they were merging with local firms. They emanated from Oxford. Three of the Sheffield firms joined to form Thornton Baker, Sheffield. And there was Pannells,[8] who were a combination of Fitzpatrick, Graham, and Pannell, Crewdson and Hardy, two firms who rather strangely only operated from London in the UK, but were active abroad. They were in the West Indies and in Africa, when they formed Pannell Fitzpatrick, and at that stage they were making contacts abroad and talking to Americans and Australians and Canadians and they were also picking up local provincial firms, but it was very democratic. It wasn't a complete partnership at that stage; it was a British Isles association. It was run by a council where every partnership up to a certain size had one member. London, I think, had three because they were quite large in those days. So we liked the idea of Pannells because we could be our own masters in Sheffield. So we went into Pannells in 1972 quite happily and stayed with them until the present day. Whether that was right or wrong is probably debatable.

How did the merger operate?

Pannells used some of our documentation. What we got was training and technical assistance and mutual discussion of problems. It operated on the basis that we had a national and an international administration, but not at local level, covering things like training, technical matters and standards. We had to adhere to national standards, national audit programmes, systems and so on. And they ran their own training courses. I was on a committee responsible for writing our introductory training manual, which was given to new students coming in. So I spent many happy hours setting that up for about a year. We were right in the thick of it right away and I was also on the British Isles Association of Pannells for a number of years.

We kept our own profits. We had an annual division of administration expenses in terms of responsibility based on turnover. There was some small profit element at the beginning but it wasn't one pot. But we developed from there on.

What was your relationship with clients?

You built up a relationship over the years with clients, because they were your personal friends, and clients would say to me,—look, you're doing a grand job for me, but I have looked at everything on my profit and loss account, and I have got to look at your fee. You would say,—well, OK if you want to pay peanuts you get monkeys. But it was tied into economic conditions because we had a depression in the steel industry in the mid-70s. That was the period we were under pressure and there was a more commercial attitude being taken by everybody. You got pressure on fees, and quotes and tendering came in the late 70s. A lot of our conferences were to do with tendering and beauty contests. How to impress at interview! We went through all the psychological jargon: how to sell and how to close a deal. The Americans were very good at that.

Was there any suspicion in your own mind that quality suffered as a result of this?

A great suspicion. I see it from the other side because I was on the Institute's Council from 1982–89, and chairman of the Institute's Ethics Committee from about 1986–89. I was chairman of the committee at the time we brought in advertising.[9] I steered it through Council and that was not everybody's cup of tea. Once you allow advertising it's like a steamroller, you can't stop it. They try and hold the line as to what is in good taste but it's very difficult. Someone's good taste is another one's bad taste.

In terms of quality has anything suffered as a result of the commercial pressures?

Well, theoretically nothing should suffer because if a firm is a member of the Institute then they are duty bound to do a proper job. But human nature being what it is, corners are cut and things do slip in. It is interesting that some audit committees are now saying that you don't take the lowest tender because it isn't necessarily the best thing for the company. But I suppose it is a matter of cutting time where you can. I have not been involved in it, but one hears all sorts of things, such as in a vast international conglomerate, the auditors will only look at subsidiaries whose turnovers are over a certain amount. They will risk the small ones. They won't look at them. That's the pressure of competition.

Born in London in 1930, the son of a stockjobber, JOHN DENZA was educated at Winchester College public school and then took a first in Classics at Cambridge. In 1952, he took up articles with Spicer & Pegler. Qualifying in 1955, he stayed with them for two years before joining Cooper Brothers, where he spent four years, mostly engaged on special work (management consultancy). In 1962, he joined the medium sized firm of Finnie, Ross, Welsh, becoming a partner in 1963. Here, he started with special work but ended up as a tax specialist. He retired in 1994, two years after the firm merged with Stoy Hayward.

What was your original motive for going into accountancy?

I really didn't know what I was going to do. I tried a fortnight with a Lloyd's underwriting brokers, and walked out in horror. It seemed to me the proportion of the average premium that went up in paper was so terrifying that I felt sick. I now realise I was very naive. I was interviewed for one or two industrial jobs, and then my father suggested accountancy. I think what probably made me not turn it down out of hand was that he had been given a complimentary copy of a book, which was a series of articles by the senior partner of Spicer & Pegler, who were the accountants of his firm, and old man Spicer used to write extremely funny articles, usually to make points about tax. I read this book and thought the idea of accountancy was not necessarily dreary. And I was in fact articled to Spicer & Pegler.

What did the job entail?

Apart from three months in the tax department at the end of my articles, which I asked for, it was for the most part going out on audits. But the variety made it interesting anyway. Sometimes it might be a solicitor, who didn't need to be technically audited. I also remember going to do Mars. That was a marvellous job in the days when sweets were rationed. We got a ration of reject Mars bars, or one of the other things they made. Anyway, they were an American firm with advanced ideas. They had to have the same canteen for everybody from the managing director down to the office boy, and the managing director clocked in like everybody else, although he had power to authorise himself not to.

Was there a very strict system of working papers?

Very strict? No. Common sense was always paramount. You were expected to produce a good set of working papers. It showed up when they went to the tax department if you didn't. If you hadn't produced, if the information they needed wasn't there, they made a complaint pretty vigorously. But the dominant consideration was professional judgment, and in my day I think we did really well.

Did your firm specialise at all in clients?

There was a jolly good range of sizes and types of client. They were particularly strong on the Stock Exchange and in Lloyd's. But as my father was a stockjobber, I was not sent where I could get inside information about another firm. I was not sent to Lloyd's, since I suspect it was not really articled clerk's level. I remember once doing a dividend audit, and checking that every single dividend paid by a fair-sized quoted company was correct. It involved a ridiculous amount of detailed work, checking that they were paying all the right amounts; all the fuss about whether the pennies were rounded up or down.

I used to be put on the audit of a dental manufacturing company in Blackpool. The fact that it was in Blackpool was most interesting—just to go up there twice a year, a fortnight for the interim, and three to four weeks for the final. By the end of my time I was in charge of the audit. That was a fair sized business.

Who did you study with to get your accountancy exams?

Foulks Lynch. All my generation did. They had been established by Spicer & Pegler. Most of the textbooks were still called Spicer & Pegler. Old man Pegler was dead, and old man Spicer was still senior partner,[10] but he was only the senior partner, I think, because he was such a venerable person. Had he been less venerable, he would probably have retired by then.

Was there a good system for supervising audits?

In retrospect, at times, I wondered if they were taking risks. But I think actually they had fairly good judgment as to whom they could trust in what. They had some good senior managers.

Did you ever uncover fraud while training?

I did once, in the dental company actually. I found some of the answers the secretary gave me about some unusual items in the petty cash rather surprising. I reported this to the audit senior, felt I'd done my job, and forgot about it. I did not know the senior audit manager had heard this conversation, and a fortnight later, he telephoned me saying,—That you Denza? Sylvester's cut his throat. Fortunately, he didn't kill himself; it was recognised afterwards that the chap simply wasn't being paid enough and they felt a bit sorry for him.

But the general level of honesty was higher than it is now, and all the text books read a bit wrong because all the temptation was to understate profit, not to overstate it; tax rates were very high, and dividends were discouraged.

What happened after you qualified?

My two years with Spicer & Pegler after qualifying were probably the times when I was most deeply into auditing in my life. At the end of that time I got the impression that I was not likely to be made a partner soon and I started looking around for other things.

Now, what we were conscious of was that when you left the profession, if you left the profession, your salary would jump but the timing was desperately important. And I was certainly considering the possibility. But in 1958, I joined Cooper Brothers for four years. I must have been pretty well trained, all round, because they promptly gave me special work. On my first day I presented myself just before nine o'clock, Coopers' starting time. I was introduced to a variety of people, shown round the office, and by ten o' clock I was in Unilever House, engaged on the consolidation of Unilever's accounts! There was a fairly senior manager above me, and life was so different. I used to keep on going in to say,—look I've found a mistake of principle, and they would say—how much is involved, and I'd say seven or eight thousand pounds. They'd say,—Not material. Whereas many of the accounts I had been responsible for up to that time had printed the shillings and the pence, the Unilever accounts appeared to the nearest thousand pounds, which was very rare then.

When the consolidation work ran out and we were waiting for more to come in, I was put on to auditing some tiny subsidiary. I immediately wanted to change the audit programme. And the junior manager said to me,—there is a process for changing an audit programme, and if you want to go through it, you're welcome, and I'll show you how to do it. But when you've tried once, you won't try it again. So I didn't try it. But that is an indication of the danger. I think one should keep to the size that's manageable by a human being. The volume of work covered by those men [Coopers partners] was enormous. I expect it still is but that aspect of giants I don't really like. They have to be too bloody over-organised and once you are over-organised, it's awfully difficult to behave sensibly.

With Cooper Brothers you did very little auditing?

I was on special work almost immediately. I was summoned and told I was going to go to Turkey for a month and Greece for three months on an audit, which was repeated the following year when I was in charge.

Which firm was it you were auditing?

The American Tobacco Company of the Orient Inc. Its head office in that part of the world was the Athenian one. There were two bases in Turkey, one on the north coast, and the bigger one on the west coast. Actually, I had an easy time. Obviously, the Turkish tobacco crop varied in both size and quality, and some years if they had a very big yield, the price would be low and the Americans would buy in a very big way. But if they had a bad year then the local needs were paramount and the Americans sometimes didn't buy at all. In fact the two years I did the audit the Americans didn't buy, so the first place I went to there was very little to do but to check that the system was working, which the Americans had made as complicated as possible. The audit notes contained all sorts of tips about what to do when you are stocktaking tobacco if you are not going to get fleas and that sort of thing.

Did Coopers deserve the reputation they had in those days for cut-throat competition?

I would do the accountant's report for prospectuses, and it was fairly obvious that the existing auditors nearly always felt that Coopers were out to get the job from them. Now, I dare say they were, but if they did it would be on the basis that they had made a good impression doing the prospectus and the merchant bank would have said,—with the company quoted now you really need a firm with a better name.

Summing up, what are the main changes that the audit has gone through?

The big thing now, particularly with anything of any size, is computerisation, and the most important aspect of an audit now is checking the system, looking for any defects in the system. In a sense that was what we did too but the system didn't dominate then the way that it does now. And that is perfectly fair. But that was before the excitement of these accounting standards that have come out about ten miles long, covering something which one would have thought could be adequately covered in six inches. It's frightening. It's so recent, isn't it? I can remember, about the time I qualified, working out the principle of the tax equalisation reserve,[11] which I thought would be rather a good idea but nobody seemed to do it. Very shortly afterwards it came in and I was already doing it because I thought it would show a true and fair view.

Has the quality of the audit changed?

It seems to me they have lost all trace of professionalism, they've thrown it away. It's beneath contempt. I think it's because they have drowned in these excessive paper regulations and they seem to equate ethics with statutory instruments on the details of VAT, or something. One example illustrates this perfectly. As I said above, my father being a stockjobber, Spicer & Pegler did not let me go to any Stock Exchange client—sensible professional ethics. Now we have an ethical guide which declares that if any partner or any person closely connected with a partner has any beneficial interest in a client, then that constitutes an insurmountable threat to the independent conduct of the audit. So, if the wife of a partner in Pricewaterhouse Coopers holds 50 shares in Shell, not one partner can conduct the audit with due independence, whether or not he knows of the shareholding. This is so absurd, so blatant, so infantile and so insulting to every chartered accountant that one both laughs and weeps. The desperate need is to overthrow the mindless idolatry of such pieces of paper and to return to training and exercising professional judgment.

Notes

1. Farming was treated as the carrying on of a trade and the profits or gains therefrom were chargeable to tax under Case I of Schedule D (Lewis, 1977: 100).
2. ' He is a watch dog, but not a bloodhound,' Judge Lopes defining the role of the auditor in the case of the Kingston Cotton Mill Co. in 1896 (Spicer & Pegler, 1925: 412).
3. Accounts in double entry form kept in the nominal or general ledger which contain summaries of the detailed accounts kept in the subsidiary ledgers (e.g. the creditors' ledger) which are outside the double entry system. The control account provides an internal check and allows the quicker preparation of accounting reports (Parker, 1992: 70).
4. A bad debt is one not expected to be received (Parker, 1992: 31).
5. Ledger containing confidential accounts which can be linked to the general or nominal ledger by a control account (Parker, 1992: 224).
6. The Sheffield Institute was founded in 1877 and amalgamation with the Institute of Accountants, the Society of Accountants, the Incorporated Society of Liverpool Accountants, and a Manchester society led to the foundation of the ICAEW in 1880 (Matthews, et al, 1998: 60).
7. John Pears was born in 1900, the son of a Cooper Bros partner. He was educated at Rugby, qualified with the family firm in 1924, and became a partner two years later. After they ousted Stuart Cooper in 1946, he became joint senior partner with Benson and they successfully built up the firm until he retired in 1971.

He was on the Institute's Council from 1946–67, and President in 1960–61 (*WWW*; Benson, 1989: 43).

8. Pannell, Kerr, Forster ranked tenth in the list of top audit firms in 1995 (Matthews, 1998: 47).

9. The ICAEW first allowed limited advertising in 1984 and restrictions were progressively relaxed in subsequent years (Jones, 1995: 301).

10. Ernest Spicer qualified in 1902, so would have been well into his 70s in the 1950s, when the firm still only had eight partners (ICAEW, *List of members*, 1950).

11. A reserve set up to cover potential tax liabilities caused by profit for accounting purposes being greater than that for tax purposes. It could be used to spread liability and is criticised for providing for tax which might never arise (Waldron, 1969: 263).

Chapter 6

Provincial Partners in the Major Firms

The son and grandson of chartered accountants, PETER PALMER was born in Northampton in 1912. After a public school education, he read Economics and Law at Cambridge and then did his articles at the Leicester office of his father's five-partner firm, A.C. Palmer. During his training he served for part of the time as secretary of his local student society. After qualifying in 1936, he moved to his father's office in Northampton and shortly afterwards was given a salaried partnership. Returning after war service, his father's ill health progressively meant Peter taking on the duties of senior partner, long before his father actually retired. In 1965, the firm merged with Coopers and Peter stayed a partner with them until his own retirement in 1975. During his career he has been President of the Northampton Society and served for a time on the Taxation and Research Committee of the ICAEW at national level. He is enjoying an active and happy retirement in his native Northampton.

What was your motive for picking accountancy as a career?

I was labelled as soon as I was born. My father was an accountant and he said,—I am and you're going to be. I had no choice. In those days parents did those sorts of things to their children. Today they would never get away with it.

How did you feel about it?

I didn't like the idea for a long time. But I was not bad at mathematics. I was reasonably bright at exams like the school certificate.

Can you describe to me the sort of jobs you were asked to do when you were training in the 1930s?

The big job that I remember so well was the British United Shoe Machinery Co. It was a vast thing. It was good experience but I did spend a lot of time there. We went down and spent days there when we had the staff available. Really, we had to do what we were told. The clients were very powerful people and it was our biggest audit; an audit we couldn't possibly afford to lose. When we joined up with Coopers, British United said to our Leicester people,—if you go in with Coopers we shall sack you because Coopers are the auditors of our parent company in America and we are not going to have spies in the camp. Leicester said,—you can't do this to us, and at that stage they separated and they didn't come into Coopers with us.

And what was the style of the audit in those days?

It was continual ticking, casting cash books and ledgers mostly. In those days when you went out on an audit you had to tick everything.

There was no sampling?

Well there was a little bit. On the big jobs, yes, we had to sample, we didn't tick everything there. The senior in charge would know what to do. I was never invited to look at an audit programme or even knowingly take part in one. There was never one prepared by the team before you started the job. There were a lot of working papers around but I never had much to do with that. The senior in charge of the audit had all that.

You found that you weren't given a great deal of initiative?

I didn't have any initiative. One partner in particular wanted to make damn sure I wasn't given any authority, maybe because of my name, in case I spoke up about him. I was really held back in Leicester. I had a fairly lean time until after I left.

Would you be expected to attend stocktakes in the 1930s?

For some clients. For example, we would go down once a week, every Monday, to a theatre where we would check the stocks in their bar. But in those days, there were so many difficulties in checking the validity of stock records. I can remember one particular client was a leather manufacturer and he kept skins in pits. It was a horrible smelly place. I had to go and try to find out how many skins he had got there, and he would just tell me. I couldn't get in and physically count them. I had to take his word. He was clever and knew how much stock he could disclose so that he didn't show too much profit. And he knew jolly well that I couldn't argue about it. But I had to ask him to sign a certificate about the stock and that was it. So although we did attend some stocktakes, there often wasn't very much point.

And you went back to Northampton when you qualified?

Yes and was paid a magnificent £5 a week, £260 pounds a year, and that was as a partner. But the war came along fairly soon after that. When I came back, I took things up where I had left them. My father was not a fit man after the war so I had to take over responsibility and gradually became the senior partner.

Can you tell me about your merger with Coopers in 1965?

We'd always had dealings with them on joint audits, and we got on. But then Henry Benson invited me and another partner to have dinner with him at his club. And he said,—bring your balance sheets and accounts for the last five years, which we did. And I remember him saying,—that's all right. Just like that. He was quite impressed. He wouldn't give much away but he invited us to merge. We joined them, and went in with their point system. Which in fact worked out favourably compared with what we had been getting in our share as partners in the old firm. But there was certainly no question of goodwill ever being paid to us.

And were there difficulties co-ordinating with London? Were decisions taken above your head?

No, not really. They would tell you what they wanted you to know. When it came to [profit share] points they made all the decisions. It had nothing to do with us at all. We were told what points we would be paid, divided down to small fractions, but we never had anything to do with the process. But we were certain we had done the right thing, and all the junior partners did well. There came a time when the junior partners were paid too much. I wasn't getting all that much when I retired. I worked three days a week and my proportionate share of profits went down.

Did the merger radically change your systems and procedures?

The audit system changed completely as soon as we joined Coopers. Coopers brought in their own manual, which was quite different to the way we conducted an audit and we had to conform. And there was all this peer review. I had to go to other offices and review other partners' work, and I hated doing that. But when it came to ourselves, we just had to submit to them and produce all our papers, and sometimes we'd get good marks, sometimes we wouldn't. We had an unqualified clerk,—actually he was Colin Milburn, the famous cricketer, who was not very bright and he used to make a real hash of things. We only took him on to help him to qualify for the county cricket club. Actually, we did employ another Test cricketer, Raman Subba Row, as an audit clerk and he was quite bright. Anyway, on one occasion, Henry Benson came down and took a partner's files that Colin had been dealing with. He went through them in some detail and then tore the partner off several strips.

Were these changes for the worse in any way?

I think you've got to be sympathetic towards a client to some extent. It's no good telling a client how he should run his business. In the old days we always had good relationships with clients. When we joined Coopers that relationship deteriorated. Coopers had their way of doing the audit and it wasn't necessarily what the client wanted. We'd begun to work out methods of sampling that were tailored to the individual client and we used to explain to the client why we were doing what we were doing. And then the Coopers manual came in and the old system went out of the window.

How important were these good personal relationships in client acquisition?

It was the clients that you got on with who recommended you to their friends. So it was responsible for quite a lot of our growth.

Was there a strong element of socialising wrapped up in this?

That was very important. If the client was having a social evening I would always go. I remember a building society that used us, and the directors took me on an association conference. All the societies used to go to somewhere or other, and they'd invite me and my wife to go along with them in their coach. It was very important to mix with people. If any client was having a social event, a dinner dance or whatever, if I was asked if I'd like to go I'd always accept.

Were you ever aware of touting going on?

Not for audits. Only in insolvency. Very much in insolvency.

That was cut throat was it?

Oh yes. I used to get a lot of insolvency work. My father had a good relationship with the Official Receiver.[1] If we got into a case where Cork Gully[2] represented a client, they would say,—we'll support you if you pay us. For any measure of their support you had to pay them. I hated cases where I found they were there. We had to pay the price; it was thoroughly immoral but it was just accepted practice. Coopers knew all this. They didn't like Cork Gully and they used to look down on us because we were involved in insolvency, and then they took Cork Gully over in 1980! That was in the name of efficiency.

STANLEY MIDDLETON also comes from a family of chartered accountants. His grandfather was an incorporated accountant, his father and uncle, cousin and he, chartered accountants, while his younger daughter became a management accountant in Canada. Born in 1921, Stanley went to a minor public school, Worksop College, and was on his way to Cambridge to read Engineering, when the war broke out in 1939. After active service with the 3rd Regiment Royal Horse Artillery he joined his family firm in Newcastle and qualified in 1947. He became a partner and in the ensuing years saw the firm absorbed into one of the then Big Six, Cooper Brothers in 1965. Stanley was active in the Institute at district society level and was already on the national Council at the time of the merger and went on to play an active role on several committees until his retirement in 1982.

Can you tell us something about your work when you were doing your articles?

It was an easy job. You were verifying assets all the time. There were accounting programmes but they weren't as sophisticated as they are today. In those days, it was the auditors who prepared the accounts! And the theory in the small firms was, did the books balance? Were they arithmetically correct? And one searched for mistakes of a penny, believe it or not. The concept of 'true and fair' didn't really get to me for a while. In small firms the companies you audited were themselves family businesses, more concerned with their bank manager and the Inland Revenue.

Tell us how your career progressed?

Gradually when my cousin, who is also a chartered accountant, and I came back from the war, we built on what our parents had left. I qualified in 1947 and my cousin and I developed the firm from then onwards. We got some fairly large companies and as auditing developed and improved so we improved. There were no big firms in Newcastle apart from Price Waterhouse. Peats were big in Middlesbrough and had a branch in Newcastle, but 'end of story' for a long time.

So how many competitors did you have?

Oh, a lot of small accounting firms who gradually became part of Thornton Baker. They took over a lot of small firms. We used to call them the Thundering Herd. Then Coopers arrived. Coopers had a branch office up here looking after some of the subsidiary companies of big clients that they had. I was elected to the Council of the Institute and saw the light. It was either go with a big firm or you were going to have trouble if you were small. You would be stuck with incomplete record jobs. Coopers were expanding in the mid-60s and wanted an office in Newcastle. They had looked at a number of firms, and eventually chose Trevor and I as a base to build on. Coopers very soon after that had offices all over the country

How did the Coopers partnership work?

Coopers was very much a family firm. Profits were divided into points. A fair assessment was made of each partners contribution to the success of the firm and an appropriate allocation of points was made to each partner. In those days Coopers had about 30 partners, so the allocation was not as difficult as I imagine it is today.

What difference did joining Coopers make to your work?

It was quite mind boggling. It was different: a) the clients were much bigger and, b) now auditing meant—were the accounts 'true and fair'? I suppose it is a bit of an admission in a way, but it matters terribly in big companies that everything is in accordance with accounting standards and Stock Exchange requirements and so on. So here were audit programmes that had to be completed and ticked by managers and gone through by partners. It was dramatic, we worked from seven in the morning until seven at night, including Saturdays and some Sundays for a while, while we were 'Cooperising' ourselves.

You gained clients from them?

Yes, whatever they had up here we dealt with in Newcastle rather than them sending people up from London. We became subject to audit reviews by other partners in other Coopers offices to control the audit quality. We carried out the requisite work as part of the firm, not as a separate office.

So what sort of clients were there?

Shipbuilding, engineering, Rolls Royce, coal and steel, Consett, for example. Coopers oversaw the demise of shipbuilding on the Tyne & Wear.

Let's focus on Consett, how did that audit go?

Auditing something as large as the Consett complex was very different. First, the task of deciding how they operated determined the audit direction. Their internal controls needed to be vetted and recorded in detail and tested for accuracy and relevance to the true and fair concept. It is the responsibility of directors to produce true and fair accounts and for auditors to express their opinion on the directors' accounts.

Would you have an audit manual from when you joined Coopers?

Yes, that was one of the things that Henry Benson did. We had an in-house audit manual and Henry had the guts to print it and let everybody see how an audit should be carried out. It was tricky because the Institute was anti-advertising, so we couldn't send it out under the name of Cooper Brothers, but luckily we had a partner called Cooper. It was published by Vivian Cooper. But it was a daring thing for the firm to do, looking back. That was in 1966, soon after we joined.

How long would it take to audit Consett?

You would audit in two main parts—interim and final, trying to cut out the heavy weight of year-end work, because, I think it's probably still true, about 70% of limited company audits have year-ends in December or March. You get a disproportionate weight of audits to do just after those year-ends, so you try to do a lot of work during the year. You might be able to audit stock, if stock is counted continuously on a monthly basis by the firm. If not, you would try to do other areas during the year.

So this is more or less a continuous audit for the big clients?

Sometimes—not very often—you can carry out an audit of that nature, but there was then much more emphasis on the interim and final audit. Continuous auditing presents great strain on limited resources and there is always the effect on costs. These need to be contained. There could be more than one interim audit—the approach needed to be tailored to the job—the beginnings of risk assessment, I think. Where were the areas which would materially effect the true and fair accounts?

With a big client how did you assess the fees then? Would you try and bump it up if they were doing well?

No—there was none of that.

Would you have to cut it if there was a bad year?

No—the audit might be more difficult in a bad year for the client. The early years of a new audit are almost always the most difficult with regard to the fee. The effort required to record and assess the system is immense in the large audit and often it was difficult to obtain even a break-even position in the first year. One learned to improve the audit and contain fees to control cost in subsequent years. And always there is competition and the absolute requirement to maintain independence.

Was the fee agreed with the client before the audit?

Yes, you would talk about it and agree it if you had a good rapport with the client; and if you found yourself getting into trouble you could go back to him and say,—we agreed £5.000 (or £50,000 or whatever the fee was) but I have got a problem. There is a problem with your stock counting, or something, and we are trying to sort it out. I am going to have to charge you more. And after discussion he normally would agree that he was in difficulty himself, and to get the accounts suitable for a quotation or even for the registrar he would agree that this was in the end, good news. And, under the worst situation—the avoidance of a qualified audit report.

When did you have to start tendering for jobs?

Oh, before I left Coopers in 1982. It was beginning to come in in the 70s. In particular, it happened with local government auditing in which we were involved in a big way. Then presentations came in, which was good. Companies asked auditors to state what you could do for them. Now, you've got the 'add-on situation.' How would you handle the tax affairs of the company? Or,—We want to move to South America: have you got an office in South America? Coopers have won a lot of audits by showing what we could do for the company in addition to the audit function without, of course, affecting the independence of the audit.

What was the purpose of the audit?

There's a definition in Cooper's audit manual—to do enough work to satisfy yourself that the accounts are true and fair. But we always added, 'and not misleading.'[3] That is there because, if you think back to a lot of these cases that occurred recently, a board of directors can mislead—hence the add-on. You can present accounts which are true and fair, but they are misleading. You can hide things 'off balance sheet' and over-state things, and depress things, and fiddle with the year-end and so forth.

How would you characterise your relationship with management in relatively big audits? Was it ever hostile?

Not that I know of. It can get hostile when you are considering a qualified audit report. One of the problems I had to handle at the end of my career was 'off-shore' insurance. Information 'off-shore' was at best sketchy—re-insurance could cause problems since this could take place in more remote countries, where standards hardly existed, and up to date audited accounts were often impossible to get hold of.

Did your extensive involvement with the Institute detract from your professional work?

Yes, it's a burden. That's why, sadly, the Institute can't get many people coming in from industry, which is important, and from small firms. Because it's three times a month down to London and back, for one or two days, and that's a lot out of a month. If you're any good you get to be a vice chairman or chairman of the various standing committees at the Institute, and that means homework. Apart from the Council papers, which are an inch thick every month, which you had to read and try to talk about intelligently if you knew anything at all about the subject that was being debated. That's where you learn how clever some people are. Brilliant people, they really are. Not just debating capabilities, but knowledge.

Who were some of the people that you worked with?

Well, I've mentioned Benson and then there was Ronnie Leach, and there were many others. They were brilliant and they could see through a problem with great clarity, which I never was able to develop. But I learnt from them I suppose.

What is your opinion of the Standards that came in the 70s and 80s? Have they been a good thing?

Absolutely. And they are the most difficult things to write because there are so many variations in business. They had to revise these accounting standards, because don't forget it's against the 'true and fair' concept of giving an opinion. You can get two sets of accounts drawn up differently, both of which you might say are true and fair. So to set a standard is extremely difficult. David Tweedie (qv) would tell you that, but he can always get something out of a problem.

The profession is often criticised when a nasty situation arises. One can go back to the old judgment that auditors are 'watchdogs not bloodhounds' and there are massive efforts to retain the highest reporting standards in support of all matters financial. There are tens of thousands of limited companies whose accounts may have been 'cleaned up' by the auditor before exposure to the public.

PHILIP LIVESEY was born in Manchester in 1925, the son of a commercial traveller. He left his local council school at the age of 14 and became an office boy for the three-partner Manchester firm of incorporated accountants, Willet, Son & Garner, and went out on his first audit aged 15. At 16, he took articles and combined working (and service with the Home Guard) with studying, first at night school for the Preliminary exam and then by correspondence course. Immediately he had sat his Intermediate examination in 1943, he joined the Royal Marine Commandos, where he saw active service overseas. On demob in 1946, he returned to Willets but left after a year, dissatisfied with the range of experience he was getting there. He completed his articles with another small Manchester firm, J.D. Hamer, (later Henry Smith, Hamer), effectively acting as managing clerk. After qualifying in 1948, he stayed with them and in 1956 was contemplating a move into industry when he was offered a partnership and became the fifth partner. In 1967, the firm merged with Cooper Brothers. From 1980 he ran their Manchester office which under his charge rose to ten partners and 200 staff. He also served as chairman of their north west of England practice as a whole. He retired in 1987 and joined the board of a number of companies in the IT field.

How closely were you supervised in the early days?

It was wartime. Very shortly after I started audit work, and certainly by the time I was 16, I was in a very senior position on an audit. All the people who would have been supervising, the senior articled clerks, had been called up. So by the time I was 17 I was the most experienced member of the audit staff. People were brought in from outside because we were short staffed but they had no experience of audit or accounting. So the only supervision was from the managing clerk who hardly went out, and to whom we reported.

What about the partners? They weren't 'hands-on' were they?

The partners were very much hands-off.

Can you tell me about some of your clients?

They were a mix of small, private companies, mainly based in Manchester or the fringes, so they included textile companies of one sort or another. We had colour manufacturers, timber importers, essence mixers, furniture manufacturers, sweet manufacturers, gold leaf beaters. No listed companies. A client's total number of staff would be ten or 12 at the most. Really it wasn't an audit. We went in essence to prepare the accounts. We were there ticking off items in audit notebooks to ensure the figures were right, because a trial balance out by even a penny was a major problem.

How different was Hamer to work for?

It was another small practice but over the years we had a number of our clients who floated. In the late 1950s, early 60s, there was a rush of flotations and a lot of family companies went onto the stock market. So within ten years we audited five listed companies, all existing clients. Before that, the Transport Act of 1947 nationalised road haulage, and our firm was appointed along with many others, by the British Transport Commission, to investigate and negotiate goodwill for a number of haulage companies. So from 1948 to 1951 most of my time was spent on investigation work into haulage companies, negotiating with the owners and settling the price to be paid in compensation for nationalisation, which was very interesting. I reported back to the partner when a deal was pretty well reached, for him to rubber stamp it. I only had the odd audit thrown in in that period.

Did you start to initiate changes in the way that things were done?

No. Except those changes forced on us by circumstances. I mentioned the flotations and we also audited Oldham Batteries, who had subsidiaries around the world. No longer could we pretend to tick everything. So we had to begin to think a little about systems and look at sampling. It was a very gradual thing and not very well orchestrated. But we were looking at procedures much more carefully by 1956. Take stock, for example. At one time, one would merely take a stock sheet supplied by a client, check the calculations mechanically and that was it. With Willet's, often the stock figure didn't emerge until the client's draft accounts were finished. Overall, the audit was still very mechanical. The major change came in 1967, when we merged with Coopers.

What lay behind the merger?

In Manchester at that time, Coopers had about 40 staff and we had about 30. They had no listed companies, we had about five. A good case was made for us joining, so we joined. Of course, then we began to really seriously do a good audit, our approach to audit changed enormously. That's when we became introduced to Coopers' audit systems, which were and probably still are very advanced. Coopers manual centred in on controls far more than we'd ever thought of doing. That was rather difficult because joining them as a partner one didn't get involved in the detailed work but one still had to go through the files and supervise audits, and look intelligent when problems were being discussed. It was centred on internal controls and logging the clients' systems. Not necessarily reviewing internal audits, since only the big clients had them in 1967; Phillips [the electrical goods company], the Dutch folk were very strong on internal auditing at the time. But a lot of clients were like Tootal [cotton manufacturers] in Manchester who had no internal auditing as such. They had a troubleshooting team, which went in when there was a problem somewhere. So often controls were not set down in a clear fashion. It was a bit like topsy. A lot of discipline was brought to controls by Coopers, with their sometimes rather tediously long reports to management on failures in systems. That was quite a revolutionary way of doing things. In some ways, even Coopers' system was mechanical in that they were looking at systems and the breakdown of systems, and logging them. But they weren't quite asking why, as they do now.

When do you think that this analytical approach took hold then?

I don't know. Heaven knows why, I went onto Coopers' audit committee as one of only two provincial partners. I suppose they wanted someone on it who had no idea what he was talking about! This committee laid down the firm's audit policies, re-wrote the manual and supervised the whole approach to audit. Looking at the workings of that committee, it changed gradually. I'm not sure analytical approach was a term that was used. I can't remember. But certainly, they began to be more interested as to why certain things had happened, why the figures turned out the way they did. They invented the term 'performance indicator'[4], which I think now is used pretty well throughout the profession and the business world. We decided to home in on performance indicators, and we got very strong on it and issued all sorts of technical circulars around the firm. We were then beginning to try to really understand what the figures meant, and forgetting the traditional use of the balance sheet as a snapshot at one point in time (which of course it still is).

How did this new style of audit actually serve the client?

For the enlightened client it gave him the comfort that his system was working. It pinpointed those areas where there was some real danger of loss by fraud or manipulation or carelessness. It helped him to re-work his systems to bring himself up to date or cut out unnecessary work. It gave a good FD the comfort of knowing his approach was right, acceptable, and what was then agreed to be the best way to disclose. So I think he got quite a lot from an audit. But to a large proportion of clients an audit was still just a costly nuisance.

What is it that keeps an auditor up to scratch?

Integrity, honesty, reputation, the knowledge that, if you do something a little bit conniving you are letting all your partners down. I remember very well a case where a major public company client had an item one year on which they had had a loss, which they only wanted to indicate in brackets in the accounts. The audit partner said that the word 'loss' had to appear in the appropriate place. They said they weren't going to change it as by this time the accounts were in proof. We warned them not to go ahead and print. I went to see the chairman and told him the word 'loss' had to appear. Such a technical thing, such a tiny thing to be arguing about; yet it was important to them and important to us. And he said,—if we have to withdraw these accounts now and re-print, you won't be auditors next year. I said,—so be it. They did withdraw the accounts and we were auditors next year. But you have to be big enough as a firm to be able to do that. I wouldn't have dreamt of doing something that would have let Coopers down. But then, you couldn't keep a client you didn't have faith in.

How frequently have you found yourself qualifying a client's accounts?

Oh, rarely. We have done of course. Often with big companies it was over lack of information, mainly relating to overseas investments, income, subsidiaries or perhaps a breakdown in accounting. At Coopers, we had a system of submitting qualified audit reports to a partners' meeting. We'd have a meeting every two months in the north with a set agenda, and one of the standard items was qualified reports. Each office that had issued qualified reports had to submit them to this meeting for all the partners to read, and there were always four or five reports. As time went on up to 1987 there were more qualifications rather than less. But the interesting thing is that no one seemed to take any notice. The company might get upset but the analysts didn't seem to read the reports in those days. The shareholders certainly didn't read them. So it didn't matter a hoot.

If you came under pressure from a client, that's when you had to go away and think about it, and consult another partner. Henry Benson was always thumping away,—consult your other partners.

How did Coopers go about building up their business?

We had our reputation, but behind the scenes there were always a lot of studies to seek out new work. All the big firms have old boys' parties because the alumni of the firm are a great source of new clients. I think Arthur Andersen were the greatest users of that technique. It's still happening an awful lot.

How does all that compare with the old days?

The senior partner of Willets was a mason and I think he got work through the masons. Henry Smith was a golfer, he got work through that. Businessmen have got to go somewhere to get the work done, and they're either introduced by someone they know, or they meet a friend or whatever. I don't see there's anything wrong in that.

Were there ever any complaints to the Institute?

Coopers opened an office in Blackburn in about 1980. One of my partners took charge. When it was all set up he fixed up a little opening party with sandwiches and drinks one evening. He invited local solicitors, local bankers, and the few clients we had in the area. A local accountant complained to the Institute that we were attempting to obtain business by nefarious means. The Institute wrote to us and I wrote back as the partner in charge, and I eventually appeared before a disciplinary committee where I was disciplined for acts likely to bring discredit upon the Institute. It infuriated me because all firms had a party when they opened new offices. And now of course they do it very publicly. So yes, there was a complaint. I was the victim of it. It affected me when I later became a director of a bank and had to fill in a form for the Bank of England where one of the questions was—Had I ever been reprimanded by a professional body? So it was a pain in the neck for me.

Do you think the introduction of accounting standards has been beneficial?

From what I hear of it, the Scottish Institute had a slightly better approach, which is,—you Mr Finance Director or Mr Chairman present the accounts as you think fit, but say in very great detail what you have done and why. And if the auditors agree with it, well and good, and if not, let them say why they don't agree. And not in stilted language. Our Institute has tried. I don't think it has succeeded because it's so regimented; they are trying to fit everything into a tight corset. You really can't use much initiative now, and sad to say Scotland has fallen into line with the rest of the accounting profession.

JOHN HEWITT was born in Leeds in 1923 but grew up in Cornwall where his father was headmaster of Saltash Grammar School. He attended his father's school until the age of 13 when he transferred to Taunton public school. In 1941, he went up to Pembroke College, Cambridge on an English Exhibition. Army service interrupted his studies in 1942 and when he was demobilised in 1947 he decided against returning. Instead he took articles with Mellors, Basden & Mellors, then a six partner Nottingham firm, whose origins went back to the 1850s (Howitt, 1965: 241). On qualifying in 1951 he expected to move into industry and so started a correspondence course in management accounting; his career developed otherwise but he remains a student member of ICMA. In 1953, he was admitted as a partner in MB&M and then, following the 1966 merger, in Price Waterhouse. Long an active servant of the ICAEW, John was President of his District Society in 1970–71 and a national Council member from 1975 to 1983. There he served briefly on the Disciplinary, Technical and District Societies committees and more extensively on the Technical Advisory, Parliamentary and Law, Investigation and Examination committees, remaining a member of the latter until the mid-1990s. Retiring from practice in 1984, he still lives in Nottingham.

When you started, how was an audit organised?

Mellors, Basden & Mellors had a four or five page printed programme to fill in. This was mandatory for all but very small charities. And it would be supplemented at times by additional features, if necessary. The working papers could be quite voluminous. Mind you, at the beginning, in the late 40s, we were still doing a great deal of accountancy. We did the audit as we went along, but the emphasis was very much on accountancy, and so the working papers were very probably initial calculations and arithmetic as opposed to verifications. And it was just about the time when it was becoming a matter of interest to observe or test inventories. Before my time, the firm audited Pimms, the drinks people, and they would only allow the senior partner to look at their inventories, to protect Pimms secret formulas; the lower level staff were not allowed to see these things. I remember one boot and shoe wholesaler where I made the mistake of checking the tiny tot shoes on the top shelf, tipping them on the floor, and then having to put them back up in pairs. And also going sometime later to Carborundum [an American abrasives manufacturer] in Manchester and seeing a stock sheet which had an enormous total at the bottom of several hundred thousand pounds. Looking closely, I realised it was industrial diamonds. So I thought I'd better look at them; this wasn't part of the programme, it was initiative. A small surplus was found.

So how routine was it for the audit team to attend stocktaking?

Quite common. The Carborundum incident would be probably 1953. But although I can't be sure about the dates we also did Ford and Raleigh, the cycle makers, who were our major clients.

Ford's must have been a huge job?

We had a resident manager at the firm and for most of the time he had an assistant. And the residents were supplemented by large groups of people at the year-end.

What was your first experience of sampling?

I went to an Institute summer school in 1952 and met a member of the Whinney family. He'd heard of sampling and lent me a book, and I came back to Nottingham and spoke to one of my younger colleagues. We were very keen on the idea of scientific sampling. I rather liked statistics. It was arranged that the colleague and I, not then partners, present to the partners some ideas on sampling, and it was quite an occasion. But I made the mistake of starting off by saying,—the first thing you have to do is to decide what margin of error you will allow. And that was fatal because the senior partner immediately said,—I allow no errors. And I think that, although I might have been interested, the concept may have given people an idea that it was a variety of non-random sampling. So we didn't do any statistical sampling for very many years, and I think that even 20 years on in Price Waterhouse in the 70s it was still more talked about than acted upon.

What were the circumstances of the merger with PW in 1966?

There were approaches to us from people like Thornton, Baker, who were marching around England at the time. We didn't like the look of them very much. But we knew quite a bit about PW and they knew quite a bit about us. Hitherto, apart from Newcastle, PW had not done any mergers with local firms. But then in 1963 they went to Birmingham and Bristol and might have come to Nottingham in 1965 but put it off until 1966. Latterly, PW did link up with one or two others. Not many were for market share or geography; it was rather more to acquire specialists like insolvency experts or tax experts.

So you actually welcomed the change?

Beforehand, sentimentally, one rather liked the idea of rowing one's own canoe. But it was sensible to merge. There had been a large number of take-overs of local businesses by holding companies based elsewhere. By then, the Ford audit we did jointly with PW had gone when Ford became wholly owned by the US company.[5]

This was a time when a lot of changes in procedures took place. Did going into Price Waterhouse accelerate that process?

It's a hypothetical question, what we might have done by ourselves. The first year was rather disappointing, in that one had hoped new ideas would come along. But PW very generously let us carry on much the same as we were. But after a while things did become much more business oriented. PW were better managed, better organised, better administered. Apart from any technical aspects, it was the management side of running a practice, the deadlines and profitability, as well as client service, which was a noticeable improvement. But certainly there did seem initially to be quite a lot of guidance papers and there were certain changes; one put one's working papers together with different numbers and letters.

This was the time when there was much greater interest all round. In public, Cooper Brothers had been the byword for regimental audit efficiency. In a quiet way, I think that other firms in the Big Eight were getting together with more thoroughgoing ideas. At that stage, I did run a number of education courses for qualified members of the District Society, on things like disclosure of accounting policies (which was number two in the Statements of Standard Accounting Practice[6]) and before that, on the verification of inventories. There was an assessment of what was important, and I'm not sure it was instantaneous throughout the whole of Price Waterhouse. I remember a seconded manager coming to Nottingham three or four years after the merger, and then later a partner came in from another office, and with them they brought various ideas which modified, accelerated, the conversion of our thinking.

But there was nothing as rigid as the Cooper Brothers Manual?

Eventually there would be something very much akin to that. But that was the byword in its day, and led the way.

I would guess that you were ahead of the times in having to deal with those companies who had their own accountants and had internal controls. When did you notice that these things were getting generalised?

Well, if we go back to the Ford Motor Company, I think probably in the 30s but certainly in the 40s Ford had an internal audit department, which was operational under the control of the external auditor, the audit manager really. And the work which had been internally audited was partly dictated by him, but also by their management. So Ford had an internal audit department which was partly out-sourced, I suppose would be the terminology used nowadays. I don't know that I can recollect many independent companies having an internal audit department. Even Courtaulds, who had many subsidiaries in this area in the 70s had quite small internal accounting departments who toured the subsidiaries.

As far as firms having their own accountants is concerned, that was quite a significant change because it meant that the accountancy aspect of the practice diminished. Companies wanted to economise on fees. They also wanted to have monthly accounts as opposed to annual accounts and to have up-to-date information. Ford Motor Company had quite a number of accountants, chartered, certified, incorporated. I don't think Raleigh had more than one until about 1950, when MB&M did help in interviewing and engaging a few. Then fairly gradually they expanded, and they later brought in a finance director. The accountants originally at Raleigh were at middle management level rather than board level. It was a novelty to bring in a finance director. But then we found family businesses started upgrading their staff, and this altered our relations.

In the course of your career do you think the purpose of the audit has changed?

That's rather a testing question. The expectations of the public have altered, and people out there would like to think that an audit provided a health certificate, a safety certificate. Which it has never been . . . and that has made auditors a little bit more defensive. There's also been a desire to demonstrate the use of the audit to the client, though that has always been the practice, really. It became a more settled part of the procedure; clients needing something helpful on internal control, say.

And what is it then that underpins the accountant's professional ethics?

There are sanctions and people may be fined or eventually struck off. I think that there is a degree of self-righteousness, possibly. One was proud to be a member of a good firm and looked at others askance, you know. It was the same kind of loyalty to a house at school or what have you. I think this does keep us up to the mark. The risks in accountancy and auditing are not so much being actively fraudulent as turning a blind eye, or interpreting features over-favourably with a client. I was fortunate enough to be with firms of sufficient size and stature not to have to worry about losing a client. Now it always hurts when you lose a client because word gets around. But there was no doubt it was comforting to be able to say,—who needs clients like that? I wouldn't wish to imply that other smaller people were more vulnerable. It was revelatory when we took over a client from another firm. In some cases they seemed to have indulged clients. In other cases I was highly impressed by what smaller competitors had provided by way of service to the client.

What is your opinion of the proliferation of accounting and auditing standards?

I think it was inevitable. One has got a consumer-oriented society, with people expecting matters to be codified and leaving too little to judgment. People didn't realise how varied accounting presentation was, and it has been useful in bringing to people's attention the underlying principles, particularly the basis on which accounts are prepared. But I do have some doubts about it becoming over-enforced, inhibiting innovation.

Some years ago, there was a lot of discussion about current cost accounting, to cope with inflation as it was then, and there were attempts to arrive at a common way of doing it. The attempts failed, they couldn't reach an agreement. I think it was desirable that people should try to present their accounts not only in the tradition of historic cost, but in something that did reflect the changing value of currency. But because we hadn't done it before, we didn't know how to do it, and I think it would have been better to have allowed a free range of opportunities. There should have been room for experiment.

Do you think the quality of auditing has got better?

Probably, yes. Auditing didn't really start significantly until about 120 years ago, and I came on the scene 50 years ago. I would jolly well hope the last 50 have added to the previous 70. I think the quality of audits has got better and perhaps there is more value for money now than there used to be. But that is a matter of opinion. It's a qualitative distinction.

JOHN COLVIN, one of a number of examples in this chapter, became a partner in the Big Six by virtue of being taken over while a partner in a smaller provincial practice. The son of the senior partner of the four-partner Liverpool firm of chartered accountants, J.W. Davidson and Cookson,

John was born on Merseyside in 1925 and went to Shrewsbury public school. He was in the army from 1943 to 1947 and then took up the articles he had previously signed up for in his father's firm. He qualified in 1951 and two years later became a partner in Davidson, Cookson. The firm merged with Deloittes in 1969 and John became a full national partner. Always an active ICAEW member, he was Liverpool Society President in 1974, also serving for some years on the national Council, with active participation on the Education and Investigation Committees. He retired in 1984 and lives on the Wirral.

What was the range of work you were asked to do in training?

I had a very good practical training because the firm had a wide spectrum of clients ranging from the small income tax client, a lot of trust work, audit and accountancy work ranging from small family businesses to three or four public limited companies. A broad practical experience, except for insolvency.

What percentage of the work would be auditing?

I would think, 60%.

What would be the typical tasks that you were asked to do on audit as an articled clerk?

Starting as junior, I would be the last man in the audit team, and gradually it evolved into more responsible work. As the junior member of the team, I would be perhaps checking bank statements with the cash-book and producing working papers on minor sections of the audit for review by the manager. We didn't call them managers in those days, but the senior person leading the audit.

Perhaps you can tell me who some of the clients were?

The clients were a broad spectrum. The public companies were the Sea Insurance Company, Simpson Roberts and Co, who became Princes Foods and a dental manufacturing company. The rest were medium-sized companies, largely based in the city and port of Liverpool. Quite a lot of firms were concerned with shipping, forwarding agents, warehousing, freight, transport, paper manufacturers, two substantial companies dealing with bag and sack manufacture. There were also service companies, cotton brokers, metal brokers, grain importers, packaging and trading of all kinds in Birkenhead and the rest of Merseyside.

What about your studies?

I studied with the BCA on a three-year course. Overall, having been away overseas for four years leading an entirely different life as an army officer, I found it very difficult to settle down to recommence studying at the age of 23. But I managed it. My father supervised me and the rest of it was done by self-disciplined study at home, five nights a week. A problem arose because they assumed that I was being coached to Intermediate standard, whereas I had been exempted from the Intermediate exam because of the interruption of my articles by four years war service. But this was spotted about a year before the exam and I passed the Final on my second attempt. I was actually awarded the Liverpool Alan Cookson prize, which was awarded twice yearly to the best student, taking into consideration exam results, service to the district students' society and service under articles.

Did you have to pay a premium as an articled clerk?

No. Premiums were just about going out at that time and I think all the Liverpool firms had come to the conclusion, especially with regard to people who had been on military service, that it was wrong to charge premiums. I had a small salary but not sufficient to live on. I depended on living at home.

So after you qualified you stayed with the family firm?

Yes. I became a partner in 1953 but I like to think I had to prove myself. It wasn't just because I was the son of one of the partners. It was quick. But again, at that time the partners recognised that I had been away for four years on army service and that my life had been disrupted.

Did you start off as a salaried partner?

Yes, I started off as a salaried partner and I remember that I had a guaranteed minimum salary of £800 a year. In actual fact my first year's profits were £900 approximately.

When you became a full profit sharing partner were you expected to put capital in?

There was a capital and goodwill requirement under the partnership articles. My father helped me.

How was the profit share itself allocated and who administered it?

One of the conditions of my coming into the partnership was that my father agreed with the other two partners that he would relinquish some of his share of the profits, since he was coming up to retirement age, although there was no requirement as to age of retirement in the partnership agreement. But he generously decided he would take a drop and started coming in less and it was all mutually agreed in that way. The partnership deal was amended to give me a share and he relinquished some of his. A senior partner, a man called Cook, wrote up the private ledger and looked after the partnership accounts.

How did the partnership progress?

We merged with Deloittes in 1969, when the firm was exactly 100 years old. Throughout the 1960s there was a very evident decline in the fortunes of the city of Liverpool, which was most unfortunate. Having been one of the great cities of the world in shipping and cotton, troubles on the docks affected a great many clients. Also, this was the time of take-overs and mergers, and the medium-sized firms such as we were began to feel the pinch.

It so happened that all three of the public companies, of which we were auditors, were taken-over. In two cases, Deloittes were involved as the auditors of the acquiring companies. Although Deloittes were entirely professional and courteous in their relationship with us, it became obvious that sooner or later a rationalisation of audit responsibilities would evolve. And so we knew we were going to lose a good deal of work in those two particular areas. The same thing happened to the dental manufacturing company. They were taken-over by a London company and the audit then went to a London firm of auditors.

At that time too the two senior partners retired. Another partner announced his intention of retiring, and the three partners who were left decided we would make an approach to Deloittes to join with them. Another factor was that Deloittes at that time didn't have a Liverpool office at all, and we were very conscious they had a lot of work in Liverpool which they serviced out of London and Manchester. So in 1967, we made an approach to Deloittes to see if they would be interested in us, and we merged with them in 1969, after they had come and given us a once over and looked at all our working papers; I think they liked what they saw. So we became Deloittes, Liverpool.

And you became full national partners of Deloittes?

We became full national partners, yes. They were fair to us. They looked at our on-going clientele and the other work which we had in the office, and they recognised that we had good personnel; the partners and the senior staff were people of quality. We came to an arrangement over profit sharing and capital that was very satisfactory to us and I have never regretted the arrangement we made.

How many Deloittes partners at it's peak worked from the Liverpool office?

There were four partners when we went in with Deloittes in 1969. Number four was a junior partner who went to London to learn the Deloitte ways from that end of the firm, and Deloittes sent up a senior audit manager from London and promoted him to a partner in Liverpool. Quite a lot of subsidiaries of American companies had moved into the industrial estates in Chester, north Wales, Kirkby, Ellesmere Port, and Bromsborough, so a lot of additional audit work came in 1969. We took on additional staff and our numbers rose from about 30 to about 60. Then in 1973, Deloittes took over a firm called Harmood Banner, the biggest firm in the city, with about 150 staff and eight to ten partners. So it became a bit of a reverse take-over and Deloittes, Liverpool became the second largest Deloittes UK office.

Did the audit itself change greatly over the course of your career?

Some things are common to all audits. But I think one of the real improvements in today's auditing is that the auditor gets much more into knowledge of his client's business. I remember when I first went to audit we never really got to grips with what the client was doing. We seldom went out of the audit room onto the factory floor. It was only in the 1970s, when management letters started to become prevalent, that the auditing profession had to pull its socks up and realise an historical audit wasn't much good to the client unless we were able to justify it by making recommendations to the client as to how he could improve the financial performance of the business.

Was that part and parcel of other big changes? Did sampling become much more important?

Oh yes. I remember substantial changes in 1971/72 when we all got into statistical sampling and random checking, rather than checking everything. The testing became much more sophisticated. One concentrated on what might be material and ignored what was immaterial. Before then we used to meticulously check the petty cash book. All to see if say £500 had gone astray or not throughout the year. Now, it would have been much better if we accepted there was £500 expenditure through the petty cash over the year, and spent the four or five hours that that had taken on the factory floor talking to personnel and reviewing factory procedures.

Did the objective of an audit change?

Instead of solely an historical audit in which one merely signed off with a report of a true and fair view for the benefit of the shareholders, it became a tool of management—an aid for the directors.

What is it that underpins an accountant's professional ethics?

It is instilled in training. It is laid down in the Institute's code of ethics. In my case it was laid down in the family. My father was a very upright accountant. I can see him now standing up for what was right between shareholders' and directors' interests. He would never be swayed by commercial interest and I tried to follow his example throughout my own career.

Did you ever experience difficulties with clients?

I had an American subsidiary where the man in the UK was English. In my opinion he was trying to overstate the profits by bringing sales forward. I wasn't happy with it, and he wouldn't give way. As soon as I rang through to the holding company in Philadelphia, I was supported 100% by the American people. That was fairly easy.

As a partner what sort of controls did you initiate to ensure that audits had sufficient quality and depth?

One would keep up to date with modern audit techniques. I went on many courses run by the Institute, the local district society and by in-house training within the firm. Auditing standards were coming out of the Institute all the time and there would be local society courses on those, and they would then be incorporated into our audit programmes. When we became Deloittes we had much more sophisticated in-house courses. In Liverpool, we had chartered accountant training set up, with classrooms and manuals as to best practice. That was topped up with courses in other regional offices and Institute courses and district society courses. An enormous amount of training took place. We inter-changed to do quality reviews in other Deloittes offices. I remember travelling to Deloittes, Newcastle and spending three or four days there. And likewise people came to Liverpool and did the same to us. I think that was a very good way of ensuring that audits were being adequately undertaken.

It sounds a fairly tight system of review and supervision. Would you say it was tighter than the supervision you were subject to at the start of your career?

Yes, I think that is so. There is much more of a requirement now for working papers to be adequate and they have to evidence reviews. I'm sure in the old days the work was reviewed but it wasn't evidenced as being reviewed. We were, I'm sure, very thorough and very particular and very professional, but not as well-evidenced in our thoroughness as we would be today. In the old days, a particularly good audit was sometimes lacking because we didn't really get to grips with what the client's business was all about.

Did you ever have to formally qualify a client's accounts?

Yes, but generally dealing with it amicably. It became quite standard to qualify and it didn't become too much of a stigma for the accounts to be qualified.

We frequently qualified charities' accounts over incomplete records. How, for example, when you have got hundreds of collectors out on the streets, bringing in material sums, can an auditor possibly say whether it's £50,000 or £60,000 that has gone into those tins? In the old days, one would accept the sum. More recent guidelines from the Institute lay down that qualifications are essential. Nowadays you can cover a wealth of problems with notes.

JOHN NORRIS was born in the north east of England in 1929, the son of an Anglican clergyman. After attending Marlborough College, he did his National Service in 1948 and 1949 and then went on to read Classics at Gonville and Caius College, Cambridge. On graduation, he was articled to the four-partner Sunderland firm of T. C. Squance & Sons. He was placed second nationally in his Intermediate exam and as a result of his obvious ability was offered a partnership with the firm prior to sitting his finals. He subsequently learnt that the original plan had been for him to be seconded to one of the international firms to gain wider experience but that this was changed owing to the ill health of one of the senior partners. The offer of a partnership proved an acute embarrassment since in the Final examination in 1955 he committed the cardinal error of spending too much time on one question in one of the accounts papers and feared that he had failed. In the event his fears were groundless and he was placed fourth. Between

1958 and 1970, he ran a new office, with one other partner, for the firm in Darlington, where for part of the time he was out of mainstream auditing doing special work for a single major client. T.C. Squance & Sons merged with Thomson McLintock in 1966, and it was to their Newcastle office that John moved in 1970; he stayed there for the rest of his career, mostly conducting audits. Thomson McLintock merged nationally with Peat Marwick in 1987 and John was a partner in the merged firm until his retirement in 1989.

What jobs were you were asked to do when you were doing your articles?

I spent a lot of time preparing clients' accounts, which I found very interesting, and it certainly taught me double entry. I also went out on the audits of large shipbuilding companies.

That must have been extremely interesting, are there any other clients that stay in your mind?

Yes. We did the audit of the Sunderland & South Shields Water Company, where we spent a lot of time checking from A to B on the rental ledgers. We were auditors of the Sunderland Working Men's Building Society, where the audit partner had the key to one lock on the strong room door and the Society the key to the other lock: a partner used to go down with the key every time that the Society needed to get deeds out of the strong room. We also audited the River Wear Commissioners so we had a spread of really good quality clients. We also had a string of smaller clients, which you'd expect.

What were the component parts of a typical audit in the earlier part of your career?

A certain amount of test vouching, mainly on the expenditure side. The verification of fixed assets and the directors' minutes. In many cases checking the whole of a bank statement. We looked at wages very carefully, particularly in the shipyards, and attended pay-outs.

To make sure that there were no dummies on the payroll?

Yes. At the shipyards we'd do six-monthly checks. The typical shipbuilding contract provided that the price of a ship comprised the cost of all labour and materials plus a fixed sum to cover overheads and profit. In those days contracts were very rarely unprofitable! We used to review the costs charged to the contract and carry out a certain amount of test vouching. The fee which we charged for the certificate which we provided at the end of the contract was fairly nominal. Later on we did it as a separate, much more detailed, exercise and charged considerably more. That was where I first met a Hollerith punched card computer.[7] As a new articled clerk I was very impressed by the fact that a second punched card operator keyed in the same information as a check and that the machine jammed if she hit a different key from the first one.

What lay behind your move to Newcastle and your return to mainstream auditing?

When we merged with TMcL, we retained their small office in Newcastle and then expanded it by transferring work from Sunderland so we ended up with three offices. It wasn't really satisfactory because the Newcastle and Sunderland offices were too close together, and the partners and/or the staff and/or the files were always in the wrong place. We decided to close the Sunderland office, which was a bit of a blow to the older partners because that was where the firm had begun, and all the Sunderland work was concentrated in Newcastle. At that stage I handed over my client work in Darlington and moved to Newcastle in 1970.

And what sort of changes did you see, coming back into auditing in 1970 compared to the earlier phase in your career? What sort of innovations were there?

There were much more detailed systems than before in terms of internal control questionnaires, permanent files, audit programmes, standard audit indexes etc and much more emphasis on putting down on paper what tests had been carried out and what conclusions could be drawn from them.

Computers were becoming more widespread and there were specialist computer auditors who wrote and ran their own interrogation programs for the larger installations. We had imported another partner into Darlington, who had been a senior manager with Deloitte Haskins & Sells, and he had shown us the way in improving our audit procedures. We had done the same in Newcastle and had, also in 1966, taken into the partnership the TMcL senior manager who had been responsible for their Newcastle office.

When I came to Newcastle one of the jobs that I took over was Common Brothers, the shipowners, where in addition to the statutory audit, we did the consolidation. I found it a fascinating company. With other clients, particularly the shipbuilding companies, we were very much looking at the outcome of long term contracts. We had quite lengthy debates with the directors about whether the contracts were going to be profitable or unprofitable. Overall, I think we began reporting more and more for the financial analysts, shareholders were pretty apathetic. But there was much more emphasis on independence and there is no doubt the standards of required conduct had improved tremendously. I remember that a number of the shipbuilding and engineering companies on the Wear were floated in the early 60s. We were the auditors of most of the subsidiaries, although TMcL were reporting accountants and auditors of the top company. One of my partners was a trustee of a number of trusts for the families of directors, and he was interested as a trustee in, I think, 40% of the capital. It was accepted then but couldn't happen now.

You sound like a very 'hands-on' partner?

I think that I was. And in part, that was because I sometimes felt that the manager was rather inexperienced or perhaps this was the first year when he had been responsible for the audit, and I wanted to get in early rather than facing any problems later on. I always went down to the client. I never reviewed anything in the office, as I knew I would be interrupted all the time. I'd just go down to the shipyards and I might be there for up to a week. And that is what I enjoyed, getting out of the office. I would generally have lunch in the managers' dining room and it was surprising how much one learnt about the progress on particular ships or the problems current at the time.

But we weren't just looking at audit problems, we were also looking at other things that had gone wrong and that needed to be drawn to management's attention. The management letter was really what the client valued in return for the audit fee. You would be telling him how to improve not just his financial systems but also perhaps his industrial systems.

Would disagreements with clients normally be resolved at this stage?

Well it depends on how serious it was. I would normally talk to the finance director, or whoever was the right person, and try to resolve things. Then the question really was what you were going to do if you could not resolve it. There were cases where you had a problem and because of its nature you could not resolve it at all. I had a client, Doxford & Sunderland, a shipbuilding company on the Wear, which was taken over by Court Line[8] in 1970 or 1971. I'd just come from Darlington. Court Line decided to clear one of the shipyards and to build a large covered building dock there instead, so that ships could be built under cover and then be floated out into the river. But they were building ships at the same time, so there was an enormous amount of dislocation. As a result, the cost of building a ship escalated; and what the client was saying was that if it had not been for the dislocation, so many thousand hours would have been required to build the ship. They had records to show the average man hours required to build different types and sizes of ships. The excess hours on this basis were costed and treated by the client as an 'extraordinary item': we took the view that we could not confirm that these costs were all 'extraordinary' in the technical sense. We qualified. Our qualification was sufficiently significant to be reflected in the report of the auditors on the group accounts. The headline on the business page in the *Daily Telegraph* the next morning was 'Auditors unhappy at Court.'

It was the usual practice for shipbuilders to receive the first instalment of the contract price when the contract to build a new ship was signed. Much of this money was borrowed by Court Line from the Doxford group. I remember going down to the Court Line head office to try to find out where the money had gone but I could not. Court Line had acquired an airline which was widely rumoured to be struggling and the suspicion was that this was where the money had gone. We qualified on the grounds that we were unhappy about the recoverability of the money from the parent company. We obtained confirmation from the parent company auditors that they were not going to qualify on going concern. The company went down four months later.

Was formal qualification a frequent occurrence?

No. But in the days when shipbuilding was in trouble and there was industrial unrest and contracts were overrunning, it became less infrequent. The 1970s were the peak years. You reviewed very carefully the projected contract costs and the provisions for contract losses. Having taken into account inflation and other factors, you were satisfied with the provisions. The following year, the provisions went up. There would then be a debate as to whether they had increased because the original provisions were wrong or because of events during the year. If it was because the provisions had proved to be understated, that was an uncomfortable feeling- had we missed a trick? On the other hand, if the provisions had gone up because of an exceptional amount of industrial unrest as opposed to, shall we say, a reasonable amount, that was an acceptable explanation—the additional cost was a proper charge against the year's results.

Did you ever come under extraordinary pressure to avoid a qualification?

I do not think so. I was surprised that there wasn't more resistance in the Court Line case, but the Court Line FD had until fairly recently been a practising accountant. I was dealing in a lot of cases with subsidiaries of national companies, and whether I qualified or not, it was not sufficiently significant to carry through into the accounts of the parent company. Court Line was the major exception. So in the main, I was not in conflict with the parent Board of Directors, with the threat of losing the audit. I think that if you were involved in a really big audit, then there would be a little bit more pressure not to qualify.

Can I ask you, starting at the beginning, how did the various firms you worked for acquire their clients?

Well, T.C. Squance & Sons was founded in 1870 and was going on for 80 odd years before I became involved. They had a series of very talented partners who were well known in the county [Durham], as well as being very competent accountants.

Social connections were important?

Yes, well certainly I am thinking of two of the partners. They were very friendly with major clients. One chairman would ring up Tom Squance to find out when it would be convenient to have the board meeting so as not to interfere with his fishing!

Ah, fishing, I see, not the golf club. Did TMcL. market themselves?

Yes we did, but we did not do it as extravagantly as some of the other major firms. We believed that good work would actually bring its own rewards. For example, we did a lot of investigations for the Price Commission and we always made a point of reporting on a week by week basis. They were very happy with this arrangement, so they kept coming to us.

Peats were big in the North East, did they do things differently?

They were more commercial and more competitive, and by and large they were more profitable and therefore they had been able to expand more rapidly.

Would you say they had a policy of poaching?

I think the answer is that they were competitive.

Did you ever feel the threat of unfair competition?

Not particularly, in my time. You were conscious all the time that your competitors would be looking to take over a number of your clients, and you would be looking to do the same to them. Everybody was asked to make a note of useful people. But despite this we were on good terms with the partners in the other major firms in Newcastle.

Would you ever cut fees in order to attract new business?

Yes.

In contrast, would there ever be a case of the fee being inflated purely because of the client's profitability?

There were very few cases like that. It is dangerous if you then find yourself in a beauty parade. It is very difficult to explain to your client why you are suddenly able to cut your previous fee by 40%.

When did tendering become a regular feature?

Probably about 83–84.

Did you find it demoralising to tender, and then not get the job?

Yes. There were occasions when we had a pretty good suspicion that there'd never really been any intention other than to get the current auditors to drop their fees.

Were you ever aware of the problem of low-balling?

No, that only happened on national tenders, so I never came across it.

Just in conclusion, did you enjoy your career?

Oh, yes. I cannot think of another profession I'd have been happier in. There was very little career guidance in the early 1950s and Classics did not obviously fit you for anything in particular. So accountancy was very much a blind choice, but a good one.

The son of a Staffordshire family businessman, GEORGE CARTER *was born in 1934. After attending Warwick School, he was articled to Loarridge, Beaven in 1951. This was a two-partner concern with offices in London and Brighton but George worked exclusively in the London office. After qualifying in 1956 he joined Price Waterhouse, was promoted to manager in 1963, and made a partner in 1966, acting as the firm's insurance specialist from 1974 to 1980. In 1982, he moved from London to become senior partner in the west Midlands until his retirement in 1994. Always active in the Institute, he served on several committees, including the Audit and Actuaries Committee from 1975 to 1980, and is the joint author of the ICAEW guide to investigations published in 1978. Outside the Institute, he has taken on many responsibilities on bodies at the heart of west Midlands commercial life, having been, for example, a member of the CBI Regional Council since 1988. In retirement he lives in the countryside just outside Worcester.*

Can you give me a resume of the jobs you were asked to do when you were training?

I don't think we had a single limited company audit, they were all widow's repayment claims or Schedule A claims[9] as they were known in those days, where you could claim an average of five years' maintenance on your house against your Schedule A assessment. Then there were sole proprietors and partnerships, and we had a lot of chemists in the East End. They used to turn up with their books once a year, usually with all the invoices rolled up into tight little rolls and stuck in a box. We had to spend quite a few hours in the beginning just unrolling them all and flattening them out.

So there would have been no pure audits then?

No. It was pretty much all incomplete records. I did have one interesting job with the solicitor who was on the floor below. He had a client who'd died about five years earlier and he still hadn't got the accounts sorted out properly. He got into a bit of a panic, and he brought about six deed boxes up to us and asked me to sort it all out. I spent nine months doing that; I found the original affidavit and I started from there. I think the estate was about £3–400,000 which in 1951 was a lot of money, and I ended up by getting quite a lot of the estate duty back. I had to write up all the investment records for five or six years, so it was quite good training.

It sounds as if you were given quite a lot of leeway?

I was given a lot of responsibility. I was the only articled clerk, and I can remember my principal's office, which was on the top floor of one of the old town houses in Bedford Road. He had a desk at one end and an old Victorian dining table the other end and a rather tatty carpet, and he used to have piles of paper on this Victorian table done up in red tape. After I had been there a year or two I used to go into his office and say,—well I'll have a go at this one or that one. I wrote all my own letters. There was a harridan of a secretary with an Imperial upright typewriter and I had to plead with her to type things for me.

What happened after you qualified?

Peats and PW both said,—come and have an interview, and I had interviews the same morning within an hour of each other. In those days Price Waterhouse were in Fredericks Place and Peats were down the lane at the back. I was interviewed in PW by Richard Bucknill[10] and then at Peats by Henry Peat; they both offered me a job at an identical salary, which I naively thought was a coincidence. £600 a year going up to £750 when I passed my exams, and I virtually tossed a coin to see which firm I was going to. I went to PW for two reasons: one was that having gone to lectures in the bowels of Winchester House as it then was, I frequently sat next to a chap called Desmond Byrne who was with PW, so I knew a bit about them, and the other thing was I knew that PW had a pool system of allocating the staff and Peats had a departmental system, where you worked for a manager in a small department, and I didn't really fancy that. So for those two fairly slender reasons I went to PW. Then when my results came through, my salary was put up not to £750 but to £800, which was quite extraordinary.

When you became a partner in 1966, the 20- partner rule would still have been in force?

Well, yes, that's right because it was the Companies Act of 1967 that did away with it. So I became a partner in Manchester, although I had never been to Manchester—I was working in London. I also became a partner in Lagos on the strength of the fact that as a manager I had done a couple of investigations in Lagos. I became a member of the Nigerian Institute of Chartered Accountants by default. In those days the Nigerian firm was run from London by two partners, and so I joined those two firms although I never went to Nigeria or to Manchester . . . (laughter). Then a year later the rule was removed, but you still had to put all the partners' names on the letterhead in those days for quite some time, and as the numbers increased space for the letters got smaller and smaller and smaller. I don't know when it was that that requirement was removed, but you had a list of all the partners on display in the office.

How was the PW office run in those days?

When I was on the staff, there was a large ground floor room which had two doors. You came in through the front door of the building and there was the door on the left into the partners' room and if you turned in through that door, across in the corner there was a table where Martin Harris[11] sat with the staff book. The staff book was a record of all the jobs that were on the go, who was on them and so on, and every Friday you went through the books and if you were the senior guy on the job, you went into the partners' room and stood in front of the staff partner. If you were doing the audit on say, Bush Radio, and you wanted another week you would say,—Bush Radio, Sir, one more week; or,—I need an assistant, or whatever. If you had finished a job you would say you were free and he would say,—right, the Albert Hall, go and see Gregson, who was one of the managers, and you would go off to see him and he would then brief you on the job.

The book started at nine o'clock and at half past nine the doors were shut. In the meantime, all the mail was being opened. There were some white-coated chaps who opened the envelopes, and then the partners went through the mail together. And if any partner had a particular problem with a prospectus or some other sort of document, after the door was closed he would say,—I have a problem and these are the circumstances. If there were ten partners there he would probably get ten different bits of advice, and then he would go off and do whatever he thought was right in the circumstances.

Tell me something about the auditing techniques you used.

As a manager in about 1962, I remember six of us being summoned by the then staff partner, Martin Harris, and we were told that the partners had decided that it was time the firm introduced some staff training. Before that there hadn't been any formal staff training, it had all been on the job. He said,—you six are going to be the lucky lecturers. So six of us were given a topic and my topic was the balance sheet audit[12] excluding stock, and I have to tell you at that stage I had never heard of a balance sheet audit. We all gulped when we were told we were to start giving lectures a month later and we had better get busy and prepare them. So I rushed off to the Institute library to find out what a balance sheet audit was, and there wasn't very much about it, but I spent the next year or so lecturing on it.

The whole ethos of the firm then was 'judgment.' The whole approach to the audit was,—what is true and fair in my judgment? To hell with the law or whatever. You have to bear in mind that was before accounting standards came into being so in any particular circumstance you faced you had to make your own judgment based on what had happened before in similar situations, and that's where you took advice from your partners who had seen it all before.

How competitive was the profession in those days?

In the 1960s and 1970s, it was still considered absolutely unethical to target anybody's clients. Michael Coates,[13] then one of the middle partners in the firm, analysed the top 100 companies in the country and discovered that at that time only about 50% or less were audited by one of the top five or six firms. He said,—this is bound to change; the companies are going to get bigger, the smaller firms of accountants aren't going to be able to cope and these are the companies we are going to go for. He had this target list and managers were given an allowance to entertain people. Somehow or other, *Accountancy Age* got hold of this list and there was a hell of a row at the time.[14] Targeting now is an every day event but when I was first a partner, being asked for a proposal for new work was a very rare event. The firm we thought the most aggressive in the 60s was Coopers.

Do you think there has been a decline in business ethics over the last 15 to 20 years?

The financial services sector has expanded at the most astonishing rate since the 50s. If you go back to the late 50s when all the merchant banks were independent, there was an amazingly strong old boy network, all based on schools. Everybody knew everybody else, almost, and my word is my bond held sway in those days. The number of people employed in the financial services sector today must be enormously greater. Hence you've got a huge range of people coming in, and the more people you have involved, the more potential you have for lower ethics, and the more potential there is for the rogue trader. When you've got this enormous extension of people involved, you have to bring in more control systems and a lot more discipline in order to protect reputations.

As far as the profession itself is concerned, how has the introduction of audit standards altered things?

It has put audits and the auditor into something of a straight-jacket. In some ways the standards helped and in some ways they hindered. They helped in the sense that you could say to the client,—you can't do that because. But then usually, if you put something in writing there's always some slight ambiguity that the client can develop and say,—well actually, you say that's what it means, but I think it means something else, and my lawyers say something else. So you get that problem. Before standards, you said,—I'm sorry, it's my judgment that the presentation doesn't show a true and fair view, and your client couldn't really argue against that. It was take it or leave it. He could say,—I don't agree; but he couldn't say,—look, the standards say this and I'm applying the standards.

People get up to all sorts of mischief. If they can get away with paying themselves several million without telling anybody, they will do it happily. If they think they have to justify it to the shareholders then they might think twice about it. But on the other hand, compliance with all the standards makes the accounts almost indigestible to the man in the street or even to a reasonably intelligent person. So how do you get across to that sort of lay investor the information you want him to have, or should he be relying on professional advisers? I don't know. The question of what accounts are really for has eluded generations of accountants.

How do you account for some of the recent spectacular audit failures?

I think it does cast a cloud over the profession. People hide behind formulas and say the object of the exercise is to express an opinion and a true and fair view in the context of materiality, and that is inevitably ambiguous. In the Barings case, Leeson made something like 90% of the group profits and somebody ought to have realised that this was suspect. If you were doing a proper risk analysis that had to be right at the top of the tree. You'd go and look at it in the greatest possible depth. But I guess it's the same old story, you listen to what you want to hear. I suspect the management didn't want to ask too many questions.

NEVILLE SIMS was born in 1933, the son of a director of a company manufacturing legal stationery in London. However, his roots were in south Wales and he was educated at Penarth County School. He then took up articles with the two-partner Cardiff firm of Phillips and Trump, qualifying in 1957. Two years after qualification, he became a partner there. In 1968, the firm merged with Whinney Murray, later to emerge as Ernst & Young. Always active in the ICAEW, Neville was chairman of the Cardiff District Society in 1974, South Wales Society President in 1977/78, and served from 1981 onwards on the Institute's national Council up to the present day, where he accumulated much committee experience. He retired from what was then Ernst & Whinney in 1985, and since then has worked as a consultant and practice co-ordinator for the seven-partner Cardiff firm of Watts Gregory. He is also on the national executive committee of the UK 200 group[15] *and is their co-ordinator in south Wales. He is adamant that he is in no hurry to retire altogether.*

Why did you choose accountancy?

In my own way I've always kept books right from early childhood. I had imaginary games of all sorts, and had this liking for keeping records. Then at Penarth County School, they were fairly forward in their thinking. When we got to form three, we had the choice of Latin, Biology, or a Commercial course which was bookkeeping and shorthand. I chose that, and I took to it like a duck to water and never looked back. So when I eventually matriculated, the career then either had to be banking or accountancy.

What sort of partnership was Phillips and Trump?

With the one partner, all of his time was spent on accountancy and the auditing side of the practice and the other partner was very much a commercial animal, with directorships and that sort of thing, and a dislike for auditing.

And who were your clients?

There weren't any big national names. It was a very typical small general practice, with a range of small clients, mostly local small family companies. But we did the audit of the non-public funds of RAF, St Athan, which was very interesting. It wasn't really a pure audit but they did prepare their own accounts. They worked to a manual themselves and they had regulations which they had to observe and we had to ensure that it was all in order. We also had a nice audit on the Treforest Trading Estate, a firm of printers who are no longer in existence, called Copigraph Ltd. I'd go up there and do interim audits. They had their own accountant, so it wasn't just incomplete records I was dealing with.

Did you have to pay a premium?

No, my father happened to know the principal I was articled to and I think they did a deal. I wasn't paid at first, but my father unfortunately died not long after I passed my Intermediate, so he never saw me qualify. We weren't a rich family and because of the circumstances they did start paying me four pounds a week which was enough for me to complete my articles.

What did you do immediately after you qualified?

Because they had been kind to me when my father died, I felt I owed it to them to stay for a couple of years after qualifying. My father's ambition for me was always to join Coopers, who were the auditors to his company in London. I talked to my principal nearly two years after I qualified asking where my future lay. He said to me,—I can't tell you now, but bear with me. I didn't quite know what that meant until a month or so later, when I was told a senior above me had handed in his notice. My principal then told me that the senior had never been regarded as partner material and therefore they couldn't offer me a partnership. But now that he was leaving, they would like to offer me a partnership. So I had that awful decision as to whether to stay with the firm as a partner, or move on to London and get experience with a larger firm. But at the end of the day, because partnerships are not offered to you every day of the week, I gratefully accepted the offer. So I became a partner of the firm I trained with.

And how did the partnership develop?

In 1968, the firm was approached by a firm I'd never heard of, called Whinney Murray, saying they had a lot of work in south Wales but didn't have an office. They had been strongly recommended to approach us because of our standards, and would we be interested in joining them? So we deliberated long and hard. The partner I mentioned, who was very much a commercial-minded animal wasn't interested. But my principal and myself agreed to join them. That's how I managed to join one of the large firms.

Did you find it a bit of a wrench after working with only two other partners?

It wasn't too bad then. We were only about 60 or 70 partners nationally in those days. You more or less knew most of your partners. Not quite as impersonal as it is now. Whinney Murray had a super client base. They still do. We used to do a lot of referred work here in south Wales. And new work, 90% of which comes through recommendation. We had very high standards and there is no doubt that helped enormously in our growth. My big problem was that the name wasn't very well known at first. It made life a little more difficult. But then as the profile of the firm grew, there was more national press and the name became better known. Especially when we got the Laker receivership.[16]

How were fees assessed?

Well, I'll let you into a secret. When I was the partner in charge of the Cardiff office, I had three grades of clients: A, B and C. The A clients were the Plc's of this world; whatever they wanted, we did at the drop of a hat. No questions asked. The B client was the largish client but by no means as—I wouldn't say important— needful of the same sort of immediate reaction. And then you had the C clients who were the rest of them, where you did the accounts as and when you could fit it in. So I had three charging scales. I used to operate what I called a tolerance level between the As and the Cs. Whatever I lost on the Cs, the As had to make up, so my bottom line wasn't affected. Now I'm afraid to say London didn't agree with that. But their way of thinking just wouldn't work. It wasn't practical. I wouldn't have had any clients left. So I stuck to my own methods.

Quite honestly clients don't want to know about compliance work and they don't want to pay for it. It's all added value today, and they are looking to their accountants to produce that added value. And if you can give them it, they don't mind paying your fees.

What do you think were the principal changes auditing underwent over the course of your career?

Compliance work has grown enormously now because of audit regulations. That's been a big change. We are now very much committed to proper systems, which are reviewed by the JMU. Therefore, whatever size firm you are there are proper procedures laid down for auditing. I think a lot of the problems with current auditing derive from the fact that you're under such commercial pressure as far as fees are concerned. But you have the use of all the modern techniques which we didn't have in my day: random sampling and all that goes with it. I remember when Ernst & Young as they are now, brought in strategic risk analysis. A great thing. We had to get to know our clients' businesses thoroughly, recognise where the weak areas were and then we homed in on them. So the whole approach has changed, and for the better quite honestly. I think a good audit should produce a lot more than the old-fashioned tick and bash.

The techniques have changed, has the purpose changed?

Oh, that's a difficult one. The public out there don't really understand what an audit means. Those who are financially aware obviously do, but not the man in the street, the ordinary shareholder, who we are supposed to be protecting.

Theoretically and in law the audit is conducted for the ordinary shareholder. Do you think that has any basis in reality?

I don't honestly think so. Talk to ordinary shareholders and I doubt if anyone bothers to read the audit report when they get these glossies [company reports] once a year. I'm talking about people now who aren't financially aware. Perhaps we don't have as many shareholders in that category now as we used to. The institutions have taken over the majority shareholdings of the large companies, and they are obviously financially aware.

In reality, audits have always really been for the management and board of the client firm, and in the case of the smaller outfits, the Inland Revenue. It's not a recent development. If the directors know their job, they should have an idea what the audit should produce. What the shareholder doesn't see is the management letter, which is written to the directors setting out areas of concern which may not be material enough to cause the auditor to qualify his report. Now companies are more and more looking to have audit committees. So they are very much aware of what the auditor should be doing, and I would like to think that if an auditor isn't coming up to scratch, then the directors will recommend that they be removed.

Commercialism has had an impact and you can't deny that. But we've had to combat that in being more efficient in our auditing techniques. If you have got a threat, you regard it as an opportunity.

Did you ever have hostile relationships with client management?

Oh, yes. On occasions I've had to take a legal opinion to support my view. I was never afraid to do that. Once we had a managing director who had borrowed money from his company, created loans and all sorts of things. We argued it wasn't in compliance with the 1948 Companies Act. He maintained it was. So we had to seek a legal opinion.

On another occasion, a decision went to arbitration on the value of stocks in an acquisition. The vendor and the purchaser didn't agree. We gave an opinion and the purchaser didn't agree with it. So it went to arbitration.

Were there ever occasions where, either by accident or design, you felt you were being denied information that was necessary for satisfactorily completing an audit?

No, I don't think so. Although there was one instance where events subsequently proved that we hadn't been given information. But that was through no fault of ourselves as auditors. There was collusion going on and it wasn't discovered until a later stage. That's the risk auditors have of course.

What is your opinion on the standards issued by the regulators?

They can be useful. There was a very substantial company where they changed the basis of the valuation of stock. They didn't want to adjust the previous year's stock and that put me in a very difficult position. I said,— I have no choice but to qualify my report. Anyway we went through the SSAP on the valuation of stock.[17] There was a sentence that said,-previous years' stock must be restated if practical. Now this was quite a complicated company with complicated stocks, so it was quite a while before we came to the conclusion that they did not have to restate their opening stock, because everyone agreed it wasn't practical. But if I had not come across that particular wording, we would have qualified the audit report whether or not the directors wanted us to.

Did you qualifying accounts often?

Not very often. I've usually managed to get management to agree to what I want it to do. It's a very serious matter qualifying an audit report. Where we did, it was usually over the valuation of stock. Also, where we felt proper records had not been maintained, and therefore you couldn't offer an opinion. They may have had a computer failure or something like that. Major companies have come up against that problem, not just the smaller companies.

Personally though, I think that if there is a difference of opinion between management and the auditor, and the auditor does qualify, it is absolutely wrong if the auditor is then asked to resign. It does undermine the independence of the auditor very much and there should be an independent body that both sides can go to as an arbitrator, whose decision both sides would be bound by, and the auditor would be allowed to continue.

I refused to take on clients for the very reason that I felt they were the sort of clients that might want you to bend the rules. I didn't want to be associated with them. I thought our name was far too important.

Born in Leeds in 1934, BRIAN ATKINSON is the son of an assurance company manager. After attending a local grammar school, he was articled to John Gordon, Harrison, Taylor (who merged with Spicer & Pegler in 1972). After qualifying in 1957, Brian moved to Price Waterhouse, working for one year in Leeds and then nine years in London as an audit manager. In 1966, he moved to the ten-partner practice of Buckley, Hall, Devin in Hull, where after three years he became a partner. In 1979, he moved back to his native Leeds, as managing partner. During his time there, the firm was absorbed by Ernst & Whinney (now Ernst & Young). Now in semi-retirement, and running a part-time consultancy from his home in the village of Thorner, just outside Leeds, Brian was for many years an activist in the ICAEW, serving as District Society chairman in Hull and as a committee member in West Yorkshire.

What was it like to work for John Gordon, Harrison, Taylor in Leeds in the early 1950s?

It was very much the local mixed practice. As the firm was involved with many different types and sizes of organisation, articled clerks were very fortunate in gaining a wide spectrum of experience, locally and nationally. I distinctly remember my first day as an articled clerk. I went to a scrap metal merchant who was based, he won't be there now, in Kirkstall Road. I thought, indeed I hoped, that my accountancy career wasn't going to be spent in places like this. It certainly was an eye-opener. It was the roughest place you've ever seen in your life. But we did a range of things, Blake's Boot Protectors, which was a well-known local company. Our biggest job was the Yorkshire Electric Company, and on nationalisation a different

Board became a client. There were also the Women's Institutes which were a popular favourite for articled clerks. I think there was a standard charge of two guineas there. So you did a lot of those to learn the nitty-gritty of debits and credits. You had to crack that particular kernel or else you'd never get the nuts sorted out. But I was closely supervised, a qualified accountant—chartered or incorporated—was never far away. And I had a paternal principal who took a close interest in my progress. Subsequently I was very grateful but at the time—in one's late teens, early 20s could get a bit tedious. I was a bit unusual because between my Intermediate and Final exams I spent the whole time in the tax department.

Was there a lot of paper work?

Not as much as there came to be later on. You'd have a trial balance, supported by debtors, creditors and the bank records and that sort of thing. There was no referencing system to my recollection. You just followed the balance sheet order, starting with the cheques and worked through. You have got to realise, we had no photocopiers. And there was still a shortage of paper back in the early 50s. So we weren't encouraged to accumulate too much paper work.

What were your hours like?

Normally speaking the hours weren't that bad. I had one terrible job, which I was going to once a month to write up the books. This was a textile manufacturer on the other side of Halifax, and you had to leave usually about half past five in the morning to get to this place, and you'd take three buses to get there, hoping, in the middle of winter, the next bus was working. I'd get back at half past seven or half past eight at night or something like that, depending on the buses again. So that always was a fairly long day. But normally speaking, you'd be finished at five, five-thirty, fairly regularly.

And did you have any problems with the exams when they came up?

I may have had problems studying, but the exams I coped with, touch wood. One of the confusing elements was, it was the time consolidated accounts were very much coming into play. And consolidated accounts were incomprehensible to everyone in those days, despite Sir Thomas Robson's famous book.[18] Our final accounts exam must have been 60% on consolidated accounts. The whole thing was very new. So I struggled with that, I must say. One was very worried whether one would pass but I got through it. I don't think the exams were that bad.

Overall, was taking articles a good preparation for your career?

In the environment of those days I think it was. But we lived in a very formalised era, and it was very much saying 'sir' to everyone for the most of it. But no, I didn't find any real problems with articles. If you chose the right firm you got a good grounding in accountancy. Whereas we might have been regarded as cheap labour, I think firms took their obligations seriously. But bearing in mind our senior partner was a highly respected member of the accountancy profession, I don't think it was surprising we were fairly well treated. When I moved to Price Waterhouse in the late 50s it was a very different world. Very impersonal compared to where I had been. I remember when they took the comma out between 'Price' and 'Waterhouse' this merited a note to the staff as to why it was being done. It seemed that the unity of the firm would be better served by taking the comma out!

What was PW's Leeds clientele like?

Subsidiaries mainly- things like ICI divisions. I think there used to be three ICI divisions audited from the Leeds office in those days. I spent a lot of time there. It was a big transformation for me because I was going straight into a quoted company that was monster-sized compared to what I had seen before, although I had seen bits of the Electricity Board. So it was a very different world; all mechanised accounting. That one was particularly fascinating because it was so different; I spent a lot of time there. It was one of the specialist oil companies, half-French and half-American owned. They had a complex management relationship between the French and the Americans. The guy who was running it in the UK wore a bowler hat, but he was an American with a name like Caesar.

And after Price Waterhouse what came next?

Well after that I decided to come back north. I replied to an advert which said 'Yorkshire' and found myself in Hull. So lo and behold, I joined a very remarkable firm, because even in those days it had three of the top 100 listed companies, all of which had started in Hull. But the specific reason they took on someone like me from a big firm was in connection with a small recently listed company called the Wiles Group, in which James Hanson had recently become involved.[19] His involvement, the partners perceived could presage major changes and that a local group, involved principally in agricultural activities, could become something different. This perception was proved correct as the Wiles Group became the springboard for the Hanson Trust. The other major listed clients were Smith & Nephew and Northern Foods, but Hanson plc was my main responsibility.

Can I ask you about the kinds of relationships you had with client management, like Hanson for instance; did it ever get hostile?

Yes, one had an occasional hostile situation. When you are sticking for dear life to the principles and they are fighting for survival, things can be very difficult. I once took over a client from another partner because the relationship had somehow broken down. Now this wasn't in terms of accountancy or auditing principles at all.

It was a personality clash, was it?

They both denied it was. You get into heated arguments, most of which get resolved at the end of the line. But having said that, you have to be prepared to stand up for your principles. If you are not, then why are you there? Ernst & Young have a panel that sits in London. The client is invited to attend, as is the client partner, and both viewpoints are heard. Ultimately, the firm establishes its opinion by which the client is asked to abide and which is then binding on the firm.

Were you ever involved in uncovering frauds?

Do you know, I never was. There was a story at Price Waterhouse in London, which may have been apocryphal, where a student found a fraud on the first job he did after he left university. This was a matter of some jealousy. I never did, and it was very disappointing; in a way, you wondered if you'd missed something. Perhaps it's not as common as people imagine. When they happen, of course, they hit the headlines.

Did you ever have to qualify accounts?

I think it is inevitable from time to time. One of the difficulties with clients is they don't quite understand what the audit is there for. Qualifying is significant for the Revenue, for banks and for City institutions, and is, therefore, a heavy responsibility, which the client perhaps doesn't see. Despite your attempts to explain, it may be hard to understand what the truth and fairness angle and disclosure really means. You try your best. But then again, you've failed if you spend your life qualifying accounts.

Did you ever feel under pressure from anybody not to qualify an account?

You did get the ultimate threat from the client which is of course,—if you do this I am going to change my auditor. So occasionally we get put under pressure, but the pressure of losing an audit is insufficient grounds for not following your conscience. But funnily enough, it doesn't mean you necessarily lose your client.

How did you set about protecting your independence?

Socialising with a client, for instance, is something that becomes very difficult. OK, you have a beer at the end of the audit. I'm not saying that you can't go to his golf tournament. But I don't think you want to make close friends with clients because that may compromise the situation, and you have to be very careful. Senior staff can, of course, have similar difficulties and one such situation led to extremely awkward interviews with a client and a staff member. I wanted to talk to him and it turned out he wanted to talk to me. We were both away in Glasgow and we were talking very late one night. It was about three in the morning and funnily enough our thoughts were exactly the same. He was very worried he was getting too close to the chap, and I was very worried the chap was getting too close to him. One of the most difficult interviews I had ever done was with this man to explain that I was taking him off the audit.

How have you found the increased competition in the profession?

Tacky isn't quite the word. Client gathering has become a very much more acquisitive thing, and in the 1980s practice development became very much an 'in thing,' perhaps due initially to American influence. One was supposed to be impressed. It was certainly a great challenge to those, such as myself, not versed in the processes. In the old days, a major part of the job was personal contacts and you still hoped for the client who walked through the door on personal recommendation. On one particular occasion a prospective client came through the door having already seen several other major firms in Leeds and appointed us—a 'beauty competition' by any other name. On the whole though tendering is a very nerve racking business and often demoralising.

Was there ever anything approaching touting?

Some tactics did surprise me, for instance, around the mid 1980s when a partner from a rival firm started handing out calling cards at a social event organised by one of my clients.

Have you any other misgivings about the direction the profession is taking?

Perhaps the potentially high rewards are encouraging too many people to enter the profession or alternatively to change their direction. Whilst I was delighted to see my brightest student win a prize, I was perhaps disappointed that he was a person with a first in chemical engineering. Certainly, I was surprised to find a number of my daughter's friends at Cambridge studying engineering went into the City after graduating. Perhaps they should have used their degrees more constructively, although such highly trained people must be good for the accountancy profession. and the City. The better the staff, the better the audit. There's no doubt about that.

BOB NIDDRIE was born in 1935. After schooling at Brockenhurst Grammar School, he was articled to the small practice of Whittaker Bailey in Southampton in 1952, qualifying in 1958. After National Service, he returned to the firm and became a partner in 1962. In 1975, Whittaker Bailey was taken over by Price Waterhouse, and Bob became partner-in-charge of the Southampton office, and four years later was given the additional responsibility of the Channel Islands practice. He retired in 1992.

What were the circumstances of your being recruited to Whittaker Bailey?

I was only the third articled clerk in 100 years of the firm's history. When I tried to get articles it was very difficult, because nearly every firm was linked to a particular local school and they only took articled clerks from there. I remember being referred to the local secretary of the Southern Society, John Mitchener, who kindly went through with me the list of local practices, and said,—this one only takes boys from King Edward's School and this one only takes boys from Taunton School and so on, and this one, Whittaker Bailey & Co., doesn't take articled clerks at all. I persuaded him to phone them and despite the fact they hadn't had a history of taking articled clerks, they agreed to an interview and fortunately employed me.

What sort of firm was it?

They were a small firm, one of the three oldest firms in Southampton, established in the 1840s with one partner in Southampton and two partners in the London office. The local partner was also involved in a local stockbrokers, Whittaker and Bailey. On the audit side, we had a lot of brown paper parcel jobs preparing the accounts from scratch. But this was combined with substantial clients such as the University of Southampton, which we effectively audited continuously, Southampton Chamber of Commerce, the School of Navigation, Lankester's, a large foundry and engineering company founded in the 1680s, and numerous companies involved in the port,—importers and wholesalers of fruit, pharmaceutical wholesalers, etc. So there was always an element of pure audit.

With only one partner, what was the level of supervision?

Managers had their own very individual styles and were left very much to themselves. There were no formal audit procedures and so often things were in the manager's head rather than down on paper. There was one manager who kept very few records, and I remember the partner finding that getting information out of that manager with regard to the audit was like getting blood out of a stone. Clients objected to change and it was a real weakness having the same manager, who was a law unto himself, being retained on the same job for up to 25 years. Most managers stayed with the firm for the whole of their working lives.

How arduous did you find your articles?

It was very tough. Studying was done through a correspondence course and little time was given off by the firm for study; as I recall it there was a month before each exam. Coming up to my Finals I was exhausted from working long hours, two hours a day commuting and studying every night and weekends. I took medical advice about my exhaustion and was told to change my eating patterns. I had to eat a large meal in the morning, a light meal at lunchtime and in the evening, so that I wasn't laden down with food when I studied. Fortunately, I passed my Finals first time.

What did you think about the training?

You had everything thrown at you and if you had the ability then you were given responsibility early on. You lived and breathed bookkeeping, accountancy, auditing. You established a sixth sense, and so you knew all the tricks people got up to because one found there was fiddling of some type on every job. The experience was first class and stood me in very good stead when I became a partner with Price Waterhouse.

What happened after you qualified in 1958?

I did my National Service, came back and became a partner of Whittaker Bailey & Co. two years and nine months later. I was a general practitioner, tackling tax, insolvencies and management advice as well as audit. The clients expected you to have that breadth of skills and business knowledge and you wouldn't have survived with any credibility in regional cities like Southampton without it.

I came back from National Service very refreshed mentally, with lots of ideas and at an age where you didn't hesitate. When I became partner, I discovered that in many cases client fees had remained the same for ten years, and I re-assessed the fees to the extent of trebling the fee charged to some clients. Most of them laughed and said they thought somebody would catch up with them some day. I only lost one client, and overnight I turned it into an extremely profitable practice. However, the fee increases came at a price and were accepted on the understanding that we would be providing a 24 hours a day, seven days a week service, which for the very small firms in those days was probably unique.

We were at a changeover time. Where previously the fathers of the generation I was servicing were quite prepared to work all night to do their own tax returns and all their own books to save on paying their accountants, their sons were wanting more leisure time and if you were prepared to provide a first class service, they were prepared to pay well for it. This led to our attracting some entrepreneurial clients, which was an exciting development as we then enjoyed the stability of the clientele of long-standing, with the addition of new and exciting younger clients.

What other changes did you make in the early 1960s?

One of the principal changes we made was insisting on proper audit planning and that audit work and file notes were properly and fully recorded. Many of the techniques and approaches to the work had been very old fashioned. For example, we looked after the bookkeeping of the church schools of the Diocese of Winchester. There was a monthly meeting in Winchester, which my principal used to take me to. We would leave Southampton by train at around 10.30 a.m., have lunch in Winchester, and go to the meeting which started at 2.15 p.m. Our part of the agenda never came on until 5 p.m. and lasted no more than half-an-hour, and yet we had devoted the whole day to this one meeting. Our fee recovery was consequently only 50%. When I took this job over, I arranged for our item to be first on the agenda, and I left Southampton at 1.30 p.m. for the 2.15 p.m. meeting and I was back in the office by 3.30 p.m. We felt we were always ahead of our local competitors and that was one of the factors which eventually made us attractive to PW.

Did your relationships with client management ever get hostile?

After PW took over in 1975, we were auditing an American subsidiary who made monthly financial returns to the States which ignored any possible over-valuation of stock. When it came to the year-end, we assessed that significant stock was unsaleable and therefore over-valued to the extent that profit would need to be slashed by 50%. The client insisted they could realise stock items at their book value, and challenged us to prove otherwise. We had three sessions to midnight with the local board and visits from the main US board. We held our ground; the figures were too significant to consider a compromise and we insisted on the write-down required. I then had a very uncomfortable eight months waiting to see whether we or our clients would be proved right. Fortunately for me, it turned out that I was right and the client failed to sell any of the stock in dispute.

Did you ever find yourself denied information you felt you really needed to complete an audit?

Only when I was in charge of the Jersey office. Jersey was at that time a potentially dangerous area for auditors. We audited banks and holding companies where the assets were often held in other countries. That was very difficult to audit. In one instance, a local bank subsidiary had been instructed by its parent company to destroy all faxed instructions, which left us with a lack of audit evidence for the local transactions.

Did you ever personally uncover fraud?

Someone once tried to bribe me; although I didn't realise it at the time. It was a new client introduced by a reputable local solicitor, where on my first visit the director having asked the company secretary to leave the room, then proceeded to say how certain he was we could work together and obviously I would need something for my expenses. I said,—fine, thank you. He then counted out a significant amount in cash. I said,—that's fine, but on the way back to the office, thinking over what had occurred, I became suspicious and having discussed it with one of my partners, he wrote a letter acknowledging receipt of the money on behalf of the practice. The next thing that occurred, the police were in our office asking what we knew about the director or company secretary concerned; it turned out to be a major fraud they were involved in.

What would usefully improve the company audit?

Try and tidy up things on the client side. I believe current audit techniques stand up but the real weakness can be with some executive directors, especially on the financial side, and some chief executives on whom the auditor has to place reliance. If that reliance proves unjustified it is virtually impossible for the auditor to overcome this. Tougher action is needed against erring directors.

The son of a Leeds textile agent, JOHN MORDY was born in 1940. He was educated at Giggleswick public school before taking up articles with Peat, Marwick, Mitchell in Leeds, where he was to remain for the whole of his career. Qualifying in 1963, he became a partner ten years later and was to see the Leeds practice grow to 40 partners. A member of the national Council of the ICAEW for 15 years, John was first chairman of the Training Standards Board, chairman of the Education and Training Directorate for four years, national Treasurer, 1990/91, and President of the West Yorkshire Society, 1991/92–1994/95. Retiring in 1995 at the age of 55, he and his wife are restoring their farmhouse on the outskirts of Leeds, and they also own a small cottage in lower Wensleydale, from which he is able to indulge his passion for walking.

Tell me about your experiences as an articled clerk at Peats?

There were very strict audit programmes. If I remember rightly there was a green book and you had to do a different page for each year. The audit was based on what we'd done the previous year, so there wasn't any audit planning. Work was done by rote; you did it last year, so you did it again this year. Clients tended not to do new things.

Could you tell me some of the clients that you were involved with?

The first one I ever went to was a wholesale grocer down by the River Aire, which at that stage was seriously rat infested. I remember knowing that he supplied my local grocer and thinking,—I ought to stop buying food there. Textile companies were important companies, because at that stage Leeds was still very much the centre of the manufacture of suits and men's clothing. I remember going to a wool merchants in Bradford, which had to be straight out of Dickens, watching the bales of wool being lifted up on what must have been 19th century cranes into the warehouses. And there I remember you worked at a sloped desk. And then there were other clients: I remember a forge which was founded by monks. Its stamp shop gave me an impression of what hell must look like. I suppose that was one of the first occasions one got out of the office and walked around the factory seeing what was happening. That was new, that was different. I was involved in that audit for seven or eight years and then it got taken over and we lost the audit at that stage.

Did you have to pay a premium?

No, I think I was the first articled clerk in the Leeds office that didn't pay a premium. There was a slightly odd set up in that there were four partners resident in Leeds at the time, of whom three were Scots, so there were problems arranging articles. The new bye-laws in 1957 made the arrangements more flexible and I became articled to an ICAEW member based in our Bradford office, but the person who started immediately before me had to take a Scottish contract.

Overall, do you think doing articles was a good preparation for your career?

It gave me practicality and taught me double entry bookkeeping. I think the basis of the system was actually quite good.

And so it's not a matter of regret to you that you didn't take the graduate route?

Yes and no. Had I known what I knew ten years later I would have taken the graduate route, but that was the advice I got from people whose views I would then respect, who I might not now respect. They said it was a waste of time. I could have gone to university, there's no doubt about that, but they said,—no, don't. My father had two more children who were coming through education and I suppose he wasn't too unhappy to see me go straight into work. I missed the general stretching of the mind you experience as a university student.

Theoretically, and for that matter, legally, the audit is carried out on behalf of and to benefit the shareholders. Do you think that's got any basis in reality?

Not a lot I don't think. It could have if shareholders were prepared to get involved, but in practice you are reporting to the very top element of management. The audit committee is something that has evolved over the last 10 years and has become a very powerful tool.

Given that then, what underpins an auditing accountant's ethics?

Ultimately litigation, although that's very much a matter of overkill. There is a general professional background, you've been taught your job, you've got ethics. The generality of ethics has been reinforced by commercial pressures. You've got your reputation. If you don't do a good job, a satisfactory job, a commercial job, then you will lose the work. You've got to do the job efficiently because your client is looking to keep his costs to a minimum, and get value for money.

Were you ever in a situation where you felt that you were being denied information that was necessary to complete an audit?

There were one or two instances. Part of the difficulty of course is knowing when you are denied information. It's easy enough to audit what's in the books, it's difficult to audit what isn't there. To an extent, the client or management may not necessarily appreciate that they're denying you. They may not fully understand the significance of the questions you're asking. I certainly recall instances where with the benefit of hindsight I might have taken a different view. Not very many of those involved clients deliberately withholding information. There may have been cases where had you known a bit more you would have asked supplementary questions.

When you were a partner what sort of controls were put in place to ensure that audits were sufficiently deep, and of sufficient quality?

The whole approach changed over that period. At the outset you tended to be fairly close and knew what was going on, but when clients got bigger then it was necessary to put in more controls, put in more paperwork. There's a lot more bureaucracy in managing the audit now.

Who made up the audit team actually doing the work?

Students would do the basic collection of data and the underlying verification work. You would have a qualified senior with them and a manager above them, reporting through to you. Latterly, we were recruiting very able people and therefore you needed to stretch them at a much earlier stage. A lot of the criticism from students at that stage is that they weren't being stretched enough. It's like a balancing act.

Was the system of supervision too tight for the people supervised?

It sometimes wasn't flexible enough. You had to have controls in place to make sure that they were doing the work and weren't making decisions or judgments beyond their competence. You needed to have somebody in place to approve the judgments that they were making. Certainly though, judgments were made at fairly lowly levels.

Did you ever uncover fraud at management or director level?

Not fraud. I think there were areas where we had major differences of opinions with senior management, and maybe they were very unhappy, but it wasn't fraud. There would have to be a certain amount of compromise, these things are never actually black and white. There are occasions where you stick to black and white and you actually make things worse.

The Companies Act gave you that discretion?

It's important to stick to 'true and fair,' and there is a certain line. I'm not sure that the present methods and standards that we have necessary help.

You now get stuck with standards that can be very precise, very difficult, very constraining.

Would there ever be a situation where you'd brandish a standard at a client to try and resolve a dispute?

That now happens quite regularly. Over the last ten or 15 years, the stock market has become much more a matter of public interest. It affects finance directors, because the financial media are all looking for a particular form of presentation and the pressure on the FD is such that the auditor has to have the standard there in place and say,—sorry, you've got to comply with that. And the FD says,—if I don't, what are you going to do? And then perhaps the FD is confronted with the financial review panel[20] and all the problems that flow from it. So you've actually got a much more powerful armoury. But on the other hand, it's almost like the nuclear deterrent, it becomes rather more difficult to deal with minor items at the edge; you may well give way on minor items in a way that perhaps you wouldn't have done earlier.

Did you have to qualify accounts frequently?

Very rarely.

In what sort of circumstances would it happen?

Where there was a fundamental uncertainty. Insufficient records. Or you might have a questionable contingent liability, if you have a difficult contract structure and the effect could be extremely material one way or another. With stock valuation, you considered materiality as well. Qualification in itself is extremely rare now because you actually have a paragraph in the audit report that emphasises that the matter should go through the accounts, so I suppose in that context qualification is less common. But audit reports are more verbose, with attachments and notes and references. You will see many references in accounts saying,—without qualification, we nevertheless refer to . . . . . That type of thing. In the old days that probably would have been a qualification. On the whole, it's better now, because at least you've still got the client, who would otherwise be offside.

Did negotiation around the management letter help bring clients into line?

It was a fascinating exercise because the internal politics of the client firm comes into play. There'd be some companies where top management just wanted to know everything, and that was fairly helpful; but when the management letter became a document that was important within the client organisation itself, then the negotiations at management letter level became much more difficult than the negotiation over the accounts. Everything has to be settled in advance, because you don't want to have a fight with management in front of an audit committee over the contents of the management letter.

The profession is much more overtly competitive than it used to be. When did you notice things starting to change?

I suppose about 15 or 20 years ago. That's when you started appreciating that you actually had a pretty big business, and you went up to certain clients saying,—can I have money on account? At that stage, you were indicating,—we are in business as well as the client. You, as a practising accountant, could no longer afford to wait for signing the accounts off before you submitted a fee.

What is your view of tendering?

I think there's an awful lot of pain attached to tendering; it's a very expensive exercise. Having said that, it concentrates your mind, and you have to make sure that you understand the client, so you do go through a learning process before you get into the audit. It's not all downside; if you've done a proper job with the tender and you win the audit, then you've done a lot of the groundwork, which gives you a flying start for carrying out the audit.

How common do you think it is for client firms to put audits out to tender, and it subsequently emerges that really the only intention is to drive down the fees of the current auditors?

I think there is a certain amount of that. There may be circumstances where you've had a falling out with the management, in which case you get invited to tender with other people. It's fairly clear they want to change and fees may not be the only consideration, although they probably will go for a reduction in fees. There may be circumstances in which it becomes quite difficult to maintain your position because if you come in with a significantly lower figure than the one you're already charging, then you're actually admitting that you've been overcharging. So it may just be that they are looking to see whatever level of service people can offer, which is not an unrealistic thing to do. There are certainly many instances where the lowest tender does not win the audit. It is a messy exercise, it's not just messy for the accountant, it's also messy for the client and it's something that shouldn't be entered into too lightly.

Born in Cwmbran in south Wales in 1954, MICHAEL CAREY is an engineer's son who is now the partner in charge of audit practice in KPMG's Cardiff office. Having failed his 11+, he first went to Llantarnam Secondary School in Cwmbran and then transferred to Croes y Ceilog Grammar School. In 1972, he was articled to the three-partner firm of Notley Pearson & Shewring in Newport and after staying there one year after qualification, he joined what was then Peat, Marwick, Mitchell in 1977. In 1987, he was made a partner.

What was your original motive for wanting to go into accountancy?

I decided I wanted to do something which was financially orientated, because I'd enjoyed Economics. I did Economics A-level. Banking didn't pay well enough and I had an interview with the Institute's educational officer in Newport and he offered me a job, so I said yes.

As an articled clerk what sort of jobs were you asked to do?

It was anything from wage preparation, preparation of accounts from incomplete records, a small element of audit. Generally speaking in that small a firm it was felt that if you prepared the accounts they were probably OK. There was an element of audit but it wasn't significant. And we did some club stocktaking and stock reconciliation.

How closely were you supervised?

Not particularly closely. The articled clerks were in a top floor room working away. We delivered the end results to a partner who met the client, and apart from very early on when I was really picking up the ropes, I wouldn't say there was any review of what I had done before it went to the partner, and not much review by the partner either.

Even in the beginning, when you went out on a job you would go out on your own? There wouldn't even be a senior clerk?

Depends on the size of the client. We had one true audit client where I was a junior member of the team. The vast majority of other jobs I remember doing, I was effectively in charge.

What about checks. Was it always a full check or would you bring some kind of sampling in?

In terms of the smaller clients, where we were preparing the accounts, it was pretty well a full check because you needed to see something to support every transaction to know how to account for it. In those clients where there was more sophistication you normally had a trial balance, there it would have been a sample check supported by quite a detailed review of the other items.

Was it the practice in those days to submit a management letter?

We never produced one. It [a management letter] assumes you've undertaken a systems audit and therefore you can comment on the systems, whereas by and large ours was entirely a substantive audit. Clearly the partner would have had a discussion with the client at the end, and if there were issues we had any concerns about he would discuss it then, but it was very rarely documented in a letter.

So what happened after you'd qualified?

I stayed for a year, partially because that was the year that I got married and I thought one big change was enough to go through, partially out of a sense of loyalty because they would have been in a degree of difficulty if I'd have left. Twelve months after qualifying it was obvious that there was no career opportunity for me, and the traditional step for somebody qualifying with a small firm was to join a big firm, have two years' experience, and then go into industry. So I applied to Deloittes, Coopers and Peats, and joined Peats.

And how long was it before you became a partner?

1987, ten years. When I joined Peats, because I had not gone to university, I was younger than most of the students who were joining Peats from university, which was an interesting position.

Did the graduate students treat you as a second class citizen?

No. Frankly, the biggest problem you have to cope with as you move through any firm, I suspect, is when I joined there were a number of people who were considerably more senior to me, and over a period of ten years I found myself catching up and moving past them. So at times they would be reporting to me. That could be a degree tricky.

Compared with your previous experience, was it very different auditing for Peats in the late 70s?

It was a much more formal audit with much more documentation required. In fact, when I joined we were just moving from a questionnaire-based audit to one which was much more free-flow, where you went in and documented the systems and produced an audit programme.

How strange was it to have to cope with firms that had systems, internal controls and finance directors?

I didn't find it too strange. What was required was a fairly rapid development of self-confidence. You join an international organisation like Peats and you are dealing with companies that are listed on the stock market, more senior people than you have ever dealt with before and it takes a little time for you to realise that you actually are as skilled, if not more skilled, than they are. And it took me a little while to realise that, and develop the confidence to know that, if I felt something was wrong it almost certainly was.

In many ways I had a better training base than those who trained with Peats because then and now they are trained in audit. They do not get much experience in actually putting the accounts together. And very often, when you come across a crunchy technical issue, the ability to do some double entry bookkeeping is extremely helpful. So all I had to do was to learn to do an audit in Peats' style. That is relatively straightforward. Learning bookkeeping takes rather more time and rather more practice, so actually I was better placed than many of my colleagues.

There have been technical changes in the course of your career; do you think these changes actually alter the purpose of the audit?

No. I think the purpose of the audit remains exactly the same as it always has been. Readers of accounts want some degree of assurance that what they are looking at bears some resemblance to reality. Whilst we only express an opinion to the shareholders, there's no doubt that banks, creditors and others in taking decisions to do business, and on what terms, place reliance on the audit report and, depending on the name on the bottom of it, more reliance on some than on others. What has changed I think, particularly through the 80s, as there is an increasing pressure on fees, has been a greater focus on what needs to be done to express an opinion. So there's been more research into where audit opinions have been expressed incorrectly, what went wrong, where did the error arise, and using that research, the audit has become much more focused. And that is continuing. We are introducing changes to our audit approach at the moment, which will take that process even further. But we always have that benchmark which is; the figures have got to show a true and fair view, so whatever approach we adopt that has got to be the end result. So all we've really changed is the way we get there.

And what underpins the accountant's professional ethics in all of this?

I'd say frankly that what underpins it is that without it we lose the credibility which enables us to earn fees. So even clients who seek to put pressure on me to form a different view to the one which I am inclined to do, will probably think less of me if I give way than if I hold my ground. Clearly, there are always commercial judgments in these things. But at the end of the day, regardless of the size of client I am dealing with, if I allowed myself, through whatever means, to be persuaded to take an unprofessional decision, or to allow conflict of interest to impair my judgment, the damage I could do to the KPMG brand name is enormous. I don't have a single client, I doubt that KPMG has a single client, that is so important to the firm that risking the brand name could be contemplated.

When I joined the profession, it was very much a gentleman's business and there wasn't much outright competition, it was very quietly done. When I joined Peats, Coopers were by far the most commercial and aggressive organisation, and they were considered to be—not cowboys because that's the wrong expression, but rather fly for the profession, if that's an appropriate way of describing it. Now everybody has recognised that that is the way of the world and has followed suit in some way, shape or form.

Have you been responsible personally for innovations in the audit that you think have gone some way to improve its quality and depth?

One of the schedules which I always insist on, and is now pretty well adopted across the firm, is a reconciliation of the previous year's profit to this year's profit, showing how that change came about. Whether it was sales volumes, sales margins, changes in overheads, and a narrative to support that which gives you some understanding of what is happening in the business. It also focuses your mind on where there may have been manipulation of the accounts. The other issue these days is that technical requirements are so voluminous in terms of accounting or auditing standards, and KPMG requirements on top of that again, that it's very easy to overlook something. The way that that is normally managed is by producing checklists, and there are times when we almost get to the point where we have checklists to confirm that the checklists have been completed!

So how do Peats go about planning an audit today?

At the beginning of every audit we have a team discussion, partner, manager, staff, to talk about the strategy for that particular audit, and there are a number of issues we address at that meeting. Do we want to retain the audit? Is the risk related to that client acceptable, for example, addressing fraud issues and many others? I was concerned that in that team discussion it was very difficult to be sure that we'd covered everything, and you can't then properly deal with it at a later date. So we produced a pro-forma agenda (because I didn't want another check list) which is only two pages long and covers all the technical issues, but it also takes you through the commercial issues, and has substantially improved the quality of that strategic discussion.

Were you ever personally involved in detecting fraud?

I remember one fraud where you had the production manager, warehouse manager, sales director and chief accountant all working together in collusion to defraud the company they were working with. That was very very difficult to identify.

How did you identify it?

It was identified simply because we started asking lots of questions about why was the profit margin declining. But that entailed having local knowledge. You can't escape the fact that there is a lot of benefit from being part of the community and knowing, for example, that your client's product is very easily obtained locally.

And did that lead to prosecution?

That led to three or four people landing up in prison.

Has the culture changed greatly, in terms of business ethics, since you started?

I don't believe that it has. Healthy scepticism is the phrase we use. I think that's because: a) accountants are human and b) they generally come from a background which has encouraged them to believe that human nature is good. So you would normally start off on the assumption that you are being told the truth, but it doesn't take you very long to realise that there is a difference between the truth and the whole truth, and the difference can often be fundamental. And therefore you will probe answers; you will keep your eyes open for facts which differ to answers to previous questions.

Clearly one of the judgments you form in planning the audit is the exposure to fraud, which not only looks at the nature of the business but also at the nature of the personalities who are running that business.

What sort of relationships have you had with clients? Has it ever got hostile?

Not often. Generally speaking, we work on the basis that there is enormous value in the audit service, and if the client is going to get the full benefit there needs to be a level of co-operation. Our style is generally open, relaxed and friendly, therefore normally clients are co-operative. If you identify a problem, you are a blockage to them presenting information in the way that they wanted it. But frankly, outright hostility from a client is as good a warning flag that there is something wrong as you are going to get. You've invariably got too close to the heart of the matter.

And does that lead to arm-twisting to avoid qualification?

Yes, there is arm-twisting. It is particularly prevalent where third parties have a focus on the accounts, for example, when the bank is interested in a set of accounts because the financial position is a little difficult, or where there are venture capital investors. Very often in those cases it is the venture capital shareholders who are pushing the company to produce accounts which show a particular picture, so the company management often end up as piggies in the middle. Clearly there is always pressure, but if at the end of the day I feel particularly strongly enough about an issue, if I know I cannot sign these accounts in compliance with standards and a true and fair view, then it doesn't frankly matter how much pressure the client puts me under, I am not going to be giving way.

Does commercial pressure not come into it at all?

I can't speak for other major firms, and clearly the pressure would be greatest in a smallish firm with one very substantial client where the loss of the account would be substantial. In an organisation the size of KPMG there are clearly some very major clients who we would not want to lose, but I don't think there are any clients the loss of whom would result in major damage to KPMG. And I go back to the point that what our clients buy from us is, in many ways, the name at the bottom of the audit report, which adds substantial credibility to their organisation and which means a lot to readers of the accounts. We wouldn't dare compromise the quality of that name by giving way to even the very largest of our clients if that client was looking to do something which wasn't appropriate. There's clearly an art of persuasion in those cases, because to get yourself to a point where there is a qualification on the table, suggests the clients are looking to pull the wool over somebody's eyes. Our view would be that it is very rarely in the interests of the client to even contemplate so doing.

Do you think that auditing standards have led to improvements?

Not in KPMG, and not in any other of the big players either, in that what standards have done is to codify what we were already doing. What I don't find entirely helpful is the trend towards auditing standards which require us to gain representation letters[21] from our clients, that is not a KPMG style. In my view the clients represent that the accounts show a true and fair view when they sign. It's our responsibility to undertake an audit which identifies any area where that judgment may be in question. To require pages and pages of representation adds a degree of unnecessary bureaucracy and undermines the status of the auditor in the eyes of the client.

The profession has been much criticised for the Maxwells, the BCCIs the Polly Pecks and all the rest. How would you respond?

Hindsight is a wonderful thing. You would think if you were auditing the petrol stock in a local garage that you should be aware if the quantity of petrol claimed to be on site is in excess of the capacity of the tanks. But you don't necessarily ask yourself that question until it happens to you. We are constantly learning lessons and improving our approach, so that we are comparing our client's performance with their industry. I had questions to answer with one of my clients for four years, because he was out-performing the industry and I was very aware of it. I spent a lot of time understanding why he was out-performing the industry, in what area he was out-performing the industry, and trying to be satisfied that it was real and not the result of manipulation. I think most firms would probably admit that where they have made a mistake, if they go back and look in their files, there is some indication somewhere of a problem that they maybe should have looked at a bit more carefully.

Notes

1. A public appointment established in 1883 to administer bankruptcy procedures (Howitt, 1965: 16).
2. Cork Gully, a merger of W. H. Cork and Gully, Stephens, Ross & Gregory in 1932, and led by Sir Kenneth Cork in the 1960s and 70s, were insolvency specialists (see Cork, 1988; Matthews *et al*, 1998: 292, and interview with Fabes and Chapman, chap. 2).
3. Cooper, 1966: 1.

4. A measure of the performance of a company, e.g. rate of return on capital employed or price/earnings ratio.

5. Ford in the UK became wholly owned by the US parent in 1960 (*Economist*, 19 Nov. 1960).

6. SSAP 2 was published in 1971 (Edwards, 1989: 125).

7. Data processing machines that could handle more complex data than the comptometer and were therefore ideal for processing information from invoices, statements and ledgers. It involved mechanically punching holes in cards, sorting the cards and then tabulating the results into printed totals or balances (Bigg and Perrins, 1971: chap XI). First invented by Herman Hollerith in America in the 1880s, they were widely adopted in Britain in the interwar period, with the two main producers being the British Tabulating Machine Company, who marketed the Hollerith machine, and Powers-Samas. They were only ousted as the main office data processors by the electronic computer in the late 1960s (Campbell-Kelly, 1989: chaps 1–9).

8. In 1974, Court Line, the travel firm, went bankrupt. The subsequent Department of Trade report in 1978 (Douglas Morpeth (qv) was one of the inspectors) was critical of the auditors, Robson Rhodes (Department of Trade, 1978).

9. Schedule A covers the taxation of rental income (Lewis, 1977: 335).

10. Born in 1918, of private means, educated at Eton, he qualified in 1947. He was made a partner in 1952, and was considered a possible senior partner, but died aged 47 in 1965 (Jones, 1995: 220).

11. Qualified in 1950, made a partner in 1956, headed the enquiry into Pergamon in 1969, but left PW to become Director General of the Panel of Take-Overs and Mergers in 1974 (Jones, 1995: 215 and 279).

12. The balance sheet audit, more common in America, operates in the opposite direction to the normal audit in that it starts with the end result, a draft balance sheet, and works backward to the underlying records. The traditional British audit starts with the detail of the profit and loss account (Woolf, 1997: 131–2).

13. Son of a previous PW partner, he qualified in 1951, and was made partner in 1959. In 1973, he produced an internal paper which set PW on a course to aggressively increase its market share. He was senior partner from 1975–82, when he became chairman of the PW world-wide firm (Jones, 1995: 215, 258–9 and 288).

14. In 1977, an internal PW memorandum was leaked to *Accountancy Age*, which indicated that a list of 100 companies had been drawn up which PW were clearly targeting. *Accountancy* mused whether the ICAEW Disciplinary Committee could be asked to decide whether entertaining an 'uncommitted' client amounted to a breach of the ethical guidelines (*Accountancy*, March 1977: 4).

15. A network of small regional accountancy practices providing mutual technical support (information from the interviewee).

16. Sir Freddie Laker's transatlantic 'Skytrain' operation collapsed in 1982 (Jeremy, 1998: 31).

17. SSAP 9, on the valuation of stock (Woolf, 1997: 193–5.

18. Robson, 1956; the first edition was in 1946.

19. James, later Lord, Hanson, with his partner V. G., later Lord, White, built up the firm of C. Wiles, which went public in 1964, into a conglomerate initially in plant hire and printing. It changed its name to the Hanson Trust in 1969 (Cowe, 1963: 297).

20. The Financial Reporting Review Panel was established in 1991, following the Companies Act 1989, to examine material departures from accounting standards by major companies, with the right to apply to the courts to order the directors to revise the accounts (Parker, 1992: 122).

21. Letter from the directors of a concern to the auditors putting on record their representations on matters affecting the accounts, e.g. that they had disclosed all contingent liabilities (Woolf, 1997: 210–214).

Chapter 7

Leading National Partners

Born in London in 1910, the son of a doctor, Sir CHARLES HARDIE attended a minor public school, where he won a scholarship to Cambridge to read Latin and Greek. However, on his uncle's recommendation he took articles with the City practice, Edward Moore and Sons, in London in 1926, qualifying in 1932. In 1934, he joined Dixon Wilson in London, which today still has only 16 partners and has never merged with another firm. He served as senior partner there until 1982, and was central in building up a large clientele of landed estates. Except in the early years, he spent most of his time as a director of public companies, at one time chairing eight Plc's. Most controversially, he was responsible for signing an unqualified auditor's report for John Stonehouse's[1] *secondary bank in 1973, about which he was reluctant to talk. He finally retired in 1995, at the age of 85. Sadly, he died not long after this interview.*

What were your experiences in training in the late 1920s?

When I started, I had to pay a premium of 500 guineas and was expected to wear a bowler hat and spats. My first job was to make what they called a Chinese copy in longhand of a trust account. It was 28 pages long, and took me about three weeks, when it was discovered that I had missed out two pages and had to start all over again. There were no typewriters then; it was a few years before the old Imperial typewriters came in and with them typists, so everything had to be hand-written in script.

I would spend weeks on end going to small public companies, professional firms and some private firms, casting day books, which was very laborious but it taught me how to add up three columns, because you had pounds, shillings and pence. You had to put a special tick on the bottom of each page. You checked postings from personal and impersonal ledgers,[2] and the cash book was cross-checked with the day book, with another man ticking the opposite entry; two clerks shouting at each other from morning till night.

How closely were you supervised?

You would be working under a senior clerk, who had been doing the same jobs for 20 to 30 years, whilst he undertook the more complicated tasks. After a year or two I graduated to being allowed to produce simple sets of accounts on my own. The hierarchy dictated that the senior clerk would present the completed accounts to the partner who would go through everything with a fine toothed comb, before taking the accounts to the client and signing the audit certificate. The partner certainly would not get involved in any checking himself.

Were there audit programmes?

There were no standard Institute programmes; each client would have his own programme, detailing the checks. These consisted of voluminous hand-written working papers, without a girl in sight, and no adding machines.

Did you come across fraud when you were a clerk?

I got a good reputation early on, because I was auditing a hotel in Jermyn Street and found that a £400 carpet had been purchased for which there was no receipt. I said to the manager,—never mind the receipt, just show me the carpet. The manager immediately blushed, since there was no carpet; it had been taken to his own house. He was sacked and I was thought to be a very bright boy.

What happened after you qualified?

In 1934, I became a partner with Dixon Wilson, and took charge of the audit side up to the war. I was paid £3,000 per annum as a 24-year old bachelor, which is the best off I have ever been. At that time there were only four partners, the older ones dressed up in morning coats and top hats, whilst I continued to wear my bowler and spats.

Did you have to bring in capital?

I borrowed £500 from the bank, but paid that off fairly quickly as income tax was only four shillings[3] in the pound in those days. The capital value of the firm depended on not withdrawing profits; most was left in because it represented the partner's book debts, with up to six months' audit fees being owed at any one time, and the clerks' wages needing to be paid. The senior partner would then expect a higher profit share than the rest of us, whose share depended on the amount of business we brought in.

How did your subsequent career develop?

I went away to war for six years, and resumed my role, only to find that women had largely manned the firm. I was able to assemble a large clientele of landed gentry whom I had met during the war. I had been close to the Guards' Division and lots of these people came to me to look after their affairs. I was an old man in their eyes, 36 after the war, and they were mostly in their 20s. We then built up a very good practice through clients' solicitors recommending us to other clients' estates; a very specialised form of auditing, although we did have some public companies.

Was there a strong social element in your acquisition of clients?

It was negligible, since I was a busy man, and so were my clients.

How did you fix fees?

Fees were calculated on a booking-out system devised by Dixon Wilson in 1910, which avoided undue fluctuations in non-labour costs. You might give some protection to existing clients experiencing difficulties with temporary discounts, but the specialist nature of our work meant we had little significant competition.

But you did not stay in auditing?

No, most of my time was spent as a director of public companies.

But you retained a perspective on the audit?

I saw it from the other end, mostly dealing with the big firms. It became a very impersonal relationship; you never knew who was going to be your audit manager the following year. A lot of the depersonalisation comes from computers. Here, a lot of figures come out, with no need to add them up, and it's difficult to detect commercial activity. In the old days you developed a feel which told you that certain gross margins should be attained, and, if not, you wondered what had happened to the money; had it gone sideways? Now, it's difficult to conduct a dispute with a machine, and there have been numerous examples of the big firms missing major frauds, because the intimacy of the audit has been lost, although this may have enhanced the auditor's independence. And there again, audits are stricter than ever before, given the standard setting of the Institute; the atmosphere of litigation makes standards inevitable, but I detest the uniformity.

How significant was the growth of internal controls?

That was the other major change, in that a client's internal audit department now does 90% of the work I did in my youth. The detection of fraud is now particularly dependent on the internal audit, and the sophistication of the controls. The adoption of sampling systems distances the external auditor from some of the evidence of fraud, and he has to concentrate on the client's systems.

The sheer size of organisations makes sampling inevitable. I was a director with Forte Hotels and they had 800 hotels, all big enough to justify a separate audit. But only 50 were taken as a sample; the names were just picked out of a hat every year.

Do you think fraud is more common now?

Not more common, but the sums are inconsiderably larger. Personally, I only came across petty stuff.

How do you view the failure of the profession to cope with some of the spectacular fraudsters like Maxwell?

When I was chairman of BPC[4] we were involved in a joint publishing venture with Maxwell in Japan, which proved unsatisfactory and the connection was severed. Later, when Maxwell's attempt to take over BPC was being resisted by us, both Maxwell and myself were summoned to a meeting at the Bank of England. To my horror, Lord Benson was there, about to chair the meeting. I immediately protested that his presence was improper. Coopers audited both Maxwell and ourselves; there was a clear conflict of interest. Benson replied that he was there to represent the Bank. Subsequently, very heavy pressure from the Bank led to the take-over going ahead.

My feeling is that despite Maxwell's poor reputation he had a great deal of support in the City and even in government circles. He was seen as a hard man capable of turning BPC around, and perhaps what he was able to do at the *Mirror* bears this out. He did sort out the print unions where we might have been a little bit timid. He had an apparently charmed life, and you can't just put this down to his larger than life personality. Given the high levels of protection he seemed to enjoy, Coopers may well have been encouraged to turn blind eyes to a number of things, not least his blatantly obvious incompetence in financial matters.

In general, I see the recent big frauds as evidence of the crippling dependence auditors have on information supplied by the client. If you are going to try and put that right, then tightening up the regulation of internal controls is likely to be much more useful than any fresh attempt to soup up auditing standards.

Born in 1915, COLONEL GERALD ASPELL's father was the leading partner in the small, Leicester chartered accountancy firm of Aspell, Dunn. After public school, he was articled to another small local firm, Wykes. Since his father had taken ill, after two and a half years Gerald joined Aspell, Dunn, and completed his articles there, qualifying in 1938. Since he had joined the Territorial Army in 1933, (his last uniform job was in 1984) he was called up early, in 1938, saw active service and was finally demobbed in 1946. His father had made him third partner in Aspell, Dunn in absentia, *in 1943. In 1952, Gerald merged the firm with Cooper Brothers, becoming a full national partner. When he retired from Coopers in 1978, he was partner number three out of a total partnership of 750. He has given long service to the ICAEW, being President and Secretary at district level and on the national Finance and General Purposes Committee and contributed to the writing of one of the early accounting standards. He was also at one time, Vice-Lord Lieutenant of Leicestershire.*

Did you have to pay a premium at Wykes?

No, it was on an old boy basis between my father and the partners at Wykes and Co. Wykes and Co. had a unique system for those days, where you served the firm as an employee for two or three years. If you showed aptitude, they would then give you your articles and you still went on being paid.

And did they pay you a wage?

No, nothing at all, no wage at all. When I left after two and a half years they gave me a check for £25.

What about when you moved on to your father's firm?

No, not from the firm. He paid me privately. All the articled clerks in my father's firm had to pay a premium. Possibly it depended on the financial circumstances.

Overall do you think your articles were a good preparation for your career?

Well, I can't think of any other way one would have sorted out the sheep from the goats. It taught you a lot of loyalty to the firm. One was slightly against graduates in those days because the firm very much reckoned to teach the nuts and bolts of the job themselves, and didn't particularly want somebody with a history. What the firm wanted was to check that the brain could encompass the range of work. University students would be rather more channelled in those days: high fliers who specialised in one subject.

I was always eternally grateful that I qualified before the war. To come back after all that and start to become a student again would have been dreadful. In fact, they were very generous in the ICAEW. They set up a lot of refresher courses for us and I went on one of those. But they also exempted those who had been articled before being called up from the Intermediate. This was an act of kindness but I don't think it did anybody any good, because they went straight through to the Final and left it till then to sort out their futures, by which time it was pretty late on in their careers.

What happened to Aspell, Dunn after the war?

We were helped by my army connections starting up their own businesses and looking for an auditor. Then I took the firm into Cooper Brothers in 1952. My father's old partner, Reginald Dunn, and I became Leicester partners. We went in because I met Henry Benson and John Pears, who were the two senior partners in those days, and they wanted to get a foot into the hosiery trade. They approached me; I didn't approach them. Out of the blue. Some people say,—how on earth did you get into a big firm like that? I say,—the answer's simple, I had dinner with them.

What controlled the ethics in the job in those days?

Well apart from being bribed by the client, which there was quite a bit of at one time—offering to do work on your house, that sort of thing—there wasn't anything to be made out of being dishonest. One might sound a bit pompous, but one was indoctrinated from the moment one went into the firm how honest one had to be the whole time. In those days there were no wide boys and ethics were paramount. It came from the training.

Did relationships ever get hostile with clients?

I think quite a lot of them thought we were a damn nuisance. You were in the way. I don't remember any punch-ups. There were plenty of disagreements but we were very civilised.

When you were conducting an audit, were there ever occasions when you felt you were being denied information that you needed?

Oh, yes. It was much more open in the later days I think. In the 1930s, the private ledger was often bound and locked and you could only get the key from the proprietor. And he was very reluctant to give it to you on occasions. It was terribly secret to him. You really came up against it when you were doing the audit report for a flotation. You wanted to go right back to everything and check the costings. They were sacrosanct and they were kept in the managing director's safe.

How did you get round that?

You tried to resolve it as you would in any dispute. The ultimate sanction was, of course, you didn't sign the audit. You had to be careful with a private limited company, because they could tell you,—just go jump in the lake. I'll get somebody else. There were a lot of people around who were not qualified, who were perfectly capable of taking the job on.

I did once resign from an audit. I was negotiating things for a client, a profitable manufacturer in the early 1950s, with the bank, and they went behind my back and told a total cock and bull story, which they refused to withdraw. They had a twisted solicitor; he was so twisted he managed to get out of it and his clerk was sent to jail. Saying that though, 90% of people were totally honest.

Was the uncovering of fraud a frequent occurrence?

No, no. There will always be people to whom, in the old fashioned expression, 'rather a shilling on the cross than a pound honest.' Staff pilfering in my day was a common thing. But one had some very dodgy clients, particularly through the war years, because there was a lack of staff, a lack of supervision and of course the Revenue weren't so tidy. But once they put on 100% taxation, there was no incentive to fiddle then.[5] They earned all they could keep by 12 noon and the rest of the day was spent in the pub.

Did you ever uncover a major fraud by client management or client directors?

Certainly, people siphoning off money for their own purposes.

Was it always followed through and did it lead to prosecution?

The Revenue tended not to prosecute if you owned up to the whole thing. But if you tell them more than two lies, then they throw the book at you.

Were you ever involved in formally qualifying a client's accounts?

Not often. Usually due to lack of true information or lack of control. I once had to qualify a theatre's accounts in the 1960s because quite rightly all the emphasis was on the production side. The administration and the canteen and the restaurant just went to hell.

Was that in Leicester?

I'd better not say.

DAVID HOBSON was the senior partner of Coopers and Lybrand from 1975–83. The grandson of a Cambridge mathematics don on his father's side and an Indian civil servant on his mother's, his own father was an economist at the Board of Trade. Born in 1922, he was educated at Marlborough and Cambridge where he read maths and then economics. His studies were truncated by the war, when he became a telecommunications officer, although he was still awarded a degree. Family connections introduced him to Cooper Brothers which he joined in 1947, 'for the purpose of getting a general business training.' However, coming first in the Institute's final exams in 1949 encouraged Coopers not to lose him and in 1953 he was made a partner. He then spent most of his career under John Pears and Henry Benson building up the practice before taking the reins himself.

What did they put you to do when you first joined Coopers?

I started by being tipped into Unilever House to deal with the books of the United Africa Company. At that time offices had batteries of clerks, whole floors of them, whether it was in Unilever or elsewhere; all those people have now disappeared.

Were there any Coopers still in the firm then?

Yes, there was Vivian Cooper, Chim Cooper (as he was known) and of course Henry Benson was a Cooper on his mother's side. Just before I went there, the then senior partner, Stuart Cooper, left the firm in 1946. That effectively ended any family control, other than that Henry Benson was one of the two senior partners jointly with John Pears, who was the senior partner when I went there. He was the recognised leader of the firm for the next 20 years.

Give us your impressions of both Pears and Benson.

John Pears was an able man. He was on the whole more popular within the firm than Henry. If you read that document[6] you will see his suggestions, just before I went there in 1945, as to the way the firm should be developed.[7] Henry went with him. Benson was a man who if he hadn't been an accountant would have been a very able lawyer. His father was a solicitor in Johannesburg, and as a man to put over a clear summary of his thoughts he was outstanding. He was not always the easiest man to work with; sometimes he was better with clients than with people within the office, and with the more junior people of the clients. He related to the senior management of companies very well and a little less well to the juniors.

Was he a bit of a bully with the junior staff?

I think that view could be taken, but not only with junior staff. He produced a great deal of work for the firm and was a man of great distinction, but not the easiest to get on with. John had a greater degree of support from more people within the organisation than Henry could command. He had more of the human touch, although he had his failings as well. I survived there for many years with two very determined people.

They were a very good partnership since they were both good business developers and good technicians. John Pears was a very able man in dealing with tax as well as auditing. He sent a good many tax inspectors into retreat. Henry Benson was recognised as a very effective technician and he worked very, very, hard. He did a lot of the work himself. He'd settle down and write the conclusions. Of course, both of them were impatient with poor work. I don't think anybody who has high standards puts up with rubbish. The firm had been asleep for about 40 years and they woke it up and put it into the first division.

Did you have a policy on recruiting women?

John Pears was never very keen on training women as accountants. He didn't think that they were very suitable for going around a steel works. There were difficulties in this in the way that clients would react. They wouldn't mind too much having women going through their personal tax returns, but to go round Babcocks [the engineering company] works at Renfrew with 10,000 workers, one girl wouldn't really be very acceptable within a very male dominated industry. That was the principal reason why people wouldn't take them on, and there weren't many demanding to come in as far as I can remember. They came in later, of course, under Henry Benson and we got up to a very large percentage of women. We had the first woman partner and we've got some there now.

Perhaps we can talk about the famous Coopers' Manual. How did that come about, was Benson closely involved in that?

I think both of them were, John Pears and Henry Benson.[8] In 1945, John Pears felt that a manual should be prepared. It took some time for it to be completed and it came out in 1948–49. It was published much later.[9] It was in use in the firm for many years before it was ever published. We were working with a manual all my time as a partner, from 1953. I can recall working on a prospectus in 1950 and we had a manual of what to do in that area at that time, which our joint auditors did not have. They just sent the people in to bat without any instructions at all.

Clearly Coopers were leading the profession in your early career. What would you say was controlling the quality of the audit then in the late 40s and early 50s?

The requirement that we followed the manual. We introduced a checklist for the 1948 Companies Act, which eventually got given to the Institute and was then published by somebody else. But in fact it was ours; Henry Benson gave it to the Institute. We also carried out test reviews of our own audits from the early 1950s. So there was a standard of quality assessment at that time. The audit manual was published in 1966 because Henry felt that we should help the profession by showing what we'd done. It had been in use for 20 years and our staff were trained on it, with specimen audit files based on it.

We were in the vanguard of getting the Institute to produce technical advice in the members' handbook. A large part of that was based on our work. They were taking parts of our manual and effectively using them to tell people how to audit the inventory or debtors or something of that kind. John Pears and Henry Benson had quite an effect in getting that done. Other people did work on the committees doing the drafting but I don't know many cases where there wasn't somebody from our firm on the committee concerned. Initially, it was John Perfect or Francis Shearer.[10] Others followed.

What would you say was the purpose of the audit when you were training and in your early career?

To see that the accounts showed a true and fair view for the shareholders. The directors were responsible for the accounts. I think there was much less done in the way of covering a world-wide situation. There wasn't the same feeling of responsibility that has grown up latterly with regard to the underlying work in other countries. At that time I don't think it would have been accepted that we could do more than send a questionnaire to the auditors of overseas subsidiary companies, unless they were part of our international firm and followed our manual.

What about qualifying accounts in the 50s?

We qualified the accounts of the Groundnut Scheme and that was all over the front page of *The Times*.[11] We qualified the British Printing accounts in the 1960s, and that was right across all the popular press. British Printing was a merger of Purnell (which was Wilfred Harvey's company) and Hazell Sun, which was a printing business headed by Sir Geoffrey Crowther. They were two distinctly different businesses, one was entrepreneurial and very close to the wind and the other was stodgy.[12] Harvey was a crook and was helping himself to money. The fraud was that he acquired various companies and paid X for them but he entered them in the books as three or four times X, and the difference went to the credit of his personal account.

In 1965, Purnell was in a mess. The auditors were Curtis Jenkins, and the senior partner, Charles Oddie, sent a copy of various queries out to each director at his home address, and that put the cat amongst the pigeons. We got called in by the bank to investigate at some length and we became joint auditors in order to strengthen the situation. I was put on the job by John Pears. The board was split four to four and couldn't meet except on neutral territory. So they met in the Westminster Bank's boardroom. Finally, we got the qualification drafted and accepted. There were then efforts at criminal proceedings, but Mr Harvey had such high blood pressure that doctors said that he might hear things that would upset him during the course of any trial and they couldn't be responsible for what might happen. It's not the only case of people who have been in trouble who managed to produce doctors who provided suitable explanations as to their health, not always justified.

What were the main grounds for qualification generally?

I don't know if there was always a main ground. We had a qualification register and potential problems used to come to the partners' meeting. Every month, probably ten or so qualifications came to our meetings in the 1960s. Later, they had to be delegated to an audit committee meeting.

Did you feel that there were any commercial pressures on you not to qualify in the sense that you might lose the client?

There were one or two cases where John Pears and Henry Benson resisted this pressure. One was with a well-known company chairman, who would resist qualifications on the grounds that he knew better how to put the inventory figures in the balance sheet than anybody else. The upshot there was that the accounts were qualified. That was an engineering company I think.[13]

As a partner were you expected to bring in work?

Yes. I went about it by doing the job properly and by getting known around the place. I did work mainly in the City of London. I used to do prospectus work for bankers and others. Sometimes clients came in from recommendations from friends or somebody else that one knew. Also, having diagnosed a problem somewhere, you'd try to ensure that you made some sensible suggestions where you could help people. That was John Pears' field and he made that remark in 1945 on practice development,— You can't be accused of touting if you offer your services to your own clients which it would be in their interests to accept.[14] He also had the idea that at every audit you should make at least one useful suggestion. That method often produced work. You suggested methods by which they could do better and they discovered that there were problems. Then you got asked in to help on it. If the audit was a purely mechanical process which did not offer extra value for the client it got nowhere.

What would you say were the main changes in the audit during your career?

In no particular order, the introduction of the Institute's Recommendations, with everybody expected to do things in a certain way and then the introduction of accounting standards. Then there was the development of international firms to meet the requirements of clients who worked all over the world.

What do you remember about your time on the Accounting Standards Committee?

It was run by Ronnie Leach, who was a good chairman, and we went through the drafts with considerable care. We had many leading members of the profession on it, people like Bill Slimmings,[15] John Grenside (qv) and others. We wrote some pretty good standards, brief, to the point, and easy to understand. I think when Ronnie Leach went off the ASC it became somewhat less effective. I don't think it carried quite the weight and there was too much wasting of time in discussions.

Then they got down to reorganising it under Ian Hay Davison.[16] He decided that the ASC should be a senatorial organisation and it would take two hours to go through everything and people would make one comment and then the meeting would close, and the result was that the stuff was not properly digested by the Committee. Senatorial was the word that Davison used. I think what he meant was that the full Committee must not do the nitty-gritty. The Committee was to have an overview, whilst a sub-committee would do all the detailed work. The trouble with that is, if the sub-committee does not put in appropriate safeguards and you don't go through the draft properly it goes wrong. The sub-committee had not got people of the same experience and standard as the ASC.

What are your views on more recent audit failures, ones involving Coopers?

I can't comment on any of them because I don't know anything about them and I might be thought to do so.

I think the basis under which auditors have unlimited liability, and they get sued on the grounds that they're the only people with any money or insurance is wrong. After the City Equitable case,[17] the 1929 Companies Act refused to allow a company to indemnify an auditor. It really has got to an absurd situation when people are arguing that all sorts of subsequent events should be blamed on an auditor. It has forced a defensive attitude which I personally regret. People now say,—this is too risky a client to have, you should dispense with him. Our feeling used to be, you should qualify the accounts and let the shareholders deal with him. It was one's duty not to turn down a client unless he was a known criminal. One took on clients that one didn't always vastly like but the idea was that it was better that somebody who was prepared to act and qualify the accounts should do so.

Do you still think self-regulation is the best way?

Probably, but I don't really know whether some of the regulation is necessary in the form it now takes. I don't know quite what an outside regulator would do; issue dog licences to auditors? I don't know the answer and fortunately I'm no longer affected by it.

The son of a railway signal engineer with the Westinghouse Brake and Signal Company, JOHN VENNING was born in Streatham, south London, in 1933. He attended Merchant Taylors public school, and was articled to Ford, Rhodes, Williams (later Robson Rhodes) in London in 1951. Qualifying in 1957, he returned to the same firm after National Service, becoming a partner in 1964 at the age of 30, and remained with them until retirement in 1994. He served as a DTI inspector in the investigation of Bestwood.[18]

What were your first tasks as an articled clerk in the 50s?

Anything. I started off on the telephone, filing, a lot of adding up, weeks and weeks of it. And then going out, mainly auditing, usually in pairs where one sat casting with the ledger, calling out enormous numbers of entries over to each other, trying hard not to fall asleep.

How closely were you supervised?

I was lucky as I got a lot of personal supervision. Everyone accepted the system. You had articled clerks and you had the old timers who weren't qualified, what I would call the sergeants, in military terms. They gave you a lot of knowledge and accepted that you were the ones who were going to go on; there was no rancour about that. I got a lot of supervision from my principal, who was always interested. He saw you and he jolly well wanted to know what you were doing and if you didn't know he'd find out. I always remember the first audit I actually took back to him. He said,—well how does the business operate? And I said,— I didn't know. So I was quickly shunted off and told to find out. In many ways this personal relationship worked—it is very sad that it has all gone. At the end of an audit the partners would put on morning suits to go and sign the audit report. It was like going to a wedding.

Did you have any interesting clients?

Castrol was our biggest audit. We handled a lot of investment trusts, a lot of rubber and tea companies. I was considered a real expert on rubber and tea. I'd never seen a tea bush or a rubber tree! But after my articles I did my National Service in Singapore and therefore was deemed to know 'the East.' The chap who used to look after our Indian offices was getting on and wanted someone to take over and I was put down to do an Indian trip every other year, and I used to enjoy that. We went there right up to about ten years ago.

Did it present interesting problems from an accounting point of view?

Rubber and tea stocks were always bought in at the sales price and you couldn't complete the accounts until the stock was sold. There was a value for deferring tax, but there was no particular calculation for it. There were nice little funds that got stuck away, and afterwards became unstuck and were taken as profit. But then people began to take these things a bit more seriously, particularly if a company was about to get taken over. And if you dealt with a subsidiary the parent company's auditors started to review you in considerable detail. We were a small, very prestigious firm, but we gradually lost lots of clients to the Big Six.

When you became a partner in 1964 were you salaried?

Very much so. There was a great debate on whether I could have the key of the partners' lavatory door; they were not sure whether that would prejudice my Schedule E status.[19]

Presumably, you did bring capital in later on when you become a profit sharing partner?

That was quite hard; and you had to buy the goodwill as well. A third of your share of profits was used to pay the partner from whom you acquired your share, an annuity for nine years. It was about £2–3,000, but that was a lot of money in those days. I had to come to an arrangement with the banks.

In the course of an audit, did you ever come across significant fraud?

I can't say that I did, but the firm did; we were very good at spotting petty cash fraud, and we did find a few of them. The big management fraud I don't think I ever spotted, although there was a tendency to worry from time to time, but somehow I managed to steer clear of it. I wasn't in the right place. Our firm got tangled up with Court Line, but I never had anything to do with it, which was pure luck. Who knows where I'd have been if I had. The investigation concluded that there were just too many discrepancies, and on balance we should have qualified. From our point of view it was a great relief.

How traumatic was it for the partners who were directly involved?

I think one retired fairly soon afterwards; but the younger one wasn't the same man ever again. He stayed with us, but I think he really suffered from it. It probably wasn't his fault, because if there was a fault it was the old boy's. It's all very well, but out of these situations come new rules and regulations and that's the way things move on. It certainly woke us up to the threat of litigation.

Have you got a view of some of the spectacular frauds that have caused some commentators to question the value of the audit?

The 'nasties' I've wondered about. In many cases the people actually doing the testing had got to the nub. It's what happened to the information as it went up the tree that worries me. In many cases, for umpteen reasons they either got boxed, or wrapped up or put on one side. I did quite a lot of forensic work, and my biggest worry was that the boys on the ground at the time dig the points up and may not know what they have dug up; things get lost as they go up, maybe through time constraints. In many cases, partners should have known that there's something not right. I've come across absolute shambles in bookkeeping, such as blank cheques being written.

DTI inspections and reports have their critics.

The criticism is made that it's draconian towards people giving evidence. They don't know what the evidence is that's being put to them and what they've got to answer. Secondly, they've got to answer and this could be used against them later. But if you're a crook I don't have any problem with that personally, and if you're not a crook then it doesn't really matter because it's useful for everybody to know what went on.

Some people think that accountants should not police their fellow professionals, that there is a tendency to be lenient?

But who else is going to police them? Clearly there still is a mess. The trouble is that DTI investigations take so long, whereas the policeman can say,—you will turn up at 11 a.m. and you will bring your documents. The fact that the QC and the accountant are busy people and have other things to do doesn't help. In our case [Bestwood] the QC got called into court for a fortnight on some big case or other, and so everything stopped. There do not seem to be so many enquiries nowadays.

Another criticism is that the reports tend to be equivocal about assigning blame.

That came, as I understand it, out of Maxwell, where they did assign some blame, and the High Court said it was unfair; from that time on everything had to be fairly bland, with the words all toned down. If the guy's a crook, I can't see why they can't say it, because the evidence is there. Maybe the answer to that is they should just be factual without offering comment, but make useful recommendations. There are no easy answers to these questions.

You took the system as you found it?

I suppose the frustrating part was the time it took for everything to happen. It took you time to get into what you were looking at; then to get the people to come; then to get them to comment on the transcript; then you'd put points to them and get them to respond, and it was going for weeks and weeks and weeks. And everyone's delaying all the time, so by the time you've got there, it's all dead anyway. It's interesting, the frauds are always set up the same, circulation of funds and creating assets, not just cheating on numbers.

Overall, how has the profession changed?

Everything has become much more regulated and complex; the most interesting thing was reaching decisions on grey areas. Now everything is thought to be black and white but there are always difficult decisions to be made. The other enormous change is the need for someone to be blamed when things go wrong. In my early days, it was accepted that people made mistakes; the important thing was to learn from them and not make the same mistake again.

Born in London in 1935, A.W. (Paul) MILNE is the son of a small businessman in the West End of London. After attending Kingsbury Grammar School he joined Deloitte, Plender, Griffiths in London in 1942, spending two years there before being called up for war service. He returned to Deloittes in 1948 and qualified in 1952, having been exempted from the Intermediate examination. He became a partner with Deloittes in 1969 and specialised in the audit of banks and oil companies, which involved him in extensive travel abroad. He spent some years on the Disciplinary Committee of the ICAEW. He retired in 1987, and lives in Buckinghamshire.

Can you give me a rough idea of some of the things you were asked to do when in training?

It was all audit work and consisted mainly in a great deal of detailed checking of bank reconciliations, vouching journal entries and postings from day books to the ledgers, Year-end stocktakings were carried out and other assets verified by inspection. It could be extremely boring. There was an accountancy lecturer in those days—W.W.Bigg[20]—and I remember him advising that you should do something that the client would not expect you to do—such as calling for their sales catalogue—something which would cause the client to wonder what the auditor was thinking. It was good advice but it shows how routine audit could be.

How closely were you supervised as an articled clerk?

Not all that closely by the partners. In those days, Deloittes was I believe the largest firm in the country, and with the legal restriction on the number of partners you can understand that partners weren't vastly hands-on. The firm had a number of senior managers who were largely responsible for the work to be carried out, in consultation of course with the relevant partners, who supervised and reviewed the work carried out.

How was the work organised?

An audit programme was prepared by the partner and manager. It specified the amount of work to be carried out by way of vouching, posting, asset verifications and bank reconciliations. It could not be called a scientific basis of sampling but was based on the experience of the partner and manager and of their knowledge of the client's affairs.

You stayed with Deloittes after you qualified?

Yes I did. I did at times go off for interviews for commercial jobs. But I never really found any that appealed to me.

How long was it between your qualifying and becoming a partner?

Quite a long time but not abnormal. The limitation to 20 partners meant you could not expect, in a firm as large as Deloittes, to become a partner before the age of 40. The Companies Act of 1967 enabled firms to bring senior managers into partnership earlier and also to accelerate the admission of bright young men.

Was it a large amount of capital you had to bring in?

It looked a large amount when you first thought about it, but as far as I can remember after all these years it was less painful than expected.

Do you think the purpose of the audit has changed over the years?

If it is accepted that the purpose of the audit is to establish whether the accounts prepared by the directors comply with the requirements of the Companies Act then it may be said there is no change, other than these requirements have become more rigorous. If however the purpose of the audit is considered to encompass other benefits arising directly or indirectly from the audit, then there has been considerable change.

Clients now expect the auditors to use their professional judgment in assessing the way the company is run and how it compares with others.

The directors look to the auditors to take an active interest in the company's activities, giving advice before it is asked for as well as when asked for, not just from the auditor but from experts in other disciplines such as taxation and consultancy. Indeed, some firms are now competing with the merchant banks in financial transactions, previously thought to be the preserve of those banks.

Did you qualify client's accounts frequently?

No. I think with the majority of clients you could always resolve the matter. Clients do not want a qualification and usually a clarification of wording or an explanatory note would resolve the matter. Obviously, if this is not possible and no agreement can be reached it seems to me you have to qualify.

You've a lot of experience in auditing banks and Ian Brindle's on record as saying you can't qualify a bank. Do you agree?

You can qualify a bank, of course you can. However, it must be recognised that a qualification could have a disastrous effect upon a bank. In my experience, if the auditor found himself in the situation where he could not avoid a damaging qualification after discussion with the directors and senior banking officials, the regulatory banking authority would be advised. In the case of a bank of substance, it would be unlikely if discussions between the parties did not lead to an acceptable solution.

The suggestion is that if you qualify a bank you're automatically pulling the plug on them?

I do not think that this is necessarily true. It depends on the severity of the qualification. However, it should be recognised that if the bank's financial situation is as weak as the question suggests, a qualification could stop further deposits being taken which would otherwise be lost.

The son of a director of a small private company, DEREK JAMES was born in London in 1930. He did his articles with the eight partner firm, Singleton Fabian, (later part of Binder Hamlyn), with the intention of going into the family business, and qualified in 1954. After National Service, however, he joined Barton, Mayhew, (now part of Ernst & Young) in London in 1956, before quickly moving on to Cooper Brothers, where he became a partner in 1963. He spent some of his career in the USA and Canada, and accordingly also looked after subsidiaries of North American companies in the U.K.; latterly, he was responsible for the firm's offices in the Middle East and the Eastern Mediterranean. He retired in 1988.

What kind of training did Singleton Fabian provide?

It was a fairly basic training. At that time it was a cheap form of labour. We paid a premium to become articled, £500 I think it was, and received it back over a period of five years, starting off with ten shillings a week. I wasn't a very prosperous man in those days. I spent about three months in the liquidation department, but most of the time I was working on audits.

Were you closely supervised during your articles?

The principal to whom I was articled used to see me at least once a month formally and discuss my progress, particularly in my studies. There was a senior clerk who was responsible for the audit when I was very much a junior. Subsequently I assumed the role of senior.

Was there always a set audit programme?

A basic programme, with a strict system of working papers.

Can you remember some of the clients that you audited in those days?

West Ham Greyhound racing track was one of them and a Hatton Garden jeweller, both very interesting. It was a very general practice.

How did your career progress?

I joined Barton, Mayhew in London for a brief time. It was quite a large firm for the period, with some very substantial clients and the full complement of 20 partners; considerably bigger than Singleton Fabian, and a definite step up for me.

What was their style of audit?

There was very little reliance on internal control. It was very much a mechanical audit. There was an audit programme and the steps that were set out in the programme were designed to test the system. There was much greater emphasis on verification of assets and liabilities, and the review of the profit and loss account.

Did you ever get involved in things like interim audits?

It was fairly common at the time. It was the only way of completing the final audit in time. There were also one or two monthly checks for smaller companies who needed reassurance about their bookkeeping.

What prompted your move to Coopers?

I answered a blind advertisement in *The Times*, which turned out to be from Coopers. It was for an assistant to a partner with the potential to become a partner oneself. That was when I settled in the profession and abandoned thoughts of a business career. They had a vast range of clients from Unilever downwards.

Did you specialise within Coopers?

I spent two and a half years in the USA, two years after joining them, and I had an international focus from then on. Often I came home on Saturday morning and left again that Sunday evening.

Did you find a significant difference in the American way of doing things in the early 60s?

Audit procedures were very similar; perhaps slightly more sophisticated than they were in England. The American profession had to develop rather faster because of institutions like the SEC. But then we were an international organisation from 1957[21] onwards. I was in America three years after that, and for the next five or ten years there was considerable international development, by which time we were doing the same things all around the world.

Can I ask you about relationships with client management? Was it ever hostile?

On rare occasions, but generally clients were very supportive of the auditor. They always have been. You had difficulties particularly where a company was not performing as well as it should have been, and did not wish shareholders to have information that would lead them to question their investment. I always questioned management, and had occasional unpleasant experiences as a result. I think that partners take much more interest in the audit than they used to.

Did you ever detect fraud?

Yes, there was more than one occasion when I detected fraud. One was just a straightforward cash fraud. It was quite interesting. The chief accountant ended up in jail.

Did you discover any frauds by management or directors?

Not really, no. Management sometimes tried to conceal information, which is not very far off fraud.

Do you think fraud is more common now than it used to be?

Yes I do. I think that the whole ethos of the business world has changed. There are an awful lot of young men about town who are keen to make as much money as they can in a short time and are not as careful in terms of their behaviour.

How often have you formally qualified an account?

At a guess, between ten and 15 times. Quite often it was due to a shortage of financial resources, and it was open to question whether the company was a going concern.

Were you ever aware of pressure from a client to try and stop you qualifying an account?

Oh yes.

What sort of pressure?

If you do this, the audit will not be yours next year.

And what was your response?

Fine.

What was it that benefited the client most by being audited by Coopers?

The greatest benefit that I ever provided to clients was improving their systems, particularly management control. Going back 20 years ago, I had a client who set up his own business. We introduced a system of management control and he became an extremely wealthy man, and always used to say that it was because of the system that we introduced in the first place. Coopers used to produce a management letter at the end of the audit, saying whether there were any significant weaknesses in control and making recommendations for improvement. This covered management techniques as well as accounting. Coopers were ahead of their time from immediately after the war onwards.

Have you formed an opinion on BCCI, Polly Peck, even Maxwell, where the profession seems to have fallen down?

Probably in all cases it's fraudulent management who were able to pull the wool over the auditor's eyes in some way or other; different ways I'm sure in different cases. But I can't talk about Maxwell because he was a client of the firm. With BCCI, it appeared that certain transactions were concealed by senior management to their benefit.

You wouldn't put it down to negligence on the auditor's part?

No, not really, no. I think there was little an auditor could do, if somebody at the top was determined to cover up what he was doing.

IAIN MUIR was the senior partner of, Moore Stephens, in the 1980s. He was born in London in 1928 but came from Glaswegian commercial stock, his father having come to London as a shipping sale and purchase broker on the Baltic Exchange. He was evacuated to Scotland in 1940 but after two years returned to finish his schooling at the minor public school, Aldenham, in Hertfordshire. After National Service he took articles with Hereward, Scott, Davies, a three-partner firm in London, and qualified in 1954. Although he intended to join his father's firm, a chance meeting at a cocktail party with Hobart Moore, the son of the founder and senior partner of Moore Stephens, led to him joining the firm where he spent the rest of his career. For 15 years he was Hobart's personal assistant and took over himself after Moore retired in 1979. Muir was thus at the heart of the process, which took the firm from relative obscurity with eight partners when he joined to being a multinational organisation with 500 partners when he retired in 1989. On retirement he bought and for ten years ran a farm in Suffolk.

What were Hereward, Scott, Davies like to train with?

They were a very good firm to be articled to because I was exposed to a lot of sole traders. Clients included every kind of shop, doctors, nursing homes, hotels, artists, wholesalers and small manufacturing units, and my grasp of bookkeeping came from having a bundle of vouchers in a paper bag thrown at me. Some of them did not even write up a cash book. Tremendous experience though, and by far the best way to get into accountancy and auditing in my opinion. Unless you understand how records are put together you can not start to audit them. By the end of the first year I was actually preparing accounts to final stages. I became a very good 'accountant.' Nobody could pull the wool over my eyes in later years about bookkeeping.

What was the biggest audit you were involved in?

A public company, Austin Veneer Plywood, shortened to, AVP Industries. They had a lot of furniture making and associated industries in several factories, and in order to get some auditing experience I was involved. I think they finished up owning hotels.

Did you have audit programmes?

We had hand-written programmes and we worked our way through them: a month of purchase invoices, a month of this and a month of that.

That was sampling.

Yes, that was the sampling procedure, absolutely (laughter) . . . very primitive. Most probably a harder look at the legal expenses, or an analysis of it for tax purposes, but pretty primitive.

Did you attend stocktaking in the early 50s?

We did attend stocktaking, yes. I would not have thought the follow-up procedures were terribly worthwhile, but perhaps at that time I was not so involved in the final stages of an audit. I had a big question mark about auditing after I had finished my spell with that firm, but when I moved on to Moore Stephens they were more auditing conscious

In what way was the auditing procedure different at Moore Stephens?

There was more thought given to the planning of the audit, in that we were trying to prove what the balance sheet meant. I look back and think I must have been very naive about what auditing was all about in those days, and in fact it really did not interest me as much as all the other ramifications of financial matters. So most probably I am a poor person to ask about auditing.

How did your work change when you went to Moore Stephens?

It was not long before I became an audit manager. We had a small office in Paris in those days where we looked after the accounts for a lot of Greek ship owners. I think the London business consisted of about 30% shipping, 30% shoes for some reason, and the rest was a good mixed bag. I was always attached to the shipping side and went straight alongside the shipping partner. But the senior partner, Hobart Moore, was keeping an eye on me. After I had been there about nine months, he said,—what are you going to do Iain? I said,—I am going to have two years and then I am going to join my father. He said,—would you stay in the firm? I said I would think about it. So he said,—would you like to become my personal assistant and sit alongside me? By that time I realised he was definitely promising an exciting future. About two years after that, he put an office alongside himself and I sat next to him for the next ten years.

What was your role?

I was in the office between half past eight and nine, and in those days he was living in the country, and used to get in about ten. Then I would stay until seven o'clock at night; I was living in Hadley Wood in those days so you can stick an hour on front and back for travelling. That was just covering him and the hours he chose to work. He was the kind of person who liked to work in the evening, so his day started later. He was a phenomenal worker. In the early days, I would go to his country house at Thornhill in Surrey at the weekends to help entertain clients. I would play tennis, pour the drinks and on a Saturday night organise Scottish country dancing. During this early period many of the overseas offices were established and I organised some of our first international meetings.

Was it a good experience for you working alongside him?

He was very farseeing and had a rapier-like mind. He was quite outstanding. He had a knack of picking up some of your own ideas as well. And the next time he promoted them as his own (laughter). I was not all that keen on that.

How had he started off?

The business was founded in 1906 when Sir Harold Moore linked up with J.R. Stephens and became Moore Stephens. Sir Harold Moore was a very respected man in the City and the hard-core was there when his son Hobart was left with the business after the war, a very nice practice by that time. After the war the shipping side of the business took off in a very big way. There were a lot of Greeks in London and we acted for about 80 families at one time. Hobart enjoyed a fine reputation with the Greek shipping community and he recognised the opportunity they presented for overseas expansion. He never missed an opportunity to open overseas offices or initiate links with overseas accounting firms. Before the war the Greek shipping community had been basically served by a single office in London, but with the great expansion of their shipping interests every family established its own office. Moore Stephens had acted for that original office and by virtue of the Greeks' loyalty to the firm we continued to act for the breakaway firms.

How did your career progress from there?

I left Hobart after I had been alongside him some ten years when one of our senior audit partners on the shipping side was taken ill and overnight somebody had to step into it. I had had enough of sitting alongside Hobart, living in his shadow, and I was keen to do my own thing. I was not directly concerned with audits. I was more concerned with the consultancy side but most of the people working for me were involved on audits. If anything went wrong on an audit I got involved rapidly. However, generally I left that side of our group's activities to our audit partners.

When did Hobart Moore take a back seat?

He retired in 1979, aged 70—somewhat reluctantly. A year or so earlier we had had to substantially re-write our partnership agreement and deal with many major issues including the sensitive issue of Hobart's retirement date. The new agreement was put together by all the senior partners, most of them in their late 50s and contemplating retirement at 60. As a result there was to be a substantial age difference between Hobart and my own age group, and succession was an issue. He had a real problem there, and in the end we overcame it by one of our partners, who was about to retire a year after Hobart, becoming senior partner for a year. It did not make any difference because that senior partner appointed me the managing partner for that year.

So was there a dramatic decline in Hobart's powers?

No, he still had a super brain and was still active with a small group of clients after his retirement, but he was autocratic and retained a role in the International firm. This could have been dangerous and possibly damaging as the London partners had always driven and directed the development of the International firm. If he had lived there could well have been conflicts in that situation.

On reflection one can well understand his reluctance to retire. He had personally led the firm from being a small City firm to a major London partnership and an international organisation with, at the time of his retirement, some 200 offices in 50 countries in the world.

I know he upset a great many people but he was a very, very strong character—necessary to build up such a business.

Was your firm ever in trouble over an audit?

I can think of a couple of occasions when we were criticised, usually when a business was sold. There was a particular case about 1975, when I was still a group senior partner. I attacked my own staff first to find out how strong we were and I was happily pleased that we had done a good job. They had absolutely no grounds against us. The purchasers complained about the balance sheet, they thought we had over-valued stock, a fairly typical sort of case. They had bought the business but since they did not offer enough on the second tranche of shares, our client had the ability to buy the company back which he did, and they suffered a loss as a result. Our client then sold the business again to another company, highly reputed in the food industry, and they opted to change the basis of valuation to the one the previous purchasers had been promoting. They insisted on doing it but instead of writing stocks down, they actually increased the value of stocks, so the case fell apart.

What annoyed me was the investigation lasted two years, from which we recovered no costs. As soon as a claim is made against you, you have to advise your insurers. The claim was logged at Lloyd's, which also irritated me. The insurers appointed solicitors who put us to a tremendous amount of work, reviewing our files and documentation. We spent the most enormous amount of time on our defence. We recovered our lawyers' costs but we did not get a penny. My audit team was thoroughly vindicated but we were massively out of pocket, and apparently we had no right of recovery, which I thought was wrong.

After I became senior partner I was very conscious of the work I thought we should not take on, of what type of work that did not appeal to me as an audit. I had privately earmarked the type of business that I would not mind losing, believing it to be fraught with danger.

In what sense?

Total inability to get to grips with the real problems. Banking in the Far East I would have put into that category.

BCCI and that sort of thing?

I met Gokal in his early days in London and we acted for some of the underlying trading companies in the UK and later in Hong Kong and Australia. At that time the trading companies were very successful and we enjoyed the work at this level, but we then had reservations about the upper structure of the group and the web of inter-company finances.

What else would you steer clear of?

We had a joint audit in the Far East, a major bank, and when you saw their 500 branches scattered through these islands I thought,—who would know what was going on there? It was impossible to know what a local bank manager might be doing. We were going to lose that major audit in the Far East, and it was an occasion when I was not particularly disturbed at the prospect.

What was the ultimate fear?

The ultimate fear was that there would be a massive hole somewhere along the line. Your audit certificate was fairly all embracing at that time, and there would have been a nasty scene anyway. We were always wary of the insurance world too (I thought that our partners having unlimited liability with the firm meant they should steer clear of being Lloyd's underwriters). We did not really go into insurance until we linked up with a firm with expertise in that sector.

What other shipping clients did you have?

I was the first outside accountant to look at the Onassis Organisation in Monte Carlo in 1960 or 61. We had three months and 12 people down there for our audit, and we went through the whole gamut of testing everything they did. There was an air of mistrust in the organisation and Aristotle Onassis was certainly concerned with the integrity of his staff, particularly in relation to the running costs of his vessels. It is an industry where many commissions are involved, apparent and not so apparent, and he clearly believed he was a victim.

Was it a straightforward job?

It was very difficult, but it was interesting. He had about 170 companies and he had never consolidated anything. Nobody else had been in there before and done an audit on that scale. I was the first person to put a set of consolidated accounts together for him, and I think he was amused. We were of course only concerned with his shipping operation and I gained the impression that although he had most probably never seen the figures presented in such a way he was very much aware of the value of his investment in shipping.

He was using many many banks, and on the occasion of one of our scheduled meetings he said,—have you any ideas? And I said,—yes, I think you should employ some banking staff and run a company within the operation to bank for the whole group. Anyway he listened and he said,—well strange you should say that because I was thinking of making an offer for the National Bank of Greece (laughter). My face just drained of any colour and I said to myself,—you are in the wrong league (laughter).

Did he take your advice?

Yes, I like to think so, about three years later he bought a small private bank based in Geneva.

Not a bad client for a medium sized firm?

I think we were the sixteenth when I left in terms of world-wide income. We were behind the Big Eight and if they absorbed anybody else above us then we would move up the list a bit. When Chalmers Impey disappeared, then we went up one. We had a dining group of the senior partners of the firms from about number 10 to twenty, and we used to keep an eye on the Big Eight.

How often did this dining club meet?

Oh, every couple of months or something like that, we used to have dinner and a chat. We thought we ought to keep an eye on what was happening. We were interested in professional indemnity and other things like that; for example, whether we were capable of setting up our own little companies and the amounts we could self-insure. We used to talk about profit shares and how you dealt with it, which you could not talk to anyone else about.

How was your relationship with clients generally?

As a firm we were very good because we had the sort of clientele where people were running their own businesses. We did not have an awful lot of public companies, where the power was not in the hands of one or two people or a family. All the public companies we acted for we were very close to the major shareholders, mainly family firms (although they might be quoted), where they had 30–40% of the shares, and my philosophy was that you stick very close to the family; our partners had an obligation to be close to them.

Did you ever fall out?

Oh, I am sure we fell out at times, I may not have heard about it. I do not think we lost any work. Oh, yes we did—I remember a couple of cases now when I do not think the partner who had the responsibility was close enough to the family and had allowed that to drift. I used to try and intercede but usually it had gone too far.

How does that square with the independence of the auditor?

I was more concerned in keeping the client in those days than with independence. Independence was just beginning to be talked about. We did stay very close to the principal shareholder. Not so that it would influence our audit, but it was important in my view to be close to them. They were our bread and butter. I was a shareholder in my client's companies, with the blessing of the Institute, in my early days. Thank God I was! (laughter) I was a shareholder in a very successful public company. We were not the auditors but we were very close to the chairman and all the directors.

Did you ever qualify these families' accounts?

There was not a lot of scope for that. If a fundamental accounting principle was at stake we would clearly take a stand on it. But the sort of work we were involved in, the valuation of work-in-progress and everything else, to me was fairly cast iron. There were fundamental accounting principles, but in shipping we had an additional set of rules for preparing accounts and auditing as well. What profit you took from what voyages in terms of years and profits, if it was a time charter or a voyage charter, was clearly set down. We had our own set of rules and we were consistently applying them. Inter-company pricing might have been subject to discussion at one time or another, but those were always very carefully looked at to make sure we were seeing it in a proper manner.

Most of the accounts were passed across my desk at one time or another, and the best audit was probably done by me in five minutes when I had the set of accounts in front of me (laughter). I had of course the benefit of having the final financial statements in front of me as well as the presence of a highly competent and experienced audit manager. That was my job. I would always be looking for areas in which there could have been error or room for discussion. But there were few problems, largely due to the nature of our client companies which in the main did not present the complexities of other businesses.

How did you view the auditing and accounting standards that started coming out in the 1970s?

I usually had trouble with them to start with but I learned to live with them. Some of the things auditors began to ask their directors to do I thought we had a bit of a cheek at the time. And sitting on the other side of the fence I still think they had got a bit of a cheek, trying to put some of the problems back to the directors with letters of representation.

Do you think standards have improved matters?

Oh I think so, I think there is more consistency about it. Most of them are very well intentioned. But there are so many notes to a set of accounts today that they most probably destroy the ability to look constructively at a set of accounts quickly. As a result, most people know less about the company than they did years ago when the statement was simpler. When you get 15 pages of notes, how many people actually read them today? I might read the small print but six items in the profit and loss account with ten pages of notes is a bit silly.

One of the last questions I ask people is their view on the recent scandals in the accountancy world. You seem to have an inside track, as you knew Gokal.

As I have mentioned, the underlying companies in the Gokal group were in the main successful but it was the source of the capital that was the problem Like many entrepreneurs the lust for growth and the resulting power is insatiable. He was arrogant and no exception. When toward the end of my career I was in Geneva I called on him to encourage the payment of some outstanding Hong Kong fees—my visit was not appreciated.

Did you have any contact with BCCI?

No, but we feared something was wrong there years ago. I cannot think how he fooled the auditors for so long. I knew how he [Gokal] operated and I could not understand how the whistle had not been blown on him. From almost the day the bank incorporated I think much of the funds that went into BCCI finished up with the Gokal group.

But Abedi was in charge of BCCI?

I am certain there was collusion. I suspect they were teeming and lading,[22] moving monies around to satisfy somebody on this day and somebody else on the next day and so on. Gokal was very brilliant on his feet, on his crocodile shoes I should say (laughter).

Do you think that possibly the auditors got sucked in and just did not want to lose their fees and were turning a blind eye?

I cannot believe that. I just wonder what we would have done in a similar situation with the people we were really close to. There has to come a point when you say,—no, I cannot live with this situation. But they were most probably very reluctant to resign, bale out and say,—we cannot continue. I do not believe that it is ever down to any single person. If it is a committee and they are arguing about a major issue with a client then I cannot think that they would not err on the side of caution. But whether the pressure is so great that they succumb, I do not know. I was never put in that position.

JOHN WHINNEY is a member of one of the most famous families in the history of accounting. His great grandfather, Frederick Whinney, became a partner in the firm which is now Ernst & Young, in 1857[23]*, was a founder member of the ICAEW in 1880, and he and John's grandfather were both Presidents of the Institute. John was born in 1931, educated at Eton, and left at the age of 18 to do two years National Service. He would have gone on to Oxford like his father, but the latter insisted that he had already had two years in the army, and 'you don't want to waste another three or four years.' So he went straight into articles, qualified with Whinney, Smith & Whinney in 1956, and was made a partner in 1959. He was a DTI inspector on the Cornhill Consolidated Group enquiry in 1977,*[24] *and a member of the Institute Council from 1973 to 1987, shortly before he retired.*

Tell us about when you started with Whinney, Smith & Whinney.

Well, I had a fairly varied experience at that time. There was one job I was given, which I was engaged on for about 18 months—a restaurant in the West End. I used to go once a month, and it was more than just auditing, I wrote up the books for them. They wrote up the cash book, but I entered all the figures into the ledger and produced a monthly trading account. And I used to go along monthly to a small firm of civil engineers, and did their PAYE and the payroll records for them. But otherwise it was mostly auditing.

Can you give us a feel of how the office ran when you were there?

There were 12 London partners. The managers then were practically without exception, unqualified; they were qualified by experience rather than by examination, and most of them had been with the firm for donkey's years. Many of them had started off life in the City as messengers running errands, and then eventually been let loose on a bit of auditing. I think there would have been probably about twice as many managers as there were partners, maybe a little more than that, so say about 20–25.

What was a typical audit like when you started? Would there be an audit programme?

Yes, but a typical file of working papers would be a quarter of the size that it is today, or even less than that perhaps. The approach depended on the senior. We started often enough with a bank reconciliation, to get the feel of what sorts of transactions were going through. And then again, depending on the size of the company being audited, there was a lot of tick and bash. We used to get through piles and piles of invoices and, bang! We had a little audit stamp with WS&W and an identifying number on it, so we knew which member of staff had examined the invoice. Often, this was done as a two man job, one thumbing his way through the invoices and bashing the thing so it couldn't be re-presented, and the other one putting a little mark in the book to say he had vouched it. Then probably for a small audit, the articled clerks would do the adding up of the cash book, and do any cross casts that were necessary. For a bigger job, we had a team of about five or six comptometer operators.

Then, you probably had a look at the sales and purchase ledger balances, and you would assess for debts and you would agree the balances on that. Sales ledger balances were usually done on a complete basis, but not on the huge jobs. It was laid down in the audit programme how many months of invoices you checked, but I suppose it was the manager who decided we would do two months or six weeks or whatever. It was probably about the mid-60s that we used to circularise debtors and ask them to agree the amount they owed a company. Then the fixed assets - we would have a look at those, and we might look at the title deeds, and the log books of motor vehicles, and usually make a physical inspection of the plant and machinery.

Would you attend stocktaking?

Yes. As far as I can remember, I think that was always on the audit programme.

And what was the end game of the audit?

I don't remember anything in the way of a post-audit letter, or a management letter in those days, although I suppose that it might well have been done on an informal basis with the partner going along, and talking to the finance director, and saying,—old chap it would be helpful if you did so and so, or you might find it better if you did something a different way, or you've got a weakness in control here and there. I might be wrong about the management letter, but I would imagine they came in in the late 1960s.

What was the general relationship with the client? Was it ever hostile?

I don't think I ever had any hostility, as far as I can remember, but I'm sure there were occasions when there were problems. I can remember at least one or two cases, going quite a long way back, where the client got in touch with the senior partner of our firm and said,—would you mind terribly taking so and so off our audit, we really can't get on with the chap? So we arranged an internal transfer, from one partner to another.

Who was the senior partner when you got your partnership in 1959?

In 1959, there was a lovely individual who was senior partner for just one year, after I joined as partner, called Sidney Mearns. He was a Scotsman, an Aberdonian, and then my uncle Ernest carried on.[25] He would have retired in 1965 or 66, but was persuaded to carry on to carry the merger with Brown, Fleming and Murray[26] through, because the other side would not have liked the senior partner elect to be the senior partner of the merged firm. It was one of the conditions of the merger that Ernest became the senior partner for about three or four years. The next senior partner was Sir William Carrington,[27] he was a great tax expert. He was there for two or three years, I think, and then there was a BF&M chap, Trevor Macdonald.

Who took the initiative in the merger with BF&M?

Whinney's were very much the larger firm, and we probably took the initiative. The huge advantage for us, was that BF&M had two very large audits, BP and Burmah Oil. I think BF&M were a little bit apprehensive that unless they grew considerably larger, and spread their portfolio, they would be in danger of losing either or both of them. Their interest was to be less dependent on one or two enormous clients.

And in 1979, we reorganised our relationship with Ernst & Ernst.[28] In a way, I was disappointed that when we did have one name, it wasn't Whinney, Murray, Ernst & Ernst, rather than Ernst & Whinney, but it was shorter, and alphabetically higher up the list.

What was your main contribution at the Institute?

I was chairman of the Ethics Committee for three or four years, during which time we issued a new guide to professional ethics. It was a slightly thankless task because, by and large, chartered accountants think they know how to behave, and my job was to tell them they were wrong. We tightened things up and we introduced, I think for the first time, a formal prohibition on shareholding in client companies. I was also a Board of Trade inspector on the Cornhill enquiry.

What was the issue over Cornhill?

This fellow was desperately trying to keep his little fringe bank afloat. Then he persuaded an American insurance company to lend him £6,500,000 on the basis of the security of bills of exchange, which they didn't really understand. Eventually, they found out what was behind this bank, absolutely nothing, so they wouldn't lend any more money, and the whole thing collapsed.

Did you have to criticise any accountants?

Yes.

Who were the auditors?

A tiny little man, a single practitioner, and then they moved to Price Waterhouse who, in fact, never signed a audit report and that was one of the reasons why the company was unable to raise long term finance because they couldn't produce any audited accounts. PW did in fact sign off the audit report for one company called CIB, which they rather regretted and which they did on the basis of an assurance they were given which turned out to have no substance.

What were your impressions as a DTI inspector?

I enjoyed that job, it was a fascinating story. It took 3½ years for us to report and 3½ years for the Department of Trade to publish it. My co-inspector was a lovely fellow called David Calcutt, who later wrote the Calcutt Report.[29]

What problems did you have?

Well it seems to be very unjust. By law you are bound to answer what the inspectors ask you, and you may be incriminating yourself in the process, which was very unsatisfactory.

Were you aware of that?

Yes, we were indeed, and David Calcutt was absolutely marvellous in the way he would try and put people at their ease and say,—look this isn't a court of law, albeit we are after the truth.

Audit failures have been in the news over the last ten years; do you have any views on that?

Well yes, I don't know where to start really. I think the problem is what the auditors are doing is adrift and it is probably our fault that it is adrift. I think the auditors themselves are skimping the work, I don't think that they think they are, but they are skimping. They don't go into depth in testing where perhaps they should do. But the most newsworthy of these collapses have been failures not at the testing level, but at the partner level. They say,—I am prepared to accept that black is black, without seeing the evidence.

Why do you think partners accept that?

I think it is because they want to keep sweet with their clients. Maybe because they want to keep sweet with their own senior partners too. I don't know, but a lot of the failures have been at top level.

Would you have, in your time, accepted that there were aspects of a company's business that you weren't allowed to look at?

Yes, I think we did. One of the big ones we were involved in jointly with Price Waterhouse was BCCI, which I was not involved in at all. Right at the end, when the audit had to be signed off in 1986, we said,—look, if it is a question of us carrying on as joint auditors next year, we must be able to see more of the group than we are seeing at the moment. There was negotiation between the client and us and in the end the client said,—I'm sorry but we are not happy with double auditing, with Price Waterhouse seeing it and you seeing it as well. In the end we said,—all right, enough is enough, and we won't seek re-election.

Weren't Ernst & Young after the whole audit?

Well yes, I suppose it would appear that way. But from what I heard inside the firm it was just that we were not seeing enough of the group. We were being asked to take responsibility for our audit report covering the whole thing, when we were only seeing less than half. So we had to take the other half on trust.

Notes

1. The London Capital Group was set up in 1972 by ex-Labour government minister, John Stonehouse, and collapsed in 1974, leading to Stonehouse's infamous bogus suicide, and later imprisonment. Sir Charles helped set up the bank which was fraudulent from its first dealings, the facts being documented in the Department of Trade report co-written by the leading chartered accountant, Ian Hay Davison (Department of Trade, 1977).
2. Impersonal ledger is another name for the general or nominal ledger (Parker, 1992: 150).
3. 20p or 20%.
4. British Printing Corporation, the printing and paper making company taken over by Maxwell in 1980, which became the British Printing and Communications Corporation (BICC) in 1982 (Greenslade, 1992: 47 and 82).
5. Excess Profits Tax was levied at 100% on companies from 1940–47 (Jeremy, 1998: 119).
6. Referring to the 125th anniversary issue of the Coopers & Lybrand house journal (*C&L Journal*, No. 31, June 1979).
7. In 1945, at the first partners meeting after the war, Pears had prepared a memorandum setting out the way in which he thought the firm should go: the desirability of writing an audit manual, the training of staff and the organisation and expansion of the practice (*C&L Journal*, No. 31, June 1979: 11). Benson described how he and Pears 'wanted to expand at home and overseas, to increase the clientele, and to build an international organisation which would hold its own with other international firms then in existence . . . We worked together on this task for the next twenty-five years' (Benson, 1989: 44).
8. Benson states in his autobiography that he wrote the manual based on his experience with a similar document in the ordnance factories during the war (Benson, 1989: 44).
9. In 1966 (Cooper, 1966).
10. John Perfect qualified in 1934; James Francis Shearer, CBE, in 1938, (ICAEW, *List of Members*, 1950).
11. The Groundnut Scheme was a British government plan, started in 1947, to grow groundnuts (to cover an expected shortage of oil) in East Africa. The nuts, however, could not be harvested and had to be abandoned. Coopers were appointed as the auditors, and Henry Benson's audit qualified the accounts on the grounds that proper books were not being kept (Benson, 1989: 122–124).
12. The British Printing Corporation was formed in 1964 with the merger of Purnell, headed by Wilfred Harvey, and Hazell Sun. Harvey was forced out in 1965 and the BPCC was eventually taken over by Robert Maxwell in 1980 (*Stock Exchange Official Yearbook*, various years; see also interview with Sir Charles Hardie in this chapter).
13. This incident is related in Benson's autobiography. He and Pears stood firm against the threat of being sacked as auditors, and they won the day by circulating a letter stating their case to all the shareholders over the heads of the chairman and the board (Benson, 1989: 49–50).
14. Quoted from Pears' 1945 memorandum (*C&L Journal*, No. 31, June 1979: 11)

15. Sir William Slimmings, born in 1913, was a leading Scots CA and a senior partner with Thomson McLintock, who while President of the Scottish Institute in 1969–70 made an unsuccessful attempt to amalgamate with the ICAEW. He died in 1995 (*The Times*, 16 February 1995).

16. Ian Hay Davison was chairman of the ASC from 1982–84 (*WW*).

17. The City Equitable Insurance Company collapsed in 1922, after which its head, Gerard Lee Bevan, was sent to prison for seven years for issuing a false balance sheet, while the auditors were found negligent for attaching a clean opinion (Robb, 1992: 143; *The Accountant*, 8 March 1924).

18. The 1994 report on The Bestwood plc, an investment and construction group, after the DTI inspectors had been called in in 1989, was critical of chartered accountants working for the company and the auditors, BDO Binder Hamlyn. (*Accountancy Age*, 3 February 1994).

19. Schedule E covered taxes on salaries as opposed to profits (Lewis, 1977: 56).

20. Qualified in 1930 and ran the two partner City firm, Wilson, Bigg, he took over the updating of a number of Spicer & Pegler textbooks (ICAEW, *List of Members*, 1950; Bigg, 1969 and 1971).

21. The year Cooper Bros first linked with Lybrand, Ross Bros. & Montgomery of America; they went on to merge and to trade world-wide as Coopers & Lybrand in 1973 (Matthews, *et al*, 1998: 55).

22. The misappropriation of cash remittances by using amounts from later remittances to fill the gap (Parker, 1992: 281).

23. Jones, 1986: 766.

24. Cornhill Consolidated Group was another secondary bank to crash in 1974, and although completed in 1977 the Department of Trade report only came out in 1980 (Department of Trade, 1980). The JDS admonished a chartered accountant director and ordered him to pay £2,000 costs in 1981. The auditor was censured and ordered to pay £4,000 costs (JDS, *Annual Report*, 1981: n.p.).

25. Ernest Whinney was the grandson of the founder of the firm and brother of John's father, Douglas (Jones, 1981: 37)

26. In 1965 (Matthews, *et al*, 1998: 298).

27. Sir William Carrington, who had qualified in 1926, was President of the ICAEW in 1955–6, and was knighted in 1959 (Jones, 1981: 210).

28. In 1979, Whinney Murray, Turquands Barton Mayhew and Ernst & Ernst, the American firm with whom Whinney Murray had had links since 1918, merged to form Ernst & Whinney (Matthews, *et al*, 1998: 55).

29. There were two Calcutt Reports: one for the Home Office on privacy (1990) and another on the self-regulation of the press (1992).

Chapter 8

The Great and the Good

Sir JOHN GRENSIDE was born in 1921, the son of a 'private family firm type of solicitor' with a practice in Westminster, and he was typical of most chartered accountants in this study in that although he went to preparatory school in Eastbourne and then on to public school at Rugby, he did not go to university and instead served his articles in a small to medium sized London based accountancy firm, Smallfield, Lindsay, Fynn (later Smallfield, Fitzhugh, Tillett) in 1939. But the war, during which he served as a captain in the Royal Artillery, interrupted his training. He returned to his firm in 1946 and qualified in 1948. He moved to Peat, Marwick, Mitchell that year and stayed there till he retired in 1986. He became a partner in 1960, a general partner and one of the top management group in 1966, finally succeeding Ronald Leach on his retirement as senior partner in 1977. The governance of the ICAEW was a long-standing commitment of Sir John's and he sat on Council from 1966 to 1983, and was President in 1975. Besides much committee work, he laid the foundations of, and succeeded Henry Benson as chairman of the Joint Disciplinary Scheme in 1979, and was UK representative on the International Accounting Standards Committee,[1] 1976–80. He became known as the UK accountancy profession's "Mr. Europe" and towards the end of his career, he became chairman of Peat Marwick International, 1980–8. On retirement, like Leach before him, he took up a number of non-executive directorships, at Allied-Lyons (a long-standing client of Peats) until 1993 and the Japanese Nomura Bank International, until 1996.

What would be a typical audit in the early days?

They were unsophisticated; you were largely following routine audit programmes which were written up and revised. It frightens you now to think what you did do, because it was very elementary by modern standards. They had a very simple Swedish calculator and much of the additions had to be done looking at the wretched thing. The audits were largely vouching. One extraordinary thing was that in those days the clients thought it a privilege to take you round their factory. Of course, today it's the first thing you do, but then they took you round at the end of the audit instead of the beginning. So it really was a very elementary procedure, and yet things didn't go wrong as much as they do today, which is quite extraordinary.

What controlled the quality of the audit in those days?

Only the quality and expertise of the firm's own system. The Institute had no kind of review or quality control at all. There was no such thing as inter-firm review which most people have now.

What would you say was the purpose of the audit then?

To give an opinion on the accounts, and it was really almost limited to that. The audit wasn't really designed to be as helpful to the client as are modern audits. If there were management letters written, and I can't quite remember when they started, they were very straightforward. Largely pointing out problems which had occurred during the audit, rather than reviews of the system and helpful suggestions as to how to run the company better.

And what would you say was the relationship with management? Was it ever hostile?

No, it wasn't hostile. Perhaps it wasn't as hostile as it should have been. Mind you, certainly at the lower levels, the people actually doing the audit weren't well treated and they weren't well respected. They were stuck in a nasty little room and they were regarded as a bloody nuisance. It was a bit better I think at the top level.

Did you detect fraud in the early days?

Yes. But it was usually more the petty type of fraud. The more major type of management fraud wasn't anything like as prevalent as it is today. I believe that business morality went into serious decline about 1970 or thereabouts. Also I think that one of the concomitants, and an undesirable one, of competition was that it led people to go from understatement to overstatement in the preparation of accounts. Understatement was usually driven by a wish to avoid paying tax, and overstatement came in with all the incentive schemes, either because managers became significant shareholders and wanted to drive up the share price, or because they had remuneration packages which depended on an incentive element.

Why did you join Peats?

To go to a larger firm. I thought the opportunities were better, the training was going to be better, and the experience was going to be better, and I had no real wish to become a partner in a medium-sized firm.

How did you get on in Peats? What made you successful?

First of all by doing work which impressed people. It really depended on the recommendations of the partners you were working for. There was a bit of luck in it because if you worked for partners who mattered, it was better than working for ones who didn't. If you got work which was rather high profile that was also helpful.

How was Peats organised when you joined them? How many partners did it have?

In those days, we were inhibited by the 20-partner rule, so the number of partners in London was about 18.[2] We always kept a little bit spare out of the maximum. But we couldn't operate with as few as 20, it was impossible. So we had to go to all sorts of lengths in order to get round it. There were a number of separate partnerships around the country, with a certain amount of inter-locking going on. We did very little joining up with people. There was a little bit in the provinces, but never in London.[3] We went a bit backwards and forwards on what size any particular office ought to be, and whether it was worth having one in a place like Exeter or somewhere. Peats never merged with what you might call a major firm until Thomson McLintock.[4] We mostly merged with significant local firms. The sort of people I was with before.

We had [in the London office] departments with managers running about 25 to 30 people, equivalent to a small firm really. In those days they were all general departments doing work of all sorts. It was very unsatisfactory. The departments didn't work for all the partners. Certain partners favoured departments which either they had been in themselves or where they thought they had good managers. Another factor was how busy the department was—whether it could take on any more work. If not, a partner had to find a different department which could take the work.

When did that change?

In the late 60s. We started having specialised departments for doing insolvency work in particular, specialised tax work as opposed to routine tax work. We also started having departments which specialised in banks, or insurance companies; one kind of industry or another. That had a big advantage from the client's point of view, except that you did start running into a certain amount of conflict. Some clients didn't like similar businesses to their own being looked after by the same people. And there was a bit of trouble with the staff because it meant that people's experience was a bit limited as opposed to being more general. But it had a lot of advantages; people became more expert in understanding particular businesses. The whole thing changed from the original days when somebody somehow wrote out an audit programme without really understanding the business. Now, in later years you don't begin until you understand the business.

How were policy decisions made at Peats when you first joined?

They were made by relatively few partners. A lot were made by the managing partner and then they were made by a group of partners who would meet once a month. Then they started to have technical partners who started to devise more sophisticated approaches to the work.

What were the Peat family themselves like to work for?

It was rather difficult because the Peats were charming people and they were quite good business developers but they weren't technicians.[5] So even in those days one of the other partners took most of the technical type of decisions. They [the Peats] were qualified, of course, but they didn't really do very much hands-on work.

Did Leach change things when he took over in the 1960s?

The real change from what you might call a rather informal, private, family business, into a highly sophisticated, multi-national, modern type operation, took place from about the mid-60s onwards. But even a bit before that a lot of research was carried out into modern techniques of auditing. Audit programmes became much more sophisticated, audit manuals and sampling started to come in, a much more careful approach to picking what you are going to do, not just taking one month. We had a number of pretty bright young people at that time. They wrote these manuals and devised a lot of the procedures. People like Graham Corbett;[6] young partners brought up on more modern ways.

There was also a much greater understanding of the business [being audited]; the development of quite long and quite detailed management letters pointing out the weaknesses of the business, areas where they could improve. There was a far greater relationship with the clients themselves. We got to a point where partners used to go to the client and just talked to them. With no audit going on, they would keep contact with these people to find out what they were doing and try and help them. They did far more tax work. Set up things like tax consultancy committees to review the budget, to review the tax planning of the company. They got involved in doing acquisitions for companies—although they have always done prospectuses and flotations.

Did this closer relationship with the client cause problems of independence?

You had to draw a slightly thin, difficult line between the independence of the auditor and participation in the company's activities. There were one or two clients, even in the old days, Reeds, the paper people, for example, who wouldn't have the same people do their consultancy work as do their audit. But they were relatively rare. Most people wouldn't worry. One of our biggest clients in those days, which Sir Ronald looked after, were the Rank Organisation. I suppose by modern standards we did over step the mark there, because he did an enormous amount as a consultant to them which was very close. But we never thought there was too much conflict of interest. I suppose because perhaps in a way we were arrogant enough to think we could act independently.

We all took the view that we should change significantly from just doing an audit to really trying to help the company to become a better company. And a lot of that, of course, involved reviewing their procedures and so on. The internal audits began in companies in the 1950s, but they became more common in bigger companies in the 1960s and 70s and then you had to get them built into the audit itself. How much will the local people [the company's own staff] do and how much does the auditor do? And again, the old boy network with the chairman disappeared very largely and it became a question of contact with the board as a whole. In particular the finance director took on a bigger role.

What about the quality of the audit? Do you see any trend in that?

One of the problems is that the public don't understand an audit really; they expect too much. But the quality of an audit today is infinitely higher than it ever was before. On the other hand the sophistication of management fraud is rather higher too. It becomes extremely difficult if management is in fact dishonest, and if they don't tell you the truth. It's high time that there were some real prosecutions against management for misleading auditors. It is interesting to see that Coopers are going to go for the Barings executives.[7]

When did Peats start targeting clients?

They always tried to target, but the change of auditor by a big company was relatively rare in those days. They might complain and have the partner changed, but they never put it out to tender.

When did that come in? I seem to remember that Peats acquired British Aerospace.[8]

Yes, I did British Aerospace. That was one of the fairly early ones put out to tender; the Trustee Savings Bank was a bit later. You first of all prepared a paper or a booklet showing the firm, how it was organised, how we would undertake that particular audit and so on. It would be quite a large report and very expensive. And then as a rule you would have an oral presentation with slides and questions from the board. It was a troublesome thing; you wasted a lot of time and money if you didn't get the thing; and you aren't going to get them all. They normally had anything up to four or five to start off with and only one firm was going to get it.

At one time companies thought it was bad publicity to change the auditor. Then it became common practice for major companies to put their audit out to tender. It started off where you had effectively a new company; maybe the result of a merger or de-nationalisation. Then it developed from that to other companies. A lot arose because finance directors came from major audit firms and said,—These people are charging us too much, or they are not doing it properly. Finance directors believed that they were going to gain from a change. Not just from a monetary point of view, although nearly every tender resulted in a saving to them, but from the fact that a fresh look would be a good thing. In order to stop that [auditor switching], it became an accepted thing that you didn't keep the same partner on an audit for more than a certain length of time, because they became too familiar, either with the procedures or with the [client's] staff.

What about the issue of litigation and limited liability?

This is the major problem facing the profession today because the numbers involved are so high and there is no way you can get insurance to cover it. I spent a lot of time on this with the Board of Trade when I was President and before, and we couldn't devise a method acceptable to them for the laundry list type of limitation. I think most of us would have been prepared to trade the limitation against joint and several liability, which is really at the bottom of this problem.[9] And you are not far off the stage, in fact to some degree it is already happening, that people are refusing to become partners [in accounting firms] because they say the risk isn't worthwhile. They probably go off and work in industry. So you are facing a very dangerous situation here.

How did your involvement with the ICAEW begin?

I first got involved with the Institute in the late 60s. What happened was, Ronald Leach was then a fairly high person on the Council, and he asked me if I would go on to one or two of the Institute's committees. Then I became Vice President in 1972 and President in 1975.

And then there was your disciplinary work?

Oh yes, that was a nightmare. There were a great deal of problems at that time, because there were threats to take away self-regulation, which might have been a good thing, but they [the Institute] didn't like it. And so I was asked to try and devise some method of improving the disciplinary procedures, and we set up this thing called the Joint Disciplinary Scheme with the other UK bodies, which was to look into major matters of complaint. We didn't deal with small things but only where people needed to be dealt with, and where a high profile had to be shown that something was being done. I put together the original basis of that; Henry Benson became the first chairman, and then later on I became chairman. It worked reasonably well to begin with, but there were objections to it and they have changed the nature of it now, probably rightly. But it was difficult to get accountants to sit on it in the beginning. Also these enquiries were not easy. It was originally thought it would all be quite cosy, really. People would co-operate and it could proceed in that kind of manner. But, of course, some of the major firms didn't like it very much when they were being criticised, and started to get very legalistic. The people concerned were often advised by their lawyers to be very uncooperative. We didn't really have quite enough legal backing; we weren't like a DTI inquiry. They [JDS inquires] are terribly expensive too. Some of these things cost hundreds of thousands of pounds, and at the end of the day there was some inadequate penalty imposed, although they became tougher later on. I think it was recognised that we were doing our best, and that this was a reasonably pragmatic and much more severe approach to the thing than had ever existed before. The ordinary Institute disciplinary committee wasn't big enough and was largely dealing with people who didn't pay their subscription or answer letters and that kind of thing.

The cause celebre in the 1970s was London and County wasn't it? But that was never investigated?

The Joint Disciplinary committee wasn't the initiator. Somebody had to complain to the Institute, and then if the Institute thought it was appropriate it would refer the thing. It was rather like referring it to the Monopolies Commission. With London and County, people didn't complain.

Was it a bit disappointing for you, having set up the Joint Disciplinary Scheme, for it to all blow up in the late 80s and the early 90s, with the Maxwells and the other scandals? Would you have hoped the Joint Disciplinary Scheme would have prevented that?

It could never do that. No, we were disappointed they became so complicated these inquiries. I think one of the criticisms was, too, that the committee was acting as inquirer, judge and jury all at the same time. But the problem was to get people who knew enough to do the job. I think now they have got some tame QC working for it. I think if we had approached it by doing that it might have been better.[10] But no, it did develop to a stage when costs really became enormous in relation to what we were getting at the end of the day. On the other hand whatever way you do it, this [Maxwell, etc] was probably going occur.

To what do you ascribe the major problems that have gone on recently—obviously there was Ferranti?[11]

Well, Ferranti, that was after I'd left, but I think that was another classic occasion where they were very badly misled, and they were given forged things. Also when you are on a defence contract the rules don't permit you to inquire into these things too much. If you are given assurances by the Minister of Defence or someone it is very difficult to query.

But there were other problems weren't there with International Signals and Control? He [Guerin] was moving money around in a rather suspect fashion. From the outside it seems rather strange that auditors don't pick this up. Why don't they?

It depends how well they are disguised, and whether the confirmations that are obtained appear to be all right or not. These things are much easier with hindsight than they are at the time.

To what extent do you have to take the uncorroborated word of management?

You don't, very much. Although with some, like Ferranti, you may have to take, or you may feel able to take, perhaps wrongly, the uncorroborated word of people like heads of government. Normally you get confirmations from people, but sometimes these are false.

But if I can run through one or two of the options. Is it usually incompetence, or are you overworked or are auditors browbeaten by strong personalities, as in the Maxwell case?

Yes, that certainly happened with Maxwell. But it wasn't just auditors who were browbeaten by Maxwell. Some were eminent City bankers and lawyers; everybody was browbeaten by Maxwell. The City as a whole made misjudgments.

But is there collusion on occasion? Do auditors get sucked in and. . .?

I don't think there has ever been a case of collusion with the auditors, but management fraud is very difficult to detect if there is major collusion amongst management themselves. They can give confirmations, and arrange for things to be done, which is not easy to detect. Many of these things look like incompetence and I suppose at the highest clinical examination they are. But I always say it's like airlines. It doesn't matter how carefully you run these things, from time to time things will go wrong, and you have to accept that.

You've said that you don't think anything can be done about these major problems. But have Peats or other firms taken active steps within their firms to try to minimise the risk in the sense of actually improving the quality of the audit?

They are doing that all the time, but if you devised the audit to be so detailed, to really improve the likelihood of it not happening, the thing would be economically impossible. And as I said, it's rather like the airlines. The airlines take all the steps they can, both mechanically and in the quality of their pilots, but every now and again something goes wrong and you have a crash. You are simply never going to stop that, no matter what you do.

Sir DOUGLAS MORPETH's was another of the most illustrious careers in chartered accountancy in recent times. He was born in Perth, Scotland, in 1924, the son of a pharmaceutical chemist who worked for Boots but who later started his own business. Douglas went to the prestigious, George Watson's College, in Edinburgh, and then served in the Royal Artillery in the Second World War. Demobbed in 1947, he took a two-year Bachelor of Commerce degree at Edinburgh University, then came to London to take articles with the small City firm of Brown, Batts and Ashurst. On qualifying in 1951 he took a job with George A. Touche, where the family of the Scottish founder still held sway. Specialising in taxation Douglas rose rapidly, was made a partner in 1958, and became senior partner in the late 1970s. Prompted by George Touche, he was appointed to the Council of the Institute in 1964, and played a prominent role in its affairs for the next 20 years. He was President in 1972–1973, and later led the protracted attempts to wrestle with inflation accounting. He was knighted in 1981, and retired in 1985 to take up several directorships.

What made you consider a career in accountancy?

My degree was Bachelor of Commerce, but I got Honours in Accounting and one other subject, which helped persuade me that maybe I ought to become a chartered accountant.

So what steps did you take in that direction?

Well, I wrote to the Scottish Institute and the English Institute and said,—who will give me two-year articles? At that time there was a possibility of getting a reduction from three to two years if you had a degree, because of war service. The Scottish Institute didn't answer, but the English Institute said,—yes. So I came down to London, with Brown, Batts and Ashurst. I do not know if it still exists or not.

What sort of a firm was it?

They had four partners. It was a very small partnership and I did quite a lot of shoe box stuff.

Did they have any big clients?

They had what later became the TSB, but not the whole of it. There was also another audit they had of a company which manufactured some awful stuff which took the place of French letters, as it were. It was a tablet which a girl put in a certain place—they gave me some for my honeymoon!

What happened when you qualified in 1951?

Because I thought I'd failed the tax paper in the Final, I said,—I must get more experience in tax. So I wrote to four firms and said,—I've sat the Final and I am not sure I passed the tax paper, could I have some experience in your tax department? And George A. Touche & Co. welcomed me with open arms and said,—providing you promise to stay in the tax department for 18 months you can come; which I did. Of course, I hadn't failed the tax paper.

What sort of firm was Touche in 1952? How was it set up?

They had a tax department and an audit department. We had a staff of just over 50 when I joined. Two or three years after I joined they set up their management consultancy department. It had quite a large secretarial department, which looked after four or five investment trusts, which was later hived off, and became Touche Remnant. That was quite a substantial part of the business. In fact, the firm had been set up largely to look after investment trusts. George Touche, son of the founder, was still largely on that side.[12] Then we had one or two quite big audits, like GEC, Rolls Royce and a number of small ones. They only had the one office—in London. But it had an association with a firm called George A. Touche in Canada, which had been set up by the founder of the UK firm and also one called, Touche Niven & Co., in the States. So we had an embryo international firm even then.

So what did you do then when you started with them?

I started in the tax department, which had about three or four people, including one very senior manager, who would have been a partner had he not been an incorporated accountant. The partners were Scottish.

That is why they took you on was it?

It was one of the reasons.

Who were the partners?

There were only three partners in the UK firm, uncle and nephew, George Touche and Anthony Touche, now Sir Anthony, and Robin Adams, who basically ran the firm; what one might call the managing partner today. And they were also partners in the Canadian and the American firms. They made me a partner in 1958.

How did you gain clients in those days?

I do not remember having to make any concentrated effort to get new clients. The Touches knew a lot of people from their City connections, in investment trusts all over the UK, in industry, and they brought in the business. And we got work from the Canadian and American firms. If they had clients that worked over here, we would generally speaking get them.

What sort of tax work were you doing?

It was a mixture of individuals, smaller clients and one or two large ones. I did not do the whole of the GEC tax, but I was involved in it with the partner in charge.

Touche were the GEC auditors and you did the tax, what was the relationship between the two?

The tax department had to oversee the setting of the provision for tax in the accounts and they worked with the audit department on that. Sometimes, with companies like GEC and Rolls Royce, we'd spend days at it. Then we had to agree the tax liabilities with the Inland Revenue.

There were discussions with Coopers in 1957 about a merger which broke down, how did the firm go on from there?

The Touche partners said,—Coopers seem to be doing quite well. They are bigger than us, so we must start to be more aggressive in building up our practice. But from that point on, when we took on new partners, we had this expression—he's got to be hungry. We felt vulnerable because the GEC account was too big a proportion of our total fees. It was about 30%, far too high. We looked around for a firm to merge with and we ended up merging with a London firm, Kemp, Chatteris, in 1963. At the time we had 12 partners, I was partner number eight, and they also had 12 partners. They had some very good clients. They had banks, insurance companies and hotel groups. So we became a 24 partner firm, and our fees doubled from £200,00 to £400,00, which is peanuts today.

How did Touche develop in the 60s? What were the policy issues arising at that time?

We were thinking of expanding in the UK by merger. I think we found two firms in Scotland, one in Manchester, one in Birmingham. These were the first four. We were also thinking about getting much closer together with the Canadian and American firms to become an international firm. We then started thinking,—we need to have a joint name. So instead of George A. Touche, we became Touche, Niven, Bailey & Smart [in 1960]. Then Bailey and Smart retired or died, and so it became Touche Ross and Company [in 1969].[13] The rest of the 60s, and 70s was spent developing and coordinating the international firm to try and get good audit procedures and service procedures throughout the various countries.

You were still the GEC auditors when there was the big kerfuffle with AEI?

In the early days it wasn't doing awfully well, the management of the company weren't very good, and George Touche decided that he ought to try and bring in some outside management. So he found Arnold Weinstock, whose father-in-law ran an electrical firm, and by a reverse take-over Weinstock became the managing director and ran the company.[14] We were auditors when the kerfuffle happened about the stock.

But that is quite an extraordinary story. You are saying that Touche, as simply the auditor, took the initiative to change the management of the company?

Well they didn't do it without management support. But George Touche happened to be the motivator if you like or the means by which it was done.

How did your involvement with the Institute come about?

One day at a partners meeting, George Touche said,—I am going to retire from the Council. I can't do it any longer, I'm too busy, but I think our firm should have somebody on the Council, and so somebody has to get on the committee of the London District Society and then work his way up from there. And I drew the short straw. I was put on the Council in 1964.

To what extent did your work on Council detract from your work for Touche? How did you find a balance between the two?

It was quite difficult, because in 1965 I found myself chairman of the Parliamentary and Law Committee, which was quite an important committee and could have taken up any amount of time I wanted. It did detract from my work, so one had problems at times. I had to justify my existence on the Council to the other partners.

What were the main issues at that time for the Parliamentary and Law Committee?

It was Government legislation, tax legislation, all that sort of stuff. Company law had to be scrutinised in draft, and comments put to the appropriate government department. That was a fairly busy committee. When Roy Jenkins was the Chancellor of the Exchequer, he brought in all sorts of new taxes, including SET,[15] VAT,[16] all run by different government departments, all with different kinds of legislation, none of which fitted together. So we started a campaign for the simplification and co-ordination of the tax system, which was quite successful because Chancellor Jenkins set up a tax committee to be chaired by the chairman of the Inland Revenue to discuss tax, and I was on that for 15 years.

Tell us something about the personalities at the top of the Institute at that time. What was your opinion of Leach, for example?

I admired him, I thought he was very good. He was very nice. He could be as ruthless as Henry Benson but you wouldn't notice it because he would be smiling all the time. He would get what he wanted but you would want to give it to him. Henry was just ruthless. When we set up the International Accounting Standards Committee, there was the question as to who would be the chairman, and I thought,—you, Morpeth, could actually choose this for yourself. But I decided I couldn't do it because I had far too much on, and I had to go back and do some work for the firm. So I asked Henry to do it. He has taken the credit for setting it up, but he didn't actually do it all.[17] He was obviously involved in it, but it was through my stimulation.

When did you become chairman of the English Accounting Standards Committee?

I never became chairman of the UK Standards; I was vice chairman or deputy chairman. The story relating to that was, Eddie Stamp, a Canadian, was an outspoken thorn in the flesh in the accounting profession, but a good thorn, if you know what I mean. He wrote an article when Ronnie Leach was President, saying that according to his calculation there were a million ways in which he could prepare a balance sheet on a true and fair basis, which is probably fairly accurate, but it certainly set the cat amongst the pigeons. Ronnie Leach decided to set up a progress chasing committee, which would chase the Technical Committee and oversee it, and make sure it brought out better Recommendations. I ended up chairing it. Michael Renshall,[18] who later became a partner in Peats (he is retired now), and I between us steered that committee. We knew that the press would be looking at us closely, and we were going to be in the hot seat, when we were only responsible, in theory, for progress chasing the Technical Committee. So we ended up by getting the committee set up as the Accounting Standards Committee.[19] So that is how it started. Ronnie Leach became chairman.

Looking back on it now, do you think the Standards have been a force for good?

Well, they were obviously a force for good, but very difficult to implement because they had no force of law. So firms with major clients who said,—we are not going to apply this standard, would not be forced to do it. There was also an inadequate reconciliation of what was true and fair and what was a standard. The standards were supposed to define what was true and fair, but then an auditor was allowed to say that the standard wasn't applied, because what was applied was true and fair. In other words, there was almost a dichotomy between true and fair and what the standard was. I never got anywhere with my idea, which was that if somebody did not apply the standard then they should say what the effect would have been had they done so. But that didn't get off the ground, so I do not think standards have really grasped that ultimate nettle.

What about your work on inflation accounting?

The first solution which we came up with, which was rejected by the Treasury, was probably the simplest to deal with, and we should have stopped there. Current purchasing power[20] was much simpler to produce, but could have been more easily misunderstood by the reader, which is why the Treasury did not like it. What we were doing was turning pounds into inflation adjusted pounds, which people called phoney pounds, and the Treasury didn't like that. With current cost accounting the problem was that there were so many ways in which business deals with transactions, and there were obviously extremely difficult circumstances that had to be dealt with by the rules of current cost accounting. You could not think of them all at that time, could you? We ended up with a set of rules which could be understood. If they were only applied to the larger companies, which is what we did, (maybe we did not apply the size criteria in the right place, but never mind) then I think everybody would have understood the accounts and the effect of inflation.

I remember Margaret Thatcher saying to me,—you're producing current cost accounting but I am going to get rid of inflation. So I said,—frankly, I would rather have no inflation than current cost accounting. And that is what happened. There was a delay in bringing in the standard because two accountants set up a campaign within the Institute to try and stop it. When the standard finally came out inflation was beginning to fall, it dropped away very quickly and so there was much less need for a standard.

Finally, do you think there are too many commercial pressures on the auditor now, as compared to when you started your career?

I am really glad I have retired from it now. It is not the same profession I used to know. The pressures and the strain on the partners to perform are immense. Most of the large firms in the last ten years have got rid of over 100 partners, if not more. So what is a partnership now? Once, if you were asked to be a partner in a firm you could say,—as long as I work hard and do my bit for the firm, this is my career. But it no longer is, necessarily.

RICHARD WILKES is another past Institute President. Born in 1928, he came from a background of old, established, family-run manufacturing businesses in Leicester, and went to the local public school at Repton. He then took articles with a leading Leicester firm, Bolton Bullivant, qualified in 1951, and within two years was taken into partnership. In 1967, Richard was senior partner of Bolton Bullivant and president of the Institute's local District Society which brought him into contact with Ted Parker, the then national President and senior partner of Price Waterhouse. This in turn led to a merger of the two firms, and to Richard heading the Leicester office of PW. Almost immediately he became the District Society's representative on the national Council, where he was very active. He was chairman of the Auditing Practices Committee[21] *in the late 1970s, and national President, 1980–81. He moved to London and became PW's Director of Communications and Professional Relations; and in 1977 he was involved as the UK's representative on the International Auditing Practices Committee and later on the Council of the International Federation of Accountants, of which body he was President, 1987–90. He retired in 1990.*

How did you find a partnership to do your articles with?

It was through the firm of solicitors that looked after my father's affairs. He happened to mention to the senior partner one day that I was wondering whether to become an accountant or not. This was while I was still at Repton. So this man, Cecil Frost, said,—well, I know just the firm you should go to. It was called Bolton Bullivant and I was asked to go and see a man called Denis Lea, who was then the number two partner in the firm (the senior partner was a man called John Bullivant). He interviewed me and I was signed up for articles immediately I left school. So I technically started my articles before I went into the army. I did two weeks in the office and then went off into the army. They were a local Leicester firm, well founded, with a good reputation, serving family owned businesses.

What did they put you to do when you first went there?

Add up columns of figures, and according to one's aptitude there was the opportunity to get on rapidly. I was given as an assistant to a man called George Grange, an unqualified accountant who had worked in the practice for over 15 years. He was a good tutor, a good mentor. But he was a technician and didn't recognise the wider issues. Anyway you were too young at that time to look at the wider issues of ethics and independence and so on.

So was it all auditing?

It was accounting and auditing; the two in those days were interwoven. There wasn't the clear distinction that we draw today. The 1948 Companies Act had only just come into being, with its clearer definition of auditors' responsibilities. They were family run businesses, and the in-house accountants of the larger clients generally were able to take matters up to the trial balance stage, then the auditors came in and put things together and then did the auditing. It was a pretty routine slog, tick all the bank statements, add up most of the columns and figures of the wage book and so on.

Did they have any quoted companies?

Not as audit clients to start with, but John Bullivant was a director of quite a big public company called Wadkin, who were world-leading manufacturers of woodworking machinery.

Would your firm also be auditing Wadkin at the same time as he was a director?

Not initially, only after John Bullivant retired as chairman. At that time they were embarking on a series of acquisitions and brought a number of companies together in northern England, and I was sent off to do the investigations prior to the purchase of these businesses. I was then appointed company secretary, a quasi finance director, which gave me an excellent insight into manufacturing industry and business. That activity would probably take me at least one day a week, and then I had a whole range of other clients, some quite small ones. A number of our clients started to go public in the post-war period, and through that we became involved with one or two London firms who used to come in as reporting accountants.[22] A local firm was not acceptable as reporting accountants in those days.

Were there a lot of boot and shoe companies?

Yes, and hosiery, engineering, printing and light engineering. Just before the war, Leicester was held to be the second wealthiest city in Europe, measured on a per capita income basis, and the main reason for this was the wide diversity of its industry. If one sector was in recession the others were booming. There was always continuous employment and there was also a high level of employment for women.

And how long would an audit take?

Impossible to say really. Some of the bigger audits would take a couple of months. We used to do the audit of John Bull Tyres. They were very sophisticated. They had a Powers-Samas or Hollerith accounting machine which relied on punch cards. We thought we were advanced, as we had a comptometer girl! You'd send for her and give her a programme of work to do, testing the additions on the payroll and things like that.

How would you compare the training you had to the training the average chartered accountant has today?

Look at the way PW trained people when I was down here in London. The number of in-house courses were phenomenal, the introduction to the system and all the rest of it. But what you learnt in my training was the essentials of double entry bookkeeping. Nowadays, these chaps with computers get themselves into a mess when it comes to looking at where the other side of the entry is, if you've got fraud and so on. Unless you have got an understanding of those basic double entry elements you can get lost. The balance sheet is still there and it's expected to balance.

Also I think those starting out now lose out because when I trained you used to have supervising principals, but then they, the partners, became increasingly involved with complex matters so they didn't have the time to give to their students, and so it was delegated. Whereas, in my training, I was fortunate, I was dealing direct with the partners from quite an early age, having demonstrated that I had the confidence. So I was learning a lot from them and their wisdom and experience. The other thing was, John Bullivant, the senior partner, used to go every morning to a little cafe around the corner from the office, called Morton's. There was a trio playing and there were palms and so on, and he and a number of other leading business people would meet there at about 11 o'clock for half an hour, with a cup of coffee. They would discuss affairs, business, prices—hosiery was uppermost in peoples' minds—and other things. From time to time I was taken along to sit with him, not expected to contribute at all but just to listen. Now you never get that happening today; so that was a great privilege, and it also gave me an introduction to some of Leicester's leading business people that was very helpful later on in my life.

Did you ever find any significant frauds in those early days?

I was doing the audit of a charity and the secretary/treasurer was a Reverend, who got himself into financial trouble, took money from the charity and committed suicide, because I was coming down to start the audit. The morning I arrived, he was found hanging in the boiler room because he knew he was going to be found out. It is strange isn't it, because I'm currently dealing with another defalcation from a charity, with a man in sole charge, the audit was due and the circumstances were almost identical. The chap committed suicide because he knew he too was going to be found out.

What was your relationship with management in those days?

Oh, very friendly. The relationship was really set by the partners in the practice. Essentially by John Bullivant, who was a well-known man of affairs in the city. Denis Lea was also well connected through family businesses.

What were the main issues when you merged with PW in 1969?

We called it amalgamation, but it was really a take-over. The main issues were: the quality of the work that we were doing, and the quality of the staff. Because we tended to make people partners at a younger age, there was doubt as to whether the junior partner was up to the same level of expertise and experience as the partners in London. So this was probably the major negotiating point. The other main partner and I had divided loyalties. We felt it was the way to go, but it meant leaving the most junior partner behind. They offered him a position as senior manager in London for wider experience, and then a decision would be made within two years as to whether he was suitable as a partner. In the end, it was felt that he hadn't got all the characteristics required. He was very good with the smaller clients, and so he went off and set up on his own, which was good because it meant that as we started to weed out clients from PW, who were not appropriate for cost and other reasons-they were too small-we were able to say,—here's somebody we can strongly recommend to you. So actually there was a happy outcome for all. But it was none the less a difficult couple of years until we got bedded down.

So what was the general culture in PW then? Did everyone get on well?

The atmosphere was good; it was very friendly, very supportive. If you wanted help there were no formal structures for getting it, you just rang up somebody. Partners' residential meetings for discussions on the firm's development, and so on, went on for five days. There were opportunities for golf and sailing or whatever it was. This was what is called 'bonding' today. That's really what it was.

You went on the Auditing Practices Committee after it started in 1973, tell us about that?

It had been going for about a year and hadn't produced anything substantial. It was still debating what form standards should take and it hadn't really been given any resources, except part-time support from what was then quite a small technical secretariat at the Institute. Into the middle of that lands the London and County banking case in 1976. Now that involved Harmood Banner, and the chairman then of the Auditing Practices Committee was David Richards, who was a partner in Harmood Banner. The Institute thought his position was inappropriate since part of the criticism that came out of the London and County affair was that there were no auditing standards. So poor David had to retire as chairman. So they were casting around for somebody whose firm appeared to be clean, and they turned to PW. They'd cleared the fact that PW were not going to be in for any criticism and asked if I could be released to be chair the committee with quite a tough brief to try to speed up the development of auditing standards.

Michael Lafferty was a Young Turk on the *FT* then, and he was really stirring it up within the profession with adverse comments in that paper. The *FT* had never had an accounting correspondent before, so he was making the most of it. I can remember him ringing me up after I was appointed wanting to know what my plans were, and being aggressively critical as to what had gone wrong. I played a dead bat; there was nothing I could say because I was not aware of all the circumstances.

Anyway, I agreed to take on the job providing they promised to deploy more resources. I wasn't going to be as exposed as my predecessor had been, and so that was agreed. I was also told that the CCAB would beef up the committee, which is what they did.

What were the main issues that confronted you?

The big debate for three or four meetings was how did you write an audit standard dealing with a matter that was essentially judgmental. For example, could you write down that you will attend stocktaking, if stock was not material; or similarly, circularise debtors? If it was not material what was the point? The level of materiality was a concept that had gained acceptance then. Lafferty was asking,—are you going to say you've got to circularise debtors? Which was one of the problems in the London and County case. Because I wouldn't give him an answer, as we couldn't resolve the matter, he didn't really think we were making any progress. But actually what we were doing was to formulate the principles upon which way we were going to go forward, and it was a good thing we did take our time. So we had essential principles, which were—you will get adequate audit evidence, for instance. That was part of the 'operational' standard. The operational standard said,-you will plan an audit, you will record what you did on the audit, you will get adequate evidence to support your opinion. Then there was an auditor's 'reporting' standard, which set out the essentials of the report, and then we gave examples. To support the operational standards, there was guidance on how you got audit evidence, and one of the ways of getting audit evidence, of course, was you circularised debtors—if they were significant. So that's how it worked. But it didn't say-you will circularise debtors or you will attend stocktaking. The standard was—you get adequate evidence. So you could pin down a chap if he didn't circularise debtors, who turned out to be material, because he had made a judgment that they were insignificant with inadequate evidence.

Tell us about your work on the Council of the International Federation?

When IFAC was first formed one of the first committees that it established was an auditing practices committee of its own. There was already in place the International Accounting Standards committee, IASC, and the one area internationally that needed attention was the question of auditing standards on a global basis.

So what did your work mainly consist of on the IFAC APC?

Well we had a blank piece of paper. From IFAC council the brief was to look at the introduction of international auditing standards. Going back to 1977, I think that the only country that had anything in place at the time was the American Institute. The UK auditing practice committee was only about one year into its work. The chairman of IAPC, as it was known—International Auditing Practices Committee—was a man called Bob May, partner in Arthur Andersen's New York, who went on to become president of IFAC. First issue was whether we were going to issue standards or guidelines. There was a big debate on this in the committee with varying views. There were many people who felt that auditing did not lay itself open to being ruled by standards, because it relied on judgmental matters. The outcome of that was that we issued auditing guidelines because there were strong feelings in other parts of the world.

Who were the dominant countries?

Well it wasn't so much the country. It was the personalities of the individuals that really drove the committee. The Americans didn't start saying,—we've got auditing standards in place and you must follow these. Not at all. Bob May was very wise in not driving for the US route, because he would have turned people off. It wouldn't have achieved what we did in a very short space of time if he had adopted that rather aggressive domineering line. It meant everybody was working to better the profession and not to further the interests of their own country.

What were the main cultural differences, if I could put it like that, between the countries, in the sense of the way they approached auditing? Was true and fair a major issue?

True and fair was not an issue really. The French had given up on it. The French were one of those arguing for the prescriptive approach, which they had done within Europe. The Fourth Directive[23] was either in place or about to come in place, which enshrined true and fair in Europe.

Because it was brand new there was an imperative to get something out to show the profession world-wide that people were doing something. So we lit upon the idea of issuing a statement on something not too controversial, on engagement letters for auditors. Not much to get too worked up about. The other debate that we had was the one which we had had in England. The independence of the auditor, should it be incorporated in the auditing standards, or should they go into ethics. We decided the independence of the auditor was something for the Ethics Committee to get it's teeth into.

So what were the other major guidelines?

The first one was called, the principles of conducting an audit, and it set out to cover the ground that the UK had gone down over standards. In other words—you will plan an audit, you will get audit evidence, you will review the accounts, and so on. This was quite novel when you looked at countries less advanced than the western world, like India, the Philippines and Mexico, where practices weren't as far developed as ours. The other thing we had to overcome was their view that the audit was not much more than accounting work, preparing the accounts and so on, rather than actually conducting the audit.

I'm surprised you say there were no major differences between the way different countries wanted to conduct their audit.

Countries like India, as a former part of the British empire, had inculcated into it quite a number of British principles in the way they went about their business. The other thing of course to remember is that most of the representatives actually came from the major international firms and had inculcated into them to varying degrees the international practices of those firms. They were the ones that had the people who could be spared to take a role on the international scene. The small accounting firm hadn't had a hope of sending anybody off twice a year for a week, and then doing other work.

So were you opposite the table to someone from PW?

Yes, the chap from India was a PW man. I hadn't met him before, but firm loyalties did not intrude whatsoever, in just the same way as country loyalties didn't.

Did you have the feeling that in fact the guidelines were being ignored when it got down to country level?

Yes, this was a major concern as to how to promote the international guidelines, particularly the auditing side, down to the individual member. There wasn't a great enthusiasm here in the UK, because bear in mind that we were busy in the UK setting our own standards, and it was much more important to educate our members. So I think the best we were able to achieve was to have all the exposure drafts and the guidelines printed in *Accountancy*. But there was a woeful ignorance of IFAC and its role, other than in this place [Moorgate Place].

Has that changed now do you think?

Oh, very much so. There is a much greater awareness of IFAC and some of the work it is doing. And it is known outside the profession as well. IFAC also funded one or two places on the board to enable small countries, that didn't have the resources to be nominated to the board, to take a role that was not too western or Anglo-Saxon orientated.

What was your connection with Lloyd's of London in the 1980s?

Ian Davison became chief executive when he retired as senior partner at Arthur Andersen. Lloyd's then was very thin on any form of regulation. Ian was horrified at what he found. There were so many devious practices at that time, the PCW scandal and there was Kenneth Grob.[24] Ian was keen to put in a framework of self-regulation. I became part of a small group who informally tried to help draw distinctions between regulations and guidance, and how you could apply them to the Lloyd's market. So that was the role, and it lasted for two years. Ian was also very concerned about the quality of the Lloyd's auditors, some of them quite small firms. The first project that I did for him was to visit all the partners responsible for Lloyd's audits to try and get some degree of uniform approach for the year-end then approaching. I toured round in conjunction with Ian Plaistowe (qv), then a newly appointed partner at Arthur Andersen; we were able to wave UK auditing standards at them because they were now in place. One other thing I did for him [Ian Hay Davison] was, with a lawyer, I gave a series of presentations to Lloyd's managing agents and members on their responsibilities and legal duties under the Companies Act and the law of agency. We were greeted with a degree of ignorance which was extraordinary. They sat there open mouthed, so that was quite interesting.

Do you think that the commercial pressures on the auditor are too great now?

I don't think so. PW has resigned clients because the client wouldn't conform. It has fallen out with clients over qualifications in the audit report. Only last year, there was a distillery which refused to re-appoint PW because we qualified the accounts; we insisted on an accounting treatment, and they didn't agree with it.[25] So I think that auditors are increasingly robust. Now maybe in the 80s, were they so robust? I don't know. It was the aggressive era of league tables, market share and so on. What has happened now is there have been other pressures; most significantly, the pressure on indemnity premiums. If your quality controls aren't right, then your indemnity insurers are likely to kick up a fuss. So there are other pressures militating in the opposite way.

DEREK BOOTHMAN is the son of an accounts clerk at a well-known Manchester textile warehouse. Born in 1932, he was a scholarship boy at William Hume's Grammar School in Manchester. Aged 16, he took up articles with the three-partner firm of J. Needham and Son in Manchester. He qualified in 1954 and after his National Service, he was made a full partner at the young age of 24 since, as a prize winner in his ICAEW examinations, he was regarded as something of a catch. He effectively stayed with the same firm until his formal retirement in 1988. Needham's was taken over by Singleton Fabian, who in 1974 themselves merged with Binder Hamlyn. Derek was a member of the ICAEW Council from 1961–91, and President in 1986–87.

Why did you choose accountancy in the first place?

My father really steered me in that direction. I don't think I ever considered anything else.

And what kind of clients did you have at Needham's?

Because it was Manchester, everything was dominated by the textile industry. We had spinners; weavers; dyers; textile wholesalers, and later in my career they had virtually all ceased to trade.

What sort of tasks were you given to do when you started?

It was all extremely mundane. I added up day books for days, and did a lot of ticking and blotting—this was before the days of the ball point pen! I was once instructed on a Monday morning to check the bank and was left on my own for the rest of the week without any further instructions. On another occasion, I was ordered to check that every purchase cheque had been stamped by the bank.

Did you have to pay a premium?

Yes. My father paid £250, which was returned over the five years in lieu of wages.

Was there a system of audit programmes in place for individual clients?

Audit programmes were effectively non-existent, but by contrast, we were expected to keep up a most meticulous set of working papers on every client.

Overall, was doing articles a good preparation for your future career?

It was appropriate for the time. I suspect that the current graduate intake into the profession is much better looked after. As a partner myself, I used to allow senior clerks much more initiative than I was ever given; I really saw my role as a co-ordinator, whilst they got on with the job of running the audit.

But then in those days, you had to make up a client's accounts for him almost without exception; a pure audit was virtually unknown. The five or six basic steps that went into the audit would vary entirely according to the nature of the client. Since almost all our clients were owner/managers, bookkeeping was the accountant's primary function—the audit was an incidental accompaniment.

How long could the whole process take?

For the smallest client, you could be in there for only a week, but with our largest client, we took three months to do the job. In my experience, we very rarely had to do interim audits and we never had a client large enough to necessitate a continuous audit.

Did you physically attend stocktakes in those early days?

No. All the checks were simply arithmetical. It wasn't till fairly late in my career that the accountant would be expected to attend a stocktake in person. This came about very much as a result of audit manuals being published in the 1970s.[26]

What did you see the role of the auditor comprising in those days? What was the purpose of what you were doing?

I've always regarded myself as an all-round financial advisor, rather than any kind of a watchdog. I've always found the audit boring in itself. I am an accountant, not just an auditor. For most clients, the main point of the audit was to agree the liability with the Inland Revenue; for others, it was just an irksome and expensive legal obligation. Because we audited practically no public companies in the 1950s, the notion that we were ultimately responsible to public, as distinct from private shareholders, was largely meaningless, although that responsibility is now the top priority.

And what is it that underpins an auditing accountant's professional ethics in these circumstances?

They derive entirely from the fact that the accountant is in a market situation. If you want to stay in business, you have to avoid failure.

Some accountants place a great deal of stress on their training as the source of their professional ethics?

I think that is easily exaggerated.

Did you ever have hostile relationships with client management?

Never in the old days, because we used to be so close to the clients. I think the profession nowadays has achieved a much greater degree of independence. In my case, the bulk of the arguments I've had with clients revolved around understanding their profit margins. I always saw it as my job to convince the client that understanding margins was necessary and that discrepancies had to be explained.

Did you ever have to formally qualify a client's accounts?

Very rarely. When we had to qualify, it would be mostly because insufficient records were to hand, or when doubts were present as to whether the client was a going concern.

And you never felt any pressure from clients anxious to avoid qualification?

Never anything untoward. As I say, I think the profession has been extremely effective in preserving its independence.

There have been spectacular examples of audit failure in recent years such as Maxwell and BCCI. How would you explain them?

In some of those cases there was clearly complex collusion within the client company to conceal important information. In those circumstances, it has to be said that the auditor's job really becomes nearly impossible, whatever expertise they employ.

The son of a small London businessman, Sir ALAN HARDCASTLE was born in 1933. After attending the public school, Haileybury College, he was articled to the two partner London firm, B.W. Brixey, qualifying in 1956. After National Service in the Royal Navy, he joined what was then, Peat, Marwick, Mitchell, in 1958, becoming a partner in 1967. He served as general partner from 1972 until 1988. Long active in the ICAEW, he was on national Council from 1974–94, and was President for an 18 month stint between 1983 and 1985. In 1989, he left Peats and took up the new post of Chief Accountancy Adviser to HM Treasury and Head of Government Accountancy Services. Knighted in 1992, he is enjoying a retirement devoted to music, theatre, fishing and the company of friends and family.

Perhaps you can give me a run down of the jobs you were asked to do when you were doing your articles?

A very wide variety, and fortunately the practice was a good one, it still had great big companies. My principal was an extremely busy accountant, so I was involved in a range of things from accounting work for clients, auditing work, taxation, all the way through to some quite complicated things. I do remember pursuing a tax case, under the guidance of my principal, right the way through to the denouement, which was when we instructed leading counsel. But my principal was a superb teacher. On Saturday mornings, once he'd opened his post, he was devoted to his articled clerks. He'd have all our correspondence course work papers returned to him and he went through them. By golly, he was wonderful; he really encouraged you to think about what you were doing. He was wonderfully encouraging.

Years afterwards, ten of his old articled clerks gave him a dinner in the Institute, some came from abroad, and it was a marvellous evening. We all thought he was deaf, his writing was indecipherable, all his suits were light grey at the front because he smoked like a furnace without an ash tray, and so that evening, we pulled his leg about things like that. And then, he got out of his pocket a great big bundle of paper and opened it out slowly. This turned out to be the contemporary notes he'd made on every one of us while we were being trained, and he went through them remorselessly.

Was there any pure audit in those days or was it always combined with doing a client's accounts?

With our reasonably substantial companies there was no accountancy at all, they were pure audit. But also I must add, that if my principal thought that any of these clients didn't perceive him as a general business adviser as well as an accountant and auditor, he would have been quite shocked.

Can you give me an idea of some of the clients you had?

I think in fact all the important clients we had at that time have now ceased to exist as separate companies, they've been absorbed. I do recall we had a firm who made corrugated casings, cardboard boxes and that sort of thing. That would have been our biggest client I guess. Another fantastic one was a complete set of lorries driving around London delivering ice. Fishmongers, butchers, all sorts of people bought ice in large two or three foot cubes; they were called Carvers of Gatwick. But those are just two that come to mind quickly and the range of clients went right down to shopkeepers, one-man bands, costermongers.

One was an Italian dressmaker who literally handed over a brown paper parcel of all sorts of strange things, she never charged properly for the services she provided.

What changes did you encounter when you joined Peats in 1958?

At the time I joined Peats and for a while afterwards, audit programmes were still tailor-made year-by-year, drawn up by the senior in charge of the job, recorded in foolscap, bound books, especially made with hard green covers, I remember. The number of times I saw people running up and down the stairs on their way to see partners to clear an audit, filling in the audit programme on the stairs as they went! It was very rare for the partner reviewing the job to spend much time going through the audit programme. So even in the early 60s anyway, it was very much the old approach, but that was beginning to change. I suppose it was the impetus from two sources really: one was the beginning of the great use of computers, which of course enabled accounting systems to be set out and consistently applied; and the other was the raising of the standard and consistency of the audit. There were enough examples of poor auditing around, it was clear you had to have a more scientific approach.

To what extent do you think an American influence was being felt?

The American influence wasn't so very obvious except in the sense that litigation was growing very fast there, making people more wary of the consequences. Also, throughout the 1960s, there was a tremendous amount of American investment in this country. They were buying up companies, investing in companies and having an influence on business here, and of course their auditors followed the new rules. And computers had taken root faster there, so there were a number of influences contributed to it.

Has the introduction of IT had a huge impact on the audit?

It's undoubtedly had its impact on the audit. In one sense it's a good thing, because it identifies the more likely areas where the greatest risk lies, and you concentrate your resources there. But I think after a few years of this more codified approach, this more scientific approach if you like, there was a bit of a backlash because it became a bit too dogmatic, and it took quite a bit of the feeling of applying judgment away from very intelligent people.

You think it became mechanistic?

I think it became a little mechanistic, and that's how it seemed to the much brighter intake of student articled clerks who were moving much more heavily into the profession at that time. Because accountancy was seen as such a hugely attractive professional qualification to have, we were attracting more than our fair share of the very best graduates coming out of the universities.[27] And we would give them very little to do. They were faced with something which involved blind acceptance, and found it deathly boring, and I think it led to quite a lot of bright young people moving out of practice. That was coupled with the beginning of the increase in specialisation, in other words, if you were an auditor you were an auditor and you didn't do other things, and that took away some of the interest of the work. One can sense the thing had gone a bit too far, but I think it has probably swung back to a more acceptable level now. So it can be quite intellectually challenging to take on a large audit; although there are the parameters clearly set out, and certain things you must pursue properly, it does demand that the young auditor uses his brain.

I know you became very senior in Peats, how involved in actual audits did you manage to remain yourself?

In the nature of things, particularly in the latter days, I was more remote because as the practice grew the more senior partners were much more involved with non-professional work, if you like, running the practices as businesses. A lot of that was a very great pity, because the very best people professionally, people who had built up years of experience, were often not dealing with clients face to face, which is your very best asset. Your experienced, grey haired people around the place were the biggest strength. You could always impress a client by walking along the small corridor we had there to guys who had been partners for years, knocking on the door and saying,—have you got five minutes, I've got a problem? And almost without exception they would say,—come in, I've got the time. Eventually, we became too busy to spare any time at all, and I think that's a great loss. A number of firms came to realise this a few years back. Massive numbers of partners were retiring early because they were just treated like shopworkers. They felt inadequate dealing with big businesses, and after a few years found it not frightfully rewarding.

You've referred to the impact of the growth of the threat of litigation on the profession. Can you expand?

The growing awareness of the possibility of being sued—you could see what was happening in the States—led to the much stricter codification and standardisation of the audit approach, but that had its down sides. People have become defensive, and I find this very sad. I've seen some examples of this in more recent years where one is seeking somebody's considered judgment and you get back the most defensive, sometimes almost impenetrable reports, which in the end weren't awfully helpful, since it's really disclaiming responsibility for anything at all. It's very sad. It's affected relationships between professionals and their clients, and in a sense has come to devalue the profession.

How competitive was the profession in your hey-day with Peats?

Everybody knew what the game was and it was done quite ruthlessly, yet it was always very discreet. From the early post-war period, right up to the 1980s, Peats and Coopers, who did not start off as the biggest firms in the audit business, were intensely competitive.[28] But it stopped short of lowering professional standards. I can't think of a case where either of those two firms would go for a job by offering, as it were, softer options of accounting standards. Now we do know in the 80s that did happen. There were companies looking to get their audit fees down and for lax accounting, who went around touting, when they knew they had a difficult accounting problem. They were looking for whoever was going to give them the softer option, and the senior partners in some firms succumbed, undoubtedly. By the time the recession reached the point that companies were going under, I believe that fees were economy driven; by then I wasn't an auditor, but I observed it.

BRIAN CURRIE was Institute president in the year prior to the interview. The son of a pharmacist and optician, he was born in Hampshire in 1934. He won a scholarship to Blundell's School and then an Open Scholarship at Oxford, where he read Greats at Oriel College. Whilst an undergraduate, he spent some time working in Fleet Street, and thought at one time that this might be his future. However, in 1959, on completing his National Service, he joined Arthur Andersen, who had only arrived in Britain from America two years previously and still had only two partners and some 40 staff in their London office. After qualifying in 1962, he crossed over to the consultancy side of the business, and in 1970 became a partner in their Glasgow office, opening up their Scottish, and then Scandinavian and South African operations. He then spent two years at Her Majesty's Stationary Office as the financial member of the board. When he returned to AA in London as deputy managing partner in 1975, and then as managing partner from 1977 to 1982, he had to rapidly re-acquaint himself with auditing. 'People like Plaistowe, (qv), who was a manager at the time, had to teach me on the job.' He retired from Arthur Andersen in 1990, but continued to be an extremely active member of the ICAEW, having been a Council Member since 1988, and President, 1996–97. He was chairman of CAJEC in 1994 and 1995. In retirement, he runs a farm on the edge of Exmoor and currently gives time to the Restrictive Practices Court[29] and various charities.

Why choose Arthur Andersen?

It was a very nice small practice in the City of London, and their training was fairly impressive; I had learned the importance of that and they lived up to their promises.

What do you remember of the training in the late 50s, early 60s?

I'd missed the introductory training, so I sat down with Ian Davison one afternoon, his brief being to teach me accounting. After an hour or two, he said,—look read this book and I will ask you questions about it tomorrow. It was all straightforward. I had some practical experience, so right from the outset I had a feel for what we were trying to do. The first task I do remember is auditing a payroll. I must have been a bit slow because I kept poking into corners even if they weren't necessary. But I very much learned on the job, and it was about a year before I finally did the Andersen induction course. That was unusual. I had a spell in my second year when I was helping to develop the training for the future, creating model audits and a set of working papers. That in itself was good training.

How did you get on with the correspondence course?

It was full of things which didn't have much to do with what I was doing, like the five Acts of Bankruptcy. I formed the view then, and I haven't shifted since, that an awful lot of the Institute's formal examining may well be of no direct relevance to people's development. Training in a high quality practice is what makes a chartered accountant. Examinations are a hurdle, and you have to have some sort of common hurdle which all the members have passed. At the beginning of the century, the Institute examined people in Latin! Formal examinations are a useful test of the ability to absorb and marshal information. You do need to test that. But we were doing that all day and every day anyway, and everyday work was really a much more important test.

What did an audit involve in those days?

There was a certain amount of ticking and bashing, but I was among the people who was attracted by the idea that one should audit systems and controls. I thought one ought to test sales in a totally different way from the massive block vouching checks which many accountants still practised. I looked for the areas of risk and possible weaknesses in control systems. For me, it was more important to work through a system and a set of controls with specimen transactions than it was to blindly check isolated stages of the system in large blocks. There was a certain amount of derision at the time, but I persevered with the ideas.

That sounds very pioneering for an articled clerk. How much initiative were you actually granted?

Oh, loads, as long as you could persuade the people you were working for that it was a better way. After all, I was 25; I had been in the army. I'd already learned a bit about accountancy, so I wasn't a young kid or anything. That was also a trait of Andersen's—you were treated with whatever respect you deserved.

Did you experiment with scientific sampling at an early date?

We toyed with the mathematics a bit. But my observation quite early on was that if you were going to apply statistical sampling to audit work, your samples had to be so big to attain the sort of probability and error margin that you needed, that it was going to be uneconomic. So after a certain amount of experimenting, I rather set my face against it. By and large, it seemed much better, and much more likely to be practicable, to assess and attack risk. Subsequently, the business was all about risk assessment.

The technical changes in audit requirements over the years are well documented. Do you think the nature of audit is changing?

The danger is that we're forever tightening regulation around the traditional modes of financial reporting and auditing, and actually they are moving out of the investor's focus. We are moving towards an era when companies will have public databases of most of the financial information that investors require. The question that investors will want answered is ,— How reliable is that database? Who is looking at the controls over it? Who is testing and sampling it? Consultants could do that just as well as auditors and their activities are not regulated at all at the moment. So in a very real sense the law needs to shift focus, because that is where the big demands and the future of professional attest services will be. People agonise about regulation and what the profession should do, and they are missing the point. We're building too much regulation in the wrong place, which risks taking the profession's eye off the new areas. We have got to free auditing from over-regulation so that it can make the shift to where it will be needed in the future.

Don't you need tight regulation to keep the profession up to scratch?

Professional regulation will always be needed. But you must take into account the many other pressures which motivate the profession to do good work and to avoid errors and mistakes. Litigation is undoubtedly a very powerful deterrent to bad work. The publicity that goes with it can be even more demoralising. If you do get it wrong or mess up, you have a hell of a job living it down, and life is bloody while you are dealing with it, bloody for everyone. Financial problems hit the headlines very quickly; so in a way auditors are more vulnerable to speculative publicity than most other professions. Because people in professions value their reputation above all financial considerations they fight very hard to maintain it.

So litigation and reputation are two economic drivers towards quality control, but there are other very powerful drivers as well. Quality control depends on integrity and independence. The partnership ethos depends on everyone having confidence in each other's integrity and independence. Most people find it very satisfying to be part of an independent and ethical profession. That 's why they stay in the profession. I used to say when I was an articled clerk that it was like being part of a crusade and that sense never left me.

What do you look for in an accountancy firm's quality control system?

The fundamental principle of quality control is a rule that if you have a problem you go and talk to another partner about it. That is the core of it all. Everything else is built around that notion. The other aspects, documentation and review, are very important, but we had relatively few problems over the years with failures in those areas.

But even the best of quality control can't protect you from all litigation. I never forget hearing about the IOS case, with Bernie Cornfeld.[30] That was a very difficult audit report to write; there must have been more talent drawn into writing that opinion than before or since. Some of the finest people in the accountancy profession, the best in Arthur Andersen word-wide, gathered in Switzerland to write it. There was still litigation.

Another crucial aspect of quality control is deciding who you will and won't work for. We were the first firm to have very strict rules about the type of work and client that we accepted. Sometimes, we said no to whole industries. There were industries where I declined to accept clients, because the risks of dishonesty or impropriety were too great.

Will limited liability help the profession?

The present situation needs changing because of the volume of speculative litigation[31] against auditors. Speculative cases are horrific. There's always uncertainty in litigation. If you take 500 cases, you can investigate them thoroughly and be quite sure that 95% haven't got a leg to stand on. Even so you may end up settling. Changing the law might reduce speculative litigation, and that will lighten one of the profession's present unnecessary burdens. But I don't think it will make much difference to professional practice, because in the end it's reputation that professionals are worried about and not money.

People have focused on the risk of bankruptcy for the partners, but I take the view that, while it could happen, it's not really likely to happen. If somebody is successful in a big law suit, they are not going to say to the partners,—Give us your grand pianos and your other personal assets. They are going to say to the partners,—What is your income stream over the last few years, and how much have you earned from that income stream? What can you pay from that stream in the future? That would be terrible but not the end of the world. So all this hoo-hah about partners' assets and so on, it could happen, but the real problem for a professional firm, if it were found to have done bad work, would be the consequent damage to its reputation.

Since the 1980s, the profession has become much more overtly competitive. How competitive was it previously?

Oh, I think it was very competitive; but not in any cut throat sense. You knew that you had to be seen or people wouldn't ask you to work for them. So from the earliest days I gave talks and wrote papers and got involved in public activities, keeping a high profile. There's not much point in being in the profession if you can't attract clients. But that never ran to soliciting business directly. I used to tell the partners they all had to become heroes, and by that I meant they had to become very visible, simply so that people know who you are.

Why were Arthur Andersen successful?

It was just our people and their talent. Some competitors used to say we grew because we were aggressive. I doubt it. I remember Don Hanson[32] once said that if the firm were really as aggressive as the world thought, we'd have long ago been a much bigger firm than we actually were. We always had an image of being aggressive and it's difficult to describe where it came from. To a degree, people like Arthur Andersen himself and quite a number of the others were fairly outspoken, and fairly publicly visible, but I don't think we were aggressive in the true sense. I have certainly been told by clients that we were never aggressive enough in asking them for work . . . (laughter).

Competitive tendering for audits is now routine. Do you think the profession has benefited from being part of this openly competitive process?

Competition is always good. But there are dangers. There is a danger that if fees get driven down, audit becomes the poor relation of the other work in the office, and that's very undesirable because it means you have difficulty in getting your best people into it and keeping your best people there. That's the trouble with competing too hard on fees. I don't think anybody ever lets price drive down quality. It is too much of a risk. But morale and things like that do come into it as well. The other allegation that often arises is that people bid low on audits in order to gain other work at attractively priced levels. I think that is nonsense. Any FD worth his salt, if he gets a good low price for an audit, is going to make damn sure that the tax work and all the rest goes out to a tender in exactly the same way.

Somebody going for a low price doesn't value the product very much anyway. Who wants to work with someone like that? You may for a time, if it is in an industry where you desperately want to gain some experience and some knowledge, but it is a temporary thing and that relationship won't last. So cross selling doesn't work in that sense.

Is there a case for preventing auditors from engaging in other services?

Other services can give rise to a threat to the auditor's objectivity. We have done a lot of work in our ethical guidance to address those sorts of threats. But I have become even more concerned about the greater problems that might arise if we were to debar auditors from any work except auditing. The big risk is that the other fields, like corporate finance or consultancy, open to young accountants, are more interesting to work in, and will in the long run starve the audit divisions of talent. That's going to lower the quality, and it's going to slow the pace of innovation. I am not sure that many people in the profession really understand these issues.

What concerns did you carry over into your work for the Institute?

I believe that the profession is primarily regulatory. I have been doing battles for many years with those who believe it should be solely a support organisation. Austin Mitchell[33] says it's a trade association.

Colin Sharman (qv) says that's all it should be.

All I can say is, if a trade association is all it is I would resign tomorrow. It is what it is because it's a regulatory organisation. In the end, the Institute is a group of people who sense that regulation is the price of membership and the key to member quality. We've allowed all kinds of other functions to come in, but it must never depart from that core. I have spent a lot of time trying to develop and streamline the regulatory structures, because a lot of them were very old. Previously, they were scattered all over the place and mixed up with the support functions. You have to make all the regulatory and disciplinary organs much more unified and transparent. The Institute has become more democratic. That sustains its ability to regulate, because only a democratic organisation can retain the commitment and support of its members in its regulatory activities. I think education—certainly examining—is part of that as well. People say education is a support activity. Of course it is in one sense but so is the disciplinary apparatus.

Do you have any sympathy for the small practitioner who complains that the proliferation of standards is making his life impossible?

Yes, lots, it's quite understandable. The trouble is we live in a civilisation which believes that rules have to be written down and interpreted and then reinterpreted, and this leads to an increasing technical burden which is getting heavier. Heavier and heavier in an area which in any case is shrinking in importance. And there isn't a good answer to that complaint.

Let me illustrate how we can seek to improve things. Take our ethical guidance. With the old guide there was a whole raft of intuitive but unrelated rules that were framed as prohibitions. In CAJEC we aimed to unify them by developing what I call a procedural framework. The aim is to group all these disparate rules around a common core of central principles from which the separate rules derive logically. If any of them don't derive logically they ought to be scrapped. Then people can see the coherence and the real reason for the rules being there. The same thing needs to be done for accounting standards.

David Tweedie (qv) is trying to develop core principles in the same way, and we all know the battles he's having there. But it's the same precept. You've got to reach a stage where you've got a common core of principles which everybody understands and knows, and which are quite brief. And then everything else, although it may be written down and interpreted, flows from it so logically that you almost don't need to read it to know what it says.

The Institute seems caught between the small practitioners' conviction that it is a mere creature of the big firms, and the big firms' growing impatience with what they see as its conservatism. What can it do to heal the wounds?

That's always been there and I doubt that it will ever change. Everybody thinks the Institute is being run by somebody else, and it's a misconception that it's being 'run' by any single person or group. It's a forum for making professional rules, and that's all it ever can be. Council is mainly a forum of small practitioners and industrial members. There are relatively few Big Five members. Their influence is probably out of proportion to their numbers, but it is unreal to see them as all-powerful. They are very persuasive, they are very hard working, they sit on a lot of committees and so on. They get a lot of the initiatives up and running but most of the decision-making committees consist very largely of small practitioners. I am sure small practitioners up and down the country think the various committees are engaged in conspiracies against them, but they are made up largely of small practitioners sitting around the table.

How do you explain the profession's apparent inability to detect some of the more spectacular frauds of recent years?

It is very difficult to discover certain types of fraud. In absolute terms it can't be done. You can't prevent all fraud. I don't think I have failed to discover one, but in conducting investigations of fraud I have often wondered whether I would have been able to uncover it from the information available at the time. The fact that there are not very many successful fraud prosecutions tells you that on the whole the fraud was clever enough to deceive anybody, including a responsible auditor. Auditors will always have difficulty in detecting deliberate and subtle fraud, especially where there's a well-organised conspiracy of people who can hold their peace. Next time there is a recession there will be a fresh crop of discoveries and there will be auditors saying,—How the hell did we let them get away with that? Business people are clever. Many of us can think of all sorts of methods of operating a fraud in ways that the most skilled auditors could never discover. Fortunately most of us don't! That's the worry about organised crime. My life long worry has been,—how would you ever know if you audited something that really belonged to the Mafia?

But some frauds like Barlow Clowes, BCCI and Maxwell are so blatant it is very difficult to see how they were missed.

People say the obvious sign of fraud is a dominant personality who gets his own way in an organisation. But think of the many organisations which are pretty reputable, but where you have dominant personalities. With hindsight, if ever anything turns out to be wrong in those empires we will say,—It should have been obvious. But there are scores of organisations with those superhuman, energetic, driving people who are honest businessmen and not crooks.

So the auditors are not to blame?

Corporate collapse will always lead to challenges about the quality of auditing, always. But auditors can't prevent corporate collapse.

The real test of the adequacy of work is two—fold. There's the disciplinary procedure and the civil liability process. The disciplinary process involves looking at the evidence that was available and saying,—Should they have discovered this for sure? In the civil liability process the standard of proof is much lower. It's based on the balance of probability. That of course is an even sterner test for the auditor defendant. Those two processes will get to the truth of the matter. Now if you investigate and as prosecutor or plaintiff you can see a defect sticking out, you don't bother with the detail, you should just hammer the defendant straight away on that.

But the fact that people have not often been hammered tells you that auditors, contrary to the mythology, don't often do bad work. If you have ever been a defendant you will know how the people suing you will devote infinitely more time, effort and expense to the detailed issues than your staff could conceivably have done in performing the original work. If there has been an omission in the work, they will find it. So that really is the true final test of quality and one has to beware of speculation before that test has been completed.

People question the point of the audit if it can't spot these outrageous frauds.

But I have discovered a number of things in my time which might have become big frauds if they had been left to develop, and I suspect that's true of almost every experienced accountant. But the public doesn't hear about them. Public attention always and inevitably focuses on the ones that got away. Auditors prevent normal things going wrong and they put right a lot of things which have started to go wrong, stopping them developing any further. That is a hell of a useful job, which I think is as well if not better conducted in this country as in most countries. It would be nice to have a profession which was perfect in everything, but I suspect that one can't. We've certainly got an audit profession which is highly motivated to do good work. Techniques and methods improve every day and will go on improving. We've probably got or are heading for the best audit profession we can have.

Some critics want the profession to be state-controlled.

My own view is that shifting audits over to the state would destroy what we have achieved. A state regulated profession would probably disappear—it wouldn't be able to recruit the people the audit profession needs. District auditors and national auditors[34] are fine people, but for many years they excelled at telling you that something went wrong quite a long time after it became public knowledge. In recent years they have learned to uncover and prevent, and they are getting very good at it. But remember that they made some of their greatest strides of innovation and development by importing methodology from the private sector professions. Government control of the auditing profession would change the way our commercial community works. We are lucky that on the whole we enjoy fairly high standards of fairness and ethical behaviour in business, and a great deal of that results from people like auditors and lawyers and other professionals playing the roles they do. So that's really one of the reasons why I gave time to the Institute. I am not an auditor. I'll never be an auditor again. I'm not even sure I very much enjoyed doing it during the long-past periods of my career when I did do it. But by golly, it's important.

CHRIS LAINÉ was President of the ICAEW at the time of the interview. He was born in London in 1936, the son of a solicitor in the civil service. He won a scholarship to the King's School, Canterbury, a public school, and after his National Service, went up to Trinity College, Oxford, as an exhibitioner, where he read Modern History. In 1960, he joined Cooper Brothers in London as an articled clerk, qualifying in 1966. In 1971, he was made a partner and given charge of all Cooper Brothers' operations on the South Coast. These had previously been looked after by the London office, but Chris was asked to open a new office in Southampton, where he stayed for the rest of his active accounting career, from 1990 being designated senior partner for the South Coast. Always an active ICAEW member, he has sat on Council since 1990 and followed Brian Currie (qv) as national President in 1997, where he continued Currie's project of democratising and modernising the Institute. After his presidency, he formally retired to his cottage outside Romsey, Hants., where he pursues his interests in cricket, golf, classical music and painting.

Given the size of Coopers'clients, presumably most of the work you were doing in the 1960s would be pure audit?

Most of it, certainly for the first year and a half it was almost entirely auditing, but I spent some time in quite a small accounts department, which was a useful experience. I decided I would never have the patience and the kind of mind to be an accounts specialist. In those days, because all sorts of investigation work was done by people who were primarily auditors, there were no specialist departments, other than tax and insolvency. Therefore, one could find oneself doing a reasonable variety of other work. Today, in a large firm people become specialists when they join.

How closely were you supervised?

The philosophy at Coopers was to throw you straight in at the deep end. I remember coming down to Southampton, when I had been only going a year, to carry out an audit of Ford's operations in Southampton on my own. The test was to see how far you could get on your own. They [a component manufacturer] had been acquired by Ford's not all that long ago, and they had to adopt the standard Ford systems. But the locals were an independent-minded bunch. So you were always stretched and you learned very fast. Don't get me wrong, if you thought you knew and you didn't, then you would be in trouble if you ploughed on. One was brought up very much with the philosophy that you consulted all the time, and if you got stuck there was always someone to help you, and very willingly. This was the disciplined way you worked. The structure was clear and the review process by the managers was very thorough. And then I always felt that the best part of Coopers' training was that they trained people to become trainers themselves.

How involved were the partners in the audit?

They were very godlike creatures in the sense that there was a distance. A partner was someone who was at a different level. But they were very much directly engaged in audits, albeit at a senior level. Some of them were better than others in engaging with the staff. Some were extremely annoying, and there was a sense of things changing throughout the 60s. There was a great breakdown in formality at the end of the 60s.

How important was the famous Coopers' manual?

We operated to set procedures and the manual came from those; like all manuals I have yet to find one that gave the answer to all difficult questions, because a manual can only advise and can't answer every contingency. However, it was a remarkably comprehensive framework.

Have the procedures changed much from when you started in the early 1960s?

After we'd done a final analysis of the P&L account, we used to do something that is no longer a recognised technique, which was to scrutinise two accounting records, which still existed in most companies; one was the cash book—simply to spot any unusual items and investigate them. Secondly, you always went to the journal to see what they had been doing to put the accounts together, to see again if there were any surprising or unusual items there. Accounting was semi-mechanical, but the world was changing with punch card machines around but very few companies had computers. The first company I went to which had a computer was Unilever and they abandoned the first attempt and went back to handwritten ledgers and accounting halls, before they did it the second time and got it right. Then new techniques started to evolve in order to examine controls. Very superficial by today's standards.

When did you first see the management letter assuming its contemporary importance?

It assumed a general level of importance in the 70s. In the 1960s, we were regarded as being pretty innovative as a firm in writing these letters. They were written in a very stylised way, and very politely. Today, they are much more robust; the issues they involve are too important. I remember vividly, about 1962, raising an issue about some controls at an interim visit to a major subsidiary of an international company. It had moved its whole undertaking from an old clapped-out site to a brand new greenfield site during the summer break, and we did our interim in September/October time. Everything got behind as a result of the move and they had a production line that had to be kept going. It had a very sophisticated stock delivery system, with some deliveries going straight to the line, which required quite sophisticated controls. To keep the thing going, and to keep the suppliers happy, they removed some of the internal controls in order to streamline the process. We reported to the management that this was extremely risky and they shouldn't do it; and it saved our bacon because four months later they had a major stock discrepancy; someone had managed to do exactly what the controls were designed to avoid. A trusted employee of many years had over a period of time embezzled something like £150,000. He was caught not by the stocktake itself but by a financial analysis that was being done in this particular area. But the first reaction was—the auditors had let them down. It was my first example of—it's always the auditors' fault. It turned out, the chief executive had received our letter and not done any thing about it. He lost his job. It was a key lesson in the need to be absolutely frank in these letters.

Can you tell me about your experiences in building up the Southampton practice in the early 70s?

It was quite a hard road. It was the firm's policy at that time that we shouldn't merge with any local practices. Interestingly, Peats had been given the same brief when they arrived in town. For a year or so the local firms were very suspicious, and then they started merging with big firms like Deloittes and so on. Peats and ourselves were the only two firms that never did a local merger, so it took a lot of energy and hard work, but once you got the momentum going it was all right—the word goes around. In those days you didn't advertise. When the rules changed, we could see no advantage in spending large sums of money; since the reaction from all our clients was,—if you boys are going to start wasting your money on advertising don't think we're paying any increase in fees. For about a year and a half, none of the local firms wasted any money on advertising at all. P.R. people were ringing up all the time and inevitably someone was persuaded to have a go. It was all futile because I don't think it has ever added one jot or tittle to our portfolio of clients. I always felt that work is gained by reputation, which is about how you do the work; and talking about it doesn't bring in the kind of people we were trying to attract.

How competitive had it been prior to that?

Well, the idea that it was an uncompetitive world then, a sort of cartel based on privilege, is nonsense. The fact that we could socialise together and be quite civilised to one another does not mean that we were not seeking commercial advantage at every opportunity. It was a complete misunderstanding of the true position, and I think the profession as a whole has not gained in public esteem from advertising. It was a sop to Thatcherism in the 80s which has done us no good. When it was coupled with the so-called scandals at the end of the 80s and the beginning of the 90s, it did a pretty thorough job of changing public perception of the profession. Now there is a wide press and public perception that anything that smacks of self-regulation is questionable.

Has increased commercialism been a recent danger?

There is no doubt that the more overt emphasis on value for money has challenged auditors to re-examine their procedures and to streamline their operations, which has been a good commercial spur. As a profession, we commissioned a completely independent report[35] a few years ago to see whether there was any good evidence of low-balling and the conclusion was there was none. All the academic work I've read on this subject would indicate that that is the case. Having said that, I can see the attraction of loss leaders to gain entrance to other work, but the legal requirement to disclose non-audit fees paid to auditors has had a very crisp effect on a lot of boards of directors who say,—right, if we have to disclose, our auditors won't be doing any other work for us.

How significant has the tendering process been?

The final decision in my view is always going to boil down to the impression that the individual doing the tendering makes on the group they are going to be working for,—that's the chap we want looking after us. It's personality and interview skills, really. In the old days that happened invisibly, now it happens more overtly.

You don't think tendering drives down standards?

There is a real problem that audit is in danger of underpricing itself. Right now, at the sophisticated end of the market, the technique of audit, and the way in which it is conducted and performed, is all up for grabs. The capacity of IT to deliver information has totally transformed auditing. The Institute and the Stock Exchange give awards every year for the best annual report, but whether we will have this celebration of historical data in five years time, I don't know. The real users of this data want it very fast, and the technology is there. What the market wants and what the operator needs is the assurance that the financial data you input from day to day is reliable, and that is the real challenge. There are a lot of people in my profession who are working on it, and the investment in technology to provide the assurance necessary with real-time systems is the next stage. At the moment, the government is trying to extend the exemption for smaller companies to be audited. Logically, while always retaining the right of third parties who have a current financial interest to have an independent assessment, an annual statutory audit is something we will lose eventually except for Plcs. It will have an overall effect on the profession, especially on the small practitioners.

Many small practitioners are unhappy.

I've been around to see it emerging, and spoken to groups from every part of the country to hear their views, and to explain why they are where they are. The capacity of the professional body to resist government is virtually nil. Most will reluctantly accept that. The second problem is an active challenge to the value of what accountants are doing. Well we've always done this—is no answer. The sole practitioner must be shrewd enough to recognise that he is aiming at a niche market and bringing specific expertise to it. I believe in the small practitioner providing financial advice to small companies as to how to set up their records, and how to provide financial information on a regular basis; providing advice on new computer systems. If they do that, many find that they have never been more successful with clients since they stopped trying to audit them. They do really well because they really work at it and they are up to speed and they give very good advice and personal service. They find that a very exciting job to do, and I think I would too. One thing these practitioners have in common is that they do not expect, and they do not want to be involved in the audit of small companies.

So you don't see any future in auditing for the small practitioner?

To small businesses an annual set of accounts, sometimes long after the event, has little or no value. But to the small practitioner the audit is seen as bread and butter work, regular income, like solicitors and conveyancing. It's their birthright. But we have to accept that the world's moved on. So there are people out there who see it as an opportunity, but most see it as a threat. More and more small groups are merging together quite simply to enable them to cope with the technical elements. An individual cannot hope to keep up to date, so it's frankly going to be hard. Some are terrified because the JMU comes round, and you only have to have one tricky experience in an area and word gets round. You will always get the sad cases, and they will always make a fuss. And yet increasingly I've found that practitioners in the last year or so have said how helpful the JMU has been, and how reassuring and how relatively unthreatening they are. But those who sit there and say,—the law says you've got to have an audit and my profession will defend that to the last breath of the last man, I think is lunacy.

Ironically, whilst many small practitioners are convinced the Institute is a creature of the Big Five, some leaders of the bigger firms are saying,—we don't need the Institute. Is there a danger of the Institute falling straight down the middle?

All this is a central concern for Council, which contains 13 sole practitioners of one sort or another, the largest group on Council. The big firms have eight, industry of various sorts has ten, academe has a couple and so on. The Council is a broad church, and does reflect most of the areas in which we operate now. We are putting in place structures that quite openly recognise that our broad church has to be segmented, with special interests that have to be looked after, quite openly and legitimately. If that doesn't work I believe it has the seeds of its own destruction. The big firms supply the knowledge and expertise that drives the Institute's technical side, the input that really matters. You are not going to find many small practitioners contributing an awful lot at that level of technical expertise.

The Big Five however do 60% of the training, and I think the crunch has come over the latest revision of the syllabus. Two years ago, an Extraordinary General Meeting narrowly voted against change and this June [1999] a similar motion at the AGM was narrowly defeated on a poll of less than 15% of the membership.[36] Now we are faced with the fact that the providers of 60% of the training are going to say,—to hell with that, what are we doing? We want to stay, but the market's moving on, haven't they noticed? You are going to have a conflict, and we want to avoid it if we can, and in a sensible way. But in the end, the doomsday scenario is that the 60% vote with their feet and say,—we'll go somewhere else. A situation where unanimous decisions and recommendations of an elected Council can be overturned or delayed by an activist seven and a half per cent of the membership argues a crisis compounded of constitutional weakness, ineffective communication and member apathy. It is a problem shared by most professional bodies and offers no easy solutions. Echoes of Hugh Gaitskell's fight as leader of the Labour Party in the 1950s; and Council is minded to fight.

Notes

1. Founded in 1973 to formulate internationally accepted accounting standards. It had representation from the accounting bodies of some 80 countries and by 1992 had produced 31 standards (Parker, 1992: 161).

2. Peats successfully circumvented the rule by each branch or group of provincial branches having the core of the London partners (minus two) with the addition of one or two partners who ran the local office (ICAEW, *List of Members*, 1950).

3. In this period Peats took over Edwin Guthrie, and the Birmingham branch of Sharp Parsons (Wise, 1982: 17).

4. In 1987, Peat, Marwick, Mitchell, merged with KMG Thomson McLintock to form Peat, Marwick, McLintock (*Accountancy*, Sept. 1989).

5. Sir Harry Peat, son of the founder of the firm, was senior partner until 1956, when at the age of 78 he gave way to his brother—Rod. The Peat family relied heavily on the partners under them, including Sir Ronald Leach. who eventually succeeded Rod, by then in his late 80s, as senior partner in 1966 (Wise, 1982: 19–20; *The Times*, 31 Aug. 1996; ICAEW, *List of Members*, various years).

6. Peter Graham Corbett, who qualified in 1957, was the son of John Corbett who had been a partner in the firm since at least 1950 (Wise, 1982: 20; ICAEW, *List of Members*, 1950).

7. In November 1996, Coopers & Lybrand sued nine executives of Barings Bank, holding them responsible for the collapse of the bank in 1995. Coopers were themselves being sued by the bank's liquidators, Ernst & Young, for the £830m lost in the collapse (*Daily Telegraph*, 30 Nov. 1996).

8. Peat, Marwick, Mitchell won the British Aerospace audit in competition with four other leading firms in 1977 (*Accountancy*, Feb. 1978: 10).

9. Under joint and several liability one party in a suit is liable for all the damages if the other parties, for example, the company directors, cannot pay. The large accountant firms almost always will have greater resources than the directors.

10. The scheme was revised in 1993, the JDS Executive Committee now passes cases to a lawyer, the Executive Counsel, who handles the enquiry (Chance, 1993: 25–26; *Financial Times*, 10 Dec 93; Boys, 1994: 15).

11. In 1987, Ferranti paid $420m for an American defence contractor, International Signal and Control Group (ISC), owned by James Guerin, which turned out to be worthless because arms contracts in Pakistan and the Middle East were bogus (*Financial Times*, 20 Sept. 1989, 17 Nov. 1989). Ferranti, which was effectively ruined by the deal, sued Peats, the auditors, for damages, settled in 1991 for £40m (*Financial Times*, 13 August 1991). The JDS investigated Peats and found in 1996, after a three year inquiry, that they had no case to answer (*Guardian*, 30 July 1996).

12. See Matthews, *et al*, 1998: 129–30.

13. Matthews, *et al*, 1998: 320–1.

14. In 1963 (Cowe, 1993: 285).

15. Selective Employment Tax, introduced in 1966 in a vain attempt to shift labour from the service sector into manufacturing (Jeremy, 1998: 120).

16. Value Added Tax replaced purchase tax in 1973 as the major indirect tax in the UK (Jeremy, 1998: 117).

17. See Benson, 1989: 107.

18. Qualified in 1957, and was under-secretary of the ICAEW in the late 1960s (ICAEW *List of Members*, 1966).

19. In 1970, the ICAEW establish the Accounting Standards Steering Committee (ASSC), and chaired by Leach it produced SSAP 1, on accounting for the results of associated companies in 1971 (Edwards, 1989: 236–247).

20. A system of inflation accounting which replaced nominal pounds with constant value pounds (Parker, 1992: 80).

21. The ICAEW first began to regulate auditing practices with the issue of Statement U1, entitled 'General Principles of Auditing', in 1961. In 1973, it set up the Auditing Practices Committee (APC) to 'develop a more rational framework of audit guidance which would provide a focus for the efforts to improve auditing' (Stacy, 1986: 17). In 1976, it became a committee of the joint Consultative Committee of Accounting Bodies (CCAB) but not until 1980 did the APC issue its first set of auditing standards: 'Auditors' Reports on Financial Statements' (Chandler, 1986: 11). In 1991, it became the Auditing Practices Board (APB) (Parker, 1992: 26).

22. Accountants who report on the financial information contained in a prospectus and other matters connected with a new issue of securities (Parker, 1992: 243).

23. A directive issued by the EU in 1978 to member countries to harmonise company law, including accepting the principle of true and fair, implemented in Britain by the Companies Act 1981 (Parker, 1992: 131).

24. PCW were a group of Lloyd's underwriting syndicates whose auditors, Angus Campbell, were criticised for their audits in the years, 1978–81, in a 1990 DTI report. Kenneth Grob was the managing director of another firm of underwriters accused of diverting funds out of the firm. The firm's auditors, Josolyne Layton-Bennett and Arthur Young, and De Paula, Turner, Lake, and Peat, Marwick, Mitchell, Bermuda, auditors of subsidiaries, were also criticised in a 1990 DTI report (Hodgson, 1984: 308; Boys, 1997: 97–100).

25. The 1995–96 accounts of Burn Stewart Distilleries were amended at the insistence of Price Waterhouse, but they retained the audit as a result of shareholders' pressure (*The Herald*, 5 and 29 Nov. 1996).

26. The first edition of Cooper's Manual (1966: 266) stated that attending stocktaking was the generally accepted procedure in the United States and Canada and therefore necessary for those clients, but it was not a required procedure in the UK, and should be undertaken where stock was material and then only periodically, normally once every three years.

27. Graduates increased from 10% of the ICAEW intake in 1963, to 72% by 1972, and almost 100% today (Matthews, *et al*, 1998: 85).

28. In 1951, Peat, Marwick, Mitchell (5.4% of listed company audits) and Cooper Bros. (2.4%) ranked third and fourth respectively, behind Deloitte, Plender, Griffiths (8.0%) and Price Waterhouse (7.2%). In 1991, KPMG (19.0%) and Coopers & Lybrand, Deloitte (17.8%) were first and second (Matthews, *et al*, 1998: 46–47).

29. Set up in 1956 to look into and adjudicate on trading agreements which may be against the public interest (Jeremy, 1998: 110).

30. Investors Overseas Services was an investment racket run by Bernie Cornfeld (Peter Clowes was one of his salesmen) which crashed in the early 1970s (Widlake, 1995: 92–94).

31. Litigation, popular in America, whereby wealthy entities are sued, often on relatively slight grounds, in the hope that they will settle out of court rather than contest a costly law suit.

32. Arthur Andersen partner, qualified in 1957 (ICAEW, *List of Members*, 1966).

33. Born in 1934, MP for Grimsby since 1977, is the chief backbench critic of the accountancy profession and an ally of Prof. Prem Sikka, with whom he has co-authored many publications (*WW*).

34. Under the Local Government Finance Act 1982, local authorities can chose to be audited by district auditors or private sector auditors, both of which are approved and regulated by the Audit Commission. The equivalent body in central government is the National Audit Office, established by the 1984 National Audit Act (Greenough, 1991: 58; Dewar, 1991: 248).

35. By Elizabeth Llewellyn-Smith, on 'Competitive Pricing,' published in 1995.

36. The Big Five firms have twice recently attempted to revise the ICAEW training syllabus to make it offer more choice and specialisation, seeing this as more appropriate to the future needs of the profession and of industry. On both occasions, this has been thwarted by the small practitioners, anxious to preserve the general nature of the C.A. qualification, an example of the big firms versus small schism, which is threatening the future of the ICAEW (*The Times*, 10 June 1999).

Chapter 9

Contemporary Leaders

Lord COLIN SHARMAN was born in 1943, the son of a regular army colonel. Brought up in the barracks town of Salisbury, Wiltshire, he was educated at the Bishops Wordsworth School, a nearby grammar school. In 1962, he took articles with the four-partner City firm, Woolger, Hennell, where three of the partners were former audit managers with Peat, Marwick, Mitchell. Moving on to Peats' London office in 1966, Colin rose from senior clerk to senior manager in four years. Between 1970 and 1972, he was a manager in the Frankfurt office and then moved to the Hague. Given a partnership in 1973, he was partner in charge of Peats' Netherlands operations from 1975 to 1981. Returning to London in that year in the interests of his children's education, he filled a number of senior posts within the firm before taking over in 1994 as chairman and senior partner of what has now metamorphosed into KPMG International. Colin is perhaps unusual amongst contemporary leaders of the profession in favouring the abandonment of self-regulation in order to safeguard the professional bodies' support function. He was elevated to the peerage in June 1999.

Can you give me a general idea of the jobs you were asked to do as an articled clerk in the mid-1960s?

Mainly small and private company audits with the occasional listed company thrown in. There was a complete run of different things, a brush manufacturer, a brass foundry, coal merchants, a pub chain, coat manufacturers, all sorts.

What sort of tasks did you actually find yourself doing?

The first year you would help somebody on a bigger job and then after a year you would have a selection of small jobs to look after yourself, preparing accounts, so you learnt quickly.

How closely involved were the partners in the firm, did they actually get out in the field?

No, I have no recollection of a partner ever going out to see a client. We went out and did the work, and brought the working papers back to the office, and the partner reviewed them and that was that. All the planning for audits was done by the seniors and ourselves. The partners didn't do any detailed planning they just reviewed and signed off. We had an office manager, and if you needed any technical help you went to him. There were no formal audit programmes. Some would involve a full check of everything, again we used a bit of statistical sampling but not a lot, and only with our bigger clients. We used to devise our own samples, based on what we read in our Foulks Lynch course.

How closely have you involved yourself with audit work since you joined Peats in 1966.

I have always had audits, even today. I don't sign any audits nowadays, though. We have what we call lead partners who manage the relationship. But I was still the main partner on Nat West, for example, for a number of years. We have a worldwide role, but we don't have any partners that have no clients. My involvement would be reviewing the audit plan, and deciding on the risk assessment plan, our most recent innovation, and then reviewing the reports, the completion memorandum and the management letters, attending all the committee meetings and the meetings of the senior executives to discuss our clients. Technically, since the early 80s we've had direct access into clients' own computer systems. We now live in their systems, auditing. Our people from locations around the world, validate information and transmit it over the same network to us, using the client's system.

Do you think the purpose of the audit has changed, along with the technical changes?

We are now very conscious of providing that extra value. I always remember a client saying to me,—I ought to get more out of my annual audit than a ruddy great bill for telling me I got my sums right. The provision of management information and the advice that comes from it is a lot more useful than even six or seven years ago. That has been caused largely by increasing competition in the market place. Most well run companies don't need someone to tell them their numbers are right; what they are looking for is more, which is not the same in every case.

Does this not impinge on auditor independence?

Independence is reflective of the nature of a relationship between two people, objectivity is a state of mind, and it is objectivity which underwrites professional services rather independence. You could be very objective, and give better advice for not being completely independent. I'm not saying independence doesn't matter, but the important thing about independence is that it's not a question of reality, it's a question of perception: how people perceive the relationship. We certainly don't have a single client in the UK who would come close to compromising our independence. It's not an issue. The financial size of the client is also not the issue; the issue is the robustness of the individual auditor. Now there have been some very frank exchanges with clients, but that's the job of an auditor, and a good relationship enables you to do it, and they will respect you for it, but if you don't have respect, you are in trouble.

Have the days gone when you could take a client at his word?

No. I think it still is there; many of our clients I'd trust absolutely. We may have disagreements, but they are honest disagreements. We tell them,—your view is conditioned by needing to show a good performance; our view is conditioned by the need to get it right or as near right as we can. Very occasionally, we've had cases where we resigned an account. There was a very interesting one last year, where we resigned as auditors, and the client then obtained an injunction preventing us from filing our reasons for resigning with Companies House. While we were getting the injunction removed, they appointed new auditors—a small firm in St Albans, who issued a clean report.

Do you think the increased threat of litigation has distorted a lot of what the profession is doing recently?

No, but we are more careful about giving advice. I was talking to the head of our lawyers' litigation department last week and he said,—I'm getting very worried about your quality; and I said,—why's that? And he said,-because we are not getting any new work from you (laughter).

Do you think limited liability status[1] has partly stabilised things?

No, I think it is a state of mind. Certainly, it has enabled us to attract better quality people to work for us than we would have otherwise have done.

There was a fear at one time that the best accountants would start to refuse to become partners?

We've had cases of people not being prepared to come into a partnership.

Were you every involved in qualifying accounts personally?

I think I went three years once without issuing an unqualified opinion and certainly for the whole of the time I have been involved in Euro Tunnel[2] we've never issued an unqualified report.

What are the special circumstances there?

Well, with Euro Tunnel you never knew if it would be there next week (laughter). In many cases there are liquidity problems.

How justified is Peats' reputation for competitiveness?

If you look at our top ten clients today I would reckon that not over half of them would have been with us six years ago. Cable & Wireless we won in 1994/95 in a competitive tender; ICI in a tender competition with Price Waterhouse; the BBC; Westminster Health Care. There is a sizeable spread of big clients that we won over the last five or six years. Advertising enabled us to spend more money. It's about corporate image basically. It doesn't actually help the [audit] business, though it does help with the other services. Corporate business is about getting major audit clients through targeting.

In the old days, if other firms weren't criticising you, you weren't pushing hard enough. I got reported to the Institute a couple of times; once over a damn stupid issue. I did some marketing and had some bags made saying,—chartered accountants and management consultants. And they [the Institute] said,—you can't say that, because you're not allowed to put anything after chartered accountants. I responded that we were actually talking about two separate partnerships, so technically its was OK. They replied,—You can do it, but you can't use an 'and' or an ampersand between the two.

How competitive were you over fees in those days before tendering? Would it be the case that you would ever drop a fee to try and attract a client?

There was partner A who would always say,—that's a bit too much, knock something off, and partner B, who would say,—oh that doesn't seem very much, he's got a lot more money, let's put some more on. So there was always a negotiation between the partner and the client.

Has tendering significantly altered the partner/client relationship?

The social pecking order has changed, with clients coming out on top. When I started out, we would always have received a client in the office; the only reason a client would come here today was if it was a matter of extreme confidentiality and they didn't want me to be seen. We get about 45% of all the tenders that we go for, so it is worth our while. And you don't always get the tender on the lowest bid; time after time when we have won work it's because we have convinced people we can supply the best service. I've seen cases where a low-ball has been refused because it's so ridiculous.

Prem Sikka and Austin Mitchell argue that the audit is a loss leader for more remunerative accounting work[3]*—how much of a problem do you think that is?*

With 87% of our big clients, other members of the Big Six have worked for them. Our biggest client spends £450m a year on professional fees, of which we get £20m. We totally rely on our reputation; as soon as we start ripping off the clients we are dead.

What are your views on the direction the ICAEW is taking?

I believe that the Institute has a very valuable role, but you have to understand what that role is, and it is either a trade association or a regulatory body. The trouble is it tries to be both things, which is not credible. This is where Sikka and Mitchell have a point. To the outside world, one day we are going around deciding what rules we are going to have, and the next day we are being judge and jury and dishing out the punishment. You just can't have it. Ultimately, regulation has got to be completely independent of the Institute, which is why we will support Swinson's proposals,[4] but only as a sensible step on the way. The Institute tried to be all things to all men, and they got themselves into a terrible tangle trying to hang on to self-regulation. Even an organisation like KPMG can't do everything, so we do a limited number of things very well. Now, the Institute has tried to do everything, and it has fallen down.

You sound disillusioned with the Institute.

Well, we have always believed that it's important to play our role within the Institute and give our support to it. But I only got involved in one thing with them, chairing a working party, and the politics of it drove me crazy. I can't get involved in it. I think the governance of the place is absolute lunacy. How can you run it when you've got 80 plus people on the governing body? I run KPMG International, which is a $9 billion organisation with an executive team of six and an international board of 12. We can make things happen. But that lot out there, they really have to sort it out. Ultimately, the important thing is sorting out the qualification; the new [training] proposals are very sensible. Trainees have to have different options; the day of the compendium qualification is gone,—its nonsense, you have to have specialisms.

What lies behind some of the high profile audit failures of recent years?

One of two things: you are either working for the wrong people or you are doing the wrong type of work. Now in some cases, it's the wrong type of work, but mostly it's because you are working for the wrong type of people. One thing, certainly in the major firms, is that risk management procedures are so much improved that the danger is that these villains will go to second and third tier firms who don't have the same sophisticated risk management procedures, and they end up being looked after by people who don't have the strength to deal with it. At the moment, because of our procedures we simply will not take them on. We just say,—no, or,- can we please check out references? And they go elsewhere. Now that can't be good for those who end up auditing them.

What happened with Ferranti?

The real problem with Ferranti was that it was a very sophisticated fraud. Even today no one can tell you what happened. Now, how do you expect an auditor to find it out in the time he's got, when after 15 years with all the investigative power that went into the various enquiries there is still no one who knows how it was done? There was collusion both within the company and with the customers, which made things impossible. Preventing future Ferrantis demands, quite simply, better risk management procedures up front.

How do you see the future of the auditing profession?

I have seen a lot of change and the pace of change is accelerating. I think it is quite feasible that in the next 15 years historical audit will be replaced by contemporaneous audit. You will see a complete change, and in many cases I suspect we will be doing audits as the reports are written. We've invested a huge amount in researching this, $50 to 60 million, this year.

Do you see that as merely a technical change or a change in the purpose?

I think its more a change of purpose, because we'll be moving away from satisfying shareholders to satisfying capital markets.

Born in 1942, IAN PLAISTOWE is the son of a mechanical engineer and company director. He attended Marlborough College and Queen's College, Cambridge, where he read Classics, 'a very unreal subject.' He took articles with Arthur Andersen in London in 1964, which at the time had only five or six partners and 100 staff in the U.K. Made a partner in 1976, Ian has had a distinguished career with the firm as it expanded, culminating in his appointment as Director of Audit and Business Advisory Practice for Europe in 1993. He has sat on the ICAEW national Council since 1983 and was national President, 1992–3. Notably, he has chaired the Auditing Practices Board of the UK and Ireland since 1994. Friends and colleagues we have spoken to refer to him approvingly as a 'purist' in auditing matters.

What did Arthur Andersen pay you as a trainee accountant at the start of the 60s?

It was a lot of money in those days, £804 a year or thereabouts. PW and Peats were offering £650. I had a friend who went and worked for Plessey's and I remember he got £900 or something, but considering I was getting a training it didn't seem to me a bad income, and certainly in relation to what the other major firms were offering, it was very attractive.

Can you give me a brief resume of the jobs you were asked to do when you were in training?

Arthur Andersen gave you a considerable amount of training, and in fact you weren't allowed out of the office until you had done about five or six weeks' training. They were the only firm at that time that gave you anything like that training, which was another reason that I found it so attractive. With that training, we were sent out and given responsibilities at a very early stage. At that time, I recall doing some things we called procedural tests, which were tests of a company's procedures, or doing simple work like auditing a bank reconciliation, or doing debtors confirmations—those sorts of things.

How hands on were the partners themselves in those days?

One didn't see much of the partners. They used to come out at the end of the audit and look to see what had been done and whether or not sufficient work had been done to enable a partner to sign off. We tended to work as a team, but there were very few partners in London at that time.

After a while you were given a fair amount of initiative?

Oh yes, I can remember in my first year there was an audit which I was given sole responsibility for, it was a tiny audit, but it was a very good way of getting an overall picture of everything that was happening.

Did you attend a client's stocktaking?

Indeed. In the 1960s, Arthur Andersen was a firm very unlike the other major firms, because it had only been operating in the UK for six years at the time, and it had all the techniques based on what had emerged in the United States. The processes the firm went through, and its structure, were very different from those of 'old fashioned' English firms. And then in the late 60s, the English firms changed and transformed themselves.

Was scientific sampling up and running in those days?

No, Arthur Andersen never went in for statistical sampling to any extent, largely on the basis that we are not trying to come up with a statistically valid conclusion. The end result of an audit is a judgment on the view given by the financial statements. That's the key thing, rather than going though a mechanical process, which some of the other firms have gone through but have tended to abandon since.

There have been considerable technical changes in the company audit over the last 20 years, especially with the accelerated use of IT: how has this affected audit practice?

It's inevitable that as companies become IT-based, so the audit has to become IT-based as well. And I think for some of us older partners, who started in the days of pen and pencil, it's quite difficult to keep up with everything the younger people are doing. I don't think that of itself has necessarily made the audit process more difficult, on the other hand in some respects it has made it easier because you have the ability to do more checking, at the press of a button.

Apart from the technical impact of change, do you think it's changed the purpose of the audit?

The purpose of an audit is to express an opinion as to whether the accounts give a true and fair view and comply with the Companies Act. That's a statutory obligation and requirement, but side benefits come out of it, like management letters, which Arthur Andersen have written since the 1950s, and advice to clients. And that has been the case for 40 years.

What underpins the auditor's ethics?

The things that underpin an accountant's ethics are to do his job with integrity and objectivity, and to do it to the best of his ability. Things like the training which an accountant got is really out of date nonsense, but it is what an older generation likes to look back, rather wistfully, as the special thing which distinguished them. The younger accountants look to the market and what the market is demanding, and that is absolutely true and absolutely right. But whatever approach you take you come back to the fact that the key thing about an accountant is that he applies his specialised knowledge to the best of his ability, on behalf of his client, with integrity and objectivity. That is something that applies to all professions.

Was your relationship with client managers ever hostile?

It happens when they think that you are raising red herrings, or they don't want matters reported to higher management in the group, or you say you're going to qualify the audit report for one reason or another, or they are complaining about your fees, all those things.

Did you ever find yourself in a situation where you felt you were being prevented from getting hold of information you were entitled to in the course of an audit?

Occasionally there were clients who wished to distort their profits, and therefore removed financial records from the accounting department.

But you always found the strength of the firm was sufficient to enable you to get what you needed?

No, no. I remember on at least one occasion we were totally fooled, and the manipulation of the financial records only came out a year later. And that was a man who wanted to survive in his job as general manager of a company, and he effectively committed a manipulation of the results to further his own career.

But was it the routine of the audit that uncovered it the following year?

Yes.

What is Arthur Andersen's system of quality control for an audit?

We plan the audit carefully. We start off with a decision as to whether we are going to retain a job, or not accept re-appointment, or resign, and we do that on an analysis of the risks to the firm which might emerge in the job. We then take this risk analysis and we consider what procedures the company has got to respond to those risks—to control them. We assign to every job a team, which always has a partner involved, and in higher-risk or listed clients they always have a control or second partner. We insist that the partner leads the process of planning the audit and supervises the audit throughout. At the end of the day the partner completes the job, and discusses it with his second partner, before deciding whether to sign off. In signing off he makes various declarations, effectively to the rest of the partnership, to say he's done a proper audit. We have in place a structure which says that on difficult decisions you involve various levels of management from within the firm, which may be the head of audit practice, it may be something we call a practice director, and on very difficult decisions we go up and up and up, until effectively you reach the world-wide managing partner of Arthur Andersen.

Have you kept in touch as a partner yourself?

Oh, indeed, because I think it's very difficult for a partner to sign off an audit unless he's actually got his hands sticky with the audit process. Not the routine testing so much as actually knowing what's been going on. I don't think a partner has to do the testing himself, he has to be satisfied that it has been done properly.

Have you uncovered fraud in the course of your career?

It depends how you define fraud. Fraud can either be stealing money or assets from a business, or it can be the deliberate misrepresentation of financial information and trying to mislead people. And the deliberate misrepresentation of financial information is quite common. It gets to an interesting question as to what the cut-off is between the company which wishes to present its results in the best possible way, and one which deliberately distorts financial information, going through completely erroneous processes. To take my earlier example of manipulation, management shipped goods out of a factory before the end of the year and recorded them as sales, and after the audit they brought them back from the completely separate warehouse they had rented for the purpose. So we were misled by that, because we saw them being shipped out. We had a short time frame within which to finish our audit and we therefore circularised debtors a month or two earlier, and we didn't pick up the error—we picked it up the following year instead. Now that is deliberate manipulation of financial information, which is not an everyday occurrence, but it happens from time to time. People stealing money or assets are relatively rare.

It has been argued that the last 20 years or so have seen a dramatic decline in business ethics generally; do you agree?

No, I wouldn't. I think people are naïve when they say that the past was a golden age. There have been some cultural changes. Margaret Thatcher promoted personal greed and personal advancement to a greater extent than it existed before, and that partly reflected the reduction of tax rates under her governments, and it partly reflected the increasing efficiency of the country and the reduction, perhaps, of the power of organised labour. But if we go back and look to see what was happening in various parts of society in the 1970s, 1960s, 1940s, I don't think very much has changed.

One thing which has certainly changed is the atmosphere in which the auditor operates. When you started was litigation of any great concern?

No.

How do you explain its being a central preoccupation of today's auditors?

Firstly, America has always been a more litigious country than the UK, and the disease, if you like, has spread from America with the increasing globalisation of the world economy; and from the UK it has spread through continental Europe. The most litigious country in the world is Australia, on a per capita basis at the present time. And it will spread throughout the rest of the world. The other thing that has happened is that the professions as a whole have become much more open to challenge by the layman. In the days of my youth a professional man, whether he was a doctor, a dentist, a solicitor or a chartered accountant, was held in some awe. People didn't challenge what he said. If a professional stated his opinion he would nonchalantly be accepted as right. Now the actions that doctors take, that solicitors take, are all subject to challenge. So you've got no-one accepting the word of a professional any more; that's just the open society we live in, and at the same time it's accompanied by an environment where people say you can sue, so that's it.

To what extent does forming limited liability partnerships offer a solution?

It will be a partial solution. It won't defend the individual partner who makes a mistake, he will still be open to being sued personally.

Is it getting to a point where it's getting difficult to persuade young accountants to take on partnerships?

I've seen no evidence of that. It [as a trend] is grossly exaggerated.

Have you found the introduction of standards has strengthened the hand of the auditor with difficult clients?

Partly the standards. The greatest things that have changed the position of the auditor, and strengthened the position of the auditor have been the changes which came in with the new Accounting Standards Board in 1991 or thereabouts. What happened in the 1980s was you had an argument with your client and your client would bring in a lawyer, and the lawyer would say words to the effect of,—Where in the Companies Act, or where in accounting standards is such and such a course of action forbidden? The accountant would say,—It's not forbidden anywhere, but I think it's wrong. And the lawyer would then say,—you have no basis for saying my client can't do this. When David Tweedie (qv) came in and set up the Accounting Standards Board, he said,—We're going to account for substance over form. The lawyers will tell you what the form is and I will tell you that's irrelevant to accounting. You will account for substance. And a lot of his early standards were designed to make accountants account for substance and not for form. So that was one step which transformed the scene. The second thing which transformed the scene was the establishment of the Review Panel, which reviews cases of accounts of public companies which don't comply with accounting standards or the Companies Act. That has given enormous strength to the armoury of auditors who can say,—If you don't do this the panel will find out and you will be reprimanded and made to restate your accounts before they're issued.

Have you ever resigned from an audit on a matter of principle?

Many times. We have no wish to continue serving a client who does not listen to what we have to say. You feel a failure, because you've failed to persuade the client to do what is right. But at the end of the day, you have tried to persuade the client—you've failed. Then you ask a friend next door to come and help, and he's failed. Then you say,—well in that case, so long Mr. Client.

Do you think there's a risk of the situation being made worse by that sort of client going down the ladder in terms of the accountants who are available to them?

Yes. We had a client the other day. We found something untoward, we asked the client to investigate it and they refused to do so, so we resigned. The client then went to two other Big Six firms, who refused to work for them. They then went to two or three medium-sized firms, and if you were to rank firms in terms of size they ended up being handled by a small firm.

Have you had to qualify a client's accounts?

Reasonably frequently, not every day.

I know that technical qualifications, because of the application of standards, have become more frequent, do you think qualifications of substance have become more frequent?

I think technical qualifications are qualifications of substance. I don't like the term technical qualifications.

Please expand.

People talk about technical qualifications if someone hasn't complied with an accounting standard, but I think that accounting standards are necessary for accounts to give a true and fair view. Therefore, the term technical qualification is stupid.

Has the auditor's independence been eroded in recent years, or is the opposite true in that in the old days auditors were too close to their clients?

Auditors have to be reasonably close to their clients, because they have to understand what their client is thinking, and in order for a client to talk to you, you have to have some form of personal relationship. So you can never get complete and utter independence. I think in the old days, particularly for the smaller based companies, people did have a very close relationship, but that's got relatively little to do with independence or objectivity. Independence is all to do with complying with rules which are designed to reinforce the public perception of an auditor's integrity and objectivity. Most of the rules shouldn't really be necessary at all, but they're necessary in order to give the public confidence in what the auditor is saying. So you can be as close as you like to your client, but you can still do a fine objective audit. And that's the object at the end of the day. What you're trying to do is an objective audit, even though you break all the rules which the Institute, or the guide to professional ethics, contains. You can break all those rules and still do the best audit in the world. What those rules or professional guidances are there to do is to help to demonstrate to the external world that the auditor has not got so close that people can make allegations that they weren't independent.

Nasty scandals like Maxwell, Polly Peck, BCCI have given the profession a lot of trouble in recent years; what do you think went wrong in those cases?

They are clients that the audit firms should never have had in the first place. The control structures didn't exist. If you have a company where you have dominant individuals, such as Robert Maxwell, with the ability to override controls, as an auditor you're on a hiding to nothing. If he's not honest nasty things will take place, and you may not discover them. One of the things which auditors find great difficulty in doing is finding fraud, and in particular manipulative fraud. So I think Maxwell is a client which in retrospect I'm sure Coopers wished they never had. With BCCI and PW, I presume the same. And most of those sorts of situations come from companies with weak controls and strong dominant management.

We haven't always avoided bad clients, I wish we had. But we are very careful about the clients we take on, and we have been careful longer than the other large firms. We put every client through the wringer before we accept them, and before we decide to retain them.

A Regular Army officer's son, JAMES CARTY was born in 1937. He attended Cotton College, a private Roman Catholic boarding school, and then went on to read Economics at what was then Kingston Polytechnic, graduating in 1965. He took articles with Price Waterhouse in London, qualifying in 1968, and worked with them until 1972, attaining the rank of manager. He then went to Lancaster University to read for his Master's degree in Accounting and Finance, following which, he spent two years on their academic staff. In 1974, he returned to London to work for the Accounting Standards Committee, becoming its secretary in 1976, and in 1981, he set up as an independent practitioner in the City, concentrating on consultancy, rather than audit work. During this time he developed close links with Robson Rhodes who invited him to become a partner in 1987.

He took over as senior technical partner in 1987. He currently sits on the Accounting Standards Board's Urgent Issues Task Force.[5]

Can you give me a run down of the kind of jobs you were asked to do when you were training with Price Waterhouse in the late 1960s?

I was mainly working with large companies. I did a lot of work on American banks like Morgan Guarantee Trust, which was the largest American bank in London, and the Chemical Bank, and then some English banks—National Westminster, the Standard Bank, Barclays. I also worked on engineering companies like Baker Perkins Engineering; by my third year that was one of the major jobs I took charge of. I did a spell at Shell in London, ICI and other major companies. Price Waterhouse always advanced people very quickly, so if you showed any talent you were given responsibility. This was a time when the accountancy profession was expanding very rapidly and the demand for accountants far exceeded the number of accountants available.

Because you showed initiative and aptitude you were given your head?

Yes. I enjoyed auditing, not everybody did, but it was a bent of mine.

As a clerk would you be involved in circularising debtors?

Yes, indeed, it was a standard practice. In those days we would circularise about 100 debtors on each assignment.

As a matter of routine would you attend the client's stocktake?

Absolutely, yes. Price Waterhouse worked very closely with the American firm (and the European firm), and therefore everybody accepted American standards of auditing.

I would have thought that in your time, scientific sampling would have been in its infancy?

There wasn't a great deal of it. Mathematical approaches to selection weren't really worthwhile, and I don't think they are today really. Samples were usually selected by judgment and one usually tried to stratify them to ensure there was a fair spread. And even as an articled clerk you would select them yourself.

Was the management letter common?

It was standard practice to offer clients management letters, but only 50% of the clients wanted them. The others didn't want to spend the money.

As a clerk would you have an input into the management letter?

From the very first moment you started an audit, you were always aware that you had to arrive at a management letter, so in the whole course of your work you were looking for suggestions you could make to the client to improve their business, or rectify problems in their accounting systems. At the end of the day, one would be asked to draft the management letter, so one had to be aware all the time of possibilities and make recommendations. So with everything you did you had to keep thinking,—can I suggest something for the client which would help?

There has been considerable technical change in the audit over the last 20 years. How, in general, do you think that's impacted on the profession?

I don't think auditing has changed as much as people like to say. When I started as an articled clerk, we were doing pretty well what we are doing now. What has happened is that more firms are coming up to the standards of the bigger firms, rather than the bigger firms changing substantially. The biggest change is in the finances, because when I qualified I was paid very little, and articled clerks were a source of cheap labour. Nowadays, here in London, we pay the equivalent of articled clerks, £18,000 per year when they start. Therefore they are a very expensive form of labour when you take into account our having to pay the colleges £4,000 tuition fees per year, and they are only with us 26 weeks of the year, when you take off all the time they are on study leave. So the economics of an accounting practice have changed very substantially. And clients are more competitive in the sense they are asking people to bid for work and fee charges are one of the things they take into account. In some cases it's the only thing they take into account, though they're rather foolish if they do that. So it's more competitive and the cost base has substantially changed.

Would you say the purpose of the audit has changed?

Well, the clients are larger. I attribute this to birth control, because when I started there were still many companies owned by a family, and the family would have a number of children who went into the business, and therefore the theme of passing the business to your children was still very common. Nowadays, I think it's quite rare. If someone has a business, with smaller families, the chances are his kids aren't interested in the business, and therefore by the time they [the proprietors] get to 50–55, they're thinking,—do I have to slog on, or can I look around for a take-over? Therefore, many businesses are sold to large corporations, and the corporations themselves have expanded in size. So the size of companies is very much larger and there are fewer important medium-sized companies around, so that is a big change. And it's not only aggressive actions by the large companies trying to take over the market; probably more impetus comes from smaller companies who have been successful and are looking to be taken over.

How does that effect the way an audit is conducted?

If things go wrong they go wrong in a bigger way. And another change is that people are all too ready to sue accountants these days. When I started off as an articled clerk it was unheard of for us to be sued. Word has got round amongst lawyers that accountants have indemnity insurance, and therefore if someone runs a business into the ground through his own management incompetence, then he tries to sue us. And of course the legal aid system is a curse because it supports anything going, and they give funds to people to sue accountants. If you're a director of a company that has gone bust then you're unemployed and therefore they pay all your costs. The accounting firm on the other side, even if they win the case, doesn't get its costs back, so you just have to grin and bear it. And the people who are on legal aid have no motive for being reasonable. They just sit there and say,—why should I do a deal with you? My claim is for £200,000, if you want to settle it, that's what I want. So you're forced to fight the cases through the courts more frequently than ever before. We've never lost a case funded by legal aid but we have put out considerable sums in defence costs. So I am all in favour of the Lord Chancellor's reform of legal aid to stop this abuse.[6]

What kinds of relationships have you had with client management over the years?

Mostly relationships are very harmonious; the clients rely on you to tell them the latest developments, and what they should be doing. Obviously, there are clients who make a mess and they wish to show profits to justify themselves to their shareholders or to the bank, and there can be items which are in dispute and you have to take a view. For example, are debts collectable? The more the provision for bad debts, the lower the profits. Similarly with stock valuations, there are situations where the client doesn't want to write-down the stock. We have resigned from audits, even of public companies, where we have found the directors were not being open and truthful with us. It's fundamental to our procedures that we have to satisfy ourselves every year that directors are prepared to prepare accounts which are in compliance with the law and accounting standards, and that they have provided full information to us. If we don't believe they are doing that then we have to consider our position. But there are many ways of dealing with difficult situations; one can explain things to clients. At the end of the day, none of our clients are of sufficient magnitude to compromise our independence. We have just recently dispensed with a list of clients. I think there is a different atmosphere now. Individuals are much more interested in themselves and their own welfare and earnings than perhaps they were in the past. That's part of the Thatcher cult of individualism.

Has anybody ever said,—if you qualify my accounts you lose the audit?

They have never put it in those direct terms, nor do I think ultimately that we have lost clients. We are quite selective in the type of clients we go for; we don't go for clients who are not within our expertise, as it were. For example, in housing associations, we wouldn't go for small housing associations, we wouldn't go for housing associations which were far away from any of our offices, because that adds to the cost with the travelling time. We don't bid for small companies. As a matter of policy we have divested ourselves of 2,000 clients at the bottom of the scale who were not paying us fees which justified the partner time.

Why has the audit business become more competitive?

When the Institute removed the restrictions on advertising that led firms to start touting for business more. Also of course there are many more chartered accountants in companies than there were before. When I started it wasn't all that common to come across a chartered accountant as the chief accountant. They were very often certified accountants or cost and management accountants who had not been through the audit process themselves and were not quite sure what was happening. Now, with so many chartered accountants around who have qualified as auditors, they know what's happening and the only bill they can really cut down is the audit fee.

Is it common for you to do non-auditing work for clients that you audit?

Yes.

Do you think that has a potential for a conflict of interest?

I'm sure it does but it doesn't normally happen. Add-on services are the biggest way of expanding the practice, but I don't think there is any case where the amount we do would prejudice our audit work. Because fees are competitive these days, the notion that you can offer a cheap audit in the hope that you get other services doesn't exist. We require every service to stand on its own feet. If you offer cheap jobs to clients they rate you as cheap and they expect you to be cheap for everything.

How has the introduction of accounting standards affected auditing?

I don't think there really has been a fundamental change over my lifetime. What you're trying to do is much more certain and understandable because it's all documented. And of course, it is a curse to an accountant because if you get hauled up in court, people cite accounting standards and auditing standards and say,—this is what you should have done and this is what you didn't do. So it's much easier to prove that an accountant has been negligent than it ever was before.

The list of apparent audit failures in the Maxwell case, BCCI, Polly Peck and the rest is quite long. Why do you think they happened?

We investigated a number of the situations you've described. What happens is that in any large organisation, where you employ a very large number of people, the vast majority of people are able to comply with the standards that you embrace as a firm, but there are a minority of people who fall down on the job. And in each of the cases that you have mentioned, I'm sure there were individuals within those firms who failed to carry out the procedure they should have carried out, failed to abide by their firm's consultation procedures and made huge errors of judgment. But I think these are very much individual cases—to advance the line that fraud is endemic is not the truth. Fraud is still a rarity, but because of the size of companies, when things go wrong they can go wrong in a very big way.

In terms of the failure of the audit, you put that down to personal shortcomings in the individual auditors.

Yes. And also weakness in their characters—they can't stand up to dominant individuals in the companies. There are situations where weak audit partners are dominated by chief executives. What we do is to ensure that no one partner is responsible, entirely, for a client, and therefore if anything is happening where we feel we are not taking the right line, we have other partners there to say,—hold on a minute, this isn't where we want to go. Where one partner is running the whole show, and he is weak, he can be dominated and pushed into making a judgment that's not entirely acceptable. People do have to stand back and look at the situation. Whenever I look at a set of accounts, I say,—where is the cash? If they say they've made £1m profit then they should have £1m more cash this year than last. And if they don't, where has the profit come from? Probably by inflating the stock and the debtors or something else. Once things have gone wrong in year one and year two, you accept it again in year three. So when it's three years down the line and it's been going wrong for some time, it's been going wrong in a very big way.

You also have to take into account that there are pressures on individuals which can affect their judgment and may not be known by their firm. And these days of course, one of the problems is divorce. If one of the partners is going through a nasty divorce action, he can't focus on things as he should. Often, the partner has been under personal pressure that perhaps his firm doesn't notice. We have a counsellor, and any person can consult him without the knowledge of the firm, we just pick up the bill. If you feel under stress you can go and get external counselling, and the firm doesn't know who has gone and what is said.

What steps do you think would contribute most to improving the profession?

Firstly, splitting the requirements for large and small practices much more than they are now, so that the regulations are more applicable to the circumstances of the company. One would want much higher standards from listed companies than the unlisted smaller ones. The cost of regulation can be disproportionate to the needs of smaller companies. The Americans do it better than we do, in that they apply regulation only to larger companies, on the grounds that larger companies have a greater impact on the economy. If a big company goes wrong, there's big damage, but if the shop on the corner goes bust, then it doesn't really matter to the economy in general.

Anything else?

I think the training of auditors has got to continue to improve. We've spent an awful lot on training but it's got to be made even more central. The difficulty is not telling people what the rules are, it's improving judgment. We try to do that through case studies, where we try to get people to recognise dangerous situations.

Everything now is on the computer and we do have two systems for analysing company reports. One is called FAME which goes back over the last six years of the company and then uses a mathematical forecast of the chances of the company going bust. So that is a very important aid which you can't ignore. It gives you quite a detailed ranking of what the chances are of companies going bust over the next three years. Also, it does comparative studies with other companies. You can immediately compare your own company with its immediate competitors. So this is useful information which is now available, which wasn't available years ago.

You also have One Source which again is another comparative system, and there are many other systems which provide information for the press. So you can interrogate a database to find what people have been saying about the company or the industry. That kind of information is much more widely available than it ever was, and it's very helpful. Of course, it's a curse because if people know you're using FAME, then if you get in trouble, people will ask,—what was the FAME analysis of the company? And if it showed that this company had dangers of going bust and you had not taken that into account in your audit, then you could have difficulties defending yourself. It's a two-edged sword but the benefits outweigh the costs.

What other problems do you have in running Robson Rhodes?

Trying to do things more efficiently all the time is a battle. There isn't so much commitment from staff as there was 30 or 40 years ago. People are always thinking these days,—well I'm off to another job which pays me more, whereas I don't think it was quite so blatant years ago as it is now. When I started I was a university graduate, but only about 5% of the trainees were in those days. Nowadays we only take university graduates and not all of them are used to hard work, put it that way. Some are highly committed, but some have probably not worked very hard at university, and when they come here it's a shock to the system, and they don't take to it very well.

What I would like to happen is for us to change over to the way that the Law Society does things, so students take all their exams before they start. You finish university and then you go on a one-year course, do all the examinations, and when you come to us you are here three years full-time. Of course, we could then pay them less, as the solicitors do. Major firms of solicitors give a living allowance to their students at law school of £4,000 per year and they pay their fees, which are about £3,500. So they are paying £7,500. We're paying £18,000 in salary and £4,000 in fees, so that's £22,000 for 26 weeks work. So economically, it's crazy. I think that pressure will build up to allow us to do that, and you could then plan your work much better. It's a menace at the moment for our operations manager trying to plan when people are available to do the work. But apart from that, I think life is just more difficult than it ever was and will continue to be so.

The son of a shopkeeper, JOHN HEYWOOD was born in Devon in 1947. After attending Sheffield College, a direct grant boarding school in his home county, he went on to read Law at University College, London. Lacking confidence in his ability to make a career for himself in the law, he decided to take articles with Price Waterhouse in 1968, with the intention of moving into industry eventually. Qualifying in 1972, he has remained with PW ever since. In 1980, he became a partner—in at the 'beginning of quite a large wave of new partners.' His principal areas of responsibility are the newly opened up markets in Eastern Europe, Russia and China, and he was appointed chairman of the firm's Eastern European board in 1993.

What jobs were you asked to do when you were training in the late 60s early 70s?

I spent about 18 months of my first two years in Peterborough, living in hotels, doing audits at Baker Perkins Engineering, and also Hotpoint, which was part of GEC. Hotpoint was interesting, with their mass of white goods flowing down the production line. That was all audit work. After that I had a spell in the small business department. I got involved with the insolvency of an aircraft firm on the Isle of Wight. I went down there every Monday and came back every Friday, which was hard. And we were always put in the tax department to do tax recovery work for long periods of time.

How closely were you supervised?

Well compared with today not very much. It really depended on the quality and the aptitude of the senior on the job at the time. I had a good relationship with a very important lady called Mrs Warner, who used to allocate staff to jobs. You got good jobs or bad jobs depending on how you got on with her.

Was there a set audit programme for every client?

We did have set audit programmes. But I remember in 1969, there was a major upgrading in the way we did an audit. We had lots of training and presentations of the new way of doing things. The old-fashioned audit programmes, which comprised of ticking and bashing, disappeared about then. We were moving into a new era. We talked lots about the business approach to audit in '69, and you see variations of that coming through more recently. I was impressed by the new systems of that time. We tended to do a lot of system checks, following bits of paper all the way through the system.

Did you stay with PW after your training?

Yes. At that stage they were introducing a new level—assistant manager. The role was overseeing the consolidation of large clients who had a large number of subsidiaries. I covered Trust House Forte and Credit International. I spent quite a bit of time on that because it wasn't as systematised as the consolidation process is now. I then went on to acquisitions checking. Then in the middle 70s, of course, there was the secondary banking crisis, and that led to a lot of investigations work.

How would you summarise the changes that have affected auditing since those days?

The context of an audit has changed in three major ways. Firstly, systems of control and information systems are much more efficient now. Secondly, we have changed our audit presentation quite dramatically from what it was. It was almost like a one liner stating the accounts were true and fair. It's now an explanation of who is responsible for what, and an attempt to outline to the reader of the audit report what aspects we as accountants are able to give assurance of. Thirdly, we are now performing in the context of much more rigorous corporate governance arrangements for major groups, which lay down much more onerous responsibilities for non-executive directors, who may want to have assurance that their systems work, particularly in key risk areas. This has changed quite a lot from the 60s. My memory is that non-executive directors had less responsibilities, and didn't feel their job was onerous.

Do you think the purpose of the audit has changed?

The purpose has evolved, yes, and globalisation will continue to alter things. So you are not only aware of the expectations of investors in a particular country. You are having to satisfy the expectations of the most sophisticated investors around the world. Take China, where the local expectations have changed dramatically over the last five years. They need this funny thing called an IS audit by one of the Big Six firms, to get the money to invest.

As a partner were you involved in developing new audit techniques?

Yes, we got more involved than our predecessors. I remember re-designing the scope of work that we were doing for three or four major groups. Myself, together with the senior manager, sat down and made our audits more efficient. The process now has developed, in that we have our managers spending more time with the partners than used to be the case, acting as a team.

Did you ever uncover fraud in the course of an audit?

Not as an auditor, but doing receivership work and viability studies of companies, I once or twice came across situations that didn't look right. On audits, we've uncovered deliberate mistakes in the sums, rather than actually taking the money or whatever, and one of my clients managed to walk away from the bank with a suitcase full of cash. That one became obvious rather early.

Have you ever been involved in formally qualifying a client's accounts?

Yes, over concern about the collectability of debts from a foreign country. There were going concern qualifications over the years, too.

Would you say qualification is more frequent now than it was?

In some ways, yes, because accounts and auditing are much more prescriptive now. There are many more regulations and rules and disclosures which need to be made, and so there are many more clear cut exceptions. Twenty years ago, they were just introducing accounting rules. There are many more reasons to qualify and, because of the nature of very large multinational groups, there is increased risk that things may go wrong with their subsidiaries.

Have you come under any pressure from a client not to qualify an account?

No client likes his accounts qualified, and you do have discussions as to why it's necessary, and they argue. Quite a lot have got wider experience than just one company, and more easily recognise the need to qualify.

Has the auditor's relationship with the client changed?

The role of the finance director has changed over the last 20 years, very dramatically in the last five years. We spend less time on strictly accounting issues. Whereas before, we had very strong relationships with them, now in a very large company the finance director's role has become much wider. He's responsible for the whole area of operational management in many ways, supporting the chief executive's strategy, formulation of policy and so on. The production of the annual accounts is much less central to his role than it used to be; most of that is delegated to the controller.

When did you start seeing tendering for audits coming in, and what do you think caused it?

Companies now have to compete more, either in the home market place or internationally, and get good value for money. I remember at an annual general meeting in 1981 a shareholder banging on about audit fees. That was my first recollection of anything other than a rubber stamp at an AGM, and that marked the time when audit fees started to come under increasing pressure. We now get involved in competitive tenders for other people's audits, and frequently defend our own. The Big Six are highly competitive amongst themselves and each firm has its own style of competitiveness. Some firms try to compete on quality and some on price and some with a mix.

How important do you think special work is in sustaining audit work?

Sustaining? In our practice less than 35% of our fee income comes from other work. But of the rest, a significant proportion of advice, which can include the client's tax, consulting, or even internal audit systems, and a whole range of other services, will not be involved with our audit clients at all. There is pressure, mainly coming from Brussels, suggesting that auditors should not be allowed to provide any other services to audit clients. I think the balance of opinion amongst our clients is that it is not a sensible way forward for their company because they value the relationship. Sometimes the auditor is in the best place, particularly in the area of tax, to give advice. I think now we organise our service lines, our product groups, increasingly independently from the audit side. So our consulting group is managed on a global basis and they move their resources around and choose to provide services or compete with services for companies which are important to them. They are not necessarily making judgments based on whether they are also our audit clients or not. So independent management of service lines is increasing.

Do you think the regime of auditing standards is working?

Yes I do, because in the last few years the Review Panel has been making sure people are complying. And of course, we have the increasing influence of the USA, where the SEC have been very strong in enforcing the rules and regulations, and that, much tougher approach, is making its mark here. The big question is whether the UK should be devising regulations which are UK orientated, or whether we should be looking for an internationalisation of standards.

How much sympathy would you have for the small practitioner who tells me that ordinary shareholders cannot understand company accounts?

For individual shareholders accounts are non-user friendly. For the institutional investor, yes, they do the job. What the individual shareholders should be getting assurance from are the corporate governance processes which are more protective of their situation than ten years ago. But the actual reading of the accounts for the shareholders is tough. Of course, many companies are now publishing a simpler version. They are coming under pressure really for openness of disclosure. As far as the small practitioner is concerned, all this is putting pressure on him as to whether he can still provide a service to the larger client. As a Big Six partner, I would say that wouldn't I. But it must be quite difficult for the small practitioner to get his people trained up in the full range of skills.

A lot of them seem to regard accounting standards as a bureaucratic nightmare.

The standards are aimed at the top 1,000 companies in the country. And so it is going to be an increasing challenge for the small practitioner to merge with others of similar size, so that they can fund the training, which is essential to specialise. The days of the old fashioned general practice are going.

Just in general would you say the standard of auditing has got better or worse?

The standard of production of accounts by companies has risen, and I think auditors have advanced hugely the whole process of managing a company's accounts. We are in an environment that dictates we must continuously improve, and two years ago we launched a whole programme of upgrading our procedures. Then we started other people thinking about what we should be launching in five years time as the next new thought. We are into much faster change brought on by internationalisation, which means the biggest firms have got to respond all the time and that is what makes for an interesting life.

Professor Sir DAVID TWEEDIE, born in 1944, is the son of a Scots mining engineer who worked all over the world. After attending Grangemouth High School and Edinburgh University, where he obtained his B.Com. and Ph.D., he was offered a lectureship in Business Administration. Feeling it was unwise to take up the post without any business experience, a two-year placement with Lever Brothers was suggested. He thought, however, that he would be more likely to find out how business worked by witnessing several businesses from inside their finance function as an external auditor. So in 1969, perhaps the first-ever Ph.D. to do so, David took articles with the then 12-partner Glasgow firm of Mann, Judd, Gordon, qualifying in 1972. From 1973–78, he taught Accountancy at Edinburgh University before becoming technical director for the Scottish Institute until 1981. He then became national research partner for KMG Thomson McLintock, until the firm merged with Peat, Marwick, Mitchell in 1987, when he became national technical partner. Since 1990, he has been full-time chairman of the Accounting Standards Board. A prolific and much published writer on the theory and practice of accountancy, David is recognised as one of the most acute thinkers about the profession and its future direction. He was knighted in 1994.

What sort of firm was Mann, Judd, Gordon?

The senior partner was the sort of man who had bottom, he wasn't one of these adventurous chaps but he was a very solid citizen. That was the style of Glasgow accountants—they were very professional and very thorough. As far as new techniques were concerned, they were experimenting with systems reviews and sampling, but it was early days for that for the profession.

Early days?

It was, but they were willing to try.

Can you give me a run down on the clients you had?

In Carlisle, the breweries and pubs had been nationalised in the First World War, when the munitions workers were frequently drunk a lot and the shells didn't explode. Things were run by the Home Office till 1971 or 1972, when Ted Heath de-nationalised them. That was one client. The Pitlochry Festival Theatre was another; this was an enormous audit. It was mainly a cash business being a theatre and it took quite a lot of money—we had a lot of experimental audit programmes in that one. Then there were quite a few motor car salesmen; I wouldn't have bought a second hand car from those firms! And there were small manufacturing family businesses in Glasgow; these were the main ones I did. I had great fun with them. I remember the first year, I did one sweat shop family business; father and son ran it. The year I went to do it the profit turned out about £30,000, and there was great consternation because it had always been about £5–6,000. We wouldn't tell them what their profit figure was at first, in case they went out and spent it. But it turned out, when we did a further investigation, that they had two products—one had a huge margin and the other a tiny margin—and they made about 90% of the tiny margin product and about 10% of the other one. For some reason, the materials ran short for the tiny margin one and they were forced to switch production to the one that made them all the profits. They didn't realise they had been making the wrong product for years. After that they transformed their business. It was pure luck!

At that time, we went in and did the audit and shot off, but there was a strong case for management advice. There should be a fee for an accountant saying how the business could be made more profitable. But then of course you're in danger of losing your independence, and this is one of the problems involved.

There has been considerable technical change over the last 20 years. How this has altered the audit?

Back in my early days, I was doing the smaller companies and you'd more of a hands-on feel for things. In the three years I was articled, we must have caught three or four frauds. I wonder if they'd catch them now. You dealt with so many more transactions in those days. Nowadays with the number of transactions going on in Glaxo say, just testing their systems is a big enough challenge. So if there's a fraud going on and the guy's any good and not too greedy, forget it. But there have been massive changes in the statistical methodology. The problem is one of trying to quantify the errors,—now what does this mean as far as profit is concerned? Have they got this wrong? It probably loses the closeness of the audit of my early days, but it's far more sophisticated now. Furthermore there is special training in fraud detection. We had to rely on standard audit techniques, which at times were very effective though. Most fraud is found out by accident, or someone silly does something dumb or somebody tells, which is the main reason fraudsters get caught.

Fraud gets a very high profile nowadays. Do you think that's the problem or do you think it's actually more common?

With classic frauds like Ferranti or like BCCI, major conspiratorial frauds, you won't find out quickly (if at all) unless somebody talks or makes a mistake. In all the textbooks, they tell you that all the systems are designed so that people don't get together to conspire, but if two people do get together in key positions, they can beat the system and you won't find out. Where you've got phoney entries and people backing them up, with foreign government involvement, or you get forged letters, you have a fraud that's very difficult to uncover, There's got to be a mistake on the part of the perpetrators.

Do you think the purpose of the audit has changed?

One of the problems the auditor's got is deciding what he is trying to do these days, and he's very, very defensive. For example, we [the ASB] produce recommendations as to what we want to see audited. Yet some auditors protest it's impossible,—we can't do that, it puts us at risk! One of the simple things is getting clients to say what they are doing about the year 2000 problem [the millennium bug]. When we get letters back from auditors saying,—we can't guarantee that there aren't any glitches, but we can't see any problems, what they are saying is, the company's statement is plausible—that's fine. But auditors can't just say,—I can't touch this and walk away, because people want some assurance. There's a lot of running for cover, because the lawyers are on the prowl.

The whole liability issue is a major problem, because investors don't just want certain statutory information, they want to know if a whole lot of things are OK. And if auditors say they can't opine on that kind of information, then they're not moving forward with market demand. There's also a big question over independence. Who appoints the auditors? The very people who negotiate with them about the presentation of accounts. So what happens if you have a fight? Seldom do the clients proceed and issue accounts qualified by the auditor. More often than not they give way, albeit grudgingly. But if they're really mad they don't have to fire you. They'll put the audit out to tender, and while you'll be asked to compete you probably won't get the job. That's how they get rid of you. Now what's the advice on that? The only solution is to remove the power of appointment from those whose accounts are being audited.

Is auditor independence at that great a risk?

No auditor's going to take a chance on something that is manifestly wrong. But I think the 1980s were an absolute disaster, and that's really the reason the ASB exists. I saw some weird things that made you ashamed. I think the auditors of the 1980s lost it. That was a bad time. There were several things happening, but broadly speaking, this was a boom period and companies were terrified about their share price because: a) they wanted to use it to take somebody over or, b) to stop being taken over themselves. So protecting the share price put terrific pressure on earnings. And then merchant bankers and others started supplying ways of 'improving' financial statements, such as off-balance sheet financing. Why don't we call debt 'equity.' Here's a scheme that can give you extra profits. All these schemes were things that auditors were supposed to cope with, and they didn't.

Why didn't they?

They hadn't got the weapons. The auditor depends on seeing financial reporting gives a true and fair view. So what is a true and fair view? Well, there's the law, there's accounting standards and there's the general practice. As for general practice you were getting a scheme that wasn't against the law, wasn't against the accounting standards, but was right on the edge. You may not have liked it but a few other auditors had let it go. Then you'd get the merchant banker and the lawyer coming in and saying,—I'm sorry, this is acceptable in your profession now, there are precedents—two or three other companies used the scheme and their auditors had accepted it. And your own QC would say,—you can't qualify, that is accepted practice. So it's not up to you what your view of true and fair is, you've got to accept the profession's view. The other guys sold you down the river. I'm not blaming any particular firms, everybody was doing it. Suddenly there was a bad scheme that was accepted, so the next scheme was even worse, you started to tumble downhill.

One of the reasons this board [ASB] was set up was to stop these practices, so we hit these schemes pretty quickly. We've got two weapons that we didn't have in the 80s. One is the Urgent Issues Task Force, where, if we see a scheme, like the ones I've mentioned, we ban it, and we can do that in a matter of weeks. So the precedent's gone. We don't allow any grandfather's rights [custom and practice] for those who used a bad scheme—it's just tough luck.

The second weapon we've got is the Review Panel; if it's really bad we'll put the Review Panel on to a company. They chew the company directors up and make them produce decent accounts. The Review Panel has stiffened the audit up. If the Review Panel finds against the company the accounts have got to be changed, and if the auditor didn't qualify, then it's an automatic submission to the disciplinary committee [of the ICAEW]. How far is the auditor prepared to support the client rather than the financial community? So there is terrific pressure. And if the auditor fails in his duty the question of course is,—OK, you're the guy who signed it, who else said you could sign it? You could pull in the technical partner, the senior partner, get the lot of them. So if there's something really bad, the Institute could really hammer a firm.

An opinion that's been expressed to me is that the disciplinary structures of the Institute are practically toothless.

Totally wrong. The only criticism is that it takes too long. People escape, we see it from the Review Panel, but ultimately in serious cases they are caught and brought to book. As for companies appearing before the Review Panel, some play a game. They say,—we received your letter and are considering our reply. But it's a long time before they reply. You get a to-ing and fro-ing of letters, and the company may try to spin it out so that you get close to the next set of accounts and it lessens the impact. It is less dramatic to restate comparatives[7] than to withdraw the accounts. So everything is deliberately delayed.

Similarly, if someone is being sued, which often is the case, court actions impede the Institute's disciplinary procedures. They have to wait until court cases are complete before it can open its procedures. This leaves the whole disciplinary process open to derision. You are dealing with cases that happened seven or eight years ago, and you're bringing in witnesses who can't quite remember what happened.

Do you think the presence of standards now will cut down the number of qualifications?

It should do, but of course you don't know where the auditor has done his job. You can see the failure in the sense that qualifications have failed to persuade, but no one outside sees the success of the auditor's insistence that the rules be applied. Usually it doesn't get to that stage—it can get pretty acrimonious and then the client concedes. Sometimes the standard does not fit the precise circumstances,—that's where the true and fair overrider[8] comes in. I've been involved with one major company,—they were obeying the standard in question, but in conjunction with another standard, it was going to release a gain of £50m, which didn't exist, into profits. This was just ridiculous; and we refused to allow it, even though the client said,—there's this line of the standard, and there's this line of the other standard, and I'm doing both of these, how can you qualify? The client eventually conceded the point.

Have you ever had any experience of arm twisting to hold a qualification at bay?

They would try to persuade you. I don't want to sound like a purist, but ultimately that's what you're there for. If it comes to the crunch, the company directors are not your employers, and that's the auditor's real problem. That's the reason I'm dubious about the process of the appointment of auditors. If you're an audit partner in one of the major firms you have probably two major clients, and what if you lose one? That's a huge chunk of the firm's income gone. Not a good thing for the individual audit partner, especially if the firm is over-partnered; some other partner could take over your remaining clients! In that situation, the individual's being put under terrible pressure, and that's caused because the client can change auditors quite easily, though not frequently. So why allow the client to do that?

So you wouldn't be impressed by the argument coming from the Big Five that there is no client that they couldn't afford to lose?

They do lose some big ones and they can afford to lose them, but not willingly. But the individual partner can't. And the senior partner doesn't like to have to stand up and confess the firm has lost more big audit clients, and answer questions like,—what's wrong with us, we keep losing clients? So there is pressure on senior management, as well as the individual auditor. I could make several suggestions. One is that the individual partner should sign his name on behalf of the firm, because I know of partners who hid behind the firm's name and did some pretty rubbishy audits and got a firm into trouble. Whereas if it had been public, it would be a case of—not him again! And I suspect the partner would have been ousted by the firm. That would make a difference.

And the other thing I think should be done is with the formal appointment. This should probably be done through the audit committee, but that could be the chairman's chums, and in most of the major scandals the boards of directors have had non-executive directors involved in audit committees. You want to have independent ones, and I think the key to that lies in the institutional shareholders starting to punch their weight. Why don't the institutions, who really own British industry, start pushing for really strong independent non-executive directors, and come up with a slate of a dozen people, given the need for the right mix on a company's board, and say,—pick any three of these as a majority of the audit committee.

Do you think the profession has benefited in the current atmosphere of fierce competition?

Not really. But I think advertising has always been there. We always used to do it, but we'd call it recruitment advertising, and put it in the wrong magazine for recruitment but one read by potential clients!

The real difference has been in how you get on in a firm. We used to divide the partners up into mandarins and samurai. The samurai were commercial animals, whilst the mandarins sat back and were wise; and you need a balance. You need people around you who put a hand around a shoulder and say,—don't do that, laddie, just slow down; you'll get us into trouble. I think that's one of the problems these days, because very few partners remain after 55, in any of the firms. You do need that hand on the shoulder, saying,—just take it easy, and think of the long term consequences, not just the short-term advantages.

You think that's been missing?

It is missing—the commercial animals are all there, but a lot of the mandarins have retired now, and the others are under tremendous pressure.

But we've got a real problem with the audit till you've sorted out the way appointments are made, because of the effect on the individual partner who is personally under pressure not to lose a client. I must say though that in recent years there have been some excellent appointments as heads of audit in the major firms, and they have emphasised quality and supported the individual partner. The tide may be turning.

You don't see any danger in the auditing firm taking on more and more special work; you don't see that as a conflict of interest?

You've still got the same pressure as you've always had before, because if the client doesn't like your opinion, then you're always under pressure, whether you are doing special work or not. I don't think acting as a consultant matters if you have the independence, manifested by a better audit appointment system.

Company accounts are different from 20 years ago, who are they for?

They're for the informed investor or would be investor. To read accounts properly, however, a sound and up-to-date knowledge of accounting is necessary. You could say accounts are for accountants and they always have been. I wrote a book with Tom Lee in '77,[9] about the responsibility of accountants to shareholders, and we checked up and found that many people don't read or understand accounts. Certainly, ordinary shareholders don't understand them; nor, incidentally, do all financial analysts-look how they were taken in by Polly Peck.

I know accountants who get very impatient with the current way of presenting company accounts; what is your view?

Part of the presentation is dictated by law, accountants have no alternative. Also, unfortunately, the profession gets the rules it deserves. Had people behaved themselves in the 80s then we would have several standards less. Standards are put in to enforce order because of the rogues, and there are more to come; those who don't want or even need direction, are suffering too. It may look complicated, and that's partly because of what some accountants have done. For example, to the profit and loss account is now added the statement of recognised gains and losses as a distinct entity, and some say,—what's the point? The problem of, for example, who gains or loses on overseas investments were recognised only in reserves (remember Polly Peck), and could be missed. A loss is now visible; it wasn't visible before but is very visible now. Another one was,—when's a debt a share? Only when a company is not obliged to pay interest or redeem it. You might think that was blindingly obvious. You don't have to be an accountant to understand it. You shouldn't have to have rules for that, but we had to have a standard to stop bad practice in this area.

Similarly with off-balance sheet financing, assets and liabilities would vanish, but the auditor would be saying,—It is legal, there's not much I can do about it. As an example of the sort of thing that was happening, distilleries keep their stock for five years, so a distillery would distil the whisky and sell it to the bank instantly. It would then have an option to call it back from the bank at the price the bank had paid plus the interest. But it never left the distillery, it was just a paper transaction. The bank never saw the stock, yet the stock was missing from the distillery's balance sheet, a sale had been recorded with possibly a profit. But there was no profit, all that happened was that cash went up and a liability goes up because, of course, the distillery had to pay the cash back plus all the interest on it. And that's how we should make them show it in the accounts. That's where I think the true and fair view, which is the guardian angel of accountancy, says,—I don't care what the law says, this is not a genuine sale. It might be a legal sale, but it's not a genuine one. You're not going to account for it as such.

If auditors let a scheme through, the next thing you know it's accepted. That's why you get the rule that says,—don't do it. And the worst scam of all, it was outrageous, involved acquisition of companies. Some of our major companies have stopped being so successful since we banned acquisitions provisions. Let's say you buy a company for £100,000 and its got £100,000 of net assets. And then you say the stock was over valued by £30,000, so you knock it down by £30,000. Then you consider that the company needs to be reorganised, and that's going to cost, £20,000 plus, so let's provide for it, and another provision of £20,000 for future losses. Suddenly you've knocked £70,000 off the company's net assets. Then you sell the stock, which was not overvalued, showing an extra margin of £30,000, and decide you don't need the provisions for reorganisation or future losses. So these are added back into profit, which is interesting, considering they were never charged against profit! Suddenly in the year after acquisition, profits are increased by 70K, all through phoney accountancy and not good management. In the year before Coloroll[10] went bust it brought back £52m of acquisition provisions, out of a profit of £55m,—it actually only made £3m! Who noticed before it was too late?

We decided you can't have a liability to reorganise an acquired company until you actually own it, and only then if you are irrevocably committed to the expenditure and can't avoid it. Providing for future losses is now banned,—you may have impaired assets, but poor future trading results do not result in a liability. And as far as the stock items are concerned, you can have stock written down, but if it goes back up again you explain to us what happened after the acquisition to produce this huge profit, when it was outside normal margins. That was the worst one. Now, you knew you were never going to stop this completely, but you could regulate against it becoming normal practice. And these are the regulations that are available now. We provide a checklist. People were making billions on this, and they are bound to kick against it. But we're saying,—forget the billions, that's a thing of the past.

These are the sorts of things where you need to produce standards and people will have to accept them.

Would you have any sympathy with the small practitioner who says he's been snowed under with standards?

Yes, I have. On Thursday [23/7/98], we're issuing another simplified version of standards but my own view is that we should not be in the business here of setting standards for small companies. But why don't we let the market decide? Why don't we just let small firms choose how to present their accounts? Then if a banker says to them,—if you want to deal with me, then I need a full set of accounts, and you have to do the full works. But only if the people want it: they may say,- do the legal minimum. But the market's driving it.

The Institute in particular has a lot of problems as a result of proliferating standards—there's practically a grass roots revolt against it, largely made up of small practitioners.

A lot of this is phoney, because we've issued 11 standards, and if you look at what we've issued, most of them don't actually affect small practitioners,—complex financial instruments, acquisitions, off-balance sheet financing. How often do they meet them? It always amuses me when they say,—we hate all these standards! Most of them don't apply.

What is the cause of their discontent?

I don't think it's the ASB causing their problems. There are several things: they've got auditing standards, they've got ethical standards, legal changes, tax changes, but we add to the feeling of pressure.

Would it be easier for some of them to relinquish the status of being a C.A. and carry on their business free of a lot of the regulation?

Some of them undoubtedly will, it's pretty tough going. Ultimately, it's government which will set the standards, and I've said in public that I wouldn't set standards for small companies. But as long as all companies are tied to a true and fair view, the lawyers tell us that they're bound by the standards. You can't have another completely different set of standards for small companies. It's up to the small practitioners to lobby for change,—there will always be a place for the small man in the market.

On the one hand, you've got the small man saying the Institute is in the pockets of the big firms, and yet when you talk to the senior partners in the big firms they are almost at the point of doing without it.

It's quite interesting, because the big firms say they are carrying all the liability. The government may not always listen to the big firms but they might listen to the voice of the professional body speaking on their behalf. Small firms feel disenfranchised, and some may try to stop anybody from the big firms becoming President, but it's the big firms who have the people who have got the time.

Going back to BCCI, Maxwell, Polly Peck and the rest; just in general, what are the lessons for the profession?

When you have a very assertive chief executive you need some damn good independent directors and auditors who can stand up to him. There's no use moaning about corporate governance if you flinch under fire. You really need guys who are prepared to stand up.

I remember going into one of our major clients on a KPMG audit. The chairman of the audit committee of the company was a very well known businessman, and while we were discussing the audit, which had been extremely difficult due to the 'adventurous' accounting of the FD and the ensuing arguments with the audit team, he [the audit committee chairman] said,—tell me, on a scale of very acceptable to totally unacceptable, where does this company stand as far as its accounting policies are concerned? Just about acceptable,—we said. And we were asked to leave [the room]. There was a hell of a row. That's the sort of guy who didn't give a damn. He didn't need his £15,000 or £20,000 non-executive's fee; he was going to challenge things. Next year there were no problems. That's the sort of person you want. If you get that sort of bloke things start to happen, and that would have helped in the Maxwell situation. With BCCI, they were out to fool everyone and conspiracies are very difficult to detect.

Except, it occurs to me as a layman, that in almost every case, there is one detail that is so glaringly obvious that you wonder how the auditor didn't spot it?

With Polly Peck the market didn't spot it either. It's interesting that a lot of the investing institutions went for Maxwell, or went for BCCI, some people were totally fooled. Everything, however, is obvious afterwards.

MARTIN SCICLUNA was born in 1950, the son of a home counties company director. After Berkhamsted School, he studied Economics, Law and Accountancy at the University of Leeds, having always planned to go into the profession. In 1973, he took up a three-year training contract with Touche Ross in London, duly qualifying in 1976. He rose rapidly through the firm, becoming a partner in 1982, head of audit, London, 1990–5, and a member of the board of partners from 1991. He was appointed chairman and senior partner in 1995, prior to the merger in the following year, which saw the firm renamed Deloitte & Touche. Between 1990 and 1995, he was an ICAEW national Council member and chaired its Auditing Committee. Martin remains an active auditor with his own clients and is an impassioned and articulate defender of the profession, in the face of its contemporary detractors.

What kinds of clients did you help audit in training?

A huge variety. They ranged from a UK bank, a US bank, a defence contractor, a cosmetics company, what is now called a utilities company, it used to be called an electricity board, and a financial institution, dealing in mortgages.

And this was obviously pure audit work?

Exclusively.

How close were the partners to the audit work in those days?

I would say pretty closely involved, actually. Our firm always had the ethos of working partners. We were not the sort of practice where the partners never leave their office and only turn up to shake hands and eat lunch. They were totally working partners. It was a good place to be because of the firm's huge amount of investment in training, which has continued to this day.

Can you give me an outline of what you see as being the main changes in the audit over the course of your career?

Obviously, an enormous investment in technology, that was a big change. When I started in 1973, I had a calculator which I thought was expensive. Today, all our people are armed with laptop computers. This is not just computers replacing the working paper files; our programmes are designed with the aid of a computer, within a computer. So you now have tailored programmes for the client. This is all investment in quality control and getting the programmes right. I think that's one big area.

Another big area of change is much, much more emphasis on internal controls within a company. That has been brought about by a number of factors: the increased investment in systems by companies, and the internal controls around those, increasing size, increasing complexity. When I started 24 years ago there was much more emphasis on doing a sample of a 120 sales invoices. You brought them down from the filing cabinet and you dusted them and put a stamp on them. There's much more emphasis now on understanding the business. There is much more understanding of the risks of the industry, the risks of the business, and therefore the weaknesses and how they control them. It is much more risk-based than 24 years ago. This change happened over a long period.

Is the relationship with the client company radically different now?

Our key contact is still the finance director. The big change that has happened in the last seven years or so is the increasing attention that auditors have paid, not just to management, but actually to the shareholders through non-executive directors, audit committees. And I find it extremely galling that we are constantly being criticised for not looking after the interests of shareholders. Compared to where we are now, when I started the shareholder was so distant you only had executive management to deal with. Now we are very insistent on proper financial information being presented, and look towards the non-execs and the chairman of the audit review, besides the finance director. So to some extent, there has been a little bit of distancing from client management. Our major critics say we are in the pockets of management, which is a load of rubbish.

You would argue that audit committees are effective?

They make you focus on what is true and fair, what is right, what are the weaknesses and controls, what are the issues, what are the judgments? They give you the right perspective. They've been very, very helpful.

Do you think the purpose of the audit has changed?

The primary purpose obviously remains the audit opinion, because it's attached to the financial statements. It is to make sure that the shareholders get a financial statement showing a true and fair view. I think increasingly now the audit is also used by the company management to get value out of it, whereas in the past they were quite happy not to. Now they have become smart buyers.

What underpins an accountant's ethics, coming into contact with smart buyers?

First of all, enormous personal and professional pride. All of us are graduates now. On top of that, we all train for three years and take another set of exams to become chartered accountants. All of us hold that qualification close, dear to our hearts, because the last thing we ever want to do is lose it. To us it is the passport to continue working in practice; or if you then want to present yourself as a finance director, you don't want to say,—I had it, but I lost it. That's the personal element. Then there is a huge amount of pressure in the firms to maintain very high standards. The firm's reputation in the market place is a key driver. You do not sell good professional services, at good rates, if you don't have a good reputation. Then, there is litigation. You not only get sued if you screw up, but if you are the partner concerned you also lose your job.

Can you tell me about your relationships with client management over the years?

You get into pretty confrontational situations where you are absolutely adamant. Again, this is something that unfortunately never gets publicised. You do get situations where you say,—I'm just telling you, you will not do that or else I qualify. Now again, our critics say,—well how many qualifications are there? And if there are qualifications they are all technical and so big deal. But the truth is, it's like nuclear war. How many nasty regimes did we knock out using nuclear bombs? The reality is the threat of nuclear war, or the threat of me qualifying a set of accounts. When I firmly believe that I'm not happy with something, I have gone to the wire with the finance director, ultimately I have always found that either it's dealt with my way, or we compromised in such a way that I was then able to withdraw the threat of nuclear war. Often the people are very sensible. Generally, we manage those situations. If I wanted ten pounds off the profit or else I qualify, the client might say,—OK, we'll give you eight, and eight I'll live with. But again there is the view—I've read and heard it enough times—the Big Six give in, because they are too interested in having good relationships with their clients. And the truth is of course we are very interested in having good relationships with our clients. Of course we are. We are a profession that serves clients. But ultimately, if something is wrong, and it's important, we stand our ground.

Do you take personal pride in any innovations of your own designed to improve the quality of an audit?

Yes, I think most of us do. As a firm, both internationally and in the UK, you tend to keep moving on your methodology in steps. You put in a new methodology, you implement it, you see how that goes, you run it for three or four years maybe, and then meanwhile, you've already started phase two. A lot of us would already be working on the next step in our own way and that drives the next stage after that.

Do you see that as a purely technical exercise, in terms of keeping up to date with what can be done?

It's actually deeper than that, more a sense of professional pride, professional service. You always try to improve the quality of client service.

You're the chairman now. In general, how much initiative do you allow underneath you? Let's go right down to the lowest level: a first year student out on the job, how much initiative is he or she expected to show?

Obviously, the lower down, the less initiative. Because to some extent you've got to make sure that people do things properly. It is a top down process now, whereas when I started auditing, it was bottom-up. The team did everything and the partner reviewed it. Now the partner says,—this is what I want done. I know my client and I want it done like so. So there is more direction. But it is in the added value area of an audit that the junior can show initiative. On one of my audits somebody pointed out that a client's two subsidiaries were wastefully using two different software packages. So you do allow those types of initiative. But to be clear, you're still making sure that the audit is done to the standards.

Do you have a system of peer review within Deloitte & Touche?

We've got the best quality control process in the world, which we introduced 20 years ago, and we have a quality control department manned by a partner, full-time, and half a dozen managers, full-time. All our work including mine, whether I am the chairman or whatever, has to go through them, and a manager can stop me issuing an opinion unless he is satisfied I'm carrying out the necessary standards. So that is what is called the hot review. That's before I issue an opinion. A lot of firms have what is called cold review; after issuing opinions, someone comes and looks into the work. The problem is, of course, if I'd screwed up it's too late.

Where do you stand on the issue of audit work being compromised by the same firm of accountants doing non-audit work? Are there arguments for the European model where audit is kept separate?

Well first of all the European separation is done by smoke and mirrors. You have got to be careful of European issues because the Europeans say they do something, but in fact they do it very differently. Firms have an audit practice and then they have a parallel practice doing the consulting or the tax. So they say they are independent but they are not really. So I think the European model doesn't work. It's a pretence.

We've had eight years of attacks on us by some critics for doing non-audit work, which is supposed to be compromising. I have said, in public meetings and letters to the *FT*, in all sorts of private letters,—Give me some evidence that proves it—and I haven't yet received any proof, number one. Number two, the critics don't understand. Forget my current position, say I'm an audit partner. I'm 46. Would anyone really think that I would purposely give a wrong audit opinion because we are getting a lot of fees? By giving that wrong opinion, I could get the firm sued mega-bucks. I could have the wrath of all the partners upon me because I ruined the firm's reputation, and probably because of the lack of insurance I could bust them. I'll be kicked out by my firm once the litigation is over and no one will touch me. I've debated with Austin Mitchell in public meetings, I've argued in bars with Prem Sikka. Look at Binder Hamlyn and what they had to pay on ADT.[11]

If I turn round to my partners and say,—I'm going to really incur the wrath of this client because I think what he wants to do is totally wrong, never in my life have I been told,—Oh no, you'd better sign, there's another million at stake, and we've got a good relationship going. Because a million today is nothing compared to the loss of reputation and future income and all the other things. So I find that criticism so unfounded. It's just people who don't understand the profession. If I knowingly signed a pile of rubbish I could be ending my career today.

But weren't the auditors partly to blame when some of the major frauds were uncovered?

If you have a bunch of crooks who are intent on collusion, it's hard. Just think how difficult it is afterwards to pin an individual down for fraud, and yet you've had years of investigation specifically on the person. Investigators have the power to subpoena the person, they can subpoena witnesses, they can go into related companies. And yet, if you think about it, how many people have been nailed properly for fraud. People expect us to find it easy to discover it when we're doing a general audit. It's like saying how come drugs still come through customs? The fact is that some people stuff them in all sorts of places and these things happen. Everyone says audit failure means that auditors were negligent. It's not true. Sometimes the fraud is so well engineered that it can take years to find it.

In most of the major frauds, though, there do seem to be glaring details of one kind or another, that cause the layman to wonder,—how could the auditor have ignored that?

Sure. With hindsight, you can point to signals. But just think, in the middle of an audit you can be given totally plausible reasons and documentation that looks right because it has been cleverly fabricated. It can happen.

So what's the answer?

There are no simple solutions, but it has come to light on more than one occasion that various institutions, it could be the DTI, the Bank of England, Customs and Excise, even the Secret Service, have had inside knowledge of what some of these crooks have been up to, way ahead of the auditors. I have publicly called on these agencies to be much more proactive, and to let us in on the dangers before the balloon goes up. For me, that would represent the single most important advance in avoiding and detecting these scandals.

Notes

1. The option of incorporation with limited liability was provided for by the Companies Act 1989, and KPMG incorporated its audit business in 1996 (*Accountancy*, Nov 1995: 11; *Sunday Telegraph*, 8 Jan 1997).
2. Euro Tunnel was a company formed in 1986 as a joint French/British venture. The cross-channel tunnel opened in 1994 but with huge problems of an undersubscribed share issue and escalating costs (Gibb, 1994).
3. Mitchell, *et al*, 1993: 16.
4. Chris Swinson, while president of the ICAEW, submitted proposals for self-regulation to the DTI in 1998. He suggested setting up an independent foundation composed entirely of non-accountants to oversee the Auditing Practices Board, a new Investigation and Discipline Board to replace the JDS, and a new Ethics Standards Board (*Financial Times*, 29 April 1999).
5. Following the 1989 Companies Act, the Financial Reporting Council was set up to preside over the Accounting Standards Board, the Review Panel and the Urgent Issues Task Force. The latter was to provide quick and authoritative inter-

pretations where there appeared to be conflicts between accounting standards and the provisions of the Companies Act, or where no provision existed (Financial Reporting Council, 1995: 6; Woolf, 1997: 17).

6. In 1998, the Lord Chancellor issued proposals designed to reduce the availability of legal aid in the UK (*The Times*, 5 March 1998).

7. The figures in the annual accounts which compare this year's results with previous years.

8. The requirement to give a true and fair view overrides the detailed requirements of UK company law relating to the form and content of financial statements, the notes thereto and accounting principles (Parker, 1992: 287).

9. Lee and Tweedie (1977).

10. A company selling household furnishing which went into receivership in 1990 (*Independent on Sunday*, 21 Nov. 1993).

11. Binder Hamlyn gave Britannia Securities a clean audit report in 1989, but when the company was taken over by ADT the following year it appeared to be worth £60m less than the accounts showed. ADT's law suit against Binder Hamlyn was finally settled in 1997 for a record £86m (*Daily Telegraph*, 22 Feb. 1997).

Chapter 10

Conclusions

As we discussed in the introduction, an oral history project of this nature is probably only justified if the data that emerges adds up to more than the sum of its collected parts. The question then arises as to what reliable conclusions can be drawn from a collection of 68 interviews, a relatively small and not randomly selected group. We would argue that, while always treading cautiously and keeping in mind the possibility that any one of the collection of responses is unrepresentative, indeed a great deal of new knowledge and a greater understanding of the trends and opinions in the history of the audit in Britain since the 1920s can be garnered. There is here a neat parallel with auditing itself—between those who put their trust in statistical significance against those who emphasis the importance of judgment. This chapter is an exercise in the latter approach. Moreover, although since to some extent we sought out the leaders of the profession and this has, as we shall see, skewed our sample socially and educationally upward, it would seem unlikely that our respondents were widely untypical in their experiences and attitudes. Indeed, the similarity of answers to many questions suggested strongly that ours was a broadly representative group. Also, as we discussed in the introduction, individual opinions may be of interest in their own right if, for example, they give a new slant on the causes of a change in audit procedure or they give the perspective of a leading insider in events.

This final chapter therefore proceeds (albeit with caution) on the assumption that an analysis of our 68 interviews is a valid exercise. Following from our declaration in the introduction, however, we must repeat that we do not see it as part of our job to comment on the validity or otherwise of the often controversial or trenchant or indeed conventional statements made in the interviews. Clearly the reader can draw his or her own conclusions as to the accuracy of the factual data and the validity of the opinions presented in the previous eight chapters. We do not seek to criticise the views expressed so much as to organise and distil as objectively as we can the complex reality presented here, and to draw some general, tentative conclusions. In other words we are not setting ourselves up as judges but as interpreters.

So what do the interviews tell us in broad outline? The two themes that emerge are the not unexpected ones of diversity and change. Without having researched the matter it would seem probable that no other profession—the law, medicine, architecture, engineering—would display quite the diversity of work that the chartered accountants undertake. They might, for example, be working for themselves looking after the tax affairs of corner shops in Kendal or employed as the finance director of Unilever. More starkly, almost certainly no profession has undergone the extent of change in the job they do, the way it is performed and who they work for, than the accountant. All of this has created tensions apparent within the profession, and which emerged clearly in a number of the interviews.

An introductory point to make is that it would seem clear that what is driving on the diversity and change within the accounting or auditing profession are the changes in the economic base of the British economy itself. This is not an original idea, and it is of course to be expected since accounting is a service industry dependent on the needs of its clients. But what it does mean is that the history of change in accountancy mirrors, in turn, changes in the economy and business, which perhaps to some extent have gone unnoticed by business historians generally.

What emerges from our interviews with accountants is indeed a transformation in the culture of business life in Britain of quite recent origin. The story that our older respondents tell is one of accountants being part of a business culture based primarily on local, personal and family networks, which holds sway down to around 1970. Our interviews indicate, for example, the young accountant in the early years choosing the profession based on family ties and often following strong paternal direction. In turn, it was personal contacts that got the articled clerk placed in a small local practice. He was trained on a personal basis by a practicing partner. That practice owed its existence to the local economy, often but not always based on family businesses. The firm got work through personal and local recommendation and it maintained close social and business ties with clients.

One of the best evocations of these local networks was given by Wilkes, describing how as a youngster in the 1950s the senior partner in his medium sized Leicester firm:

> used to go every morning to a little cafe around the corner from the office, called Morton's. There was a trio playing and there were palms and so on

> and he and a number of other leading business people would meet there at about eleven o'clock for half an hour, with a cup of coffee. They would discuss affairs, business, prices - hosiery was uppermost in peoples' minds, and other things . . . Now you never get that happening today.

These local economies are repeatedly reflected in the interviews, whether it be Beard's firm in the 1950s servicing the hotels of Southport or later the steel trade in Sheffield; Norris's four partner Sunderland practice auditing large shipbuilding companies in the 1960s; Colvin's firm reliant on the fortunes of the port of Liverpool or Passmore's two-partner firm dependent on the local Exeter economy. Even the largest companies in the country were still part of the local business networks of which the accountants formed an essential element. Companies like BMC, the motor manufacturers, for example, were still at their Cowley operation audited by Thornton and Thornton, firmly rooted in the city of Oxford, and who incidentally trained up the Haddleton brothers in the 1950s and Atkins in the 1960s.

This picture cannot, of course, be pushed too far. Some leading accountancy firms operated from the City of London on an international stage and for multinational clients since before the First World War, as, for example, Cooper Bros did for Lever Bros (Edwards, 1984: 781). But again the City also had its own local and personal character. Burlingham who worked there in the 1950s reported:

> It was an interesting place to be, because you were in the City of London in its respectable hey day. Peats dealt with Slaughter and May; that was the level—top accountants working with top solicitors. And the articled pupils in the office: one was connected with the Stock Exchange; one with the Baltic Exchange. There was a network, and it was a small world. And there was a wonderful buzz about that.

Clearly, also, the personal and local character of the economy and British business culture has not disappeared entirely. There are now many more small local companies and small local accountancy practices[1] than there ever were. But just as small companies are now less important to total output in the economy, so small accounting firms hold a smaller share of the total audit market.

So there has been a profound transformation in the economy, in business, and the accountancy profession in particular, in the last two or three decades. Young chartered accountants, for example, almost certainly do not now enter the profession on their parents say so; they are recruited not by personal contact but via advertising and recruitment drives at the universities, which are national if not international in scope. Most recruits are trained rather impersonally by the training courses of the multinational accountancy firms, who acquire customers nationally or internationally often by the impersonal process of the tender or 'beauty contest.'

The previous dominance of the local business networks within most industries, as Wilkes said, has gone. What lies behind this change which accountancy reflects? One factor has undoubtedly been structural change in terms of the decline of manufacturing in Britain, indeed, continuing the examples used above, the hosiery trade in Leicester, shipbuilding on the Wear or steel making in Sheffield. Related to this has been the decline of the family firm often by the process of merger, amalgamation and take-over.[2] As Brittain put it: 'Small manufacturers were ten a penny fifty years ago because there wasn't a concentration of power in industry, as there is now.' As their clients grew bigger so did the accountancy firms, and by the same process of merger and take-over.[3]

This economic change has meant that the key commercial decisions are not now taken in Leicester, Sunderland or Sheffield but in London and beyond. Hence the end of the local, personal, culture. The changed perspectives reflected in the accountancy world were exemplified by Rawlinson's experiences in a merchant bank in the 1970s:

> Our clients' businesses was becoming more and more international, and the capital markets were becoming international, so one was dealing with preparing accounts in a variety of currencies . . . One was having to cope with the problems, for the first time, of how to reconcile accounts prepared in accordance with American principles with accounts in accordance with British principles, let alone Italian or Japanese . . . Morgan Grenfell had more than half of its business denominated in foreign currencies . . . So we then had to start thinking very imaginatively about how to manage this situation.

And as Heywood of Price Waterhouse said: 'globalisation will continue to alter things. So you are not only aware of the expectations of investors in a particular country. You are having to satisfy the expectations of the most sophisticated investors around the world.'[4]

These themes of diversity and change, focusing more narrowly on the auditing profession, will be pursued more fully in the following sections looking in turn at: the background and training of the chartered accountant; women in the profession; the process of auditing; the audit as a business; relationships with clients and the issue of independence; the quality of auditing; fraud and the purpose of the audit; regulation, and finally the scandals of the 1980s and 1990s.

BACKGROUND AND TRAINING

Although, as we have said, while not strictly statistically significant it is nonetheless of interest to give a breakdown of our 69 respondents with regard to their social background, education and training.

Seven interviews were with accountants who trained in the 1920s, and five with those who qualified in the 1970s, but most came in the decades in between (the median year of qualification was 1952 and the mode 1951). The vast majority of respondents sprang from middle class business and professional backgrounds, with fathers being small business owners, company directors, merchants, doctors, solicitors, or bank managers. Only eight (or 11%) were the sons or daughters of accountants. None of the respondents came from exceedingly wealthy families and few if any were poor. Eight had fathers who, in an undoubtedly imprecise way, can be identified as working class, with a railwayman, coal miner, postman and more debatably, a post office clerk and a commercial traveller, among them.[5]

Based on this background, 40 of our interviewees (or 56%) went to public schools (including three who attended what might be better classified as 'private' schools).[6] A good proportion of these went to the top public schools, the so called Clarendon Nine, two to Marlborough, one each to Rugby, Winchester and Eton; and an almost equal number in the lower rank such as the two at Haileybury and one each to Aldenham, Warwick, Taunton, and Worksop. Twenty five interviewees (35%) went to grammar school. Typically, these public and grammar schoolboys stayed on in school until the age of 18 before starting their articles. Only six respondents (9%) received only an elementary education, typically leaving school aged 14, corresponding closely with the 11% from working class backgrounds noted above.

Nineteen interviewees (27%) went to university or its equivalent with (apart from the Scots, Morpeth and Tweedie, who went to Edinburgh University) a preponderance of Oxbridge graduates (nine, Cambridge; four, Oxford).[7] No graduate interviewees came from outside the ancient seats of leaning until the 1960s and 1970s, when Kingston Polytechnic, London and Leeds played a part. Again the broad typicality of our interviewees is confirmed by the fact that of the 15 who qualified in the 1960s and 1970s, 60% were graduates, compared to only 18% of those entering the profession before 1960.

In general then, our accountants were from the middle-middle classes, educated at public and grammar schools and, before the 1960s, non-graduates. Equally typically their fathers had a strong hand in their choice of career, and clearly one of the reasons for this was that without father's help many aspiring accountants would not have got started. Down to the 1950s, articles with a chartered accountant's firm was offered in a buyer's market. The payment of a premium was usual (typical was the £500 paid by Stanley

Jones in 1949) although this would usually be paid back to the clerk as wages during his or her articles. Our working class interviewees either qualified in paid employment as incorporated accountants, the so called bye-law candidates, like Sanders or Winch, or were just lucky, like Kenwright, who took articles during the second war when: 'a lot of clerks were whistled off into the services. So they were looking for people, and premiums weren't applicable.'

So fathers had a big say in the career choice of their offspring. As Thornton said, 'I listened to my father,' or Boothman: 'My father really steered me in that direction.' But perhaps the matter was not usually as predetermined as that for Palmer in the 1930s: 'My father was an accountant and he said,—I am, and you're going to be. I had no choice. In those days parents did those sorts of things to their children. Today they would never get away with it.' And, as noted above, fathers or family usually used personal contacts to get their offspring into their first position, as was the case with Wilkes in the late 1940s where: 'It was through the firm of solicitors that looked after my father's affairs,' or Sims in the 1950s where: 'my father happened to know the principal I was articled to and I think they did a deal.'

Training has been in the forefront of debate in the Institute in recent years, which gives added interest to the data revealed with regard to our interviewees' instruction. The first point to make is that our respondents overwhelmingly trained with small or medium sized firms. Of our 69 respondents, only 14% qualified with the big national firms, 37% trained with medium sized firms, most of which were at the lower end of our arbitrary definition (four or more partners) and 49% with small firms (three partners or less). Even among the six contemporary leaders in chapter nine, qualifying in the late 1960s and 1970s, only two did so with major firms. This is in sharp contrast, of course, with the situation today where the Big Five firms dominate training within the profession and small firms do very little.

This, what we might call the traditional system of training, seemed to work well, and was brought about to some extent by the limitation (until 1967) of the number of partners in even the largest firms to 20; and the limit on the number of pupils each partner in these firms could train to two or, from the late 1950s, four (Jones, 1981: 169 and 241). But probably more importantly the situation was sustained by the vitality, discussed above, of the local economies, where the big City based firms usually had no particular competitive advantage over the local firms. The latter therefore had sufficient work to justify taking on large amounts of cheap labour, training them up and releasing them when they qualified. The newly qualified clerk may hold out hope of a partnership but there was usually no room for them. They found, as Keel said somewhat ironically, that the existing partners 'thought it a better idea if I went somewhere else and got some wider experience.'

Often the subsequent career path of the newly qualified accountant was therefore to move on and gain experience with one of the Big Six firms, who were expanding and keen to take on the qualified staff they could not train themselves.[8] Accountants commonly would then take two years with the big firm and either stay with them, hoping for a partnership and future fame and fortune, like Grenside and Hardcastle at Peats, or Morpeth at Touche, or else, with the big name firm on their CV, move out into industry, as did Edey, Davies, and Rawlinson. Significantly, this move was also very often made via the personal networks discussed above, with numerous examples of auditors joining the staff of their client companies. For example, John Haddleton was recruited by Morris Motors from Thornton and Thornton, Edey moved from Deloittes to their clients, the Pearson group, while Evans went from Peats to Richard Thomas and Baldwins.

The traditional chartered accountants 'on the job' practical training did not find universal favour among our respondents. The correspondence courses, which involved long hours of largely rote learning to cram for the examinations, generated little affection, as did the mechanical work of casting, vouching and checking, although perhaps ironically Brittain thought: 'everybody should have a two year course on coping with boredom.' Kenwright's view was also sceptical in that: 'Basically, you trained yourself. You didn't get very much training in a formal sense at the office'; while Palmer, who qualified in the 1930s, complained: 'I didn't have any initiative.' Generally, however, the respondents viewed their training with approval and, while they may be indulging in nostalgia, they tended to make a coherent case for the traditional training, and on occasions made unsolicited contrasts with today's regime.

The declared advantages of the old system can be analysed under four headings. First, the variety of the work while training was valued. Articled clerks could be involved in taxation, insolvency, special work as well as auditing. On the other hand, they might have been dealing with clients who were sole traders right up to the large quoted companies that even small and medium sized firms might audit in those days. A typical experience was described by Colvin, who trained with a four-partner Liverpool firm in the 1940s: 'I had a very good practical training because the firm had a wide spectrum of clients ranging from the small income tax client, a lot of trust work, audit and accountancy work ranging from small family businesses to three or four public limited companies.' This range of work has only recently disappeared; as Lainé, who trained in the early 1960s, put it: 'In those days . . . one could find oneself doing a reasonable variety of other work. Today, in a large firm people become specialists when they join.' The present day viewpoint of the big firms was expressed by Sharman of Peats:

'Trainees have to have different options; the day of the compendium qualification is gone, its nonsense, you have to have specialisms.'

The second valued attribute of the traditional training was that the tuition was personal one-to-one contact with a practicing partner. As Wilkes, who trained in the late 1940s and early 1950s put it: 'I was dealing direct with the partners from quite an early age . . . learning a lot from them and their wisdom and experience . . . [T]hose starting out now lose out because . . . then they, the partners, became increasingly involved with complex matters so they didn't have the time to give to their students, and so it was delegated.'

Third, the old system seemed to give the articled clerks their head very quickly. In the 1920s, Sanders remembered: '. . . after I passed my R.S.A. exams, I was thought competent enough to cope, and under his [the partner's] instruction I used to take another unqualified bloke with me, and do the audit in a leather factory and many other businesses.' And this was the experience of many respondents. Simkins reported: 'After my Intermediate exam I took charge of the whole audit, reporting to the partner concerned, but very much left to my own devices. Even when I dealt with the local authority audits there was comparatively little supervision of the way I carried out the work. I frequently wrote audit programmes.' Thornton, who qualified in the 1930s, said: 'I was encouraged to use my initiative,' and Carter 'was given a lot of responsibility' by his small firm in the 1950s. Niddrie, with a similar training, found:

> You had everything thrown at you and if you had the ability then you were given responsibility early on. You lived and breathed bookkeeping, accountancy, auditing. You established a sixth sense, and so you knew all the tricks people got up to because one found there was fiddling of some type on every job. The experience was first class and stood me in very good stead when I became a partner with Price Waterhouse.

Moore, who qualified with a small firm in 1950, said: 'I was given a great deal of freedom to work on my own and to do as much as I thought I was able to tackle. And that gave me independence.' The big firms also pushed their youngsters on. As Lainé recalled of the early 1960s: 'The philosophy at Coopers was to throw you straight in at the deep end. I remember coming down to Southampton, when I had been only going a year, to carry out an audit of Ford's operations in Southampton on my own.' At Arthur Andersen in the mid-1960s Plaistowe was also 'given responsibilities at a very early stage . . . I can remember in my first year there was an audit which I was given sole responsibility for.' Of the same period, Carty remembered: 'Baker Perkins Engineering; by my third year that was one of the major jobs I took charge of. Price Waterhouse always advanced people very quickly, so if you showed any talent you were given responsibility.'

Again, perhaps this early blooding of trainees has changed significantly. As Scicluna explained it: 'Obviously, the lower down, the less initiative. Because to some extent you've got to make sure that people do things properly. It is a top down process now, whereas when I started auditing, it was bottom-up. The team did everything and the partner reviewed it. Now the partner says,—this is what I want done. I know my client and I want it done like so.'

Finally, perhaps the aspect of the traditional regime which our respondents felt was now lacking most in the accountant's training was a thorough grounding in the basics, that is the elements of double entry bookkeeping, particularly applied to incomplete records, the so called 'brown paper parcel' jobs. Muir among others became lyrical on the subject:

> my grasp of bookkeeping came from having a bundle of vouchers in a paper bag thrown at me. Some of them did not even write up a cash book. Tremendous experience though, and by far the best way to get into accountancy and auditing in my opinion. Unless you understand how records are put together you can not start to audit them. By the end of the first year I was actually preparing accounts to final stages. I became a very good 'accountant.' Nobody could pull the wool over my eyes in later years about bookkeeping.

The situation was still the same when Spens trained in the 1960s, where his medium sized firm: 'were also very good at teaching their students on small operations where you had incomplete records. So you had to physically write up all the books using double entry. You learnt accountancy the hard way, as opposed to the theoretical way.'

This viewpoint was very often voluntarily combined with a regret that the basics had now been lost. This was well articulated, again by Wilkes, talking of the 1970s:

> Look at the way PW trained people when I was down here in London. The number of in-house courses were phenomenal, the introduction to the system and all the rest of it. But what you learnt in my training was the essentials of double entry bookkeeping. Nowadays, these chaps with computers get themselves into a mess when it comes to looking at where the other side of the entry is, if you've got fraud and so on. Unless you have got an understanding of those basic double entry elements you can get lost. The balance sheet is still there and it's expected to balance.

As Beard, who also trained in the 1950s put it: 'We had a very good grounding in double entry bookkeeping which helped us no end and this is my fear of today's students . . . some of them don't understand what basic double entry or the end product is all about.' Even someone like Carey, who trained with a small firm in the 1970s, before moving to a large one, shares this view: 'In many ways I had a better training base than those who trained with Peats because then and now they are trained in audit. They do not get much experience in actually putting the accounts together. And very often, when you come across a crunchy technical issue, the ability to do some double entry bookkeeping is extremely helpful.'

John Haddleton both identified the problem and came up with a solution:

> Sometime previously at Cope Allman, I had had my first experience of inadequately trained, university-qualified auditors, when one came to audit my group accounts, and told me that I'd got the figures on the wrong side of the sheet. This was a qualified auditor, full of his own importance, who was entirely wrong. It was the first experience I had of over-confidence and a total lack of understanding of the basic elements of bookkeeping and accounting, which I have noticed ever since. That was in 1959/60, when I first saw this problem arising. It should have been dealt with by the Institute requiring auditors, requiring all accountants, to conduct work at a very low stage in the game, and to actively prepare accounts properly - before they qualify.

The traditional system was on the way out and formal training by the larger firms seems to have got underway in the 1960s. Carter discussed the rather amateurish training introduced at Price Waterhouse in the early 1960s, probably part of the progressive training scheme extending over several years' noted by Jones in his history of the company.[9] According to Plaistowe, who trained in the 1960s: 'Arthur Andersen gave you a considerable amount of training, and in fact you weren't allowed out of the office until you had done about five or six weeks' training. They were the only firm at that time that gave you anything like that training.'

As indicated by a number of the interviews, the transformation in the way chartered accountants have been trained in the past 30 years might have significant implications. The dangers of taking university graduates and giving them a theoretical rather than 'on the job' training are made clear by Carty of Robson Rhodes: 'The difficulty is not telling people what the rules are, it's improving judgment. We try to do that through case studies, where we try to get people to recognize dangerous situations. Nowadays we only take university graduates and not all of them are used to hard work.'

WOMEN ACCOUNTANTS

The experience of our seven female interviewees also reveals a world of considerable diversity. Women did not become chartered accountants in any numbers until the 1970s, but the precise reasons for this are unclear. Kirkham and Loft (1993), with their theory of gendered social closure, argued that the very creation of the accounting profession was based on the exclusion of women. They have analysed the barriers that have been placed upon women entering the male dominated profession and our study goes some way to confirm their findings. However, our admittedly limited evidence would argue that there was a much greater spread of experience than Kirkham and Loft's model would allow. Our sample is too small to sustain any firm conclusions but reveals enough to indicate that a more extended programme of interviews would be a worthwhile project, and would almost certainly yield more definite results unlikely to be found in the documentary evidence.

We have evidence that girls were discouraged from both pursuing their education and entering accountancy. As Partridge, who had to continue her schooling in distant evening classes, related: 'I left [school] at 14. In those days parents were funny. Girls weren't expected to do anything except to eventually get married.' And when Burgess's widowed mother sought the advice of her solicitor about a career in accountancy for her daughter he said: 'Waste of money Mrs. Burgess, she'll get married by the time she gets qualified.'

Those that did get into accountancy, as Kirkham and Loft (1993: 547) noted, did so through family ties, either as the daughters of accountants like Pearce, Paterson or Burlingham, or like Burdett, who had an uncle who brought her into the profession. As Partridge attests: 'In the early days, there was terrible prejudice. There didn't appear to be any prejudice once you got established. I was all right because I had done my articles with my brother. So I got in, but I wouldn't have got in otherwise, I am quite sure of that.' She related the case of a woman in about 1960 who: 'had been trying to get articles for months and had written hundreds of letters and been to scores of interviews and never managed to get in. She had some foreign connection, so she said,—Do you think it was because of that that they wouldn't take me on? And I said,—No. It's because you're a woman.'

There was some suggestion that fellow accountants were not keen to work with women. Winch's experience was that: 'The unqualified men wouldn't work if I did the audit. The departmental head just couldn't use me, so I had ten years after qualifying either working for others or on the comptometer, which was delightful!' Another viewpoint of some firms was that clients would object to a women. Burgess felt that: 'Some of them had to be pre-prepared that a woman was coming along.' There was evidence of this attitude in the Big Six firms like Coopers, where Hobson stated that in the 1950s and 1960s:

> John Pears was never very keen on training women as accountants. He didn't think that they were very suitable for going around a steel works.

> There were difficulties in this in the way that clients would react. They wouldn't mind too much having women going through their personal tax returns, but to go round Babcocks [the engineering company] works at Renfrew with 10,000 workers, one girl wouldn't really be very acceptable within a very male dominated industry.

This was also the experience of Paterson where for: 'some of the jobs you had to go away and stay, say down to West Wales, but again I never went away because I was a woman. Of course, the war changed all that, with so many men being called up, clients had to accept women accountants.' Again, there was diversity of experience. Burgess recalled that this negative attitude to women was uncommon: 'We did have a man who refused to work with me, about three years before I retired [1977] but usually the attitude was - there's a woman there, but it's all right, she does the same thing you'd expect the chaps to do.'

The general view among the interviewees was that once established in the profession the attitude of the clients was not a problem. Perhaps their privileged position was something of a shield, as with Burlingham where: 'I was my father's daughter, and they [clients] had too much respect for him to have any nonsense like that.' Equally as a sole practitioner Partridge found:

> With clients, if they came to me there was no question about it, they were quite happy. Sometimes they even came to me because I was a woman. One of them told me to my face. He said he went to the Inland Revenue and asked them who they recommended as an accountant . . . and when he saw that I was the only woman amongst them he thought that if a woman was able to compete with all those men she must be good.

This was also the experience of Burlingham working at Peats in the City in the 1950s, where the attitude seemed to contrast with that at Coopers. Her response was:

> Oh fine, I got on very well with clients. I think that's why Peats liked to have women because they got on well. There were three girls in the firm . . . Once they'd got used to the idea of a woman, most of the clients were far too well mannered to say anything . . . The ethos of the place was very favourable for a female. I could have stayed there. Peats were very good employers, and they specifically liked having women.

At the same time Burlingham hints at the reason more women did not get on in the profession in that period, and even perhaps today, since although Peats 'made it quite clear, I could have stayed there more or less forever . . .

I decided I ought to move, and then I got married.' Only two of our seven female interviewees followed her example.

THE AUDIT PROCESS

As much as any aspect of the business, the actual process of auditing today has changed out of recognition from what we will call the traditional methods, which reigned down to 1970. But again the story is laced with a variety of experience.

The traditional auditing process had certain essential characteristics. One of these was that it was commonly inextricably bound up with simple accounting or bookkeeping, in that the auditor very often made up the clients' books as part of the audit. As Burlingham, talking of the early 50s in a small provincial practice, put it: 'With small or medium sized firms you did all the work for the accounts, and the tax work. Under those circumstances you were also doing the audit, you didn't divide the two.' Indeed, the client bringing his often incomplete records into the office to be written up was the common experience of Wilde, Sanders, Pearce and Burlingham, among others. The larger the client, of course, the more likely they were to employ qualified accountants and the less work that was left for the auditor. As Davies, training with a small firm in Swansea in the 1940s and early 1950s, also remembers it: 'The firm had few pure audits. Generally, the smaller the client the more likely it was we would be doing the total job. If the client was bigger then quite often it would have a trial balance, or possibly even full accounts for us to work on.' But even at large companies making up the books was a common role for the auditor. As Keel recalled, at 'Carreras, the major tobacco group, (now part of Rothmans) audit . . . I still prepared their accounts first, although they were a quoted public company in the early 1950s.'

Another common feature of the traditional audit was that making up the accounts or auditing them was a mechanical, largely arithmetically based, process of casting, vouching and checking, affectionately (or otherwise) known variously as: 'tick and bash' (Sims and Whinney); 'ticking and blotting' (Boothman) or 'tick and touch' (Winch). As Middleton put it: 'the theory in the small firms was, did the books balance? Were they arithmetically correct? And one searched for mistakes of a penny, believe it or not.' This was still the rule when Spens was auditing relatively large companies in the 1960s. He was sceptical of its value: 'We spent weeks adding up with comptometers. All right, so they were a few pennies out but it did not prove anything. It did not solve any problems. It just proved that human beings are fallible.'

There was a large variety of practice as to whether during these endeavours the auditors followed set audit programmes. Brittain reported that while training with a small firm in the 1940s there were: 'No strict systems at all. You just went out and did the job, and nobody told you what you'd got to do.' Niddrie remembers that even in the 1960s: 'Managers had their own very individual styles and were left very much to themselves. There were no formal audit procedures and so often things were in the manager's head rather than down on paper.' Denza reported that Spicer & Pegler had no strict system in the 1950s: 'Common sense was always paramount. You were expected to produce a good set of working papers. It showed up when they went to the tax department if you didn't. If . . . the information they needed wasn't there, they made a complaint pretty vigorously. But the dominant consideration was professional judgment.'

But the more common experience throughout the early period was that some form of programme, often hand written, was followed. Keel in his small firm: 'worked from pre-prepared audit programmes in the 30s.' To Davies: 'Audit programmes started becoming more fashionable towards the end of the 40s and early 50s. Many accountancy practitioners introduced printed audit programmes, and these included questions aimed at ensuring that internal checks were properly in place, with a view to avoiding fraud and making sure the accounts showed a true and fair view.' As Beard describes it, in the 1950s: 'The actual audit programme itself was in a long book, which you kept from year to year, using the same book. You'd tick off each item and if you did a month you'd put down which month you did.' To Moore in the same era: 'We had a fixed audit programme written up by the partners for each particular client. We didn't have an audit programme blue print which applied to everyone . . . The programme would establish for instance roughly what percentage of sampling and other checks was to be done. It would be part of the programme to list discrepancies, missing documentation and missing vouchers.'

What emerges strongly from the collected interviews is the big influence on the development of auditing generally, and on the more systematic approach in the post war period, that the Coopers manual had. The manual was written and in use by the firm from the late 1940s, but not published, as Henry Benson's gift to accountancy, until 1966. According to Goodwin, the main motive behind writing the manual had been control of labour: 'I remember talking to Henry Benson and their big worry was keeping control of the staff. There were huge numbers of people, they didn't know what they were getting up to, they were scared out of their wits and this was the origin of the audit manuals.' Whatever the reason, a number of interviewee attested to the fact that Coopers were leading the way in auditing in the 1950s and 1960s based on the manual. Hewitt, for example, felt that Coopers and their manual headed Price Waterhouse and the other big firms in the 1960s: 'Cooper Brothers had been the byword for regimental audit efficiency . . . and led the way.'

Coopers' influence spread through the profession. Atkins reported that in the 1960s on the BMC audit, where Thornton and Thornton were joint auditors with Coopers: 'we followed their audit manual and so they were very influential on my auditing. My father had been with Coopers for four or five years in the 1950's before he joined Thorntons, so he was well ahead of his time in the way auditing was done.' Firms that were taken over by Coopers were forced to adopt the manual, or experienced 'Cooperising' as Middleton put it. When Livesey's firm was taken over in 1967: 'Coopers' audit systems . . . were and probably still are very advanced.' But the process was not always viewed with favour, as Palmer reported when they were taken over in 1965:

> The audit system changed completely as soon as we joined Coopers. Coopers brought in their own manual, which was quite different to the way we conducted an audit and we had to conform . . . and it wasn't necessarily what the client wanted. We'd begun to work out methods of sampling that were tailored to the individual client and we used to explain to the client why we were doing what we were doing. And then the Coopers manual came in and the old system went out of the window.

The interviews make clear that the traditional process of the audit was transformed from the 1960s on, and there seemed to be four main causes in play. First, as we have noted, clients were becoming larger and national and international in scope. Second, and less frequently discussed, labour was becoming more expensive. From the 1950s to the present day audit labour went from articled clerks paying for the privilege of being trained, to the 1990s when the trainees were being so well paid that Carty at Robson Rhodes argued that the training system should be changed: 'We're paying £18,000 in salary and £4,000 in fees, so that's £22,000 for 26 weeks work . . . economically, it's crazy.' The cost of labour had clear implications for the way the audit was conducted. The traditional audit could be highly labour intensive. As Engel put it: 'We were paid badly, and time wasn't of the essence. If you spent another week or so on an audit, it wasn't a question of being cost effective.' Kenwright also made the point: 'in those days labour was cheap . . . An audit could be much more labour intensive than it is today, and I think we would take on a lot more detailed work than would be affordable today.'

Third, there was a transatlantic influence on practice. Plaistowe, who trained with the American firm who came to England in 1957, was of the opinion that: 'In the 1960s, Arthur Andersen was a firm very unlike the other major firms because . . . it had all the techniques based on what had emerged in the United States. The processes the firm went through, and its structure, were very different from those of 'old fashioned' English firms. And then in the late 60s, the English firms changed and transformed themselves.' Fourth, technological change in the form of computerisation meant that the old manual ways of auditing had to change.

The growth in the size of companies simply made the old style of audit untenable. As Livesey put it: 'No longer could we pretend to tick everything. So we had to begin to think a little about systems and look at sampling.' In Stanley Jones' view:

> from 1946 to 1966, everything went up a scale and the number of transactions increased tremendously. As the volume went up and the systems and the nature of business itself became more complex, obviously the audit procedures had to change. You had, on the one side, businesses merging, integrating, taking over, consolidating, and making technical changes, and on the other side you had the profession . . . struggling to keep the lid on from the audit point of view . . . You couldn't carry on casting all the books yourself.

But the growth in scale also made the traditional audit probably unnecessary because it meant that more and more firms employed their own qualified accountants. This, Hewitt of Mellors, Basden & Mellors, explained:

> was quite a significant change because it meant that the accountancy aspect of the practice diminished. Companies wanted to economise on fees. They also wanted to have monthly accounts as opposed to annual accounts and to have up-to-date information . . . I don't think Raleigh [the bicycle makers] had more than one [qualified accountant] until about 1950.'

The external auditors were then involved less in making up the books and more in pure auditing, but also as companies installed internal audit controls for their own benefit this gave the external auditor the option of reducing their work to testing that the internal system was sound. Hardie recalled that: 'a client's internal audit department now does 90% of the work I did in my youth.' As to when this change took place, Hewitt noted that: 'probably in the 30s but certainly in the 40s Ford had an internal audit department'; and Brittain went to work for ICI's Metals Division internal audit department in 1951. According to Grenside of Peats: 'internal audits began in companies in the 1950s, but they became more common in bigger companies in the 1960s and 70s and then you had to get them built into the audit itself.' Again Coopers seemed to lead the way, but the change was not rapid. Livesey noted: 'Coopers' manual centred in on controls far more than we'd ever thought of doing . . . Not necessarily reviewing internal audits, since only the big clients had them in 1967; Phillips, the Dutch folk, were very strong on internal auditing at the time. But a lot of clients were like Tootal in Manchester who had no internal auditing as such.' Even at Price Waterhouse, Heywood remembers: 'in 1969, there was a major upgrading in the way we did an audit. The old-fashioned audit programmes, which comprised of ticking and bashing, disappeared about then . . . We tended to do a lot of system checks, following bits of paper all the way through the system.'

The inability to check as much as had been done in the past also put an increased reliance on sampling. A form of sample or test checking had probably always been necessary for the audit of large companies. Certainly Keel remembers in the 1930s:

> Most of the audit work . . . was on a sampling basis. If the company's own controls were strong then the sampling would be limited. If they were weak then the sampling was much more extended. We'd probably select a month or two, and having worked through, if too many difficulties, errors or weaknesses did not occur we would accept that evidence. On the contrary if the outcome was unsatisfactory checking would then be extended.

Selecting one month and a different month each year was common, but another method was used by Evans at Peats in the 1950s, who would take 'for example, 20% of purchase invoices, 10% of sales invoices, etc.'

Statistical sampling was probably American in inspiration. Winch remembers being taught it at the London Business School using an American textbook in the 1970s, but again it had a slow and patchy uptake. Hewitt had a frosty response when he brought the good news back to Mellors, Basden & Mellors:

> I went to an Institute summer school in 1952 and met a member of the Whinney family. He'd heard of sampling and lent me a book, and I came back to Nottingham and [presented] to the partners some ideas on [scientific] sampling, and it was quite an occasion. But I made the mistake of starting off by saying,—the first thing you have to do is to decide what margin of error you will allow. And that was fatal because the senior partner immediately said,—I allow no errors . . . So we didn't do any statistical sampling for very many years, and I think that even 20 years on in Price Waterhouse in the 70s it was still more talked about than acted upon.

This was confirmed by Carty, who was at Price Waterhouse in late 1960s: 'There wasn't a great deal of it. Mathematical approaches to selection weren't really worthwhile and I don't think they are today really. Samples were usually selected by judgment and one usually tried to stratify them to ensure there was a fair spread. And even as an articled clerk you would select them yourself.' Tweedie recalls that at Mann Judd in the early 1970s: 'As far as new techniques were concerned, they were experimenting with systems reviews and sampling but it was early days for that for the profession.' According to Plaistowe:

> Arthur Andersen never went in for statistical sampling to any extent, largely on the basis that we are not trying to come up with a statistically valid conclusion. The end result of an audit is a judgment on the view given by the financial statements. That's the key thing rather than going though a mechanical process, which some of the other firms have gone through but have tended to abandon since.'

To Currie, another Arthur Andersen man:

> my observation quite early on was that if you were going to apply statistical sampling to audit work, your samples had to be so big to attain the sort of probability and error margin that you needed that it was going to be uneconomic. By and large, it seemed much better and much more likely to be practicable to assess and attack risk. Subsequently, the business was all about risk assessment.

The declining ability to check all or most transactions also led the focus away from the profit and loss account to the balance sheet and the verification of assets, as well as to concepts such as materiality. Davies recalls that when Coopers became auditors at GKN in 1960: 'The biggest change was probably their emphasis on a balance sheet audit . . . they placed a lot of emphasis on stocks.' The balance sheet audit and the emphasis on stock valuation were also largely American led, but attending stocktaking in Britain was no new thing, of course. Sanders recalls them doing this at a hospital in the 1920s. And Palmer talking of the 1930s stated:

> I can remember one particular client was a leather manufacturer and he kept skins in pits. It was a horrible smelly place. I had to go and try to find out how many skins he had got there, and he would just tell me. I couldn't get in and physically count them . . . I had to ask him to sign a certificate about the stock and that was it. So although we did attend some stocktakes, there often wasn't very much point.

Davies thought stocktaking 'was regarded as a standard requirement in the 40s and early 50s'; while Whinney stated: 'I think that was always on the audit programme' at Whinney Smith & Whinney in the 1950s. Keel said they attended the Carreras stocktake in the early 1950s. To Hewitt, talking of the same decade, thought it was: 'Quite common' and Muir did attend but said: 'I would not have thought the follow-up procedures were terribly worthwhile.' Probably then, although it was done under certain circumstances, attending stocktaking did not become the general rule with the larger clients until the 1960s. Boothman recalled that in his medium sized firm: 'It wasn't till fairly late in my career that the accountant would be expected to attend a stocktake in person. This came about very much as a result of audit manuals being published in the 1970s.' Fabes at Cork Gully thought: 'We didn't physically attend stocktaking until well into the 1960s.' And Carty remembered that at Price Waterhouse in the late 1960s they attended the client's stocktake as a matter of routine because by then 'everybody accepted American standards of auditing.' Plaistowe said that Arthur Andersen attended stocktaking in the 1960s, but as an example of how advanced they were over their English rivals. And to Elwyn Jones:

> The Americans went into far greater depth than we did, and even now I don't think we have gone as deep as they do. In 1959–60, I was involved with a take-over of a company in marine corking . . . After the take-over, I had to meet the auditors of the new company who were shocked that I hadn't done very much on the stock . . . Then it came out that in America they would have had chemists in. [Then] we came to do far more stock checking, sending chaps down on the final day to check the count, a lot more than we used to in the old days.

As with attending stocktaking, circularising debtors was no innovation in the 1960s. Chapman discussed circularising debtors on one job in the 1930s. Burgess also noted they did so in the 1930s, and that indeed it was how she discovered a fraud at the beginning of the Second World War. Fabes' experience was that: 'When I was articled we never circularised debtors, but I had to in my first audit with CG [Cork Gully] in the early 1950s. But probably it did not become standard practice until the 1960s.' Wilde thought that it: 'was not a practice that was seriously taken up until the 1960s.' Whinney felt: 'It was probably about the mid-60s that we used to circularise debtors and ask them to agree the amount they owed a company.' Spens did so in the 1960s, but: 'always considered those awful routines of circularising debtors to be a total waste of time. The debtors never replied.' For Carty at Price Waterhouse in the late 1960s: 'it was a standard practice. In those days we would circularise about 100 debtors on each assignment.' However, it must be noted that although the interviews make reasonably clear when the circularisation of debtors became the rule, it is not obvious why it did so. Again it may have stemmed from transatlantic prompting but this requires further research.

Finally, regarding the process of the audit, we must note the huge change brought about by technological progress in the shape of computing, which again came into common business usage in Britain from the late 1960s. As Plaistowe put it: 'It's inevitable that as companies become IT-based, so the audit has to become IT-based as well.' Many of the interviewees were upbeat with regard to the impact of computing, since there was apparently now no need to worry about arithmetical accuracy. To Hardcastle it: 'enabled accounting systems to be set out and consistently applied.' To Kemp: 'Used intelligently the computer can serve to make the audit less tedious.' Sharman outlined the current situation where: 'Technically, since the early 80s, we've had direct access into clients' own computer systems. We now live in their systems, auditing. Our people from locations around the world, validate information and transmit it over the same network to us, using the client's system.' Scicluna also made clear that this: 'is not just computers replacing the working paper files; our programmes are designed with the aid of a computer, within a computer. So you now have tailored programmes for the client.'

But others noted the dangers. Talking of the 1970s Burdett admitted: 'I wasn't computer literate at first but became knowledgeable about the advantages and limitations of computers through experience. We still prepared the accounts for all of those firms. One firm in particular, which had computerised their records, were in great difficulty as a consequence, and I had to devise a manual back-up system which was successful in restoring order to chaos.' Spens talked of a lot being 'hidden' in computers; Fabes of: 'less information of origin.' Kenwright argued: 'There's a lack of transparency now - computers have made it very, very difficult to be able to trace an awful lot.' John Haddleton, who had sorted out a stock fraud at BMC in the 1950s said: 'I wonder if that sort of thing is as easily picked up today, by people going through endless computer lists, because, unless you have your stock sheets, and you know what it is that you ought to be comparing, you can never find it.' Stanley Jones worried that, 'technical improvements were keeping people at arm's length.' Hardie also noted:

> A lot of the depersonalisation comes from computers. Here, a lot of figures come out, with no need to add them up, and it's difficult to detect commercial activity. In the old days you developed a feel which told you that certain gross margins should be attained, and, if not, you wondered what had happened to the money: had it gone sideways? Now it's difficult to conduct a dispute with a machine, and there have been numerous examples of the big firms missing major frauds, because the intimacy of the audit has been lost.

The implications for fraud were also noted by Wilde: 'fraud is more sophisticated now, mainly because of computers.'

The current leaders, interviewed in chapter nine, sketched truly revolutionary computer led change in the near future, whereby companies will supply continuously updated accounting data and the year-end audit will be a thing of the past. To Sharman at Peats: 'it is quite feasible that in the next 15 years, historical audit will be replaced by contemporaneous audit . . . we will be doing audits as the reports are written. We've invested a huge amount in researching this, $50 to 60 million, this year.' While Lainé at Coopers maintained:

> The capacity of IT to deliver information has totally transformed auditing. The Institute and the Stock Exchange give awards every year for the best annual report, but whether we will have this celebration of historical data in five years time, I don't know. The real users of this data want it very fast and the technology is there . . . There are a lot of people in my profession who are working on it and the investment in technology to provide the assurance necessary with real-time systems is the next stage.

Currie of Arthur Andersen agrees: 'We are moving towards an era when companies will have public databases of most of the financial information that investors require. The question that investors will want answered is,—How reliable is that database? Who is looking at the controls over it? Who is testing and sampling it? And so on.

THE BUSINESS OF THE AUDIT

Although there has been much discussion lately of the increased commercialisation in accountancy, our interviews indicate that this element has always been present (Hanlon, 1994). However, the commercial aspects of the audit business were perhaps more muted in the past, and again it is clear that from the days of the traditional audit down to the present day there has been a transformation.

If we look first at how clients were acquired and practices built up prior to the relaxation of the prohibition on advertising in the 1980s, there was, our respondents indicated, little touting for business. Elwyn Jones maintained there was some: 'We have reported two or three firms to the Institute because of what they were up to. Posting letters to our clients and so on. I mean, the clients would be up in arms too.' By reputation at least, according to Palmer and Goodwin, the insolvency practitioners were the worst offenders. But it is clear that overwhelmingly audit business was won by personal contacts within the local networks, and by recommendation. Sanders explained: 'You were associated as Rotarians or golfers or masons.' To Engel too: 'it was purely by recommendation, word of mouth and clubs, pubs, sociability. And doing charitable work. We had quite a number of clients where there was no charge, voluntary organisations, and I am sure that helped. It's the wideness of your own circle that matters.' Typical was how Elwyn Jones went about building up his firm in the 1960s:

> When I started, I got myself into the Rotary Club. There was a businessman's luncheon club called the Friday Club, and I also fairly soon became secretary of the Chamber of Commerce to get myself known in Epsom and around . . . It then grew from contacts made in Epsom like solicitors and banks. You saw the bank managers in those days of course and knew them

> all, and if there was a change they would come and see you. That's changed today of course.

A further, more direct, method of acquiring clients was, as Moore noted 'by buying out other practices.'

Personal contact also worked for the largest firms. Some partners were known as good practice developers who operated by getting to know, for example, company chairmen who might be interested in changing auditors. Grenside, talking of the family firm in the 1940s and 1950s, recalled: 'the Peats were charming people and they were quite good business developers but they weren't technicians.' While Hobson explained the success of Coopers in the 1950s and 1960s due to the fact that the leaders, Pears and Benson: 'were a very good partnership since they were both good business developers and good technicians.' Currie at Arthur Andersen explained: 'from the earliest days I gave talks and wrote papers and got involved in public activities, keeping a high profile.' Livesey of Coopers noted a further method: 'All the big firms have old boys' parties because the alumni of the firm are a great source of new clients. I think Arthur Andersen were the greatest users of that technique. It's still happening an awful lot.' But more formal techniques of client acquisition gathered pace in the late 1970s when the big firms began to target clients they would like to attract. Perhaps, as Carter discussed, the move was led by Price Waterhouse, who gained national publicity for their efforts in 1977. But Grenside also said of Peats: 'They always tried to target, but the change of auditor by a big company was relatively rare in those days.' To Atkinson of Ernst & Young: 'in the 1980s, practice development became very much an 'in thing' perhaps due initially to American influence.' Finally, of course overt advertising arrived in the mid-1980s. Tweedie, however, thought that the innovation was not that big a break with the past: 'I think advertising has always been there. We always used to do it but we'd call it recruitment advertising, and put it in the wrong magazine for recruitment, but one read by potential clients.' Sharman also played down the impact of the advent of advertising in the 1980s, and Lainé saw drawbacks:

> When the rules changed, we could see no advantage in spending large sums of money; since the reaction from all our clients was,—if you boys are going to start wasting your money on advertising don't think we're paying any increase in fees . . . I don't think it has ever added one jot or tittle to our portfolio of clients . . . the profession as a whole has not gained in public esteem from advertising. It was a sop to Thatcherism in the 80s which has done us no good.

The extent of the commercial nature of the traditional audit can also be gauged by the way in which audit fees were fixed. Here again the evidence is mixed. Many respondents maintained that audit fees were assessed strictly on the hours worked and the seniority of the staff. Pearce, practising from the 1930s to the 1970s, maintained: 'I would always charge fees strictly in accordance with time spent, I never had any squabbles with clients over fees.' Middleton also said that in the 1940s, 1950s and 1960s there was no bumping up fees for clients doing well or cutting them for those having a bad year. Others like Moore said that in the 1950s fees might be flexible at least in one direction. They were not based 'on any perception of what the business might stand, although we might make some reduction of fees if we perceived the client was in considerable financial difficulties.' Hardie at Dixon Wilson from the 1930s agreed: 'You might give some protection to existing clients experiencing difficulties with temporary discounts.' Other respondents spoke of flexibility in both directions. It is not possible to establish trends over time in the receptiveness of audit fees to market forces, but certainly to Simpkins as a sole practitioner after the Second World War:

> just occasionally it came to 'what the traffic would bear.' It's easy to say it's based on so much an hour and time spent, but what do you do when you have only spent an hour or so on something but that has saved the client £20,000? Do you charge him for an hour's time? Then occasionally it is the other way round: you devote a vast amount of time to someone and achieve nothing.

Niddrie said he tripled fees at a stoke when he became a partner in a small practice in 1962, and individual fees were clearly a subject of debate within firms. Sharman described how at Peats in the 1960s and 1970s: 'There was partner A who would always say,—that's a bit too much, knock something off, and partner B, who would say,—oh that doesn't seem very much, he's got a lot more money, let's put some more on. So there was always a negotiation between the partner and the client.' Spens had no doubts how fees were set in the 1960s: 'Try a figure—if it works, it works; if not you had to negotiate a compromise. I think it has always been done on that basis, even today.' Norris, at Thomson MacLintock in the 1970s and 1980s, admitted that they did cut fees to attract clients and put fees up for profitable clients, but that assessing fees in this way 'is dangerous if you then find yourself in a beauty parade. It is very difficult to explain to your client why you are suddenly able to cut your previous fee by 40%.'

Client acquisition and the setting of fees came together in a formal way, of course, with the system of tendering which, according to Grenside, came in at the end of the 1970s:

> At one time companies thought it was bad publicity to change the auditor. Then it became common practice for major companies to put their audit

> out to tender. It started off where you had effectively a new company; maybe the result of a merger or de-nationalisation. Then it developed from that to other companies. A lot arose because finance directors came from major audit firms and said,—These people are charging us too much, or they are not doing it properly.

As Heywood described it: 'I remember at an annual general meeting in 1981 a shareholder banging on about audit fees. That was my first recollection of anything other than a rubber stamp at an AGM, and that marked the time when audit fees started to come under increasing pressure. We now get involved in competitive tenders for other people's audits and frequently defend our own.'

Generally, tendering was not liked by past and current practitioners. 'It was a troublesome thing; you wasted a lot of time and money if you didn't get the thing; and you aren't going to get them all,' said Grenside. And as Norris put it: 'There were occasions when we had a pretty good suspicion that there'd never really been any intention other than to get the current auditors to drop their fees.' Others, like Mordy of Peats, took a more a positive view: 'It's not all downside; if you've done a proper job with the tender and you win the audit, then you've done a lot of the groundwork, which gives you a flying start for carrying out the audit.'

MERGERS

Another central aspect of the change confronting the audit profession, particularly from the 1960s on, was the merger movement among firms. The motives behind the changing structure of the business were, as we discussed above, a reflection of the changes in the client companies, who were getting bigger and needed a different service to the one small accountants could give. In particular, they needed firms who could offer a national and increasingly an international range of services, and were trained to handle their ever more complex businesses, could give advice on, for example, information technology and, more and more importantly, had a name which was known in the international capital markets, to which they increasingly had to appeal.

For these reasons our interviewees reported that in growing numbers the smaller firms were losing clients to the bigger firms in the 1950s and 1960s. As Stanley Jones described it: 'We started off with quite a number of biggish companies, but after the war when mergers accelerated, it seemed that I would be invited out to lunch somewhere, and by the time I came back, I'd lost another audit to one of the big boys.' And Engel also made clear: 'We always worried as our clients grew that we would lose them to the big four or five at the time, firms like Price Waterhouse and

Deloittes, and in fact we did lose our biggest client because we just couldn't cope with the work.'

The very small local firms could and have survived, of course. It was the small to medium sized firms, with some large clients, who were most vulnerable. To hold on to these clients they had to move one way or another into larger practices. Hewitt explained the Nottingham based, Mellors, Basden & Mellors, merger with Price Waterhouse in 1966 as follows: 'There had been a large number of take-overs of local businesses by holding companies based elsewhere. By then, the Ford audit we did jointly with PW had gone when Ford became wholly owned by the US company.' Beard's firm moved early to ward off the problem in 1972 with their merger with Pannell, Kerr, Forster: 'we had clients who were growing all around the country, we could see that whilst we were big for Sheffield, we were at risk from the big boys, particularly with our public companies.' Beard also emphasised the resources for training which the larger firm provided.

But the big firms themselves also felt vulnerable (as their largest clients got even larger) and were keen to expand and increase their geographical coverage. Whinney ascribed Brown Fleming & Murray's merger with his firm in 1965 as follows: 'The huge advantage for us, was that they had two very large audits, BP and Burmah Oil. I think BF&M were a little bit apprehensive that unless they grew considerably larger, and spread their portfolio, they would be in danger of losing either or both of them. Their interest was to be less dependent on one or two enormous clients.' Similarly, Morpeth explained why Touche Ross merged with Kemp, Chatteris in 1963: 'We felt vulnerable because the GEC account was too big a proportion of our total fees. It was about 30%, far too high.'

So the smaller firms approached the larger with proposals of marriage and vice versa. Colvin's family firm approached Deloittes in the late 1960s:

> It so happened that all three of the public companies, of which we were auditors were taken-over. In two cases, Deloittes were involved as the auditors of the acquiring companies. Another factor was that Deloittes at that time didn't have a Liverpool office at all, and we were very conscious they had a lot of work in Liverpool which they serviced out of London and Manchester. So in 1967, we made an approach to Deloittes to see if they would be interested in us.

Middleton's firm on the other hand was approached by one of the Big Six in the 1960s, but the benefits of a merger were already apparent to him: 'It was either go with a big firm or you were going to have trouble if you were small. You would be stuck with incomplete record jobs. Coopers were expanding, and wanted an office in Newcastle and had looked at a number of firms, and eventually chose Trevor and I as a base to build on.' Likewise for Sims: 'In 1968, the firm was approached by a firm I'd never heard of called Whinney Murray, saying they had a lot of work in south Wales but didn't have an office.'

INDEPENDENCE

The auditor's relationship with his or her clients has also undergone change, and again our respondents reported a range of experiences and contradictory attitudes. In the traditional audit, at the lowest levels, as Grenside said: 'the people actually doing the audit weren't well treated and they weren't well respected. They were stuck in a nasty little room and they were regarded as a bloody nuisance.' At the same time, however, these auditors often clearly engendered a degree of fear as they entered their clients' premises. As Kenwright remembers it: 'I don't think the arrival of the auditors is taken as seriously as it used to be in the old days. When we used to go in people knew we were looking for trouble. We were in there and if anybody had been naughty they were going to get caught. I think there was quite a strong terror that has gone nowadays.' Indeed, Fabes, Paterson, and Wilkes all reported suicides among staff resulting from a fear of what an imminent audit might find.

The relationship was usually different at senior management and partner level. There was a consensus among our interviewees that auditors, prior to say 1970, tended to get their way with clients more easily. As Brittain described it:

> There was very little input from the client in those days. Auditors were treated with more respect in that the auditor was the sole arbitrator of what was true and fair. There was no negotiation because you had to get it right without fear or favour. In my day, the auditor was a semi-god. I know it sounds daft but even as a humble clerk you could go and ask for information, and you got it.

Thornton could not remember any disagreements over the presentation of accounts, because, as he said, he would expect clients to do exactly what he wanted; while Paterson recalls: 'we tended to get our own way with clients: the auditor was the great god.'

Yet at the same time, somewhat paradoxically, audit partners were usually close to their clients in a way that throws latter-day concerns with auditor/client independence into relief. According to Sanders: 'The clients all became personal friends. The whole relationship was cordial.' Asked if the relationship was ever hostile Boothman replied: 'Never in the old days, because we used to be so close to the clients.' Norris agrees that in the North East in the 1960s: 'They were very friendly with major clients. One chairman would ring up Tom Squance [the senior partner] to find out when it would be convenient to have the board meeting so as not to interfere with his fishing!' Muir of Moore Stephens pointed out: 'All the public companies we acted for we were very close to the major shareholders: mainly family firms . . . I was more concerned in keeping the client in those days than with independence. Independence was just beginning to be talked about. We did stay very close to the principal shareholder. Not so that it would influence our audit.'

Muir held shares in client companies, others like Hardie, Burlingham's father, or the partners in Sims' and Wilkes' firms in the 1950s, would hold directorships, although not in client companies. Norris, however, reported that in the 1970s: 'One of my partners was a trustee of a number of trusts for the families of directors [of the client company], and he was interested as a trustee in, I think, 40% of the capital. It was accepted then but couldn't happen now.'

Again the auditors were often also the close business advisors to clients. As Boothman, who qualified in the 1950s, said: 'I've always regarded myself as an all-round financial advisor, rather than any kind of a watchdog.' Hardcastle, talking of the 1950s, also noted: 'if my principal thought that any of these clients didn't perceive him as a general business adviser as well as an accountant and auditor he would have been quite shocked.' Morpeth related how, such was the influence of George Touche, whose firm were the auditors of GEC, the struggling electrical company, that he engineered the take-over that brought in Arnold Weinstock as managing director in 1963.

Yet despite this closeness to clients these traditional auditors maintained, as Muir did above, that nonetheless they remained independent. As Grenside at Peats recalled of the 1960s:

> One of our biggest clients in those days, which Sir Ronald [Leach] looked after, were the Rank Organisation. I suppose by modern standards we did over step the mark there, because he did an enormous amount as a consultant to them which was very close. But we never thought there was too much conflict of interest. I suppose because perhaps in a way we were arrogant enough to think we could act independently.

So whether or not auditors are independent of their clients today they are probably not more nor less so than in the past. Today, a number of mainly small practitioners are as sceptical of the independence of the large firms as are their critics (see for example, Mitchell, *et al:* 1993: 15). David Haddleton argued:

> I once bought some shares in a company which was audited by an internationally known firm of auditors. Their audit fees were about £1m and their consultancy fees £13m. I thought they were inextricably interested and could not possibly be seen to be independent auditors. But they said

> they were. We would never allow that. If the accounting or consulting fees that we got from a client got anything like that big, we'd say,—look we can't carry on auditing your accounts. I cannot imagine how any qualified accountant can get 13 times as much in consultancy fees as his audit fee and maintain his independence. I think it's laughable.

But Plaistowe put the counter viewpoint:

> Auditors have to be reasonably close to their clients because they have to understand what their client is thinking, and in order for a client to talk to you, you have to have some form of personal relationship. So you can never get complete and utter independence. I think in the old days, particularly for the smaller based companies, people did have a very close relationship, but that's got relatively little to do with independence or objectivity. Independence is all to do with complying with rules which are designed to reinforce the public perception of an auditor's integrity and objectivity. Most of the rules shouldn't really be necessary at all, but they're necessary in order to give the public confidence in what the auditor is saying. So you can be as close as you like to your client, but you can still do a fine objective audit.

Sharman agreed: 'Independence is reflective of the nature of a relationship between two people, objectivity is a state of mind, and it is objectivity which underwrites professional services rather independence. You could be very objective, and give better advice for not being completely independent.'

The acid test of the auditor's independence is perhaps the willingness to qualify the audit report. The general consensus among respondents was that qualifications are more frequent now than they were in the past, but the attitude of the clients or the readers of the accounts to qualifications seemed to vary. Passmore remembered: 'there were other times when we qualified accounts, but to be blunt about it nobody seemed to take any notice of the qualification.' And this view was backed up by Wilde: 'It [qualification] became more and more common as time went on, because standards were becoming so much more rigorous, and because of the increased threat of litigation, which was never a concern when I started. On the whole though, clients didn't take qualification seriously because they did not bother to consider what it meant.' And Livesey concurred: 'As time went on, up to 1987, there were more qualifications rather than less. But the interesting thing is that no one seemed to take any notice. The company might get upset but the analysts didn't seem to read the reports in those days. The shareholders certainly didn't read them. So it didn't matter a hoot.' Spens was cynical on the matter: 'Although you can threaten to qualify you never do. You always reach a compromise. I have never seen qualified accounts, except under very obvious situations.'

The general view that qualifications have become more frequent in recent years is explained by Engel as due to: 'the whole question of indemnity insurance and the tremendous liability put upon the larger firms of auditors.' Most respondents who commented explained the increased incidence of qualification as due to technical qualifications resulting from infringements of accounting standards, but the present day leaders are defensive on the matter. Scicluna made the point: 'Now again, our critics say,—well how many qualifications are there? And if there are qualifications they are all technical and so big deal.' But Plaistowe argues: 'I think technical qualifications are qualifications of substance. I don't like the term technical qualifications. People talk about technical qualifications if someone hasn't complied with an accounting standard, but I think that accounting standards are necessary for accounts to give a true and fair view. Therefore, the term technical qualification is stupid.' Scicluna maintains today's auditors are robust, and makes the point that a great deal of good work is done with only the threat of a qualification:

> You get into pretty confrontational situations where you are absolutely adamant. Again, this is something that unfortunately never gets publicised. You . . . say,—I'm just telling you, you will not do that or else I qualify. But the truth is, it's like nuclear war . . . [when] I have gone to the wire with the finance director, ultimately I have always found that either it's dealt with my way, or we compromised in such a way that I was then able to withdraw the threat of nuclear war.

AUDIT QUALITY

All the interviewees were asked what kept up the quality of the audit, and again a diversity of views were held, dependent to some extent on the vintage of the respondent. There have always been, of course, a variety of controls on the work of the auditor. As Livesey, who trained in the 1940s, noted there was always some control by the Institute: 'There are sanctions and people may be fined or eventually struck off.' Also to Sanders, who took out his articles in the 1920s, after the accounts were drawn up and audited: 'we then agreed the tax liability with the Inland Revenue; so to some extent there was a kind of cross check.' But in the days before the plethora of regulation by the Institute and not much in the way of the litigation there is today, the quality of the audit depended largely on self-discipline, or, as Grenside said, on: 'the quality and expertise of the firm's own system.' To Hewitt: 'I think that there is a degree of self-righteousness, possibly. One was proud to be a member of a good firm and looked at others askance . . . It was the same kind of loyalty to a house at school.'

The importance of the training in the traditional firm was often mentioned: 'One might sound a bit pompous, but one was indoctrinated from the moment one went into the firm how honest one had to be the whole time. In those days there were no wide boys and ethics were paramount. It came from the training,' was how Aspell, who qualified in the 1930s, put it. 'My father's high standards stayed with me though, throughout everything' was the view of Paterson, who took articles in her family's firm in the 1930s. 'It is instilled in training. It is laid down in the Institute's code of ethics. In my case it was laid down in the family. My father was a very upright accountant. I can see him now standing up for what was right between shareholders' and directors interests. He would never be swayed by commercial interest and I tried to follow his example throughout my own career' was the explanation of Colvin, who trained in the late 1940s early 1950s.

This reliance on the skill and integrity of the individual based on their training as the primary control over the quality of the audit was very eloquently put by Stanley Jones, who qualified in the late 1940s. You used 'intuition,' 'a sixth sense' and 'until you reached the point where you were satisfied, you didn't sign off the accounts.' 'The audit was effective where people had that rather old-fashioned approach to things, a personal feeling that you had to be satisfied things were right . . . reaching a point where I would have been very surprised to find that I was wrong in giving a clean bill of health to a company.' In later years, however:

> Everything was so systematised that they were lulled into a false sense of security. I still feel the danger that we get carried away by the ticks on every page as being the be all and end all when it isn't. You have got to have someone there, a responsible person who makes it a point of honour, if you like, to reach that sense of satisfaction with the audit, over and above the ticks on every page.

Wilde thought: 'You really need a nose for things to audit properly.' Paterson talked of 'a horse sense.' To some extent Carter said that this also applied in a large firm like Price Waterhouse in the 1950s and 1960s:

> The whole ethos of the firm then was 'judgment.' The whole approach to the audit was,—what is true and fair in my judgment? To hell with the law or whatever. You have to bear in mind that was before accounting standards came into being so in any particular circumstance you faced you had to make your own judgment based on what had happened before in similar situations, and that's where you took advice from your partners who had seen it all before.

Many interviewees mentioned the reputation of the firm. 'The quality was very high and the main motivation was protecting the reputation of the firm' was how Goodwin expressed it. To Burgess:

> One was conscious of the fact that if you hadn't done your job properly it could be trouble. You've got at the back of your mind that the last thing you wanted to do was to say that you considered the accounts were showing a true and fair view of the company's affairs and find a few days later something would come along to prove that they were disastrously wrong. That would do your firm absolutely no good whatsoever, or your own professional reputation

At Peats, Burlingham thought quality came from: 'Having to retain their credibility. They've got to deal with the Revenue. They've got to deal with everybody else. They've got to be ethical.' Thornton noted that in order to protect his reputation: 'I had to resign occasionally. How could you do the job properly without the client being straight?'

But significantly, underlying this concern for reputation, even in the traditional audit, were the commercial implications. As Simpkins put it: 'most clients were reasonably alert and they would decide if they were getting satisfactory service from their accountants or not, and if they weren't then they would go to somebody else. After all there was a free market.' To Boothman, professional ethics: 'derive entirely from the fact that the accountant is in a market situation. If you want to stay in business, you have to avoid failure.' Rawlinson also linked reputation with the market:

> coming back to market forces, whether you are a 14th century wool merchant in Ghent or Bruges or you are trading on the London Stock Exchange in 1998, if you get a reputation that you are rather sharp and tricky to deal with, it won't be good for your business. And so maintaining integrity, objectivity and independence of mind is something which is a chartered accountant's stock in trade.

The quality controls, that the later generations look to, have a somewhat different, but not an entirely different emphasis. Interestingly, Plaistowe attacked the value of the traditional training: 'Things like the training which an accountant got is really out of date nonsense, but it is what an older generation likes to look back to, rather wistfully, as the special thing which distinguished them.' None of the other present day leaders felt as strongly as this, but neither, despite the amounts their firms spend on training, did they list this as a source of quality control on their audits. Nor, interestingly, did they often cite as a controlling influence the panoply of self-regulation that distinguishes their working environment from that of the old timers.

Internally the larger firms, among a range of measures, introduced peer review of their own audits. We have already noted that Coopers manual was an early move to control quality, and Hobson said that their peer review started from the early 1950s. It is not clear how many or when other firms followed suit, but Colvin stated: 'We inter-changed to do quality reviews in other Deloittes offices' in 1970s. But the common threads that ran through the testimony of the present practitioners when asked what kept up the quality of the audit was: the growing threat of litigation, reputation and the pressure of the market, and, perhaps somewhat surprisingly, and in common with their forebears-personal integrity.

The threat of litigation is now apparently felt even among the contemporary small practitioners like David Haddleton:

> I think the effective pressure is fear. I don't want to be sued, I don't want to lose my qualification, otherwise I won't be able to audit anymore. I don't want to lose face in front of my friends. I think there's another one and you come across it occasionally,—I'm not going to let this rogue push me around. I've lost audits for that reason. I think we've all got to be prepared to lose work for that reason.

Inevitably, the present day leaders showed similar fears. To Scicluna, among other factors: 'there is litigation. You not only get sued if you screw up but if you are the partner concerned you also lose your job.'

But apart from litigation today's practitioners argued that what controlled quality was a heady brew of high morals stiffened by the market place. Scicluna stirred lofty sentiment in with hard headed realism:

> First of all, enormous personal and professional pride . . . All of us hold that qualification close, dear to our hearts, because the last thing we ever want to do is lose it . . . Then there is a huge amount of pressure in the firms to maintain very high standards. The firm's reputation in the market place is a key driver. You do not sell good professional services, at good rates, if you don't have a good reputation.

Currie too mixed the cynical with the lyrical:

> Financial problems hit the headlines very quickly; so in a way auditors are more vulnerable to speculative publicity than most other professions. Because people in professions value their reputation above all financial considerations they fight very hard to maintain it. So litigation and reputation are two economic drivers towards quality control, but . . . [q]uality control depends on integrity and independence . . . I used to say when I was an articled clerk that it was like being part of a crusade and that sense never left me.

Carey agreed:

> I'd say frankly that what underpins it [professional ethics] is that without it we lose the credibility which enables us to earn fees . . . Clearly, there are always commercial judgments in these things. But at the end of the day, regardless of the size of client I am dealing with, if I allowed myself, through whatever means, to be persuaded to take an unprofessional decision . . . the damage I could do to the KPMG brand name is enormous . . . I doubt that KPMG has a single client that is so important to the firm that risking the brand name could be contemplated.

FRAUD AND THE PURPOSE OF THE AUDIT

The interviewees were all asked what they considered the purpose of the audit and whether that had changed over time. Again the responses demonstrated the transformations that have taken place, reflecting to some extent the changing nature of the clients and their demands. We have already noted the degree to which the traditional audit was bound up with also 'doing the books,' and Middleton spoke for many when he also emphasised the mechanical nature of the purpose of the early audits: 'the theory in the small firms was, did the books balance? Were they arithmetically correct? And one searched for mistakes of a penny, believe it or not. The concept of 'true and fair' didn't really get to me for a while.' Tax also loomed large in the process. To Boothman:

> For most clients, the main point of the audit was to agree the liability with the Inland Revenue; for others, it was just an irksome and expensive legal obligation. Because we audited practically no public companies in the 1950s, the notion that we were ultimately responsible to public, as distinct from private shareholders was largely meaningless, although that responsibility is now the top priority.

Other respondents mentioned the fraud detecting role. For Edey talking of the 1930s: 'In my day, quite a young man in my 30s, one would have thought of the audit very much in relation to fraud, the prevention of fraud, internal or external fraud, and much less to anything else. One would not have been thinking of it in terms of ensuring that the accounts when read would enable people to decide whether to buy and sell shares.' Engel also echoed this common view of the audit in the 1950s: 'It was more of a cash control check than anything else, to see that funds went into the right slots and that there were no frauds among the staff themselves. That appeared to be the main objective-to be satisfied that to the best of our knowledge the books and records were in good order.'

However, in view of its declared importance, it is interesting that the general view was that the frauds found were, firstly, rather uncommon and secondly—small-time. To Hardie it was: 'petty stuff,' and Atkins found: 'Only minor frauds, mainly on things like social and athletic clubs'; or in Kenwright's telling words: 'I think fraud has gone up market, you are talking big stuff now, I think there is more fraud at high levels, now, than there was in the old days. In the old days, I think, it was a lot of petty stuff.'

A number of older interviewees, however, down-played the 'fraud buster' role, and indeed articulated early forms of the much discussed 'expectations gap' (Sikka, *et al,* 1992). As Simpkins put it:

> I don't think the public's perception of the audit has changed much; they still look upon it as a device to catch out a bookkeeper on the fiddle. We always tried to make it clear that the prevention of fraud was as much the directors' own responsibility as it was the auditor's. But the larger the business the less practicable it became to do the checking in that way anyway. The primary purpose is still to get the accounts right.

Respondents across the generations, who trained with large firms with large clients, of course, could be expected to follow the standard view that, in the words of Hobson, who was articled with Coopers in the 1940s, the audit was: 'To see that the accounts showed a true and fair view for the shareholders. The directors were responsible for the accounts.' To Plaistowe of 1960s vintage: 'The purpose of an audit is to express an opinion as to whether the accounts give a true and fair view and comply with the Companies Act. That's a statutory obligation and requirement.' And to Carey of the 1970s:

> I think the purpose of the audit remains exactly the same as it always has been. Readers of accounts want some degree of assurance that what they are looking at bears some resemblance to reality. Whilst we only express an opinion to the shareholders, there's no doubt that banks, creditors and others in taking decisions to do business, and on what terms, place reliance on the audit report and, depending on the name on the bottom of it, more reliance on some than on others.

This legal and textbook focus on the priority of shareholders in the purpose of the audit was, however, frequently challenged by the accountants themselves. To Kenwright the beneficiary of the audit: 'has always been company management. We know all about the rights of shareholders, but that has always been notional.' Spens felt that: 'So long as directors appoint auditors and pay them, the auditing system can never work effectively.' Scicluna, who qualified in 1976, argued that today the reality conforms to the theory more than in the past:

> I find it extremely galling that we are constantly being criticised for not looking after the interests of shareholders. When actually, compared to where we are now, when I started the shareholder was so distant you only had executive management to deal with. Now we are very insistent on proper financial information being presented, and look towards the non-execs and the chairman of the audit review.

It is, however, difficult to square Scicluna's view with the one trend in the purpose of the audit that the interviews make clear, which is that at some stage audit firms took a conscious decision to increase the value of their audits to their client's management. Grenside at Peats in the 1960s articulated this trend: 'We all took the view that we should change significantly from just doing an audit to really trying to help the company to become a better company.' As we noted above, the auditors had always given advice to clients over and above the audit, however this advice was probably not usually the central focus of the audit, which Grenside described it becoming from the 1960s. Auditors came to make a much greater attempt to understand all aspects of the client's business, whereas as Colvin, referring to the 1950s, said: 'I remember when I first went to audit we never really got to grips with what the client was doing. We seldom went out of the audit room onto the factory floor.'

The practical manifestation of this changed attitude was the innovation of the management letter. Again this was not completely novel. Although not called a management letter, Passmore remembers: 'We did that in 1934. It was one of the things that the partners insisted upon, and we were very much judged on the quality of what we wrote . . . It was a letter that went out with the final accounts and the audit report. It might say,—we think that your recording of petty cash is rather loose . . ..' But again the management letter as such seemed to emanate from America, since Plaistowe maintained that the transatlantic immigrant, Arthur Andersen, had written them since the 1950s. Carty remembered that by the late 1960s: 'It was standard practice to offer clients management letters, but only 50% of the clients wanted them. The others didn't want to spend the money.' Whinney said of the management letters: 'I would imagine they came in in the late 1960s.' To Lainé at Coopers they: 'assumed a general level of importance in the 70s. In the 1960s, we were regarded as being pretty innovative as a firm in writing these.' Colvin at Deloittes noted: 'It was only in the 1970s, when management letters started to become prevalent, that the auditing profession had to pull its socks up and realise an historical audit wasn't much good to the client unless we were able to justify it by making recommendations to the client as to how he could improve the financial performance of the business.' Perhaps, however, in small provincial firms like Wilde's: 'It only became an integral part of the audit in the late 70s, although it was originally called a report not a management letter. It came from the Institute laying down standards.'

It is not immediately apparent from the interviews why this change in the focus of the audit did take place when it did, but it undoubtedly was a reaction to the common and long standing view of many clients that, as Aspell, who qualified in the 1930s, phrased it, the audit was a 'damn nuisance.' To Kemp, one of the class of '68: 'The vast majority of clients feel that the audit is imposed on them by statute and regard it as a financial burden that they have to suffer, and really they don't want it.' Sharman recalled: 'I always remember a client saying to me,—I ought to get more out of my annual audit than a ruddy great bill for telling me I got my sums right. The provision of management information and the advice that comes from it is a lot more useful than even six or seven years ago.' Scicluna, referring to the present time stated: 'The primary purpose obviously remains the audit . . . to make sure that the shareholders get a financial statement showing a true and fair view. I think increasingly now the audit is also used by the company management to get value out of it, whereas in the past they were quite happy not to. Now they have become smart buyers.' Finally, Heywood noted the even wider dimension: 'The purpose has evolved, yes, and globalisation will continue to alter things. So you are not only aware of the expectations of investors in a particular country. You are having to satisfy the expectations of the most sophisticated investors around the world.'

STANDARDS

The views of the respondents were also divided on the benefits of standard setting and regulation generally by their professional body. There was the well know criticism from the small practitioners. David Haddleton, still practising, is probably speaking for many small firms:

> A family company is a different animal from an international company . . . I feel a lot of the work we do is pointless. That cupboard behind you is full of files which weren't there before. Each limited company file starts 100 pages thick . . . Does that really contribute to a true and fair view? Are you as an investor happier because of it? I don't think so, because you could never invest in my family companies anyway. You are not allowed to, they won't have you.

Spens also articulated a common view: 'The paper work which is thrust on you, the conditions you have to comply with to get a registration are making it very difficult for individuals to make any progress.' Kemp was equally strident: 'I've been in the profession 30-odd years, and I'd resent some of the impositions. So there is an attitude out there,—Who the hell are they to tell me how to run my practice?' And Carty also highlighted the well known differences between the small and large firms when it comes to standard setting. He advocated:

> splitting the requirements for large and small practices much more than they are now, so that the regulations are more applicable to the circumstances of the company . . . The cost of regulation can be disproportionate to the needs of smaller companies. The Americans do it better than we do, in that they apply regulation only to larger companies, on the grounds that larger companies have a greater impact on the economy.

Tweedie, the principal architect of the present regulatory system, however, had little sympathy for the complaints of the small firm: 'A lot of this is phoney because we've issued 11 standards, and if you look at what we've issued, most of them don't actually affect small practitioners,—complex financial instruments, acquisitions, off-balance sheet financing. How often do they meet them? It always amuses me when they say,—we hate all these standards! Most of them don't apply.' Engel thought: 'I think the codes of practice and the standards and the regulations are of paramount importance' and as for the small practitioners' complaints: 'They are just making excuses.'

But there was plenty of general criticism of the accounting and auditing standards. 'I think they have been disastrous . . . they haven't stood the test of time . . . Over time the Institute have been politically inept, and most of the accounting guidelines have had to be revised quite drastically,' was Berry's view. There were reservations over the growing complexity of the accounts. '[T]hings have definitely gone overcomplicated' as Paterson noted. John Haddleton felt that: 'Company accounts are less true and fair than they have ever been. More has meant less. The more detail brought in, meant the less being understood.' To Carter: 'compliance with all the standards makes the accounts almost indigestible to the man in the street or even to a reasonably intelligent person.' Even Muir, who felt the standards had improved matters because there was more consistency about the accounts, stated: 'Most of them are very well intentioned. But there are so many notes to a set of accounts today that they most probably destroy the ability to look constructively at a set of accounts quickly. As a result, most people know less about the company than they did years ago.'

A number of interviewees complained of the inflexibility imposed by the standards, which Hewitt said might inhibit change: 'I do have some doubts about it becoming over-enforced, inhibiting innovation.' Kenwright also felt that the standards made auditing too rigid. Referring to a preregulation example where he had persuaded his auditors to be flexible over the accounts of his then struggling company he argued: 'If today's rules had been applied with their full rigour on that occasion, that company would not have survived, and a lot of people would have been out of work. It's very difficult.' Mordy agreed: 'There are occasions where you stick to black and white and you actually make things worse . . . I'm not sure that the present methods and standards that we have necessary help. You now get stuck with standards that can be very precise, very difficult, very constraining.'

Mordy noted one role for the standards, which was that they were 'quite regularly' brandished at a client to try to resolve a dispute. But both Plaistowe and Carter pointed out that standards could cut two ways when negotiating with clients. As the latter put it:

> It has put audits and the auditor into something of a straight-jacket. In some ways the standards helped and in some ways they hindered. They helped in the sense that you could say to the client,—you can't do that because. But then usually, if you put something in writing there's always some slight ambiguity that the client can develop and say,—well actually, you say that's what it means, but . . . my lawyers say something else . . . Before standards, you said,—I'm sorry, it's my judgment that the presentation doesn't show a true and fair view, and your client couldn't really argue against that. It was take it or leave it.

To Carty too: 'it is a curse to an accountant because if you get hauled up in court, people cite accounting standards and auditing standards and say,—this is what you should have done and this is what you didn't do. So it's much easier to prove that an accountant has been negligent than it ever was before.'

There was a common feeling too that the standards had been introduced at the expense of the auditor's own initiative, of common sense, and of (a word interviewees very often applied to the audit role) judgment. This feeling was stated with passion by Denza:

> It seems to me they have lost all trace of professionalism, they've thrown it away. It's beneath contempt. I think it's because they have drowned in these excessive paper regulations. So, if the wife of a partner in Pricewaterhouse Coopers holds 50 shares in Shell, not one partner can conduct the audit with due independence, whether or not he knows of the shareholding. This is so absurd, so blatant, so infantile and so insulting to every chartered accountant that one both laughs and weeps. The desperate need is to overthrow the mindless idolatry of such pieces of paper and to return to training and exercising professional judgment.

To Simpkins: 'It should all be replaced by one standard, and that's,—you ought to get it right! I've always had a sneaking fear that the temptation is to follow the audit programme mechanistically, and not bother to apply one's common sense. Rigidly set schedules are partly, if indirectly, the cause of the Maxwells and the Polly Pecks.'

Finally, an up to the minute criticism of the standards came from Currie. In view of the apparently imminent brave new world of instantly accessible databases of financial information, he worried that: 'The danger is that we're forever tightening regulation around the traditional modes of financial reporting and auditing and actually they are moving out of the investor's focus. We're building too much regulation in the wrong place, which risks taking the profession's eye off the new areas.'

But these heartfelt criticisms must not obscure the fact that there was also considerable acceptance of the need, if not outright support, for the standards. This view was, however, often hedged around with caveats, or couched in terms of their being irrelevant. Elwyn Tudor Jones, for example, said: 'I can well imagine the new regulations have increased the standards overall, but for our firm the only genuine improvement in our practice came from the introduction of peer review.' Or as Carey, a partner in the Big Six, replied when asked if the standards had improved his firm: 'Not in KPMG, and not in any other of the big players either, in that what standards have done is to codify what we were already doing.' Morpeth, personally heavily involved in setting standards in the 1970s, saw at least two flaws:

> they were obviously a force for good but very difficult to implement because they had no force of law. So firms with major clients who said,—we are not going to apply this standard, would not be able to force them to do it. There was also an inadequate reconciliation of what was true and fair and what was a standard. The standards were supposed to define what was true and fair, but then an auditor was allowed to say that the standard wasn't applied because what was applied was true and fair. In other words, there was almost a dichotomy between true and fair and what the standard was . . . so I do not think standards have really grasped that ultimate nettle.

To others the standards were seen as a necessary evil. As Kemp, who is still closely involved in the regulation of small firms, said: 'There was an awful lot of form filling that involved time and cost, which got increasingly difficult to recover from the client. Accountants do feel that things have become too bureaucratic, but they have to realise that auditing standards, particularly at the small firm end of the market, left an awful lot to be desired, and that regulation *has* met the objective of raising standards.' Wilde highlighted another angle: 'All these new standards are a burden on the small practice and mostly irrelevant in any case. But they had to come in because people are so eager to sue these days.' Hardie agreed: 'audits are stricter than ever before, given the standard setting of the Institute; the atmosphere of litigation makes standards inevitable, but I detest the uniformity.' Tweedie felt that in an ideal world there would have been fewer standards but, 'unfortunately, the profession gets the rules it deserves. Had people behaved themselves in the 80s then we would have several standards less. Standards are put in to enforce order because of the rogues, and there are more to come.'

There was also division among our respondents on the role of the Institute and self-regulation. There was a general consensus in support, and many took the view that self-regulation is practically the definition of a profession, and certainly the main role of a professional body. To Currie: 'All I can say is if a trade association is all it is I would resign tomorrow. It is what it is because it's a regulatory organisation. In the end, the Institute is a group of people who sense that regulation is the price of membership and the key to member quality.' A more practical point was also made that those doing the job are the only ones who have the knowledge and experience to regulate it. But Rawlinson pointed to the fact that accountants are themselves divided:

> There are members who complain that the Institute is too much a regulator and not enough a trade union. They'd like it to be more of a body representing them and helping them to get business and they resent the fact that the Institute has a disciplinary role. I'm afraid a profession must have a self-regulatory function. No matter how many external regulators there are, if you are a civil engineer, or a chartered accountant or a doctor, your own professional peers are the best people to decide whether you're doing it right or wrong and behaving yourself appropriately.

But there were some strong views against self-regulation. Sharman, for example, again noting the divisions said:

> I believe that the Institute has a very valuable role, but you have to understand what that role is, and it is either a trade association or a regulatory body. The trouble is it tries to be both things which is not credible. This is where Sikka and Mitchell have a point . . . Ultimately, regulation has got to be completely independent of the Institute . . . [which] tried to be all things to all men and they got themselves into a terrible tangle trying to hang on to self-regulation . . . the Institute has tried to do everything, and it has fallen down.

Others like Berry felt that regulation should not only be taken out of the hands of accountants but enshrined in statute: 'The grammar of accountancy ought to be law.' Atkins agreed:

> If you are going to get to the stage where you have a limited number of accounting firms, I would go for state control, which I advocated some 20 years ago. You have to have independent bodies looking at the particular problems and taking fairly direct action, like suspending accountants from ever auditing again. If you take a strong enough line initially, as has happened to an extent in America, it cleans up malpractice.

Spens put this view even more forcefully:

> I think self-regulation is a nonsense, a real nonsense. It's a bed of patronage . . . Unless you are big you have got no hope of getting anywhere . . . We need a situation where decisions in the self-regulatory system are justifiable in court. The Securities and Exchange Commission in America has demonstrated how to work a statutory system effectively . . . The danger of the self-regulatory system is that if the authorities act improperly it is very difficult to do anything about it. With the statutory system you can always go to court . . . I think the accounting profession is probably finished as an independent profession. I guess it will come under statutory control very quickly. Like the Police Complaints Authority no one really believes that the professionals can discipline their own profession.

THE SCANDALS

We conclude with a survey of the views of the interviewees on the causes of the scandals that rocked the profession in the late 1980s and early 1990s. As we noted in the introduction, this was the topic on which respondents were most likely to exercise the right we granted them to excise their views from the historical record. But enough remains to give the opinions of a good cross section of the profession.

A common reaction, when our respondents were asked to comment on or explain the well publicised audit failures, was to express incredulity as to why and how they could have been be allowed to happen. Interestingly, this reaction was more common among practitioners in the smaller firms. Typical responses came from Burdett who said: 'I found it very difficult to understand, for example, how the Maxwell pension funds were allowed to go 18 months without an audit.' Winch's reaction to the Maxwell case was: 'I just don't understand it.' To Goodwin, Barlow Clowes: 'didn't begin to add up.' But again there was the familiar wide difference of opinion, and the collective explanations for the audit failures of a decade ago can be analysed into: first, inevitability and the expectations gap; second, passing the buck; third, faults systemic in the audit process and its personnel; and finally, growing commercial pressure.

First then, there was a distinct air of fatalism to many of the responses, which indeed could be interpreted as complacency. These arguments were also often mixed with pleas that the quality of auditing only looked bad with hindsight. As Tweedie said: 'Everything . . . is obvious afterwards'; to Carey: 'Hindsight is a wonderful thing,' and for Grenside 'These things are much easier with hindsight than they are at the time.'

A common point of view was that big audit failures from time to time are inevitable, a fact which unfortunately the public do not grasp. As Grenside argued:

> One of the problems is that the public don't understand an audit really; they expect too much . . . But I always say it's like airlines. It doesn't matter how carefully you run these things, from time to time things will go wrong, and you have to accept that . . . The airlines take all the steps they can both mechanically and in the quality of their pilots, but every now and again something goes wrong and you have a crash. You are simply never going to stop that, no matter what you do.

Many respondents argued that spotting some frauds was just too difficult, if not impossible. This is particularly the case, apparently, where management collude. For Plaistowe: 'One of the things which auditors find great difficulty in doing is finding fraud and in particular manipulative fraud.' Tweedie maintained: 'conspiracies are very difficult to detect . . . With classic frauds like Ferranti or like BCCI, major conspiratorial frauds, you won't find out quickly (if at all) unless somebody talks or makes a mistake.' Boothman agreed: 'In some of those cases there was clearly complex collusion within the client company to conceal important information. In those circumstances, it has to be said that the auditor's job really becomes nearly impossible, whatever expertise they employ.' And James: 'I think there was little an auditor could do, if somebody at the top was determined to cover up what he was doing.' Grenside emphasised the point: 'It becomes extremely difficult if management is in fact dishonest and if they don't tell you the truth.' With regard to Ferranti: 'that was another classic occasion where they were very badly misled, and they were given forged things . . . If you are given assurances by the Minister of Defence or someone it is very difficult to query.' Sharman agreed: 'The real problem with Ferranti was that it was a very sophisticated fraud. Even today no one can tell you what happened. Now, how do you expect an auditor to find it out in the time he's got when after 15 years, with all the investigative power that went into the various enquiries, there is still no one who knows how it was done?' As Scicluna put it:

> If you have a bunch of crooks who are intent on collusion, it's hard. Just think how difficult it is afterwards to pin an individual down for fraud and yet you've had years of investigation specifically on the person. Investigators have the power to subpoena the person, they can subpoena

> witnesses, they can go into related companies . . . People expect us to find it easy to discover it when we're doing a general audit. It's like saying,—how come drugs still come through customs?

There was also a fair amount of passing, or at least attempts at sharing, the buck. Grenside argued: 'Some were eminent City bankers and lawyers; everybody was brow beaten by Maxwell. The City as a whole made misjudgments.' And Tweedie agreed: 'With Polly Peck the market didn't spot it either. It's interesting that a lot of the investing institutions went for Maxwell, or went for BCCI, some people were totally fooled.' Interestingly, this argument seems to imply that auditors themselves do not view their reports as the City's principal alarm bell.

But the main recipients of the auditors' blame are the directors or dominant owners. That they were either the instigators or took prime responsibility for detecting fraud was a truism that respondents often felt it necessary to point out. Some argued that business ethics had deteriorated. Grenside went as far as to date this: 'I believe that business morality went into serious decline about 1970 or thereabouts.' And he had a model in explanation for this:

> one of the concomitants, and an undesirable one, of competition was that it led people to go from understatement to overstatement in the preparation of accounts. Understatement was usually driven by a wish to avoid paying tax, and overstatement came in with all the incentive schemes, either because managers became significant shareholders and wanted to drive up the share price, or because they had remuneration packages which depended on an incentive element.

Denza also offered a similar analysis of the relatively fraud free era in the 1950s and 1960s: 'all the textbooks read a bit wrong, because all the temptation was to understate profit, not to overstate it: tax rates were very high, and dividends were discouraged.' Another piece of the jigsaw was that as tax rates came down encouraging manipulation, clients were getting bigger so that, as we have seen, where previously frauds were petty now they were big. As Hardie put it, now fraud was: 'Not more common, but the sums are inconsiderably larger.' And Carty made the same point: 'Fraud is still a rarity, but because of the size of companies, when things go wrong they can go wrong in a very big way.'

A further aspect of the situation alluded to was the problem of the tyrannical chief executive. As Plaistowe among others explained: 'If you have a company where you have dominant individuals, such as Robert Maxwell, with the ability to override controls, as an auditor, you're on a hiding to nothing. If he's not honest nasty things will take place, and you may not discover them . . . most of those sorts of situations come from companies with weak controls and strong dominant management.' Currie also argued that the auditors are not to blame in these cases:

> People say the obvious sign of fraud is a dominant personality who gets his own way in an organisation. But think of the many organisations which are pretty reputable, but where you have dominant personalities. With hindsight, if ever anything turns out to be wrong in those empires we will say,—It should have been obvious. But there are scores of organisations with those superhuman, energetic, driving people who are honest businessmen and not crooks.

Both Grenside and Niddrie argued that, in the words of the latter: 'Tougher action is needed against erring directors.' But Spens points to the relationship between the directors and the auditor as a fatal flaw in the audit process: 'It's the same old fallacy of all audits - if you accept an audit, by definition you trust the directors. And if they ask you to trust them, you feel you have to do so.'

The answer to the problem of rogue directors comes loud and clear from present day practitioners. To Sharman the problems stem from: 'working for the wrong type of people.' According to Plaistowe: 'They are clients that the audit firms should never have had in the first place . . . Maxwell is a client, which in retrospect, I'm sure Coopers wished they never had. With BCCI and PW, I presume the same.' At Arthur Andersen, Plaistowe continued: 'we are very careful about the clients we take on, and we have been careful longer than the other large firms. We put every client through the wringer before we accept them, and before we decide to retain them.' Currie of Arthur Andersen claimed: 'We were the first firm to have very strict rules about the type of work and client that we accepted. Sometimes, we said no to whole industries.'

But while the answer for the individual firm is evident, Sharman does see the dangers for the commonweal: 'One thing, certainly in the major firms, is that risk management procedures are so much improved that the danger is that these villains will go to second and third tier firms.' And the dangers of rejecting clients for a profession that on occasions claims to be performing a public service are not lost on older heads. To Hobson, Coopers' senior partner in the 1970s and 1980s:

> People now say,—this is too risky a client to have, you should dispense with him. Our feeling used to be, you should qualify the accounts, and let the shareholders deal with him. It was one's duty not to turn down a client unless he was a known criminal. One took on clients that one didn't always vastly like but the idea was that it was better that somebody who was prepared to act and qualify the accounts should do so.

Others, or sometimes even the same interviewees, who pointed the finger of blame away from the profession, admitted that at least some of the fault for the scandals lay within the audit process itself. These alleged weaknesses had many aspects to them. There is, of course, the time honoured problem of human error. Burdett made the point: 'an audit is only as good as the people on the spot who carry it out. You can have a terrific capability as a partner, but you are still reliant on the staff on the site.' 'Well in any sphere of life some are average and some are below average' was how Goodwin phrased it. To Sanders there was a more structural problem: 'There must have been a lack of supervision by the principal partners. They depute too much work to their managers.' Keel also blamed the performance of individuals or the firm's procedures in one key audit failure - Barlow Clowes: 'Spicer & Pegler, the auditors left the responsibility to a single partner. He failed critically in the exercise of his judgment of the actions and word of Peter Clowes, the chief fraudster . . . being more than prepared to accept his assertions without adequate and reliable evidence.' Carty at Robson Rhodes also took this line:

> I'm sure there were individuals within those firms who failed to carry out the procedure they should have carried out . . . and made huge errors of judgment. But I think these are very much individual cases . . . where weak audit partners are dominated by chief executives. You also have to take into account that there are pressures on individuals which can affect their judgment . . . If one of the partners is going through a nasty divorce action, he can't focus on things as he should.

But blaming individuals or the divorce rate hardly explains the scale and timing of the scandals, or accounts for other more systemic weaknesses in the audit. A number of respondents followed the nostalgic line that the great leaders of the past like Pears, Benson or Leach were sadly missed, and perhaps would have done better. More interestingly a number of interviewees noted that early retirement may be a problem. Tweedie offered a somewhat mixed oriental metaphor:

> We used to divide the partners up into mandarins and samurai. The samurai were commercial animals, whilst the mandarins sat back and were wise; and you need a balance. You need people around you, who put a hand around a shoulder and say,—don't do that, laddie, just slow down; you'll get us into trouble. I think that's one of the problems these days, because very few partners remain after 55, in any of the firms.

At the other end of the career span, a question mark was put by some over the training of accountants in recent years. We noted earlier the value put by the traditionally trained accountants on elementary bookkeeping, on the variety of the work, on being trained on the job by experienced partners, and on the inculcation of high standards and, perhaps as importantly, what were variously known as, horse, sixth, or common sense, intuition, or again the key word—judgment. Many of the older auditors felt much of this may have been lost in the present training regime. As Atkins noted: 'People can be very good technically, there are many more graduates joining the profession now, but they suffer from a lack of judgment. It's a skill.' A skill which apparently, as Carty said, they try to teach present day trainees by classroom case studies.

A somewhat contradictory point might be made that our sample revealed that the audit partners at senior level at the time of the scandals were probably in large measure trained in small or medium sized firms which, while having the advantages noted above, had the disadvantage of giving relatively little experience of auditing large multinational companies, which many of those companies involved in the collapses were. Also, as Spens pointed out, qualifying in the 1960s or even later they still would have had little or no training in computers. Therefore, unless this training had been picked up in mid-career, there would be a problem when auditing a computer based company like, for example, Barlow Clowes.

This leads on to the general problem of auditing and computers, and the depersonalisation and lack of transparency discussed above. Allied to this, of course, has come the obvious problem of the size and complexity of the clients dealt with. As we noted above, some accountants came close to saying that the present day auditors cannot cope. Scale, as Kenwright from the other side of the fence in industry, said, has led to: 'a tremendous reliance on sample checking and . . . I think there's quite a lot of disadvantages in the fact that they just do not do the work and I imagine an awful lot of avoidable frauds take place . . . I haven't noticed anybody seriously checking enough transactions, in the businesses I was with, to really get down to whether anybody was on the take or not.' Whinney thought: 'the auditors themselves are skimping the work, I don't think that they think they are, but they are skimping. They don't go into depth in testing where perhaps they should do.' Hardie agreed: 'The detection of fraud is now particularly dependent on the internal audit, and the sophistication of the controls. The adoption of sampling systems distances the external auditor from some of the evidence of fraud . . . In general, I see the recent big frauds as evidence of the crippling dependence auditors have on information supplied by the client.' Again, Beard stated: 'in a vast international conglomerate, the auditors will only look at subsidiaries whose turnovers are over a certain amount. They will risk the small ones. They won't look at them.' But this loss of control that many of the older auditors felt is also articulated by current leaders like Tweedie, and will come as good news to the dishonest:

> Back in my early days, I was doing the smaller companies and you'd more of a hands-on feel for things. In the three years I was articled, we must have caught three or four frauds. I wonder if they'd catch them now. Nowadays with the number of transactions going on in Glaxo say, just testing their systems is a big enough challenge. So if there's a fraud going on and the guy's any good and not too greedy, forget it.

The last explanation for audit failure offered by the auditors themselves was the most controversial one - the effects of growing commercial pressure on professional standards. Atkins was outspoken on the issue of commercialism: 'look at the big firms now, they charge ridiculous fees - £300 an hour. It is just not acceptable and it drives them to bend over backwards to manipulate their own opinions to justify things, do the thing as quickly as possible and make the biggest profits.' And some more senior respondents were surprisingly candid about this. Wilkes said: 'auditors are increasingly robust. Now, maybe in the 80s were they so robust? I don't know. It was the aggressive era of league tables, market share and so on.' Hardcastle argued that competition between firms in the past had: 'stopped short of lowering professional standards' but 'we do know in the 80s that that did happen. There were companies looking to get their audit fees down and for lax accounting, who went around touting when they knew they had a difficult accounting problem. They were looking for whoever was going to give them the softer option, and the senior partners in some firms succumbed undoubtedly.' Whinney felt:

> 'the most newsworthy of these collapses have been failures not at the testing level, but at the partner level. They say,—I am prepared to accept that black is black, without seeing the evidence . . . because they want to keep sweet with their clients. Maybe because they want to keep sweet with their own senior partners too. I don't know, but a lot of the failures have been at top level.'

Or as Tweedie put it: 'I think the 1980s were an absolute disaster, and that's really the reason the ASB exists. I saw some weird things that made you ashamed. I think the auditors of the 1980s lost it. That was a bad time.'

As we noted above when discussing independence, the usual defence against the accusation of being influenced by commercial pressures is that for the major firms no one client is so large that they could not afford to lose them. But Tweedie saw the obvious problem with this argument: 'They do lose some big ones and they can afford to lose them, but not willingly. But the individual partner can't.'

> If you're an audit partner in one of the major firms you have probably two major clients, and what if you lose one? That's a huge chunk of the firm's

> income gone . . . In that situation, the individual's being put under terrible pressure and that's caused because the client can change auditors quite easily, though not frequently. And the senior partner doesn't like to have to stand up and confess the firm has lost more big audit clients . . . the individual partner should sign his name on behalf of the firm, because I know of partners who hid behind the firm's name who did some pretty rubbishy audits and got a firm into trouble. Whereas if it had been public, it would be a case of - not him again! And I suspect the partner would have been ousted by the firm.

Interestingly, admissions of weaknesses in the 1980s by the leaders of the profession past and present tends to be followed by the assertion that standards have improved since. This, of course, remains to be seen. We can leave the last word to Spens who had personal knowledge of the 1980s scandals: 'Obviously, auditors trust the boards less these days, although I expect the wheel is going back full circle, and the next recession will bring out a whole lot more horror stories, where the auditors have failed, simply because they have gotten out of the habit of distrusting the directors.'

SUMMARY

The evidence offered up by our 68 interviews revealed a history of the auditing profession since the 1920s down to the present day characterised by change and growing diversity. In the decades prior to an apparently pivotal period around 1970, the accounting practice was firmly embedded in a business culture made up of the other professions, the banks and service or manufacturing companies, even the branches of large quoted companies, which nonetheless were local or regionally based and did business largely by personal contact. Within the space of two decades at most, this scene, which dated back at least to the industrial revolution of the 18th and 19th centuries was blown away for ever. Probably few professions were transformed by this process more than accountancy.

Prior to 1970, change was slow and the working experience of the accountant, though various, was by and large part of a homogenous profession. The accountants got their start in the profession by family or personal contacts. They received training in the small practices, sustained by the local economies, which gained business by personal recommendation and sank or prospered by personal reputation. Our interviewees who went through the process valued the personal 'on the job' nature of the training by practicing partners they received, the variety of the work they were involved in, the early responsibility given them, and above all the grounding in the basics of double entry bookkeeping, all of which they felt the present day training lacks. The personal way of doing business gave way to the recruitment of graduates, inducted into formal training schemes. And another major change has been the increasing employment of women, perhaps related to the increasing shortage of suitable male recruits that the big firms encountered. The experience of our female respondents was to some extent mixed. Some met prejudice but one, for example, found Peats in the 1950s a very congenial place to work.

The technical process of the audit itself was transformed. The old, mechanical, 'doing the books,' 'tick and bash,' check everything audit was abolished, the interviews testify, by the growth in the scale of the clients, the increased cost of labour, influences coming from America and the advent of computers. But another major trend in this period, the growth in the employment of qualified accountants by industry meant that the external audit now could often confine itself to checking the internal system. Many interviewees worried about the loss of control all these changes implied.

Auditing as a business also changed out of recognition. Quite simply as their clients became competitive multinationals so too by necessity did the accountancy firms. However, the interviews indicated a cautionary note to the picture of the commercialisation of a once unsullied profession. Auditors had always competed for clients in an informal way, often charged what the market would bear when setting fees, and sometimes had a close, anything but, independent relationship with their clients. Also, while the traditional auditors did place more emphasis on their training and on the application of individual judgment as factors affecting the quality of auditing, they were often as aware as the present day practitioners that quality and their reputations had to be kept up ultimately because of their value in the market place. But again in the pivotal, late 1960s and 1970s period, audit firms apparently took a conscious decision to offer more formal 'value-added' to the audit, in addition to the well documented growth in separate consultancy services. Major clients were now won or lost to some extent by advertising, targeting and the so called 'beauty contests,' and not as previously in the local Rotary or golf club. Help to management, as well as the perhaps lesser role of providing comfort for investors, had clearly replaced seeing that the accounts were accurate and no fiddling was taking place, as the focus of the audit, outlined by our older interviewees.

With regard to the major frauds of the 1980s and 1990s the interviewees variously took the view that some frauds are simply too difficult for the auditor to be expected to detect, while the directors or overbearing managers were mainly to blame. Many others, however, did see some weaknesses in the audit process caused perhaps again by a certain loss of control brought on by the growth in scale and complexity of their clients and by computerisation. Others admitted that in the 1980s some auditors had succumbed to the commercial pressures and bent too readily to the clients' sometimes fraudulent wishes.

Also demonstrated in the interviews was that rapid change had created growing divisions within the profession, principally between the powerful multinational firms and the large number of small firms struggling to survive. These tensions have focused on the accountant's training and on standard setting. The self-regulatory measures brought on by the scandals, while being seen as necessary by some, upset many. Paradoxically, they are viewed as irrelevant both by the leaders of the big firms, since they say they already had high standards, and to the small practitioners as not applicable to their work while requiring unnecessary expense. Several of our respondents hinted that these tensions threaten the continued existence of the profession. Whether this will happen of course remains an open question. Oral history makes no claim to foresee the future.

Notes

1. In 1960, there were 393,494 limited companies in Britain; by 1995–6 there were 1,036,200. In 1958, there were 8,000 accountancy firms in the UK and by 1996, 17,136 (Matthews, *et al*, 1998: 39 and 90).
2. Jeremy (1998: 209), dates a major wave of mergers to the period 1956–73, which reached a peak in 1972. Partly as a result of this, Channon, found that of the 100 largest manufacturing companies in 1950, 54% were family controlled, but by 1970 this had fallen to 30%. Moreover, the 100 largest manufacturing companies accounted for 23% of net output in 1950; by 1978 this had risen to 41% (Matthews, *et al*, 1998: 187).
3. In 1951, the top five auditing firms held 18.8% of the market for quoted company audits; by 1991 they held 66.7% (Matthews, *et al*, 1998: 47).
4. According to Channon, 29% of British companies were multinational enterprises (with at least six overseas subsidiaries) in 1950; by 1970 it was 58% (Channon, 1973: 78).
5. Poole and Groves (1982: 113) found that in a random sample of chartered accountants surveyed in 1981, 31.5% came from working class backgrounds. The discrepancy with our figures has two possible sources. Firstly, since to some extent we sought out the leaders of the profession this is likely to skew our sample socially upward; and secondly, possibly the social profile of the chartered accountant has gone down the social scale somewhat in recent decades, since many of our respondents had retired by the time of the Poole and Groves survey.
6. In the Poole and Groves (Ibid.) survey 31.6% went to independent schools and 58.5% to grammar schools.
7. 18% of the Poole and Groves (Ibid.) sample were graduates, and only 12.6% of these went to Oxford or Cambridge.
8. Price Waterhouse, for example, were finding it difficult to recruit qualified staff in the 1940s and 1950s, but were doing so in large numbers; 253 in 1939 and 280 in 1960 (Jones, 1995: 224).
9. Price Waterhouse established a training department based on a tutorial system in 1968; opened their first training building in 1975, and in 1978 appointed their first full-time training partner (Jones, 1995: 225 and 299). Whinney, Smith

and Whinney began courses for articled clerks in 1960, and in 1967 employed their first full time training manager, with a training department (Jones, 1981: 241).

Bibliography

Adams, James Ring and Douglas Frantz, (1992) *A Full Service Bank: How BCCI Stole Billions Around the World,* London, Simon and Schuster.

Aranya, Nissim, (1970) 'Auditors in Britain: Patterns of Role Continuity and Change, A Study in Economic and Accounting History,' Unpublished PhD Thesis, London School of Economics and Political Science.

Baber, C. and T. Boyns, (1985) 'Hodge, Sir Julian Stephen Alfred' in D. J. Jeremy (ed.), *Dictionary of Business Biography,* vol. 3, London, Butterworth.

Barchard, David, (1992) *Asil Nadir and the rise and fall of Polly Peck,* London, Victor Gollancz.

Benson, H., (1989) *Accounting for Life,* London, Kogan Page.

Bigg, Walter W. and R. E. G. Perrins, (1971) *Spicer & Pegler's Bookkeeping and Accounts,* 17th ed. London, HFL (Publishers).

Bigg, Walter W., (1969) *Spicer & Pegler's Practical Auditing,* 15th ed. London, HFL (Publishers).

Boyns, T., (1998) 'The Development of costing in Britain, c.1900-c1960,' *Enterprises et histoire,* no. 20.

Boys, P., (1994) 'The Origins and Evolution of the Accountancy Profession,' in W. Habgood (ed), *Chartered Accountants in England and Wales: A Guide to Historical Records,* Manchester, MUP.

Boys, Peter, (1997) *Raising Auditing Standards: The Impact of DTI Inspectors' Reports 1971–1995,* Milton Keynes, Accountancy Books.

C&L Journal, no. 31, June 1979.

Cadbury Committee Report, (1992) *The Financial Aspects of Corporate Governance,* London, Gee.

Calcutt Report, (1990) *Report of the Committee on Privacy and Related Matters,* London, HMSO.

Calcutt Report, (1992) *A Review of Press Self-regulation,* London, HMSO.

Campbell-Kelly, Martin, (1989) *ICL: A Business and Technical History,* Oxford, Clarendon.

Chance, M. S., (1993) 'The Accountants' Joint Disciplinary Scheme' *Journal of Financial Regulation and Compliance,* vol. 2, no. 1.

Chandler, Roy, (1986) 'Laying the foundations,' in *APC—the first ten years,* London, Auditing Practices Committee of CCAB Ltd.

Channon, D. F., (1973) *The Strategy and Structure of British Enterprise,* London, Macmillan.

Chartered Accountants Joint Ethics Committee, (1994) *Report to the Councils of the Three Institutes, 1994,* London, CAJEC.

Collins, M. and R. Bloom, (1991) 'The role of Oral History in Accounting,' *Accounting, Auditing and Accountability Journal,* vol. 4, no. 4.

Cooper, V., (1966) *Manual of Auditing,* 1st ed., London, Gee.

Cork, K., with H. Barty King, (1988) *Cork on Cork,* London, Macmillan.

Cowe, R. (ed.), (1993) *The Guardian Guide to the UK's Top Companies,* London, Fourth Estate.

Department of Trade and Industry, (1992) *Blue Arrow plc,* London, HMSO.

Department of Trade and Industry, (1995) *James Ferguson Holdings plc, Barlow Clowes Gilt Managers Limited,* 3 vols., London, HMSO.

Department of Trade and Industry, (1997) *Guinness plc,* London, HMSO.

Department of Trade, (1976) *London and County Securities Group Limited,* London, HMSO.

Department of Trade, (1977) *London Capital Group Limited,* London, HMSO.

Department of Trade, (1978) *Court Line Limited,* London, HMSO.

Department of Trade, (1980) *Cornhill Consolidated Group Ltd (in liquidation),* London, HMSO.

Department of Trade, (1989) *County NatWest Limited, County NatWest Securities Limited,* London, HMSO.

Dewar, David, (1991) 'The Audit of Central Government,' in Michael Sherer and Stuart Turley (eds), *Current Issues in Auditing,* 2nd ed., London, PCP.

Edwards, J. R. (1985) 'William Plender, Lord Plender of Sundridge, Kent (1861–1946) Accountant,' in D. J. Jeremy (ed.), *Dictionary of Business Biography,* vol. 4, London, Butterworth.

Edwards, J. R., (1984) 'Sir Francis d'Arcy Cooper (1882–1941). Accountant and industrial manager,' in D. J. Jeremy, (ed.), *Dictionary of Business Biography,* vol. 1, London, Butterworth.

Edwards, J. R., (1989) *A History of Financial Accounting,* London, Routledge.

Edwards, J. R., Roy Chandler and Malcolm Anderson, (1999) 'The "Public Auditor": an experiment in effective accountability,' *Accounting and Business Research,* vol. 29, no. 3.

Financial Reporting Council, (1995) *The Financial Reporting Council, The Auditing Standards Board, The Financial Reporting Review Panel: A Brief Outline,* London, FRC.

Garrett, A. A., (1961) *History of the Society of Incorporated Accountants 1985–1957,* Oxford, Oxford University Press.

Gibb, R. (ed), (1994) *The Channel Tunnel: a Geographical Perspective,* Chichester, John Wiley.

Glynn, Sean and Alan Booth, (1996) *Modern Britain: an Economic and Social History,* London, Routledge.

Glynn, Sean, (1998) *Sir John Cass and the Cass Foundation,* London, Sir John Cass's Foundation.

Greenough, John, (1991) 'The Audit Commission,' in Michael Sherer and Stuart Turley (eds), *Current Issues in Auditing,* 2nd ed. London, PCP.

Greenslade, R., (1992) *Maxwell's Fall,* London, Simon and Schuster.

Grele, R. J., (1998) 'Movement without aim: methodological and theoretical problems in oral history,' in R. Perks and A. Thomson, (eds.), *The Oral History Reader,* London, Routledge.

Gwilliam, David and Tim Russell, 'Polly Peck: Where were the analysts?' *Accountancy,* Jan. 1991.

Hammond T., and P. Sikka, (1996) 'Radicalising accounting history: the potential of oral history,' *Accounting, Auditing and Accountability Journal,* vol. 9, no.3.

Hanlon, G., (1994) *The Commercialisation of Accountancy: Flexible Accumulation and the Transformation of the Service Class*, London, St. Martin's.

Helmore, L. M., (1961) *The District Auditor,* London, MacDonald and Evans.

Hindle, Tim, (1991) *The Sultan of Berkeley Square: Asil Nadir and the Thatcher Years,* London, Macmillan.

Hodgson, G., (1984) *Lloyd's of London: a reputation at risk,* London, Allen Lane.

Howitt, Sir H., (1966) *The History of the Institute of Chartered Accountants in England and Wales 1880-1965, and its founder accountancy bodies 1870-1880*, London, Heinemann.

ICAEW, *List Of Members,* various years, London, ICAEW.

Ilersic A. R. and P. F. B. Liddle, (1960) *Parliament of Commerce: The Story of the Association of British Chambers of Commerce 1860–1960,* London, Newman Neame.

Jenkins, Keith, (1995) *On "What is History?": From Carr and Elton to Rorty and White,* London, Routledge.

Jenkins, Keith (ed.), (1997) *The Postmodern History Reader,* London, Routledge.

Jeremy, D. J. (ed.), (1984–6) *Dictionary of Business Biography,* vols 1–5, London, Butterworth.

Jeremy, David J., (1998) *A business history of Britain,* Oxford, OUP.

Johnson, Christopher, (1991) *The Economy under Mrs. Thatcher, 1979-1990,* London, Penguin.

Joint Disciplinary Scheme, (1981) *Annual Report*, London, JDS.

Joint Disciplinary Scheme, *News Release,* 11 April 1995 and 7 July 1995.

Jones, E., (1981) *Accountancy and the British Economy 1840–1980: The Evolution of Ernst & Whinney,* London, Batsford.

Jones, E., (1986) 'Whinney, Frederick (1829–1916). Accountant,' D. J. Jeremy, (ed.), *Dictionary of Business Biography,* vol. 5, London, Butterworth.

Jones, E.,(1995) *True and Fair: A History of Price Waterhouse,* London, Hamish Hamilton.

Kelly, Tim, (1987) *The British Computer Industry: Crisis and Development,* London, Croom Helm.

Kirkham, Linda M. and Anne Loft, (1993) 'Gender and the construction of the Professional Accountant,' *Accounting Organisations and Society,* vol. 18, no. 6.

Kitchen J. and R. H. Parker, (1980) *Accounting Thought and Education: Six English Pioneers,* London, ICAEW.

Kochan, Nick and Bob Whittington, (1991) *Bankrupt: The BCCI Fraud*, London, Victor Gollancz.

Kochan, Nick and Hugh Pym, (1987) *The Guinness Affair: Anatomy of a Scandal*, London, Christopher Helm.

Lee, T. A. and D. P. Tweedie, (1977) *The Private shareholder and the Corporate Report*, London, ICAEW.

Leeson, Nick, (1997) *Rogue Trader*, London, Warner.

Lewis, Mervyn, (1977) *British Tax Law*, London, Macdonald and Evans.

Loft, A., (1986) 'Towards a critical understanding of accounting: the case of cost accounting in the UK, 1914–1925,' *Accounting Organisations and Society*, vol. 11, no. 2.

Loft, A., (1988) *Understanding Accounting in Its Social and Historical Context: The Case of Cost Accounting in Britain, 1914–1925*, New York, Garland.

Loft, A., (1990) *Coming into the Light: A study of the development of a professional association for cost accountants in Britain in the wake of the First World War*, London, CIMA.

Lummis, T., (1998) 'Structure and validity in oral evidence,' in R. Perks and A. Thomson, (eds.), *The Oral History Reader*, London, Routledge.

Magee, Brian, (1951) *Auditing: a Practical Manual for Auditors by the Late Lawrence R. Dicksee*, 17th ed., London, Gee.

Matthews, D., M. Anderson, and J.R. Edwards, (1998) *The Priesthood of Industry: The Rise of the Professional Accountant in British Management*, Oxford, OUP.

Mitchell, A., P. Sikka, T. Puxty and H. Wilmott (1993) *A Better Future for Auditing*, London, University of East London.

Morrissey, C. T., (1998) 'On oral history interviewing,' in R. Perks and A. Thomson, (eds.), *The Oral History Reader*, London, Routledge.

Mumford, M. J., (1991) 'Chartered accountants as business managers: an oral history perspective,' *Accounting, Business and Financial History*, vol. 1, no. 2.

Parker, R. H., (1992) *Macmillan Dictionary of Accounting*, London, Macmillan.

Perks, R. and A. Thomson, (eds.), (1998) *The Oral History Reader*, London, Routledge.

Poole, M. and R. Groves, 'The modern accountant: anatomy of a species' *Accountancy*, August 1982.

Portelli, L., (1998) 'Work ideology and consensus under Italian fascism,' in R. Perks and A. Thomson, (eds.), *The Oral History Reader*, London, Routledge.

Pugh, Peter, (1987) *Is Guinness Good for You? The Bid for Distillers—The Inside Story* London, Financial Training.

Reid, Margaret, (1982) *The Secondary Banking Crisis, 1973–75: Its Causes and Course*, London, Macmillan.

Robb, George, (1992) *White-collar Crime in Modern England: Financial Fraud and Business Morality, 1845–1929*, Cambridge, CUP.

Robson, Sir Thomas, (1956) *Consolidated and Other Group Accounts*, 3rd ed. London, Gee.

Rotary International in Great Britain and Ireland, (1997) *Rotary in Brief*, Alcester, Rotary International in Great Britain and Ireland.

Russell, Peter, (1991) 'Department of Trade and Industry Investigations' in Michael Sherer and Stuart Turley (eds) *Current Issues in Auditing*, 2nd ed., London, PCP.

Samuel, R., (1998) 'Perils of the transcript,' in R. Perks and A. Thomson, (eds.), *The Oral History Reader,* London, Routledge.

Seventy Five Years of Progress in Accountancy Education, H. Foulks Lynch & Co., (1955), London, HFL (Publishers).

Sherer, Michael and Stuart Turley, (eds), (1991) *Current Issues in Auditing,* 2nd ed., London, PCP.

Sikka, Prem, Tony Puxty, Hugh Willmott and Christine Cooper, (1992) *Eliminating the Expectations Gap?* London, Certified Accountants Educational Trust.

Soroptimist International of Greater London, (1995) *Information for Members,* London, Soroptimist International of Greater London.

Southgate, Beverley, (1996) *History: What and Why?* London, Routledge.

Spicer, E. E. and E. C. Pegler, (1925) *Practical Auditing,* 4th ed., London, HFL (Publishers).

Stacy, Graham, (1986) 'The first four years—Building the foundations,' in *APC—the first ten years,* London, Auditing Practices Committee of CCAB Ltd.

Stock Exchange Official Yearbook, various years, London.

Terkel, Studs, (1989) *Hard Times: An Oral History of the Great Depression,* London, Random House.

Terkel, Studs, (1974) *Working: People Talk About What They Do All Day and How They Feel About What They Do,* New York, Pantheon.

Thompson, E. P., (1978) *The Poverty of Theory and Other Essays,* London, Merlin.

Thompson, P., (1978) *The voice of the past: oral history,* Oxford, OUP.

Truell, P. and L. Gurwin, (1992) *BCCI: The Inside Story of the World's Most Corrupt Financial Empire,* London, Bloomsbury.

Waldron, Robert S., (1969) *Auditing: a Practical Manual for Auditors by the Late Lawrence R. Dicksee,* 18th ed., London, Gee.

Who Was Who

Who's Who

Who's Who in Accountancy, (1987), London, Chapter 3 Publications.

Widlake, Brian, (1995) *Serious Fraud Office,* London, Little Brown.

Wise, T.A., (1982) *Peat, Marwick, Mitchell and Co. 85 years,* New York, Peat, Marwick, Mitchell and Co.

Wood, Bruce, (1976) *The Process of Local Government Reform, 1966–74,* London, Allen and Unwin.

Woolf, Emile, (1997) *Auditing Today,* 6th ed., Hemel Hempstead, Prentice-Hall.

Index